Yamashita's Ghost

Yamashita's Ghost

War Crimes, MacArthur's Justice, and Command Accountability

Allan A. Ryan

University Press of Kansas

Published by the University Press of Kansas (Lawrence, Kansas 66045), which
was organized by the Kansas Board of Regents and is operated and funded by
Emporia State University, Fort Hays State University, Kansas State University,
Pittsburg State University, the University of Kansas, and Wichita State
University

Library of Congress Cataloging-in-Publication Data
Ryan, Allan A.
  Yamashita's ghost : war crimes, MacArthur's justice, and command
accountability / Allan A. Ryan.
      p. cm.— (Modern war studies)
  Includes bibliographical references and index.
  ISBN 978-0-7006-1881-1 (cloth : alk. paper) 1. Yamashita, Tomobumi,
1885-1946—Trials, litigation, etc. 2. War crime trials—Philippines—Manila.
3. Command responsibility (International law) 4. World War, 1939–1945—
Atrocities. 5. MacArthur, Douglas, 1880-1964. I. Title.
  KZ1184.Y36R93 2012
  341.6′90268—dc23

                                    2012024202

British Library Cataloguing-in-Publication Data is available.

Printed in the United States of America

10 9 8 7 6 5 4 3 2 1

The paper used in this publication is recycled and contains 30 percent
postconsumer waste. It is acid free and meets the minimum requirements of
the American National Standard for Permanence of Paper for Printed Library
Materials Z39.48–1992.

To my father, Allan A. Ryan (1922–2004),
United States Army, 1942–1946,

and his brother, John P. Ryan (1921–),
United States Army, 1942–1946,

and my father-in-law, Raymond E. Foote (1920–2009),
United States Army Air Forces, 1942–1945

Contents

Illustrations follow page 192.

To rule well a king requires two things: arms and laws, that by them both times of war and of peace may rightly be ordered. For each stands in need of the other, that the achievement of arms be conserved by the laws, [and] the laws themselves preserved by the support of arms. If arms fail against hostile and unsubdued enemies, then will the realm be without defence; if laws fail, justice will be extirpated, nor will there be any man to render just judgment.

—Henry de Bracton, *On the Laws and Customs of England,*
translated from the Latin by Samuel E. Thorne
(Harvard University Press, 1968)

★★★

It is during our most challenging and uncertain moments that our Nation's commitment to due process is most severely tested; and it is in those times that we must preserve our commitment at home to the principles for which we fight abroad.

—Justice Sandra Day O'Connor,
Supreme Court of the United States,
Hamdi v. Rumsfeld, 542 U.S. 507 (2004)

Cast

General Tomoyuki Yamashita, Commanding General, Fourteenth Area Army,
Philippines 1944–1945
General of the Army Douglas MacArthur, Commanding General, Southwest
Pacific

Members of the military commission:
Major General Russel B. Reynolds, presiding
Major General Leo Donovan
Major General James A. Lester
Brigadier General Egbert F. Bullene
Brigadier General Morris Handwerk

Members of the prosecution:
Major Robert Kerr, chief prosecutor
Captain William N. Calyer
Captain Delmas C. Hill
Captain Jack M. Pace
Captain M. D. Webster
Lieutenant George E. Mountz

Members of the defense:
Colonel Harry E. Clarke, chief defense counsel
Lieutenant Colonel James G. Feldhaus
Lieutenant Colonel Walter C. Hendrix
Major George F. Guy
Captain A. Frank Reel
Captain Milton Sandberg

Justices of the Supreme Court
Chief Justice Harlan Fiske Stone
Associate Justice William O. Douglas
Associate Justice Hugo L. Black
Associate Justice Wiley Rutledge
Associate Justice Frank Murphy
Associate Justice Stanley Reed
Associate Justice Felix Frankfurter
Associate Justice Harold Burton
Associate Justice Robert H. Jackson on leave, 1945–1946

Preface

The first war crimes trial after World War II took place in Manila. The accused man was General Tomoyuki Yamashita, commander of the Japanese army in the Philippines in the final year of the war, a year that saw horrendous atrocities committed by Japanese troops in Manila and elsewhere in the islands. Yamashita was arraigned in Manila on October 8, 1945, five weeks after Japan's surrender in Tokyo. General Douglas MacArthur accused Yamashita of the crime—if it was one—of failure to control his troops. Five American generals, none of them with any legal training, were appointed as a military commission to hear the evidence and render a verdict on 123 separate counts describing ghastly murders, tortures, rapes, arson, and other crimes. After five weeks of testimony, much of it in the anguished words of the victims themselves, the commission convicted Yamashita and ordered him executed. On February 23, 1946, on a scaffold in the predawn darkness near Manila, a hangman placed a noose around Yamashita's neck and he dropped to his death.

But Yamashita was no ordinary criminal, and this was no ordinary trial. He was Japan's most accomplished military leader, whose brilliant campaign against British and Australian troops in Malaya and Singapore in 1942 had delivered what Winston Churchill called the most devastating defeat in the history of the British Empire. No friend of the warlords in Tokyo, he had been exiled to a backwater command in Manchuria for two years, to be recalled only in 1944 and sent to the Philippines, where he fought MacArthur's vastly superior American forces to a standstill, finally surrendering in the hills of the island of Luzon only when the war was finally, irretrievably, and officially lost.

He was a dignified and thoughtful man who earned the respect and even admiration of the American military lawyers who defended him vigorously at the trial. Had Yamashita ordered these appalling crimes, his conviction and execution could not have come too soon. But he did not. He maintained stoutly and consistently from the witness chair in Manila that he had not ordered these crimes, and that he had in fact ordered his subordinate commanders to abandon

Manila as the American army approached and to retreat to the hills where he himself had already fled, hoping desperately only to hold off MacArthur's forces long enough to allow Japan to prepare its homeland defenses against inevitable invasion. The evidence fully supported his account.

After his conviction, his lawyers took the extraordinary step of asking the Supreme Court of the United States to hear his appeal, and that Court, taking an extraordinary step itself, agreed to do so. It upheld the conviction in what remains today its only decision on the responsibility of a military commander for the actions of his troops. It did so over the impassioned dissents of two of its members, who wrote eloquent opinions, invoking for the first time in that Court's history the concept of international human rights.

The precedent established in *In re Yamashita* has proven to be both troublesome and embarrassing for the United States. Had it been followed faithfully in the 1960s and 1970s, it might well have justified the trial and conviction of American generals of the Vietnam War. Were it to be followed faithfully today, it might well justify the conviction of American generals and political leaders for the tortures at Abu Ghraib prison in Iraq. Conversely, however, it would also justify a decision by the Supreme Court that the so-called unlawful enemy combatants at Guantánamo were entirely the business of the military and its commander in chief, entitled to none of the due process of law guaranteed by the Constitution of the United States. In fact, the Supreme Court has ruled that just the opposite is so.

The question at the heart of the Yamashita case is as important today as it was then—perhaps even more so in a vastly more sophisticated military environment with vastly more complex command structures, where soldiers in Nevada and civilians at the CIA in Virginia can carry out lethal attacks on terrorists in Afghanistan. The question is this: can a commander be held accountable before the law for the crimes committed by his troops—crimes that inflict agonizing cruelty and death on innocent civilians, including women and children—and yet crimes that he has not ordered, not stood by to allow, and may well not even have known about or had the means to stop?

The doctrine of command responsibility—or command accountability, which I think is a more accurate term—was born in that Manila trial in 1945, but today it has been added to the Geneva Conventions, it has come to dominate several major trials in the international tribunal for the former Yugoslavia, and it has been adopted by the International Criminal Court established in 2002. It has been embroidered and restated, but it is an outgrowth of the trial that MacArthur ordered for Yamashita in 1945.

By order of five American generals, General Douglas MacArthur, and the Supreme Court of the United States, General Tomoyuki Yamashita, no depraved monster but an accomplished and professional combat commander, went to his execution over sixty-five years ago, for what his soldiers did. But his ghost hovers over our law, and our troops, and our commanders.

This book is my telling of the case of General Yamashita, and my attempt to address this question and some others related to it. My aim in writing it is to take a new look at the trial, its consequences, and its lessons for today. I have taught the case for many years in my course on the law of war at Boston College Law School, but despite the importance of the issues it raises, little has been written about the trial, and nothing very recently. Except for the account written shortly afterward by one of Yamashita's defense counsel—an invaluable but hardly objective work—this is the first book written by a lawyer with reference to the 4,000-page transcript of the trial. The value of this work is for others to determine, but my goal in writing it has been to present the facts and the law as accurately and completely as possible and to provide as full an account of the case and its context, then and now, as I am able, so that readers may judge for themselves what happened, and why, and what lessons it holds for us today.

This case lies at the heart of the intersection of the military and the law. My military service in the 1970s as a U.S. Marine Corps lawyer was far from battle, but I believe that my experience as a Supreme Court law clerk, later an advocate in several cases before that Court, and later as the head of the Office of Special Investigations in the U.S. Department of Justice, the office charged with the investigation and prosecution of Nazi war criminals in the United States, and as a trial lawyer and teacher has given me a perspective on the issues that I hope will be useful to the reader in understanding the events and their importance. I have not been shy in setting forth my opinions and conclusions, but I have tried to do so clearly, allowing the reader to take them for what they are worth, distinct from the accurate telling of what happened.

All quotations from the trial are taken verbatim from the official transcript.* The trial was extensively covered by leading American newspapers and wire services, particularly the Associated Press, the *New York Times*, and the *Chicago Daily Tribune*, as well as by the *Manila Times*, and to a lesser extent by British and Australian newspapers, the latter made available by the National Library of Australia. My descriptions of the setting and of the appearance and conduct of the lawyers, the commissioners, and the witnesses during the trial are based on those accounts, on the films recorded by the U.S. Army, on the near-daily letters of one of the prosecutors, and on other contemporary accounts of witnesses to the event.

I could not have written this account without the assistance and support of a good many people. I am particularly grateful to Lea (Walker) Wood, formerly

---

*There are two surviving copies of the transcript that I know of. One is at the National Archives; the other, which I used, is at Harvard University's Yenching Library.

of the Women's Army Corps, who was a member of the defense support team at the trial, and to Colonel Harry Pratt, USMC (ret.), who was the trial's chief interpreter, for their willingness to share their accounts of the trial with me. As far as I know, they are the trial's only surviving participants. I am enormously grateful also to Angelia Herrin and George Farrell, generous hosts in allowing me the use of their home in Vermont. It was there that I first conceived the idea of this book and returned often to write a good portion of it. Richard D. Sullivan, my colleague in the Marine Corps and in the Justice Department, a former military judge, and my friend of forty years, read draft after draft, and his acute knowledge and thoughtful questions kept me focused on the story to be told. To all of them, my thanks for making this book a better one than I could have done on my own.

I am also indebted to the Harvard University Library, and particularly the librarians at Widener, Baker, and Yenching Libraries, and to the Harvard Film Archive, for leading me to the right sources and for obtaining documents from other libraries; to James Zobel at the MacArthur Memorial Library and Archives in Norfolk, Virginia; Brian Stiglmeier of the Library of the Supreme Court; Andrea Hackman of the Court's curatorial staff; Rebecca L. Collier of the National Archives; and the Robert H. Jackson Center in Jamestown, New York. The U.S. Army films of the trial at the National Archives in Suitland, Maryland, provided valuable visual information on the venue of the proceedings and the actions of the lawyers, commissioners, and witnesses as they went about the business of the trial. The UCLA Film Archive provided me a copy of the rare *Orders from Tokyo* film, and the Oregon State University archivists were diligent in searching for information about chief prosecutor Robert Kerr, whose father was president of that university. Edwin J. Peterson, former Chief Justice of the Oregon Supreme Court, generously shared insights on Kerr, his former law partner. Professor Toshiyuki Tanaka of the Hiroshima Peace Institute translated Yamashita's essay written on the day of his execution, which is quoted with the kind permission of Professor Tanaka and the *Asia-Pacific Journal: Japan Focus*. Fred Borch, John W. Dower, Eugene Fidell, Louis Fisher, Gary Solis, Ronald H. Spector, and Thomas Zeiler likewise were generous in sharing their insights and expertise, as were Robin Rowland and Brian Farrell on matters touching Singapore.

The Division of Continuing Education at Harvard made research assistants available, particularly Teresa Sullivan, who tracked down the many cases and law review articles that have cited the Yamashita decision, and Kay Makino, who translated several useful Japanese documents. Emily Kanstroom, my student at Boston College Law School, provided thoughtful research. The family of Dan Shaw generously shared their late father's recollections of his experiences in the Philippines. The valuable letters of Lieutenant George Mountz are quoted through the courtesy of Peter Mountz and Pamela McDonald, the Allen County (Indiana) Public Library, and the Garrett (Indiana) Public Library, which have posted the letters on their website. Professor Jenny S. Martinez of Stanford Law School first used the metaphor of a ghost in describing the Yamashita case, in her thoughtful 2007 article. I am much indebted to Mike Briggs, Kelly Chrisman Jacques, Kathy Delfosse, Susan Schott, and Karl Janssen at the University Press of Kansas for bringing the book to completion.

My thanks also to Manuel Monteiro, Susan Ingram, Steve Mott, Missy Gerety, Judy Enright, Mary Jean Martindale, Peter and Janyce Kittler, Bob and Patty Bryant, Franklin Schwarzer, Elizabeth Soutter Schwarzer, Tom Eagen, Chris Griffin, Mark Brodin, and Connie Gilson for their friendship and encouragement as I plugged along. Mimi, Elisabeth, Andrew, and Erin always knew that some day, probably way in the future, I would finally be done with this book.

Above all, I cannot adequately express how much I owe to my wife, Nancy, without whose support and unfailing love, patience, and good humor I never would, or could, have written this.

Prologue

The frail priest in a white cassock gripped the arm of the metal chair and sat himself carefully to face his interrogator. A breeze billowed the thin white curtains behind him and stirred the humid air in the once-grand ballroom with its sweeping view of Manila Bay. Just to his right, five uniformed generals of the U.S. Army watched as the priest readied himself.

When he was seated, an army captain standing before him spoke.

"Will you state your name and address, please?"

"Francis Joseph Cosgrave, Redemptorist Monastery, between Dewey Boulevard and Taft Avenue extension."

"Your age, Father?"

"Forty-eight years of age."

"And you are a Catholic priest?"

"A Catholic priest," he answered. "Yes."

It was October 30, 1945, not quite two months since the Japanese army that had occupied the Philippines for three years had surrendered to the American army under the command of General of the Army Douglas MacArthur. In the ballroom of the U.S. High Commissioner's Residence in Manila, an extraordinary trial was under way. Father Cosgrave was there to describe what he had survived eight months before.

In February 1945, the Japanese occupation was coming to a brutal and violent end in Manila. The U.S. Army had landed on the island of Luzon the month before and was fighting its way into the city known before the war as the Pearl of the Orient, its stately marble buildings and broad boulevards, its walled old quarter of Intramuros, its tree-shaded universities and monasteries crumbling under fierce combat. But the Americans were still on the outskirts of the city, and the Japanese were dug in. In the boys' high school known as De La Salle College, Father Cosgrave and seventeen Christian Brothers teachers, along with fifteen Filipinos, were under siege. But the threat was not from artillery fire between the approaching Americans and the resisting Japanese.

The prosecutor asked, "Will you tell us about the Japanese who came on the 12th of February to La Salle College?"

Father Cosgrave told the story. "Well, just as we had finished lunch," he said, "this officer with, as far as I remember, about 20 men, Marines, entered, and they spoke in Nippongo. The officer spoke in Nippongo and seemed quite excited. I learned afterwards, from Brother Maximin, who was killed, that the officer asked if there were snipers or guerillas there, and he was assured that there were not, which was the truth. But he took off two of the boys, two of the servant boys. They were outside for a few minutes and we heard a shot, and a few moments later they were brought back again. I saw one of them brought back again wounded, and immediately the officer gave a command, and at once the soldiers, with their bayonets, began to attack us."

"Where were you at this time?" the prosecutor asked.

"I was sitting with an old Irish brother at the entrance to the wine cellar," Father Cosgrave continued. "The Japanese soldiers were bayoneting all around us, and Brother Leo looked at me and said, 'they are going to bayonet us,' and he asked me to give him an absolution. And I raised my hand to give him an absolution and the bayonet of the Jap passed under my arm into his heart or his chest, and he immediately slumped down dead on my legs, on my knees. Before I could move I received two thrusts from the bayonet."

"What happened to you after that?"

"Immediately after that the Japanese continued bayoneting, the officer slashing with his sword. One poor woman there tried to defend her little child. Her husband was already killed, her two big boys were dead, and a boy about ten. She tried to defend the little boy. She was slashed across the shoulder, across the arm, and a big piece was taken out of her leg. She lived until the following day, as far as I remember, suffering intensely."

The priest went on.

The Japanese then followed some of the brothers and some of the people up the staircase. Some were able to run up. Shots were fired and others were bayoneted on the staircase. Others reached the top of the stairs to the entrance to the chapel and they were bayoneted or shot there. Those of us who remained at the bottom of the staircase were told by the Japanese if we were able to do so, to lie down on the floor. Those who were not able to do so were thrown down on the floor. We were thrown onto those mattresses that were there that we had been sleeping on the night before. And there I remained on those mattresses from about, I suppose, a little after twelve until eleven o'clock that evening. There were a couple of dead men lying over my feet and a dead woman on my head. I was unable to move because of loss of blood and because of the people around me.

As a Catholic priest I felt that I was not doing enough for the people, so I tried to make my way upstairs and to administer the last rites of religion to those who were still alive but dying. And I extricated myself and managed to administer the last sacraments to many of them, and I went upstairs, and I saw lying halfway up the stairs some dead bodies. When I reached the entrance to the chapel there were other bodies there, dead bodies, and a number of people who were wounded. And I made my way creeping into the chapel and there I saw inside the chapel some brothers lying in the passageway. I went up towards the altar and there was one brother lying before the communion rails, dead. In the corner were two other brothers with a little boy, the second youngest son of Judge Carlos, lying with them, dead. I was pretty exhausted when I reached near the altar, and I entered the sacristy there, and as far as I remember I must have collapsed, because when I awoke the sun was streaming in.

He paused to identify some photographs of the wounded and some sketches of the floor plan of the school for the five American generals.

At a table a dozen feet from Father Cosgrave, a sixth general sat. In the faded but neatly pressed uniform of the Imperial Japanese Army, Tomoyuki Yamashita, Japan's best field general and the last commander of Japanese forces in the Philippines, was on trial for his life. He listened carefully as Father Cosgrave continued.

Hiding behind the altar, the priest emerged once or twice to see if anyone was still alive and needed help, or last rites. Three days after the invasion, he heard voices. American voices.

"I managed to creep down through the church and told them what had happened and told them about my companions behind the altar and in the sacristy. They treated my wounds and gave me a shot of whiskey and put me on the ambulance, assuring me that within a few minutes they would have rescued all my companions." One teacher survived. "All the other brothers were killed," he told the generals. "Without exception."

On August 6, 1945, some three months before Father Cosgrave testified in Manila, a U.S. Army Air Force plane dropped an atomic bomb on the Japanese city of Hiroshima. Three days later, a second plane dropped another one on Nagasaki. For a military empire on the precipice of defeat, they were the final, crippling blows. On August 15, Emperor Hirohito addressed his subjects on the radio, to inform them that Japan had been defeated and had accepted the "joint declaration" of the Allies that had demanded unconditional surrender.

In the remote and beautiful green mountains of the Philippine island of Luzon, General Yamashita may well not have heard the emperor's proclamation.

Japanese communications were all but destroyed. But if he did hear it, he heard no instruction to the empire's military commanders to lay down their arms and surrender, and Yamashita, for thirty-nine years in the Imperial Japanese Army the emperor's loyal servant, did not.

American forces were all over northern Luzon and had been for months, driving the Japanese army and its commanding general from one mountain to the next in fierce combat. But they did not know where Yamashita was. For that matter, they were not entirely sure that he would surrender at all. In three years of offensive operations, from Guadalcanal in 1942 through Tarawa, New Guinea, Saipan, Iwo Jima, and Okinawa, American soldiers, sailors, and Marines had learned a hard fact about Japanese soldiers: They did not surrender. They fought until they died. And so to get the word out, to Yamashita and whatever subordinate commanders might be still up in the hills with him, American planes dropped thousands of leaflets in the days following and fitted out a small plane to fly over the mountaintops, trailing a 30-foot-long sign: "Hirohito has surrendered." But sporadic fighting continued, and Yamashita did not come out of the hills.

One American knew where Yamashita was. He was Captain Dan Shaw of Poteau, Oklahoma, a twenty-six-year-old pilot who had been shot down behind Japanese lines in Luzon just hours after the announcement from Tokyo. He was taken to Yamashita's headquarters near the village of Kiangan in the mountainous Cordillera in north Luzon. Eleven days later he was released, unharmed, the first step in a courtly exchange that led to surrender.

Yamashita gave Shaw a letter, praising him for not disclosing any information during questioning in captivity. Shaw brought the letter to Major General William Gill, commander of the Thirty-Second Division, which had been chasing and battling Yamashita's forces for months. Gill replied in kind, writing a letter to Yamashita expressing appreciation for his humane treatment and release of the pilot. He gave the letter to Shaw, who took off the next day and flew over the village where he had been held, dropping the letter and instructions on how to surrender. Soon afterward a Japanese detail made its way to an American outpost with a letter to Gill, written in English and signed by Yamashita.

"I am taking this opportunity," the letter read, "to convey to you that orders from Imperial headquarters pertaining to cessation of hostilities have been duly received by me Aug. 20 and I immediately issued orders to cease hostilities to all units under my command insofar as communications were possible. I also wish to add at this point my heartfelt gratitude to you, fully cognizant of the sincere efforts and deep concern you continuously show with reference to the cessation of hostilities. I failed to receive orders from Imperial headquarters authorizing me to enter into direct negotiations here in the Philippines with the United States army concerning carrying out the order on cessation of hostilities but I am of the fond belief that upon receipt of this order negotiations can immediately be entered."

The commander of all Japanese soldiers in the Philippines may have been of the fond belief that negotiations could immediately be entered, but Major General Robert S. Beightler was not interested in that. As commander of the Thirty-Seventh Infantry Division of the U.S. Army, Beightler's job was to take custody of all the Japanese soldiers on Luzon, and that meant Yamashita above all.

At nine o'clock on the morning of September 2, Yamashita and twenty-one Japanese officers and enlisted men walked slowly down the steep path of the mountains and were met by an advance party of American officers. The Japanese had divided themselves into two groups—the Imperial Japanese Army and the Imperial Japanese Navy. A U.S. Army reporter noted, "The Army and Navy groups were made necessary because of disunity between the commands, each service jealously guarding its own rights and not recognizing authority of the other to surrender the combined forces."

"As he walked toward me," Beightler wrote of Yamashita a few months later, "he proffered his hand. I refused to shake hands; he then stepped back, saluted and bowed. I could not help but feel a sense of satisfaction that standing before me, beaten and submissive, was the man who had wrought havoc, destruction and bloodshed throughout the Philippines with a vile and cruel hand, now compelled to surrender all the fanatical Japanese forces who had carried out his diabolical plans."

Beightler loaded Yamashita and the others onto a pair of C-47 transports and flew to the west coast of Luzon, where they began a rugged three-hour journey by car, jeep, and truck to Baguio, to the elegant mansion that had been the summer retreat of the American High Commissioner.

Baguio, 130 miles from Manila by air but longer by tortuous mountain roads, was a place Yamashita knew well, for it had been his headquarters just a few months earlier. In January 1945, when MacArthur's imminent landing on Luzon had led Yamashita to abandon Manila and head for the hills, Baguio was the natural retreat: elevated, protected by the mountains, adjacent to the enemy's avenues of approach.

At five o'clock in the evening of the day he walked out of the jungle, Yamashita and the Japanese party arrived at Baguio. He surrendered his sword and asked one question: When will we be executed?

He was told that there would be no execution there.

The next morning, just before noon, Yamashita was led to the dining room, filled with army technicians setting up radio, teletype, and telephone connections to broadcast the ceremony to the world. Lieutenant General

Jonathan Wainwright, who had surrendered American forces at Bataan in the spring of 1942, ending the American defense of the Philippines, and Lieutenant General Arthur E. Percival, who had surrendered British forces to Yamashita at Singapore in February of 1942, entered the room, surrounded by dozens of American and British officers. "Yamashita's face twitched and he noticeably gulped," Beightler recalled, when he saw Percival, whom he had last seen across a similar table in Singapore when Percival had been the vanquished one.

Yamashita was shown the instrument of surrender. Perhaps thinking that this was the time for negotiation, he began to seek changes in the language, but an American lieutenant interrupted, speaking firmly in Japanese. "General," he said curtly, "we are not asking you to sign this surrender. We are telling you that you will sign."

"Clearly and emphatically," the official army reporter wrote, the terms of the document were read "while the Japanese representatives listened impassively." The terms were blunt. "We hereby surrender unconditionally to the Commanding General, United States Army Forces, Western Pacific, all Japanese and Japanese-controlled armed forces, air, sea, ground and auxiliary, in the Philippine Islands," the instrument stated. "We hereby command all Japanese forces wherever situated in the Philippine Islands to cease hostilities forthwith.... We hereby direct the commanders of all Japanese forces in the Philippine Islands to surrender.... We hereby undertake faithfully to obey all further proclamations, orders and directives deemed by the Commanding General, United States Army Forces, Western Pacific, to be proper to effectuate this surrender."

Four parchment copies of the instrument were placed before Yamashita. He signed, and the ceremony was concluded. It had taken barely fifteen minutes.

Yamashita was escorted from the room under armed guard, a prisoner of war now. He was flown that afternoon to Manila, where he would be taken to New Bilibid Prison. As the plane began its approach over Manila Bay, Yamashita gazed out the window at the armada of ships that had been assembled for an invasion of Japan and at the docks piled high with weapons, munitions, vehicles, and supplies. He turned to a military policeman escorting him. "How could we win," he said through a translator, "when you had all that?"

Yamashita's Ghost

1

Law and War

The marriage of war and law has always been uneasy. The essence of war, after all, is killing people. War is everywhere accompanied by violence, some necessary to the accomplishment of the objective, some not. Yet war is not supposed to be mere gratuitous violence; it has always been an act of state, a decision made and implemented by political authority to accomplish a public purpose. Sometimes that decision seeks to aggressively control weaker adversaries; sometimes it seeks to defend against such imposition. But whether the decision is wise or unwise, whether we deem the war just or unjust, the distinction between war and violent outlawry lies in the political nature of the decision, the undertaking by the state to wage war using its citizens and public funds. The tension between war and the law arises from what many see as the unnatural union of lethal violence and legal restraint. A "law of war" seems an oxymoron, an ill-suited and perhaps even hypocritical attempt to distinguish among murderous acts.

Telford Taylor, the American deputy prosecutor at the International Military Tribunal at Nuremberg, explained the distinction:

> War consists largely of acts that would be criminal if performed in time
> of peace—killing, wounding, kidnapping, destroying or carrying off other
> peoples' property. Such conduct is not regarded as criminal if it takes place
> in the course of war, because the state of war lays a blanket of immunity
> over the warriors.
>
> But the area of immunity is not unlimited, and its boundaries are marked
> by the laws of war. Unless the conduct in question falls within those
> boundaries, it does not lose the criminal character it would have should it
> occur in peaceful circumstances. In a literal sense, therefore, the expression
> "war crime" is a misnomer, for it means an act that remains criminal even
> though committed in the course of war, because it lies outside the area of
> immunity prescribed by the laws of war.

1

But this concept—this rationalization, perhaps—is of relatively recent origin. The Roman Empire and the city-states of ancient Greece, both deeply acquainted with military conquest, gave little thought to war as a subject of secular law. Greece had certain military customs—respecting the sanctity of temples, halting combat during the (Olympic) games, allowing the vanquished to claim their dead from the battleground—and Rome had certain expectations for the conduct of professional soldiers and their generals, but the source of these customs and expectations was tradition, honor, religion, or the expectation of reciprocity, not law as given by secular or political authority. "Inter arma enim silent leges," wrote Cicero: "In times of war, the law falls silent."

The idea that war should be subject to law did not emerge in the Western tradition until the late Middle Ages in Europe, and its roots were in both the church and the crown. Here a distinction must be made between two concepts that are often commingled. One is whether a war is indeed "just"—that is, undertaken for a righteous purpose, and only when other means of diplomacy or persuasion have failed. The other is the lawfulness of the combat itself—that is, whether the war is carried out according to accepted standards of behavior, limiting as much as possible the collateral damage to noncombatants: civilians, the wounded, and the soldiers who surrender.

The two are conceptually distinct, even distant. The question of the just war occupied Cicero and other ancients, but in the Middle Ages it became firmly a theological doctrine—what medieval scholars called "jus ad bellum." God favored only the righteous warriors, and for God to be on one's side, the war had to be lawfully declared, carried on by the lawful authority of a sovereign prince or king, and, most importantly, dedicated to a rightful purpose—the defense of one's own lands or the reclamation of lands or a crown wrongfully held by the adversary. Given the confluence of secular and religious authority wielded by sovereigns, it was easy—indeed, inevitable—to cast the justness of going to war as a legal issue.

Nowhere is this more dramatically illustrated than in Shakespeare's *Henry the Fifth*, a remarkably accurate portrayal of the tension between law and war in the fifteenth century. The young and restive English king, coveting France, fixates on the denial of the crown to his great-grandmother, a French princess. But he fears that the law in France denies any right of succession through the line of the female, which if true would preclude his claim to recover the crown and strip his ambition of its righteousness. He summons the Archbishop of Canterbury, who, in an elaborate and masterful display of legal analysis, proclaims that the law is invalid—indeed, it has been disregarded repeatedly by French kings, who themselves have inherited the crown from female ancestors.

Shakespeare's Henry is steely-eyed. "May I with right and conscience make this claim?"

The archbishop, himself covetous of extending his churchly realm, assures Henry that he can, thus giving him a divine cover for his ambitions. "Now are we well resolv'd, and by God's help / . . . France being ours, we'll bend it to our awe or break it all to pieces." Victory, he is sure, "lies all within the will of God, to whom I do appeal and in whose name . . . I am coming on, / To venge me as I may and to put forth / My rightful hand in a well-hallow'd cause."

This doctrine of the just war is distinct from what became known as *jus in bello*—the idea that law should restrain the actions of soldiers on the battlefield, restricting their killing to enemy soldiers, leaving the populace undisturbed. That has always been a political doctrine, not an especially theological one. Although it is evident as early as the eleventh century, in a decree that the clergy should be spared the vicissitudes of war, it was not yet fully developed even up to the late Middle Ages. Knights made much of the concept of chivalry, including fair combat when they fought each other for their respective princes in England or France or Germany, but no chivalrous concepts restrained their conduct when they beheaded infidels in the Crusades or pillaged their own countrysides, hiring themselves out to warlords and oligarchs when no prince had need of their services.

As Henry's army marched through France toward the climactic battle at Agincourt, in Shakespeare's telling, Henry presides over the hanging of a soldier who stole a chalice from a church, then tells his assembled army, "We would have all such offenders so cut off. And we give express charge that in our marches through the country there be nothing compell'd from the villages, nothing taken but paid for, none of the French upbraided or abused in disdainful language." Henry's motivation is not spiritual, but secular, even tactical: "For when lenity and cruelty play for a kingdom," he advises his troops, "the gentler gamester is the soonest winner."

And when, in the battle, French soldiers slip behind the English lines and kill the boys who are guarding the army's supplies, Henry's lieutenant is outraged: "'Tis expressly against the law of arms," he cries. Henry too: "I was not angry since I came to France / Until this instant." Yet this gentle gamester could, and in fact did at Agincourt, order that French prisoners be slain in cold blood, and he sends a warning to the French that if they continue the battle, he will take more prisoners, warning, "We'll cut the throats of those we have, / And not a man of them that we shall take / Shall taste our mercy." The slaughter of noncombatants, it seems, was wrong when the other side did it.

In 1648, the Treaties of Westphalia ordained a Europe of nations that gradually displaced a plethora of duchies and kingdoms, and this fostered the growth of the "law of nations," which we now call international law. By that was meant not a regime of law that transcended national boundaries—that idea of transnational law was still struggling for acceptance in the twentieth century—but rather the law *of* nations, the law *among* nations, a means by which nations could deal profitably with each other as equals, adopting common expectations and customs and rules to advance each nation's parochial and often competitive interests. By agreeing on the sovereignty of the high seas, the safety of neutral nations' vessels during war, the exchange of ambassadors, and the benefits of trade and commerce among nations, "customary international law"—the unwritten but important practices and expectations that nations voluntarily follow in their dealings with each other—became a way of advancing national interests.

International law never held war to be illegal. It hardly could, given war's prevalence. It accepted war as a legitimate if sometimes regrettable form of intercourse among nations. In the famous words of Carl von Clausewitz, war is diplomacy—or politics, or policy—carried on through other means.

In this context, the medieval *jus in bello*—the behavior expected of soldiers in combat—became an important part of customary international law. Two guiding principles emerged. The rule known as distinction reflected a belief that wars should be fought between armies, not between peoples, and required that soldiers distinguish between military objectives and civilian lives and property and confine their arms to the former to the extent possible. But recognizing that war inevitably causes disruption, harm, and death to civilians too, the rule of proportionality required that such collateral damage not exceed the value of the military objective: no widespread destruction in pursuit of a military objective of little value.

In practice these rules were quite elastic, leaving much to the discretion of military commanders. Because they arose from behavior and expectations rather than from positive law, they came to be known as the "customs of war." They developed gradually and on the battlefield were often ignored. Not until the middle of the nineteenth century did treaties—formal and binding agreements among states—emerge as explicit rules of humanitarian constraints in warfare and take their place with the customs of war to form the international law of war.

The original Geneva Convention in 1864 laid down rules more specific than anything seen so far: In war on land, those who were wounded in action and those taken prisoner were to be treated humanely; and those on the battlefield tending to the wounded were to be immune from hostile action. To signify their protected status, medical attendants were to wear the emblem of a red cross on a white field. The body created to oversee compliance was called the International Committee of the Red Cross. A second Geneva Convention later extended the same principles to warfare at sea.

These Geneva Conventions were among the first multilateral international treaties, and each nation, by ratifying the treaties, took upon itself the obligation to enforce their terms. But there was no semblance of any international means for doing so. Each nation was sovereign; as in all international matters, other nations could ask or plead or bargain or pressure or threaten or even go to war, but no nation could bring another's soldiers, much less its king, into its courts to answer for violations of the treaties. Instead, each nation pledged in the conventions to make violations crimes under its own laws and to hold accountable, in its own courts, any of its citizens who violated them.

That did not work out very well. Once in a while a government might put its own soldiers on trial for mistreatment of prisoners, for depredations against civilians, or for other crimes in war, but such cases were rare. In 1863, President Abraham Lincoln issued "Instructions for the Government of Armies of the United States in the Field," known as the Lieber Code after its author Franz Lieber, a German-born professor of law at Columbia University. It was the first actual code of the laws of war meant to govern an army, and it was influential in shaping thought on the subject for decades afterward, but no one was ever actually tried for violating it.

Very occasionally, nations victorious in war, including the United States, haled before its courts the defeated enemy and put *them* on trial for violations of the law of war. The law that was invoked was not the formal language of the treaties but the customary law of war, those precepts of humane treatment but uncertain boundaries. In 1865, for example, Henry Wirz, the commandant of the Confederacy's prisoner-of-war camp at Andersonville, Georgia, was tried by the United States for gross mistreatment of U.S. soldiers captured and held there. He was convicted and hanged. But those cases were exceptional (and anyway, the United States considered the Confederacy a rebellion, not a nation). The law of war, though well understood in principle by scholars and sovereigns, rarely found its way into court.

While the Geneva Conventions addressed the treatment of noncombatants, in the latter part of the nineteenth century, there were any number of international conferences designed to go one step further: to regulate the tactics and weapons by which warfare itself could be waged. Several treaties emerged, culminating in the Fourth Hague Convention of 1907, which proclaimed that "the right of belligerents to adopt means of injuring the enemy is not unlimited" and outlawed tactics intended to "kill or wound treacherously," such as poisoned weapons and "arms, projectiles or material calculated to cause unnecessary suffering." The Fourth Hague Convention also prohibited the pillaging or other destruction of property not "imperatively demanded by the necessities of war" and the targeting of historical, cultural, or educational sites.

Other treaties followed, on all manner of wartime subjects—treaties banning the dropping of weapons from balloons; treaties requiring that submarines give fair warning to their targets before letting loose the torpedoes. Many of them were ineffectual; others did not survive World War I. But it was only after that

Great War, in the proceedings at Paris leading to the Treaty of Versailles, that the international community—the "civilized world" or "league of nations," as it called itself—seriously discussed what would have been a significant advance: a means by which those who had violated the treaties or the customary laws of war could be called to account in a court of law.

In June 1918, a German submarine had torpedoed the *Llandovery Castle*, a British hospital ship, off the Irish coast, killing 234 people. The vessel bore a prominent red cross, and there is little doubt that the attack was deliberate. There was common understanding among the victors' delegates in Paris that such a crime should be punished and that the submarine's captain should be held accountable. Many also urged that responsibility for these and other war-time misdeeds be carried up the chain of command, even to Kaiser Wilhelm, and that the case go to court.

But just *what* court was a problem. Proposals for a permanent international court were successfully opposed by the United States, whose embrace of the sovereignty of nations was far too strong to countenance a true international court. Nor would the United States delegation endorse the idea that a victorious nation could bring before its courts the military or political leaders, much less the heads of state, of the vanquished ones.

The conclusion in Paris, therefore, was that the Germans themselves must put on trial those responsible for the sinking of the *Llandovery Castle*. The resulting proceedings in German courts were, to put it gently, ineffective. The captain of the submarine escaped before trial, and two of his lieutenants, convicted and sentenced to four years' imprisonment, escaped soon afterward.

The failure of international law at this important juncture was surely due in part to the aversion of German judges to punishing German military officers for acts carried out in a war against Germany's enemies. But in part it was due to a fundamental difficulty. From the time of its inception in the seventeenth century, international law had been a regime to regulate the conduct of nations, not of men.

The laws that governed war, to the extent they did so at all, were like the laws that governed trade or diplomacy or the high seas: understandings among nations as to how they would conduct their affairs with each other. Even when these understandings were codified and formalized in treaties, as they were at Geneva and The Hague, no one seriously suggested that the treaties were an international criminal code. The idea first broached in Paris—that individuals should be tried and punished in a criminal trial—was a failure, as the *Llandovery Castle* case showed. Soldiers were accountable only to their own governments, if indeed they were accountable at all.

There was thus a considerable abyss between the international regime of law that had emerged over hundreds of years, the result sometimes of custom and sometimes of treaties, and any actual enforcement of that law. There matters stood when World War II began in 1939, with Germany's invasion of Poland and its blitzkrieg through Europe, and Japan's simultaneous attacks two years later on the United States at Pearl Harbor, on Great Britain in Malaya, and on the American commonwealth of the Philippine Islands.

2

Tomoyuki Yamashita

Japan's war began long before December 7, 1941, the day that it simultaneously attacked Pearl Harbor, Hong Kong, the Philippines, and Malaya. The 1930s were a decade of increasing nationalism, expansionism, and militarism in Japan. It solidified its hold on Manchuria on the Chinese mainland, setting up a puppet government subservient to the Japanese army, while at home a cabal of young military officers attempted to overthrow Japan's civilian government, setting off a prolonged power struggle between two factions of the army—the Imperial Way movement and the Control movement—each seeking influence over the emperor and control of the political arms of government. Violence erupted in 1936 when, in the midst of a snowstorm, two armed regiments led by captains and lieutenants in the Imperial Way faction attacked the home of the prime minister and murdered several prominent government leaders. They claimed to be acting out of loyalty to the emperor.

The emperor did not see it that way. He ordered the minister of war to put down the mutiny, and after four days of tense negotiations, the Imperial Way surrendered. A key figure in ending the standoff was General Tomoyuki Yamashita, a respected and resolutely apolitical officer aligned with neither faction, who managed to garner the trust of the young officers by his sympathetic understanding of their frustration with politicians, while at the same time stoutly maintaining the imperative of loyalty to the emperor.

Yamashita (three syllables: Ya-mash-ta) did not show early promise of being a leader of fighting men. Born in 1885, the second son of a country doctor in remote Shikoku, the smallest and least populous of Japan's four Home Islands, young Tomoyuki preferred writing poetry and strolling through the island's cedar forests to applying himself to schoolwork. He happily left to his older brother the rigors of studying medicine, though he later mused, "If I had only been cleverer or had worked harder, I would have been a doctor like my brother." Believing the boy to be in need of discipline, his parents enrolled him at age twelve in a school operated by a former Samurai warrior. Military drill

8

and the study of Japan's military history and traditions were as much a part of the curriculum as mathematics and geography, and when the boy returned to his parents two years later he told them he had made up his mind to become a soldier. He enrolled in a military academy in Hiroshima, where he immersed himself in the way of Bushido—the ancient Samurai tradition of chivalry—and of loyalty to the emperor, to which he would adhere until his death.

Yamashita thrived in this environment, and three years later, at age eighteen in 1903, he won a place in the Central Military Academy in Tokyo. He graduated with a lieutenant's commission at age twenty-one, only to find himself posted to a regiment in Hiroshima, far from combat in Manchuria, where the Japanese army defeated Russia and took over the new domain. Restive and unoccupied, he passed the examination for the War College, the gateway to advancement for officers, and after several years of study and training, he graduated in 1917 at age thirty-two, a captain, and married a general's daughter the next day. Fluent in German, he was posted as a junior attaché at the Japanese embassy in Bern, Switzerland, where he spent three relatively carefree years before coming back to a desk job at Imperial Japanese Army headquarters in Tokyo.

Yamashita was earning a reputation as a sophisticated and capable officer, and at age forty in 1925 he was made chief military attaché at his country's embassy in Vienna—the best years of his life, he later recalled. He enrolled in economics courses at Vienna University and, his wife back in Japan, took in the city and the many social and cultural pleasures of a diplomatic envoy, which put noticeable weight onto his exceptionally tall frame. "Before Vienna, I knew little of the world outside the military life," he later said. "There I read many books and made many good and interesting friends." But after three years, at age forty-three in 1928, he was recalled to Tokyo, where he was promoted to colonel and given his first command, a regiment in Tokyo, many of whose prior commanders had advanced to higher rank and larger commands.

He was in a fateful place at a critical time. His sojourns in Europe had kept him largely removed from the roiling unrest and the warring cliques in the army, and his service as a regimental commander and his lack of political baggage led to the coveted post of chief of military affairs, responsible for mobilization and budgeting for the army. It was in this capacity that he was summoned in the middle of a snowy night in February 1936 to meet with the rebellious young officers of the Imperial Way and to dissuade them from their determination to depose the ruling clique of officers.

It was a highly delicate and dangerous mission. Japan was verging on anarchy. The emperor refused to treat with the Imperial Way mutineers, summarily ordering them back to their barracks, leaving Yamashita to persuade them to go. They were in no mood to be pacified, and the blood of those they had already killed was still on their swords as they sat with this general officer, at fifty-one so much older than they. Yamashita acknowledged the sincerity of their dissent and promised, "We will not let you die alone" if entreaties to the emperor failed.

It was a bold tactic, suggesting though not actually promising that if the emperor continued to ignore their demands, Yamashita would die with them, though whether on the streets or by the ritual suicide of hara-kiri, he did not say. Thirteen of them were executed, though Yamashita intervened with the emperor to spare many others.

Yamashita had made no friends during the ordeal—each side harbored suspicions that he was secretly loyal to the other—but the emperor had good words for him and promoted him to the ranks of general officers. He spent eighteen months in occupied Korea and then was promoted again and given command of an infantry division in northern China, an assignment about which little remains known. It was a time of fierce fighting in China, but in Nanking (now Nanjing), Japanese soldiers raped 20,000 women and murdered as many as 200,000 civilians, according to the postwar findings of the International Military Tribunal for the Far East. If Yamashita, 1,000 miles away, knew of it or had any response, there is no record of it.

By late 1940, the Japanese military was nearly at the height of its power, its domestic rivals dispatched and its influence over the emperor virtually complete. Hideki Tojo (the minister of war and later premier) and the rest of the military leadership were already at the planning tables of war, seeking to expand the empire throughout the Pacific. Their only obstacles were the fortified but isolated British naval base in Singapore at the tip of Malaya (now Malaysia) and the somnolent U.S. Pacific Fleet in Hawaii. The Dutch in the East Indies and the distant Australians seemed little threat. In September 1940, Tojo, who had served in Bern with Yamashita, named him head of the air force and, at the very end of the year, sent him on a military mission to examine Germany's war machine and its strategies in a major war.

Yamashita and his delegation and Hitler and his high command spent the next six months trying to find out as much as they could about each other's plans and capabilities while disclosing as little as possible about their own. Yamashita reportedly concluded that Hitler was an unimpressive little clerk whose vaunted Luftwaffe was not up to the challenge of a modern air war, but that Japan could nonetheless learn much from Germany's industrial prowess. He concluded that Japan's military leadership was grossly underprepared for a major war and that Japan would need two years to prepare for its greatest threat—not the United States or Great Britain but its chronic adversary, Russia. Returning home in June 1941, just as Germany began its invasion of the Soviet Union, Yamashita urged that Japan modernize its armed forces and adopt the model of a unified military command, ending the tradition of an army and navy each with its own direct chain of command to the emperor, each suspiciously eyeing the other and sharing little information about plans and strategies. Tojo would have none of it. Intolerant of rivals and fearful that Yamashita might replace him as war minister and bring the plans of war to an end, he dispatched him again to Manchuria, far from the military's nerve center, as planning for war accelerated.

Poor itself in natural resources, Japan needed to turn southward for the riches of tin, rubber, bauxite, and, above all, oil to be found in Malaya and in Sumatra, Java, and the rest of the Dutch East Indies (now Indonesia). To protect its access to these resources and the oceans around them, Japan needed to dominate a vast sphere from the mid-Pacific to the Indian border, from the Bering Sea through Manchuria and into China, and through all of Southeast Asia. To secure those areas, it needed to do three things: take over the Philippines, the American commonwealth exactly in the middle of the shipping lanes between Japan and the southern resources it coveted; establish a defensive perimeter around the islands ranging from north of Australia—New Guinea and the Solomons—up nearly to the Aleutians between Russia and Alaska; and eliminate the threat of the United States and the British Empire.

That meant driving the United States out of the Philippines, Britain out of Singapore and Malaya, and Australia out of anything that was not Australia. Japan had no need or desire to conquer either the United States or Britain; such objectives would have been quite impossible. Rather, the Chinese and the Filipinos, the Manchurians and the Malayans, the Indochinese and the Micro-nesians, would all become part of a vast pan-Oriental empire ruled from Tokyo, which the white man would never again enter as a colonial overlord. Japan named its expanding empire the Greater East Asia Co-Prosperity Sphere.

Tojo, now premier, put his rivalries aside. He recalled Yamashita from Man-churia in November and gave him command of Japan's Twenty-Fifth Army, then training on Hainan Island in the South China Sea—the tropical forests of occupied China. With a muscular navy, hundreds of thousands of men in land armies, and advanced fighter aircraft—and with both the British and the hated Soviet Union fighting for their survival against Hitler's Germany—1941 was Japan's time. And Tomoyuki Yamashita was Japan's general.

3

Malaya and Singapore

Yamashita's goal was Singapore. In London, conventional wisdom assumed that any attack on that city at the tip of the Malay Peninsula, which snakes southward from Thailand, would necessarily come by sea. But on December 8, 1941—December 7 in the United States and more than an hour before the first bombs fell on Pearl Harbor—landing craft of Yamashita's Twenty-Fifth Army plunged through high surf and heavy rain to a beach a mile or two south of the Thai border. Indian troops under British command, startled by the landings and the simultaneous air attacks on sleepy British airfields nearby, put up some resistance, then quickly retreated into the jungle. Within hours, Yamashita began moving his forces south.

No campaign was as challenging as that in Malaya, and no Japanese victory in the war was as skillful or as astonishing. "Singapore was Britain's pivotal point in the domination of Asia," recalled Masanobu Tsuji, Yamashita's military operations chief, after the war.

> It was the eastern gate for the defence of India and the northern gate for the defence of Australia. It was the axis of the steamship route from Europe to the Orient, north to Hong Kong and through to Shanghai, and to the treasures of the Dutch East Indies to the south and east. Through these two arteries alone, during a period of many years, Britain controlled the Pacific Ocean with Singapore as the very heart of the area.

Singapore's crown jewel was its naval base, whose back was to the Malay Peninsula, its guns trained on the sea. "Fortress Singapore," it was called—at least in London—and it was the heart of British strategy to protect their Pacific empire. Prime Minister Churchill was succinct: "Beware that troops required for ultimate defence Singapore Island and fortress are not used up or cut off in Malay Peninsula," he warned his Ministry of Defence as Yamashita's forces began their advance. "Nothing compares in importance with the fortress."

Yamashita's Twenty-Fifth Army was a formidable one, well trained for jungle warfare and well equipped with tanks and artillery. The Imperial General Staff in Tokyo had offered Yamashita four divisions. No, said Yamashita, I'll take three. And 18,000 bicycles as well.

No other general in the emperor's forces would have been as shrewd and daring, and certainly none as unorthodox. Three divisions, because in the jungles of Malaya, speed, mobility, and maneuverability would be the keys to success and a fourth division would have meant more supplies to transport, more weapons to carry, more communication lines to maintain. Officers and men who were not riding on trucks were given the bicycles, some 6,000 for each of the three divisions. Not since Hannibal crossed the Alps on elephants had an army chosen such unlikely transport. The British had built paved roads down the west coast of Malaya to the capital of Kuala Lumpur and thence to Singapore. Bicycles would be fast and light, and they used rather less fuel than trucks.

Putting troops on bikes also minimized traffic congestion on the narrow peninsula. "Wherever bridges were destroyed the infantry continued their advance," Tsuji wrote, "wading across the rivers carrying their bicycles on their shoulders, or crossing on log bridges held up on the shoulders of engineers standing in the stream. It was thus possible to maintain a hot pursuit of the enemy along the asphalt roads without giving them any time to rest or reorganize." Outmaneuvered and outgunned, "the long-legged Englishmen could not escape our troops on bicycles. . . . They were continually driven off the road into the jungle, where, with their retreat cut off, they were forced to surrender."

With three infantry divisions, a tank brigade, and engineers and artillery and support troops, Yamashita had but 36,000 men at his command, significantly fewer than the 100,000 or so Allied troops—British, Australian, and Indian brigades under British command—in Malaya and Singapore. Yamashita was taking a bold risk in bringing fewer combat units than he could have. But he had several advantages: his troops were far better trained than Britain's, who had little experience in jungle fighting, and the British had no tanks at all. The Japanese army air force had over 600 planes, more than twice the number the British had, and every one of the Japanese aircraft was faster and more deadly than Britain's slow and aged force in Malaya. They quickly dominated the skies, demolishing airfields and outmaneuvering and then destroying the British and Australian air forces.

Tokyo had allocated few big ships for the campaign, calculating—correctly, as it happened—that Allied naval power would be weak. When Malaya was attacked, the British fleet in Singapore prepared to engage the enemy. But the British fleet was mostly two battleships: the brand new *Prince of Wales* and the World War I–vintage cruiser *Repulse*. On December 8, twelve hours after the Japanese landings, they sailed north without fighter protection. On December 9, they reached the landing area. On December 10, Japanese torpedo bombers sank them both. The British lost 845 sailors and their Far East fleet. The knockout punch horrified Churchill when he got the call from the Admiralty. "In all the war I never received a more direct shock," he wrote. "As I turned over and twisted in bed the full horror of the news sank in upon me. There were no British or American capital ships in the Indian Ocean or the Pacific except the American survivors of Pearl Harbour, who were hastening back to California. Over all this vast expanse of waters Japan was supreme, and we everywhere weak and naked."

Churchill should not have been surprised. The entire strategy for the defense of Singapore, and thus of the British Empire in the Pacific, assumed that the enemy would oblige by mounting a seaborne attack. Yamashita's army simply went where it was not expected. Yet there was more to its success than an inexperienced adversary caught unawares. American observers accompanying the British troops noted that Yamashita's soldiers exhibited "considerable initiative, vigor and physical stamina" and "an unusual aptitude for overcoming terrain obstacles" thanks to well-equipped engineer battalions. Yamashita's soldiers appropriated what they called "Churchill's supplies"—the trucks, fuel, weapons, and food left behind by the retreating British. A British officer, hiding in the jungle, marveled at the speed of their advance. "The majority of them were on bicycles in parties of 40 or 50, riding three and four abreast . . . travelling as light as they possibly could." When tires blew out, the bikers rode down the paved roads on the rims. "The resulting clatter sounded like tanks," wrote John Toland, "and at night the defenders, particularly the Indians who were terrified of any kind of armor, would shout 'Tanks!' and break for the rear."

The troops helped themselves to the food and supplies not only of the British Army but of the villagers as well—conduct that became a significant concern for Yamashita, who called in his subordinates and demanded swift punishment of any soldier taking advantage of the locals. He wrote in his diary, "I want my troops to behave with dignity."

Yamashita prized and emphasized discipline in his ranks. Soldiers engaged in pillage were soldiers who were not fighting and advancing, and Yamashita moved swiftly to punish them. On the island of Penang, he ordered three such soldiers executed and gave their battalion commander twenty-eight days in confinement. "We must encourage the sort of outlook that will make us proud of our nation," he wrote. "Those who have come to Malaya without this outlook may be debased. This is one of the things I must keep a careful watch over." Once, coming upon three captured British soldiers, Yamashita stopped and cautioned his troops: "Do not despise these men. After fighting bravely, they have been unfortunate enough to be captured. Treat them kindly."

Writing in 1952, long after Yamashita had been executed, Tsuji recalled his former commander as "one who enforced upon all under his orders a military and moral discipline as rigorous as the autumn frost." He recalled an English officer, wounded in the chest, who had been brought to the Japanese field hospital, where he was treated. "It is a fine thing that enemy wounded should receive the same treatment as the wounded of one's own side," Tsuji wrote. "This was the policy of General Yamashita, and it was carried out"—though if it was carried out for other British wounded, neither Tsuji nor others mention it.

By January 7, a month into the invasion, Japanese tanks and infantry had demolished British and Indian troops trying to hold the line at the Slim River and pushed on toward Kuala Lumpur, two-thirds of the way to Singapore. They never stopped, never dug in, never regrouped. When the British blew a bridge, Japanese engineers built their own or plunged into the river, lined up, and braced logs on their shoulders as soldiers trooped across, bicycles held high.

Finally, in mid-January, the Japanese came face to face with Australians and Indians in ferocious combat, with heavy casualties on both sides. But it was too little, and way too late. The advance was slowed, not stopped. On January 31, the last of the British, Australian, and Indian troops had been pushed off the Malay Peninsula.

The unremittingly bad news frustrated and angered Churchill. "Here we have been absolutely outmanoeuvred and apparently outfought on the west coast of Malaya by an enemy who has no warship in the neighborhood," he fumed in January. "This command of the western shores of Malaya by the Japanese without the possession of a single ship of war must be reckoned as one of the most astonishing British lapses recorded in naval history."

At the end of January, Yamashita's conquest of Malaya was complete. The British and Australians, after two months of nearly constant retreat, crossed the narrow Johore Strait onto Singapore, where their hopes of making a last stand were rapidly diminishing. They blew up the causeway connecting Singapore to the mainland, only to see the Japanese, barely slowing down, rebuild it, all the while sending troops in small boats across the water and into the mangrove swamps and onto solid land. "The battle must be fought to the bitter end at all costs," Churchill cabled Field Marshall Sir Archibald Wavell on February 10. "Commanders and senior officers should die with their troops." The answer from Wavell was worrisome. "The chief troubles are lack of sufficient training in some of [the Australian and British] reinforcing troops and [the] inferiority complex which bold and skilful Japanese tactics and their command of the air have caused," he cabled. Churchill was dismayed. He recalled after the war:

> I had put my faith in the enemy being compelled to use artillery on a very large scale in order to pulverise our strong points at Singapore, and in the almost prohibitive difficulties and long delays which would impede such

an artillery concentration and the gathering of ammunition along Malayan communications. Now, suddenly, all this vanished away and I saw before me the hideous spectacle of the almost naked island and of the wearied, if not exhausted, troops retreating upon it.

By the first week of February 1942, Yamashita was on the outskirts of Singapore. He had twenty-seven combat-tested infantry battalions, plus tanks, artillery, and crack engineers who had overcome one obstacle after another in the drive down the peninsula. But though the British hold on Singapore had become precarious, so too had the advance of Yamashita's army. It had been traveling at a breakneck pace for over two months, living largely on "Churchill's supplies" and what of its own it could carry. It was low on ammunition and was outnumbered three-to-one by the British, Australian, and Indian troops in Fortress Singapore. As he later would in Manila, Yamashita faced the possibility of a prolonged and destructive street-by-street battle in a city teeming with civilians.

His control of his own troops was at times precarious as well. One of the worst atrocities of the campaign was carried out at Singapore's Alexandra Hospital as Japanese troops closed in on the city. "Indian troops had very likely fired on the advancing Japanese from the hospital grounds before retreating to safety," historian Alan Warren wrote.

A [British] corporal was bayoneted on the operating table, and a number of others killed on the spot. The patients in the wards were rounded up and taken outside. The immobile were bayoneted where they lay. About 150 patients and medical personnel were roped together in groups of four or five, and sent to servants' quarters behind the hospital. During the night some of the prisoners were led away. Screams were heard in the distance, and Japanese guards returned wiping blood from their bayonets.

With Singapore at his mercy, Yamashita took a bold step that was both compassion and bluff. On February 10, he had an English-speaking intelligence officer on his staff draft a note to the British commander in Singapore, General Arthur Percival. Yamashita signed it and had twenty-nine copies inserted in wooden boxes, each 18 inches long. The next morning a Japanese plane, flying low, scattered the boxes over British forces in the city.

I, the High Command of the Nippon Army, based on the spirit of Japanese chivalry, have the honour of presenting this note to Your Excellency advising you to surrender the whole force in Malaya.

My sincere respect is due to your army which, true to the traditional spirit of Great Britain, is bravely defending Singapore which now stands isolated and unaided. Many fierce and gallant fights have been fought by your gallant men and officers, to the honour of British warriorship. But the developments of the general war situation has [*sic*] already sealed the fate of Singapore, and the continuation of futile resistance would only serve to inflict direct harm and injuries to thousands of non-combatants living in the city, throwing them into further miseries and horrors of war, but also would not add anything to the honour of your army.

I expect that Your Excellency, accepting my advice, will give up this meaningless and desperate resistance and promptly order the entire front to cease hostilities and will despatch at the same time your parliamentaire according to the procedure shown at the end of this note. If on the contrary Your Excellency should neglect my advice and the present resistance be continued, I shall be obliged, though reluctantly from humanitarian considerations to order my army to make annihilating attacks on Singapore.

In closing this note of advice, I pay again my sincere respects to Your Excellency.

It was signed "Tomoyuki Yamashita." He added two instructions:

1. The Parliamentaire should proceed to the Bukit Timah Road [Yamashita's headquarters].
2. The Parliamentaire should bear a large white flag and the Union Jack.

Percival did not reply immediately. His superior, Wavell, safely distant in Java, was demanding that Percival's "gallant stand . . . must be continued to the limit of endurance," but by February 15 those limits had been reached. Singapore had no fuel, no water, no food, no ammunition, no resupply, and no hope. Churchill was by now in despair. "I was sure that it would be wrong to enforce needless slaughter, and without hope of victory to inflict the horrors of street fighting on the vast city, with its teeming, helpless, and now panic-stricken population." He authorized Wavell to allow Percival to surrender.

And so, on the morning of February 15, following Yamashita's instructions, Percival sent out a flag of truce to Yamashita's command post just west of the city, and that evening he and his interpreter, Major Cyril Wild, sat across from Yamashita at a long table at the Ford Motor Company factory on the outskirts of Singapore.

Yamashita's choice of the Ford plant may have reflected only that it was the biggest building still intact, but it was a portent, in more ways than he could have known. Lee Kuan Yew, a university student in 1942 and later the first prime minister of independent Singapore (1959–1990), recalled that when he heard the explosion of the causeway connecting Singapore to mainland Malaya, after the British had retreated to Singapore, he turned to a friend and said, "That's the end of the British Empire."

The verdict was premature, but it proved to be accurate. The fall of Singapore severed the arteries of the British Empire, and it bled to death over the next twenty-five years. Today the old Ford factory, refurbished, is a national monument in Singapore, to commemorate not Japan's victory but rather Britain's defeat.

A Japanese officer met Percival and Wild at the door of the factory and escorted them into a room, surrounded by dozens of Japanese photographers and reporters gathered for the event. Yamashita entered and shook hands with the British officers.

Yamashita's ruse was now put to the test. His troops were poised at the edge of the city, seemingly ready to move in if Percival were to stall on the surrender. Percival did not know that in fact the Japanese forces were only a third the number of his own, or that they were low on fuel and especially on artillery shells, because Yamashita had ordered his artillery to keep shelling the city as if their ammunition were endless.

His strategy was to close the deal on surrender before Percival could discover just how precarious the Japanese position was. Yamashita betrayed no weakness, projected no uncertainty. It was "a bluff, a bluff that worked," said Yamashita. "I now realized that the British army had about 100,000 men against my three divisions of 30,000 men. They also had many more bullets and other munitions than I had. . . . I was afraid in my heart that they would discover that our forces were much less than theirs. That was why I decided that I must use all means to make them surrender without terms."

Percival tried to buy a few hours. "I fear that we shall not be able to submit our final reply before ten-thirty PM," some three and a half hours later, he said.

Yamashita was having none of it. "Reply to us only whether our terms are acceptable or not," he replied. "Things must be settled swiftly. We are prepared to resume firing."

Percival folded. "We shall discontinue firing by eight-thirty PM," within the hour.

Yamashita pressed for closure. "You have agreed to the terms but you have not yet made yourself clear as to whether you agree to surrender or not."

Percival could only nod. It was not good enough for Yamashita. He wanted an answer. The two interpreters got into a discussion about the nuanced translation of "surrender," and Yamashita grew still more impatient. He scolded his interpreter: "There's no need for all this talk. It is a simple question and I want a simple answer." He turned to Percival and raised his voice: "We want to hear only"—here he switched to English and chopped his hand against the tabletop—"yes or no!"

Percival paused, and then whispered, "Yes, I agree." He signed the surrender.

Yamashita later explained his outburst:

On this occasion I was supposed to have spoken to Percival rather abruptly. . . . I am afraid that in my anxiety I emphasized the "yes or no" in English too much. The interpreter also emphasized the words very loudly when he repeated them to the British commander. This, however, did end the matter quickly and Percival agreed to my demand for unconditional surrender.

Churchill minced no words: "the worst disaster and largest capitulation of British history," he called it. "Perhaps the most disastrous campaign in the history of British arms," said the *Times* of London. "It was the greatest land victory in Japanese history," wrote Toland.

Yamashita in only seventy days had achieved his victory by doing almost everything right, although he was certainly aided by what the British did wrong. Their intelligence was poor. Many of the troops had been hastily trained, and none of them had encountered jungle warfare. They had no tanks. Their motley collection of slow fighter planes was no match for Japan's crack Zeros. Their military leaders, Percival chief among them, were dutiful but neither imaginative nor decisive; they lacked both command experience and the command presence that inspires troops, and they were not held in high regard in London, which gave their needs short shrift. They underestimated the skill of the Japanese soldiers and were flummoxed by Yamashita's unorthodox strategy. Had the British and Australians been better equipped, better prepared, and better led, defeat would not have come so swiftly and completely, and perhaps might never have come at all. But effective military leaders identify and exploit the enemy's weaknesses, and that Yamashita did, superbly.

Yamashita and Percival, the victor and the vanquished, stood and shook hands as the cameramen snapped away at the historic photo opportunity. Yamashita's adjutant wrote, "He told me afterward that he wanted to say a few kind words to Percival while he was shaking hands with him, as he looked so pale and thin and ill. But he could not say anything because he does not speak English, and he realized how difficult it is to convey heartfelt sympathy when the words are being interpreted by a third person." If Percival got the message through the handshake, he ignored it. Saying nothing, he left the room.

In an interview with radio's Mutual Broadcasting System during his captivity in 1945, Yamashita said through an interpreter, "It was surprising to me that Percival surrendered at all. It was by sheer luck that my entire force was not annihilated at Singapore. The British could have annihilated us. I don't know why they did not." Yamashita was being overly deferential. In February 1942 the British were not only outmaneuvered and outfought; they were outgeneraled.

After he surrendered, Percival had one request of Yamashita. There would be great confusion in the city that night, Percival said, adding, "If by any chance the Japanese Army should make a triumphal entry into the fortress, it will be impossible to guarantee that unforeseen happenings will not occur. Please wait until tomorrow morning." Yamashita listened, and agreed. Two days later Imperial General Headquarters in Tokyo sent a telegram asking Yamashita when he planned to hold his victory parade, suggesting that the following day would be nice. Yamashita said no. "The Army will not hold a celebration," he told Tokyo. "Instead of a triumphal-entry ceremony, a ceremonial commemoration service for the dead will be solemnized on 20th February, and immediately thereafter we will begin operations in Sumatra." Tokyo was astonished—who could imagine the general who had led Japan to its greatest victory refusing to celebrate his success, and refusing in the bargain to let Tokyo show the triumphal films to pump up its cheering crowds at home?

On February 20, the army still outside the city, Yamashita assembled a group of representatives from each unit. Together they built an altar to honor their fallen, and Yamashita read a solemn message of sympathy and remembrance. He gave little thanks or praise to those who had secured the victory; instead he gave citations of valor to those who had been killed. Later, when British prisoners were put to work on the monument, Yamashita allowed them to erect a cross to honor their own dead. Six feet tall, it stood until the end of the war.

In fact, Yamashita never let his combat units enter the city. Well aware of the danger of rampage and determined to avoid it, he sent in police units, known as the Kempetai, supported by selected infantry companies to keep order, which by and large they did. No other soldier was allowed to enter without a pass. The Japanese soldiers who did were tightly controlled; they refrained from looting and generally treated both civilians and prisoners civilly. In the immediate aftermath of the surrender, one Australian observer noted "a holiday spirit about the whole affair." Given the destruction created by a week of warfare, that might have been too cheery a description, but there was no disorder, no rampaging troops, no indiscriminate violence.

One day a clerk in a watchmaker's shop pulled aside Colonel Tsuji, Yamashita's military operations chief, and complained that three soldiers were taking their pick of expensive timepieces with no intention of paying. Tsuji went inside and ran them out, not before taking names. He reported the misbehavior to Yamashita, who the next day "ordered a parade of all officers and, standing in the scorching sun, gave a scathing address on the enforcement of military discipline." The action over a common theft was not lost on the staff, Tsuji wrote later: "To the extent that there were in this campaign weak persons who were robust in the path of theft, so to that extent there would be weak units in the war, and the transgressions of military discipline would be more numerous."

Following the capitulation, British and Australian soldiers were removed to the old British fort at Changi on Singapore Island, colonial mansions on landscaped grounds. Conditions were crowded and food was skimpy, unfamiliar to British and Australian tastes, and often spoiled, but for the next few months the Japanese authorities under Yamashita's command allowed the men to conduct education classes and put on theatrical shows for themselves, later permitting them to grow food in makeshift gardens and generally letting them be, under the command of their own officers. "Some of our men don't know how to treat British officers," Yamashita noted at the time, "and their behavior seems impolite to me. I have given instructions that they must be more polite to surrendered officers."

This was certainly an exception to Japanese policies toward prisoners of war (POWs) throughout the war. Japanese training was rigorous and doctrinaire. Soldiers were to fight until victory or death. Surrender would bring shame upon them and—much worse—upon their families. Lacking any other perspective, therefore, they despised enemy troops who fell into their hands and especially those who surrendered, humiliating their families in Britain or Australia or America, or so Japanese soldiers thought.

But neither Yamashita nor Imperial Headquarters in Tokyo anticipated that more than 50,000 British and Australian soldiers would be surrendered, and so there was no formal Japanese POW administration in place, and none arrived from Tokyo until August 1942, six months after capitulation and weeks after Yamashita's departure for his next command. Captivity that had been tolerable under Yamashita then abruptly turned worse. Many of the prisoners were shipped out to Japan, or to Burma to build the notorious Burma-Thailand railroad, made famous in the 1957 film *The Bridge on the River Kwai*.

Yamashita's swift and successful campaign led someone—it is not clear who, though Yamashita thought it was "the British"—to give him the title "Tiger of Malaya," a name that followed him to his death but one he never cared for. "The tiger attacks its prey in stealth," he once said. "But I attack the enemy in a fair play," said the leader of one of the stealthiest attacks of the Pacific war.

Before leaving Singapore, Yamashita sought out Percival and shook his hand. He left behind a package for him, with a note:

Dear General Percival: As a small token of my personal interest in your welfare, and a practical contribution to your own comfort, I send you thirty tins of butter, thirty tins of cheese, 150 bottles of beer and two bottles of sherry.

With compliments and best wishes,

Yours sincerely,
Lieut. General Yamashita

But for all the civility, restraint, and courtesies, the campaign and conquest were certainly not unmarred by atrocities. Two incidents in particular shed light on the question of what Yamashita knew about the conduct of his troops—the question that would hover over his trial in the Philippines.

On January 29, 1942, near the village of Bakri in southern Malaya, two battalions of the Australian army were desperately trying to slow the advance of Japan's famed Imperial Guards Division toward Singapore, only 80 miles distant.

It was a brutal battle. Food gone, medical supplies destroyed, ammunition scarce, sleep impossible, burdened by the wounded and incapacitated, the soldiers fought their retreat through swamp and rubber trees to the settlement of Parit Sulong. "The area became a frightful shambles," an Aussie soldier later recalled. "Wounded and killed were lying everywhere. Wounded were being twice and thrice wounded in the trucks. . . . During this time, messages were coming through by wireless encouraging us with news that relief was coming. But as time went on, we lost hope."

Caught between the enemy pushing them from the north and the enemy awaiting them in the south, the commander of the beleaguered and exhausted force made a grim decision: those still able to walk would turn to the east and try to reach their army's troops 50 miles away. They would leave the injured and wounded behind, surrounded by the enemy, but hopeful that the Japanese soldiers, seeing the casualties so obviously unable to put up further resistance, would give them aid, or at least bypass them on their advance to Singapore.

It was a desperate hope, and a futile one. The Imperial Guards moved into the village and found the 145 soldiers—110 Australians and 35 Indians—dirty, famished, thirsty, and nearly naked, with their wounds bleeding or clotted with matted blood. The Japanese gave them no merciful treatment, no medical care. They jeered and kicked the fallen soldiers, stabbed them with bayonets and swords, rifled through their few remaining belongings. A lieutenant who appeared to be in charge ordered them to assemble first in front of one building, then inside a shed down the road. Some of the wounded could barely walk the distance; many simply could not.

"The more able-bodied were forced to walk over the helpless," wrote Australian historian Lynette Silver years later.

> Those wounded in the lower body, and therefore unsteady on their feet, fell on others. Screams of pain mixed with groans and shrieks of the delirious, the volume increasing as prisoners, already crushed beneath two or three bodies, felt the pressure of yet another on top of them. Those on the bottom tried desperately to fight off suffocation, as more and more were herded into the stinking, writhing hell-hole. Determined to force all the

prisoners into the building, the guards began hitting and kicking those nearest the doors. . . . The groans and screams of those inside the shed died down, only to be replaced by pleas for water. Those who had nothing to drink for a day or more were bordering on madness and shrieked in their delirium.

The Japanese lieutenant and his staff paid no attention to their pleas as the soldiers of the Imperial Guards Division passed through the village on their march south.

An hour or so later, a dozen Japanese cars and trucks came in convoy along the road, bringing up the rear of the march. Inside was a raft of senior Japanese officers, and the most senior of all wore the three stars of a lieutenant general. He was later identified as Takuma Nishimura, the division commander, one of the most senior officers in the Twenty-Fifth Army. He reported to only one man—Yamashita.*

The commander, hearing the cries and screams of the prisoners inside the shed, got out of his car, walked up to the shed, and peered inside. "The sight of the wounded men was bad enough; the stench of the blood, unattended wounds and unwashed bodies wafting from the room was nauseating," Silver wrote. As the commander turned away and headed back to his car, the lieutenant asked him what was to be done with the prisoners. "After some consideration, Nishimura turned to his aide and, in full hearing of all present, said 'Tell Lieutenant Fujita to "dispose" of the prisoners of war.'" His chief of staff added, "The bodies of the prisoners are to be cremated on completion of the execution." The commander and his entourage drove away.

That afternoon, some 145 prisoners were bound, dragged to a nearby field, arrayed in front of machine guns, and murdered—save two who fell wounded to the grass, feigned death, and lay motionless for hours. Their work done as ordered, the Japanese soldiers formed up, left the village of Parit Sulong and resumed the march southward.

This was not the only war crime the Japanese army committed in Malaya, but it was the largest, and the most brutally cold-blooded. What made this notable was the permission, indeed the order, of the commander—Nishimura, if indeed it was he—to execute the prisoners. Did Yamashita know of this brutal crime?

---

* In 1951 an Australian military commission tried, convicted, and executed Nishimura for ordering the massacre at Parit Sulong. The verdict has been controversial, however, because the sole survivor of the massacre, an Australian lieutenant, was unable to identify Nishimura as the senior officer, and because the lieutenant, who spoke no Japanese, was unable to relate what the senior officer, whoever he was, had said or ordered during his stopover. There have also been allegations that Australian investigators concealed evidence and falsified witnesses' statements in order to build the case against Nishimura.

If the accounts are accurate, he surely did not order it. On the day in question, Yamashita was on the banks of the Johore Strait, some 75 miles away, preparing for the imminent assault on Singapore Island, and he would have had no knowledge of, or interest in, an isolated force of Australians far to his rear. Whether he ever learned of it is a less certain question. There is no evidence that it ever came to his attention, and the only time he was questioned about it, in captivity in 1945, he said he had never heard of it before, and his interrogator, as shall be seen, found him credible. His denial is at least plausible—no contemporary report of the event has ever come to light, if indeed any was ever made. His subordinates might not have considered the matter worthy of report, or they might have purposely concealed it or sanitized any report they did make. If he did learn of it, he did nothing, which would have been out of character for him. Still, the question must remain an open one.

But another event is more troubling. It was called by the Chinese *sook ching*, "a purging," and it took place in the immediate aftermath of the surrender. In the recent words of Japanese historian Hayashi Hirofumi, based on thorough research:

> On the night of 17 February 1942, Maj. Gen. Kawamura Saburo [Kawamura is the family name], an infantry brigade commander, was placed in charge of Japan's Singapore Garrison. The next morning, he appeared at Army Headquarters and was ordered by 25th Army commander, Lt. Gen. Yamashita Tomoyuki, to carry out mopping-up operations. He received further detailed instructions from the chief of staff, Lt. Gen. Suzuki Sosaku, and Lt. Colonel Tsuji Masanobu. Kawamura then consulted with the Kempetai [military secret police] commander, Lt. Col. Oishi Masayuki. The plan to purge the Chinese population was drawn up in the course of these meetings. Under this scheme, Chinese males between the ages of 18 and 50 were ordered to report to mass screening centers. Those deemed anti-Japanese were detained, loaded onto lorries, and taken away to the coast or to other isolated places where they were machine-gunned and bayoneted to death.

The *sook ching* campaign in Singapore lasted three or four days, though it continued sporadically on the mainland. An investigation immediately after the war concluded that 5,000 Chinese had been killed. Other estimates range from 800, a figure put forth by the Japanese Ministry of Justice in 1963, to 50,000, the number "generally believed" in Singapore itself. Hirofumi concludes that neither of the latter figures is close to accurate. He estimates that a minimum of 5,000 died, and that there is no reliable evidence of a maximum number. "The issue of numbers remains unsettled."

Japan and China had been at war for years, and some "overseas Chinese" in Singapore did take up arms against Yamashita's army, but their impact was slight and in any event would have entitled those rounded up either to prisoner-of-war status or internment under comparably humane conditions as enemy aliens. There would be no justification whatever for summary execution, whatever their role or status, even if they had been given a trial or hearing of some kind, which they were not. They were apprehended and executed based on informants' tales, a suspicious appearance, or the whim of the Kempetai.

It is not clear whether Yamashita actually ordered these executions. He had a legitimate interest in identifying and neutralizing potentially hostile elements of the population. "Mopping-up operations," if ordered by Yamashita, could mean any number of things, including rousting out pockets of continued enemy resistance, though there is no evidence that any resistance continued beyond the surrender on February 15. And the Kempetai, the military police who actually carried out the killings, were within Yamashita's command.*

Hirofumi cites a diary entry of the Singapore garrison commander stating that he gave Yamashita a report on the purge and was told to continue. Just what the commander told Yamashita is not clear, however. Ian Ward, longtime Southeast Asia correspondent for the *London Daily Telegraph* who has written extensively about the crimes of Singapore and the trials that followed, concluded, however, that the entire massacre was devised and carried out by Tsuji, Yamashita's military operations chief. Tsuji was not chosen by Yamashita; he was inserted by the General Staff and was seen as a plant in Yamashita's command, put there by Tojo, who had long been Yamashita's rival. Tsuji had a direct channel to Tojo that he regularly used to circumvent Yamashita. It was Tsuji, Ward concludes, who "meticulously planned the mass killing programme and ultimately ordered it." He adds, "Historical research"—not otherwise cited or described—"has now established, beyond all doubt, that the massacre of Chinese civilians in Singapore had nothing whatever to do with orders issued by Yamashita. Orders issued surreptitiously by Lt. Colonel Tsuji—without the knowledge or consent of Yamashita—were what triggered the slaughter."

The available evidence does not justify such certitude. Tsuji was certainly at

---

* "The methods of torture that became the Kempetai hallmark," wrote historian Paul Kratoska, "included beatings with a piece of wood—sometimes while the person was suspended from a rope—placing lighted cigarettes or heated pieces of iron on sensitive areas, and extracting fingernails. The Kempetai made frequent use of the water torture, which involved pumping vast quantities of water into their victim, and then placing a board across the stomach and standing or jumping on it. One man who endured this torture said afterwards that water came out of every opening of his body. 'Words cannot convey the pain.'"

the heart of the massacre, but whether he undertook it with Yamashita's knowledge and approval or without it remains unclear.* Tsuji left Singapore shortly after the *sook ching* massacres and went to the Philippines, where, in the aftermath
of the surrender at Bataan, Tsuji ordered that all American prisoners be slaughtered—without bothering to inform General Masaharu Homma, the Japanese
commander. When Homma issued orders forbidding his troops from mistreating
American prisoners or disrespecting the local Filipinos, Tsuji countermanded
those orders, in Homma's name, unbeknownst to him. He later circumvented
Homma again and in the name of "Imperial Headquarters" ordered the Chief
Justice of the Philippines executed despite Homma's orders to the contrary.
Homma was stunned and furious when he learned of it, but Tsuji was far too
connected with the Imperial General Staff to be cashiered, especially by Homma,
whose moderation toward prisoners and civilians made him suspect in Tokyo.

It is not hard to imagine, therefore, that Tsuji could have carried out the
massacre without Yamashita's authority, even appropriating his commander's
name to give the orders. Tsuji, unsurprisingly, makes no mention at all of the
massacres in his memoir, though he reportedly told friends years later that it was
all his doing and that Yamashita did not know about it.[†]

Still, could Yamashita *not* have known about the roundup and execution of
thousands of people in Singapore? The action was coordinated not only by
Tsuji but by Yamashita's own chief of staff and the commander of the troops
in Singapore proper, even if Tsuji was the brains behind it. The severed heads
of suspected Chinese "looters" were impaled on pikes on bridges crossing the
Singapore River, after all. And if Yamashita read Singapore's new Japanese-
controlled newspaper, he would have seen a large notice in the name of the
Nippon Army:

> As already announced in the declaration of the Commander of the Nippon
> Army, it is hoped, under the divine protection of the universal and imperial

---

* Tsuji was himself one of the most enigmatic and malevolent figures of the war, consumed in "operations and intelligence, mass murder, and political chaos," in the words of
Michael and Elizabeth Norman in their recent and definitive story of the Bataan death
march. "In an army of ultraconservatives, Tsuji was among the most arch, an intriguer who
apparently knew no bounds. He believed his country was fighting a race war, and he hated
whites (save Germans and Italians, Japan's Axis partners) and any Asians allied with them."

† Tsuji's strange and curious career did not end in 1945, as nearly all Japanese officers'
careers did. After the surrender, he fled to Thailand disguised as a Buddhist monk; there he
lay low, evading prosecution. Hirofumi states that he was "protected by the US military." In
any event, he eventually returned to Japan, where he wrote several best-selling memoirs and
was elected to the Diet. In 1961, he disappeared again, this time evidently to Laos, and never
returned. He was declared dead in 1968.

glory, to realize the new order and to establish the co-prosperity sphere as well as the eternal development of Malaya. Anyone who disturbs this great idea is the common enemy of the human race and shall severely be punished without any exception. . . . A part of Chinese have run away and it becomes very clear that another part of them, disguising themselves as good citizens, appear to try to have a chance of wriggling. Should it remain untouched the bright Malaya would never come forever. Thus it is the most important thing to sweep away these treacherous Chinese elements and to establish the peace and welfare of the populace.

General Sosaku Suzuki, Yamashita's chief of staff, who despised Tsuji—a "poisonous insect," he called him—later told a fellow officer that he had advised Yamashita "to punish Tsuji severely and then dismiss him." But, said Suzuki, Yamashita "feigned ignorance." Was Yamashita's ignorance feigned, or was it genuine? What exactly Yamashita was told, and what he knew or should have known, defies proof by any available extrinsic evidence.

In 1945, Yamashita was interrogated about the *sook ching* and the massacres at Parit Sulong and the Alexandra Hospital by Major Cyril Wild, the British officer who had been Percival's interpreter at the surrender of Singapore in the Ford plant in February 1942. After the surrender, the Japanese had taken him prisoner and sent him to the Burma–Thailand railway. He knew well how the Japanese treated their POWs.

Very soon after the Japanese surrender in September 1945, Wild was made the British War Office's chief investigator of war crimes in Malaya and Singapore, on the staff of Admiral Lord Louis Mountbatten. Wild was well regarded, honest, and thorough in his work. Educated at Oxford, he had joined Royal Dutch Shell after university and was sent to Yokohama, where he was tutored in Japanese and lived for several more years before being inducted into the British infantry and posted to Malaya. Fluent in the language, familiar with the culture, and educated by hard experience as a prisoner, he was certainly qualified to investigate Japanese war crimes, and he did so zealously and professionally. "I have a wider knowledge of these matters, probably, than anyone," he said shortly after the war. "I have been the recipient of countless stories in captivity from the victims of ill-treatment: I can identify a large number of criminals, and when I interrogate them they dare not lie because I know the facts."

With the permission of American authorities, Wild flew to Manila and sat down across a table from Yamashita, just the two of them, on the morning of October 28, 1945, one day before Yamashita's trial began. Consulting his list of war crimes against British and Australian soldiers, Wild asked Yamashita about each. As to Parit Sulong, Yamashita had not heard of any massacres there, but he told Wild that Nishimura's Imperial Guards Division was moving down the west coast of Malaya and would have been in that area on January 20, the date Wild gave him. "He agreed that the troops of this Division must be considered responsible" for the Parit Sulong massacres, Wild reported.

As to the Alexandra Hospital, "I never heard of this until today," Yamashita told Wild. "He spoke strongly of 'the fools who had done this senseless, brutal thing,'" Wild wrote. Yamashita surmised, correctly in the event, that it would have been the Eighteenth Division in that area and that its commander should be interrogated.

Turning to events following the capitulation of Singapore, Wild asked first about the execution of fourteen Australian prisoners on February 19, 1942. "He expressed his disapproval," Wild reported, "and said with some emphasis that if he had known of this incident at the time he would 'of course' have punished those responsible."

And what of the *sook ching* killings of Chinese in Singapore? The interrogation, parts of which Wild recorded verbatim, is instructive. Yamashita initially displayed no awareness of the scope of the massacres. After the surrender, he explained, the city was the responsibility of the Kempetai. They were "entitled to kill bad characters, such as robbers and those in possession of weapons," Yamashita said. But many thousands were killed, Wild told Yamashita, almost all of them innocent Chinese civilians. "Innocent?" answered Yamashita. "It should have been only the robbers and those with arms."

Who gave the orders to kill? Yamashita answered that the Kempetai needed no orders; they had "full discretion and powers." The implication was that the Kempetai did what they thought necessary; they needed no orders from Yamashita's staff, or him.

Wild pressed Yamashita: "Was the commander of the Kempetai in Singapore in February 1942 then solely responsible for killing these civilians?"

"Yes. He was responsible."

"What was his name . . . ?"

"I do not now remember."

"Were you informed of these killings?"

"No. I was not informed."

"Was that because you were too senior an officer to be troubled with such trifling matters?"

"That is correct."

Wild, pressed for time, did not pursue the matter. As they parted, Yamashita told him, "Until today I had truly never heard of any of these matters. Please tell Admiral Mountbatten that. Tell him, too, that on learning that Japanese soldiers did these things I have been astounded."

Wild's sarcastic reference to "such trifling matters" may have been intended to get a rise out of Yamashita. But it did not, and Wild came away convinced that Yamashita was not being evasive. His report to Mountbatten said, "Yamashita gave the impression of speaking the truth when he disclaimed previous knowledge of these Malayan atrocities. It is of course possible that an officer of his rank in the Japanese army would be told nothing of the behaviour of his troops towards prisoners and civilians and would consider it beneath his dignity to inquire." He noted that his experience in interrogating Japanese since the end of the war (which, he did not note, was limited to a few weeks) had convinced him that "senior officers are generally willing to give away their subordinates, [and] junior officers and other ranks are [also] ready to incriminate their seniors. This abject reversal of the long tradition of personal loyalty is one of the most striking proofs of their awareness of defeat."

It is difficult to know what to make of Wild's conclusions. On the surface, even a neophyte investigator would not have been surprised—indeed, should have expected—that someone in Yamashita's position would be quick to claim ignorance and put the blame on subordinates. Yamashita was facing an American military trial in which he would disclaim knowledge of widespread atrocities in Manila in 1945; he would not have helped his case by acknowledging to an Allied investigator that he had known of atrocities in Malaya and Singapore in 1942. He certainly would have been aware that if, by some miracle, he were acquitted in Manila, he would have been a prime candidate for a British trial in Singapore.

And yet Wild's conclusion that Yamashita was being honest and truthful cannot be dismissed as the gullibility of a naive investigator. Wild was no fool. His experience with Japanese commanders had been gained the hard way. He knew Singapore and Malaya, and he had interrogated Yamashita face to face, for several hours—in Japanese. No one could accuse him of being an easy mark for wily Japanese officers. He believed Yamashita.

Yamashita's departure from Singapore, the city he had taken in a near-flawless military campaign, was as curious as anything in his career. On April 29, 1942, the emperor's birthday and a major holiday on the Japanese calendar, a local children's choir put on a dutiful performance of Japanese songs, including the national anthem, at City Hall. At the reception that followed, attended by hundreds of Singaporeans, an ebullient Yamashita took the podium. "Today we celebrate the Emperor's birthday with you," he told them. "You have just become our new subjects. It is my great pleasure to be with you on this auspicious day. I want the people of Malaya and Sumatra to carry on with their affairs, for they are now our new subject people."

It was an embarrassing thing to say. The Malayan and Sumatran people were not Japanese subjects, at least not that Japan wished to acknowledge. Japan claimed to be their liberator, not their new colonial master. When word of Yamashita's gaffe reached Tokyo, his old adversary, Hideki Tojo, now both premier and war minister, pounced. He ordered Yamashita transferred to Manchuria, to take command of the First Army Group there. That was not to be a combat command; First Army Group's mission was to keep an eye on the Russians, who in the spring of 1942 were engaged in furious combat with Hitler's Wehrmacht on their west and in no position to pick a fight with Japan. Furthermore, in a final humiliation, Yamashita was to proceed directly from Singapore to northeastern China, with no stopover in Tokyo to see his wife or—a greater blow to Yamashita—to have the customary audience with the emperor on the occasion of his brilliant victory.

It is unlikely that the citizenship blunder sent him there; Tojo was both jealous and suspicious of Yamashita, and he followed a time-honored tradition of promoting a rival into virtual exile. But any war minister acting in the best interests of Japan would have sent Yamashita to the Philippines the moment Singapore was stabilized. In the spring of 1942 those islands were the most important land theater for the Japanese army. Manchuria, though a vast area with a huge army facing a feared opponent, was as rustic a command as a general of Yamashita's rank could be given.

General Tomoyuki Yamashita, ever the emperor's loyal soldier, packed his bags and got on a plane to distant Manchuria to take up his duties. He did not go by way of Tokyo.

4

Leyte

In the spring of 1942, Yamashita confronted the Russians across a barren land-scape as commanding general of the First Army Group, some 200,000 men. In theory, commanding an army group tasked with holding back Japan's old-est enemy was an important post, but it did not prove to be so for Yamashita. Japan had occupied Manchuria, which it called Manchukuo, for a decade, but the Soviet Union in 1942 was fully engaged on Europe's eastern front with the Wehrmacht and had neither the interest nor the might to invade a muscular Japan. The two armies eyed each other at the border of Siberia and Manchuria, and that was all they did. For Yamashita, it was a quiet but unwelcome respite from the battlefield, brightened only by his promotion from lieutenant general to full general, the Japanese equivalent of a fourth star.

But as Yamashita kept a lookout in Manchuria, the war in the Pacific was turning against Nippon. The U.S. Navy had battered the Imperial Navy at the Coral Sea and Midway, and its submarines were devastating Japan's merchant shipping. America's industrial strength was turning out thousands of fighters and one aircraft carrier after another to challenge the Zeros' domination of the skies. On June 15, 1944, nine days after D-Day in Europe, the U.S. Marines went ashore at Saipan in the Marianas and secured it within a month, giving the United States an air base 1,300 miles from the Japanese home islands, within the range of American B-29 Superfortress bombers.

Japan was on the verge of defeat, and its high command knew it. The objec-tive was no longer to repel the Americans from the Western Pacific but to stall the U.S. Advance while fortifying the homeland against invasion. Japan could then seek a negotiated settlement that would preserve its sovereignty and its emperor.

Key to this plan was a "decisive victory" that would force the United States to reappraise the cost in blood and treasure of unconditional surrender. Japan desperately needed to convince the United States that an invasion of the home islands could not succeed at any price the Americans would be willing to pay,

31

and thus to force them to negotiate terms of surrender. In the summer of 1944, the Imperial General Staff had devised four options for a "decisive battle," with air, sea, and land defenses. The plan to be implemented would depend on where the Allied offensive would aim first. Each plan was called *Sho*, "Victory." Sho Number 1 was for the Philippines. The headquarters of Field Marshal Hisaichi Terauchi, commander of Japan's Southern Army, sent urgent messages to Tokyo, demanding that Sho Number 1 "be commenced immediately, even though rough preparations had not been completed."

The strategy had only the narrowest chance of success. Japan's navy, battered and bloodied, no longer ruled the seas; it had lost too many aircraft to dominate the skies; and its shipping and supply lines were far too vulnerable to U.S. submarines to ever again extend through the Southwest Pacific to Australia. But the Philippines might be defended. Japan's warships were still robust enough to give the Americans a battle in the narrow straits, and its armies of hundreds of thousands could be a formidable fighting force, if properly led.

In Tokyo, the defeat at Saipan meant curtains for Tojo. The Imperial General Staff replaced him with Kuniaki Koiso, a retired soldier with sense enough to realize that Shigenori Kuroda, commander of Japan's forces in the Philippines, a rear-echelon general with neither the skills nor the experience to lead men to a decisive victory, had to go. And Japan needed a skilled and battle-proven general in places more critical than Manchuria.

On September 29, 1944, Yamashita was recalled to Tokyo. After two days of hurried conferences with the Imperial General Staff—which, with Tojo gone, could at last acknowledge him as "a superb tactician and excellent leader"— Yamashita was presented to the emperor and named the commanding general of the Imperial Japanese Army's Fourteenth Area Army, in Japan's most critical theater: the Philippine Islands.

On October 7, he arrived to a commander's nightmare. Kuroda had already beat his exit from the Philippines, leaving no briefing on plans or details for his successor. There were some 250,000 Japanese troops on the islands, scattered over 800 miles from Luzon through Leyte and down to Mindanao, many of them in small units. Untrained, undisciplined, and untested, lacking weapons, vehicles, ammunition, and supplies, their morale was poor. Strangers to defensive combat, they were not even properly dug in for the assault that was sure to come. Communications were precarious; American air raids had destroyed roads and rendered many airfields unusable. As commanding general of all Japan's Fourteenth Area Army, Yamashita was part of the forces under Terauchi's command. But Yamashita, out of action for two and a half years, knew few of his subordinate commanders. "The source of command and coordination within a command," he said later, "lies in trusting in your subordinate commanders." His challenge in the Philippines was to assign responsibilities for the future of the war to "subordinates whom I did not know and with whose character and ability I was unfamiliar."

For Yamashita, "under the great disadvantage of knowing next to nothing about terrain and troop conditions of my new field of operation," the first priority was to get quickly out into the field to see for himself the mountains and the jungle, the roads and the rivers, the emplacements and the equipment of his troops, and the plans of his infantry and air commanders. With only rudimentary communications, he was surrounded by an unfriendly population growing ever more hostile and guerrillas growing more aggressive with the fervent hope and rising expectation of an American invasion.

Yamashita's only hope for repelling an American assault—much less forcing the decisive battle that the Imperial General Staff believed could still turn the tide in the Pacific—required a coordinated effort by land, air, and naval forces. But the Japanese army and navy had no common command, nothing comparable to the American Joint Chiefs of Staff. They operated not only independently of each other, but often with mutual suspicion and dislike, in separate and complex chains of command that placed decision making by the Imperial General Staff over flexibility, maneuverability, and coordination by field commanders. Japanese officers were entwined with domestic politics, and personal rivalries were endemic. "Imperial General Headquarters was, in fact, two separate headquarters, an army command and a navy command," wrote historian Stanley Falk. "The rivalry, animosity, and at times outright antagonism between the Japanese army and navy was so strong as to preclude any really joint headquarters setup or even any close coordination between the services." As a naval staff officer put it, "The Army and the Navy always quarreled with each other."

Yamashita had led an army through Malaya and on to Singapore with little interference from Tokyo and little need to coordinate closely with air and naval commands, but things were different in the Philippines. He commanded the soldiers, but neither the Fourth Air Army, Japan's air force in the Philippines, nor the Maritime Transport Command, responsible for getting ammunition and weapons and supplies to the Philippines, and certainly not any of Japan's naval forces. Yamashita later recalled that "the line of command among the various units operating in the Philippines was so diversified that before I could carry out any strategic plan I was forced either to consult the Commanding Generals of the independent units or take the indirect and roundabout step of having orders issued from my superiors." And the month after Yamashita arrived, Terauchi removed himself and his Southern Army headquarters from Manila to the safer climes of Saigon, further complicating the already difficult line of communication.

Yamashita lacked even a chief of staff, until General Akira Muto landed in Manila on the night of October 20, which as it happened was the very day of the American invasion on Leyte. Told of this event, the new chief of staff had one question: "Where's Leyte?"

Of all the challenges Yamashita faced, few were as pressing as Tokyo's inability to replenish his rapidly diminishing supplies. Nearly everything an army needs was in critically short supply—ammunition, fuel, food, medicine, and spare parts for the dwindling force of planes, tanks, artillery, and radios. And most of what Tokyo was able to send did not survive the voyage. "The transports," Yamashita recalled as he awaited trial, "were, with a few exceptions, practically all sunk or damaged by the American Air Force while en route, and it was my misfortune to receive discouraging reports of these disasters day after day. . . . I was so occupied with these difficulties that I had hardly time to turn my attention to other business."

One might reasonably assume that Yamashita's recollections of his difficulties, coming as he sat imprisoned in Manila awaiting trial, were meant to bolster his defense by shifting the blame. But Samuel Stratton, a Japanese-speaking navy lieutenant who debriefed Yamashita for several days in September 1945 (and who served as a congressman from Schenectady, New York, from 1959 to 1989), recalled in 1954: "None of his answers on tactical questions, for instance, the defense of Manila, the extent of his command authority, and so on—answers which might be, and in fact were, used against him later on—were made with any hesitation or apparent wish to be cagey."

Despite the problems plaguing him as he prepared for the invasion, Yamashita took time to order the commander of the military police—the Kempetai— "to pay particular attention not to incur the enmity of the civilian Philippine population. This order was issued because I considered the cooperation of the civilian Filipinos vitally essential for the execution of my military functions," Yamashita explained in 1945. When the Philippines' collaborationist president José Laurel complained to Yamashita that the Kempetai were aggravating an "anti-Japanese feeling" among Filipinos, Yamashita ordered his chief of staff to summon its commander and "to issue strict warning on this matter to tighten up on the control and supervision over the latter's subordinate officers and men"—a warning that Yamashita said he repeated frequently in the following months. This was a particularly sensitive matter, because the Kempetai were, at least in theory, the soldiers responsible for seeing that other soldiers behaved themselves, particularly when dealing with civilians. But the complaints from the Filipinos continued, and Yamashita, unwilling to divert attention from the front to conduct an internal-affairs investigation of the police, dealt with the Kempetai problem summarily. He sacked its commander.

When Yamashita arrived in the Philippines on October 7, he thought he would have three months to prepare for the American invasion—precious little time to acquaint himself with his tactical situation, strengthen supply lines, replenish vital resources, revitalize a sagging army, and set his defenses. As it happened, he had two weeks. General Douglas MacArthur was on his way.

For MacArthur, it was the campaign of his life. Commander of the paltry U.S. And Philippine forces in December 1941, his air force had been all but wiped out when the Japanese attacked on December 8. He had retreated with his forces to the Bataan peninsula in Manila Bay and then to the tiny island of Corregidor as the Japanese army under General Homma overpowered his outnumbered and exhausted troops.

On orders from President Franklin D. Roosevelt, he left the Philippines on March 11 with his wife and four-year-old son aboard a PT boat on a harrowing journey through 500 miles of enemy-patrolled waters, to the southernmost Philippine island of Mindanao, and from there he escaped on an airplane to Australia. As he climbed down from the plane in remote Alice Springs, he faced a gaggle of reporters. There was no talk of escape. "The President of the United States," he told them, "ordered me to break through the Japanese lines and proceed from Corregidor to Australia for the purpose, as I understand it, of organizing the American offensive against Japan, a primary object of which is the relief of the Philippines. I came through, and I shall return."

On Corregidor, General Jonathan Wainwright held out as long as any man could have, but he eventually surrendered his 15,000 troops on May 6, 1942. Then followed the infamous Bataan death march: wounded, exhausted, half-starved Americans and Filipinos were forced to march over 60 miles to Japanese prison camps. Thousands died along the way; those who survived spent nearly three years in brutal captivity.

Two years later, having led the American offensive that subjugated the Japanese in New Guinea and the smaller Solomon Islands, MacArthur fixed his eyes on the prize of the Philippines. "The Philippines is American territory," MacArthur told the Joint Chiefs on June 18, 1944, "where our unsupported forces were destroyed by the enemy. Practically all of the 17,000,000 Filipinos remain loyal to the United States and are undergoing the greatest privation and suffering because we have not been able to support or succor them. We have a great national obligation to discharge."

Not everyone agreed, and particularly not Admiral Chester Nimitz, commander of all U.S. forces in the Western Pacific—which is to say all U.S. forces north of MacArthur's theater in the Southwest Pacific. Nimitz urged Washington to bypass the Philippines and send his navy due west to Formosa (Taiwan), hundreds of miles closer to the Japanese homeland than the jungles of Mindanao and Leyte and Luzon.

MacArthur was beside himself. The Philippines were not merely a military objective; they were a moral one. For MacArthur, an army brat, they were as close as he had to a true home: his father's command, his first duty station, and the scene of his humiliating defeat in 1942, the fortress he could not hold and was forced to flee. For him the "great national obligation" was also a great personal obligation as well. Summoned to Pearl Harbor in July 1944 for a conference with Nimitz and Roosevelt himself, MacArthur made another plea for the Philippines. And in September, General George Marshall, the U.S. Army chief of staff, with Roosevelt's approval, acquiesced. MacArthur could return to the Philippines.

MacArthur, Commander in Chief, Southwest Pacific Area, led over 200,000 U.S. ground troops—half of them in the battle-tested Sixth Army under the able General Walter Krueger—supported by carrier-based aircraft under Admiral William Halsey's Third Fleet and Admiral Thomas Kinkaid's mighty Seventh Fleet of over 700 warships—"MacArthur's Navy," as it was dubbed. In the words of the U.S. Army's historian, he had at his command "more men, guns, ships, and aircraft than had been required for any previous operation in the Pacific. For the first time ground troops from the Central Pacific and Southwest Pacific were to join and fight the foe under a common commander. General MacArthur, who had left Luzon in a motor torpedo boat, was to return to the Philippines with a vast armada—the greatest seen in the Pacific up to that time."

Imperial Headquarters' original plan for the defense of the Philippines, which Yamashita himself had reviewed and approved in his brief stopover in Tokyo en route to Manila, called for his Fourteenth Area Army to await MacArthur on Luzon, the largest and northernmost of the islands, and to leave the small Japanese garrisons to put up what resistance they could against the expected landing of MacArthur's troops on faraway Mindanao. Luzon as the stage for the decisive battle of the Philippines suited Yamashita well. He observed that it was "impossible to execute any real ground operations on islands as small as *geta*"—the Japanese wooden clog.

MacArthur had no interest in Mindanao. The capital city of Manila on Luzon was his goal, and the first step in that direction was to secure the mid-Philippine island of Leyte as a base for air strikes against Luzon. Occupation of Leyte would also cut the critical Japanese supply lines south to the Dutch East Indies, with its rubber, oil, tin, and rice.

Landing at Tacloban on the eastern coast of Leyte on October 20, 1944, after days of ferocious air and naval bombardment, U.S. troops found the Japanese opposition so light that MacArthur was able to wade ashore on the first day and to deliver a typically orotund rallying cry to the Filipinos:

> I have returned. By the grace of Almighty God our forces stand again on
> Philippine soil—soil consecrated in the blood of our two peoples. We have

come, dedicated and committed. . . . The hour of your redemption is here. . . . Rally to me. Let the indomitable spirit of Bataan and Corregidor lead on. As the lines of battle roll forward to bring you within the zone of operations, rise and strike. Strike at every favorable opportunity. For your homes and hearths, strike! For future generations of your sons and daughters, strike! In the name of your sacred dead, strike! Let no heart be faint. Let every arm be steeled. The guidance of divine God points the way. Follow in His Name to the Holy Grail of righteous victory!

The lack of concerted opposition at Tacloban was not due to the Japanese being caught napping. Yamashita knew that he was in no position to repel the superior American air and naval forces on the beaches; his objective was to hold the Philippines as long as possible, turning the mountains and jungles to his advantage, slowing the American advance with artillery and infantry counterattacks. Success would keep Manila's broad harbor open to receive supplies and would buy time for Japan to prepare its defenses against American invasion of the home islands.

Luzon was the island Japan had to hold. To lose Luzon was to lose the Philippines, and so the strategy for Leyte was to slow the advance toward Luzon for as long as possible. But as MacArthur landed on October 20, Yamashita received stunning news. Imperial Headquarters ordered him to confront MacArthur head-on and seek a "decisive victory"—on Leyte.

Yamashita was shocked and furious, not only at the decision itself—which he believed to be both dangerous and wrong—but at the fact that it had been made without even consulting him. There was only one division on Leyte, and many of the frontline soldiers were recent draftees. "The communications network," in the words of one Japanese officer, "was like a broken spiderweb." Logistics and resupply, difficult enough already between Japan and still-secure Luzon, would be almost impossible to extend southward through 400 miles of hostile terrain and dangerous waters, and a Leyte counteroffensive would strip Luzon of precious arms needed for the certain landing of the Americans there. Yamashita would have all he could handle just to hold Luzon. He could not do that and hold Leyte too.

Yamashita was "dumbfounded and indignant," his chief of staff Muto (who had learned quite quickly where Leyte was) later recalled. At the very least, Yamashita urged, any decision on where to fight a "decisive battle" should await the outcome of the naval phase of Sho, as the Imperial Fleet prepared to deliver a knockout blow to the American navy.

His protests were ignored. He was ordered to "muster all possible strength to totally destroy the enemy on Leyte." Yamashita spoke his mind, but he was no renegade. He took his orders and followed them. He sent word to Lieutenant

General Sosaku Suzuki to get the rest of his Thirty-Fifth Army—five divisions and three independent brigades—from Cebu to Leyte and to await the overwhelming air and naval support that would surely be his within a few days.

It did not happen. The Imperial Japanese Navy launched its section of the Sho operation, sending a heavy force of aircraft carriers, battleships, and destroyers against Halsey's Third Fleet and Kinkaid's Seventh. The Battle of Leyte Gulf was the largest naval battle of the war, and a resounding Japanese defeat from which the Imperial Navy would never recover.

Losing dominance of the sea and air made the ground effort too little, too late, and Yamashita knew it. With the air force and navy decimated, supply lines were precarious and unreliable. Japanese communications throughout Leyte were knocked out; Yamashita was unable to communicate with the island for two full days, while MacArthur landed over 130,000 soldiers.

"The guidance of divine God points the way," MacArthur had proclaimed after wading ashore. Now, guided by God or not, American forces took Leyte hill by hill, ridge by ridge. But it was a punishing campaign. As they did throughout the Philippines, Japanese soldiers fought furiously and without surrender. They survived on scavenged coconuts and bananas, and they suffered the stress of continuous combat, lack of provisions, and poor nutrition, but the Americans learned that "as long as any officers remain alive, the remnants of a . . . force are capable of determined action." The Japanese had outstanding fire discipline, which often offset their small and diminishing numbers. Their defensive positions were stoutly fortified in the convoluted mountainous ridges of Leyte (and "beautifully camouflaged" too, an American colonel noted), and they made excellent use of the inhospitable terrain, concealing themselves so well in the caves and tall grass that American forces were often unable to locate the enemy until they were a few feet in front of him.

The soil—when it was not overlaid with swamps, jungles, or rice paddies—was poorly suited to heavy American trucks and tanks; even mortars were difficult to stabilize in the soft soil. And the weather seemed to have only two settings: punishing sun or torrential rain. General Robert Eichelberger, commanding the Eighth Army, wrote afterward, "It was bitter, exhausting, rugged fighting—physically, the most terrible we were ever to know."

By early December, however, the Japanese were clearly losing the battle, and Leyte. Nearly all of their offensive power was on the ground, and nearly all of that was in the infantry. Communication was awful. When Yamashita in Manila had an important message for Suzuki in Leyte, he had to send it by hand and hope the messenger could survive to deliver it. His order to Suzuki to pivot his front from north to east was sent on November 5. It arrived on November 12. Telephone and telegraph wires were routinely destroyed by weather or

Americans, and radios in such terrain were so unreliable that many orders were never received at all. One division lost all contact with its higher headquarters in mid-December and did not reestablish it until March. Relying primarily on foot soldiers to deliver messages to lower echelons, commanders left much unsaid.

Finally, in mid-December, the Americans reached the outskirts of the port of Ormoc, Japan's headquarters and resupply point in western Leyte, and the jaws began to close. Japanese morale was low, and their physical condition was dire. A Japanese colonel recalled after the war that his troops were living off the land, "forced to eat coconuts, various grasses, bamboo shoots, the heart fibers of coconut tree trunks, and whatever native fruits or vegetables they could forage. . . . They were literally in a starved condition, . . . many instances occurred in which men vomited seven to ten times a day because they could not digest some of the food due to their weakened stomachs." The wounded suffered from such a lack of even rudimentary treatment that officers told them to commit suicide rather than suffer lingering death or, worse, surrender. "It was pitiful," a Japanese officer recalled. "However, the majority died willingly. Only Japanese could have done a thing like this and yet I could not bear to see the sight."

On December 15, Allied troops landed on the island of Mindoro, separated from Luzon only by a narrow strait and barely 100 miles south of Manila. Four days later, Yamashita sent word to Suzuki on Leyte that the Thirty-Fifth Army could expect no further assistance or supplies from Luzon. It would have to make do with whatever it could find as it retreated into the mountains of western Leyte. Suzuki sent his chief of staff to Yamashita's headquarters outside Manila for clarification of Yamashita's intentions; it took him a month to get there, and by that time Yamashita's intentions had become all too clear. He sent his message to Suzuki:

> The enemy, who has increased his material power and war potential, now threatens, solely on the strength of his material superiority, to bear down on Luzon Island despite the heroic and desperate efforts of our sea and air forces as well as of [Suzuki's] 35th Army. In view of the sudden change in the situation, we shall seek and destroy our enemy on Luzon Island, thereby doing our part in the heroic struggle of the Army and avenging many a valiant warrior who fell before the enemy. As munitions have not been supplied adequately, I cannot keep back tears of remorse for tens of thousands of our officers and men fighting in Leyte Island. Nevertheless, I must impose a still harder task upon you. Please try to understand my intentions. They say it is harder to live than to die. You, officers and men, be patient enough to endure the hardships of life, and help guard and maintain the prosperity of the Imperial Throne through eternal resistance to the enemy,

and be ready to meet your death calmly for our beloved country. I sincerely instruct you as above.

Yamashita had written off Leyte at a catastrophic cost. By the best estimate, there had been some 60,000 Japanese troops on Leyte; nearly 50,000 had been killed. A mere 828 had surrendered or been captured by the Americans. American forces had numbered 258,000 at their peak; 3,500 had been killed and nearly 12,000 wounded.

"In their determination to make Leyte the decisive battle of the Philippines," concluded the official U.S. Army history of the campaign,

> the Japanese had committed the major portions of their fleet and air force in a vain attempt to stay the American advance. In the Battle of Leyte Gulf the Japanese Navy suffered irreparable damage—all of the carriers were lost and most of the capital ships were sunk or damaged. The air force was now almost completely dependent upon the suicidal kamikaze pilot. Finally, the dispatch of reinforcements and supplies to Leyte had seriously crippled the defenses of Luzon—the strategic heart of the Philippine Archipelago.

For Yamashita, as one historian summed it up,

> the Leyte campaign was a tragic nightmare. Sent to the Philippines barely two weeks before [the invasion], saddled with a last-minute change of plan—an impossible plan, at that—and inadequate means to carry it out, he did his best. . . . He did everything in his power to prevent the tragedy on Leyte, while at the same time conscientiously carrying out his orders to make that island the scene of decisive victory. In the latter effort, he sent many of his best troops and sorely needed supplies to Leyte, weakening himself critically on Luzon.

Interviewed by an American reporter during a break in the trial, Yamashita looked back on Leyte as the key. "We never had a chance to get in our reinforcements," he said. "We simply had no shipping." He paused. "The continuous perfect coordination of your air, naval and ground forces—that's what crushed us."

In Tokyo, the people were told that their army was fighting valiantly to repel the American invaders. Some of the high command entertained among themselves a similar fiction: that Americans might yet tire of the struggle and seek a negotiated end. Yamashita was under no such delusion. "After the loss of Leyte," he testified at his trial, "I realized that decisive battle was impossible."

5

Luzon

Furious at having been ordered into the disaster of defending Leyte, Yamashita now dictated to Tokyo the way he would fight in the Philippines. The Fourteenth Area Army would engage the enemy on Luzon in a delaying action, not a "decisive battle" but a campaign to slow the American advance to Japan. All reinforcements of troops, weapons, ammunition, and supplies that Tokyo had been planning to pour into Leyte would be diverted to Luzon, if they were not torpedoed by American submarines or blown out of the ocean by American warships and carrier-based aircraft or destroyed from the skies by the American air force. Whatever their misconceptions about American resolve, Imperial General Headquarters, badly burned by Leyte and humbled before the emperor, was not willing to overrule Yamashita a second time. It sent a general to Manila with the order: effective immediately, strategy in the Philippines would "be left to the discretion of the commander of the area army."

But just who the commander of the area army would actually command in the last seven months of the war was an ever-changing riddle. Yamashita was no Commander in Chief, Southwest Pacific, as MacArthur was. The rivalry between the army and the navy, time-honored by Japan's tradition and nurtured by Imperial General Headquarters, saw to that. His army numbered over 200,000 soldiers—a formidable force on paper, but considerably less so in the field, where it was plagued by virtually every problem that could weaken a fighting force. It was chronically short of critical supplies; its transportation system was inadequate to move men or supplies; and the troops themselves were, in the words of the U.S. Army's history, "understrength, underfed, and underequipped ground combat forces, the leadership and organization of which left much to be desired."

But the Fourteenth Area Army was only about half of Japan's armed forces in and around the Philippines, and the shifting and uncertain limits of Yamashita's command were to become critical issues at his trial. On his arrival in October, he realized he had no command over the air arm of the army, nor over the maritime transport command that controlled Japanese shipping to and from the islands. He certainly did not control the navy's warships, or what was left of them after the Battle of Leyte Gulf. They reported only to Admiral Denshichi Okochi, who reported only to Tokyo. Nor did he control Rear Admiral Sanji Iwabuchi's naval special forces, sometimes called naval landing troops or by some, less accurately, "marines." Indeed, he did not command some 30,000 army troops stranded and essentially leaderless on Luzon as a result of shipwreck, interrupted deployment, or injury.

December 1944 was a critical time for Yamashita and for Japan. Leyte was lost. U.S. planes had been strafing Japanese positions on Luzon since September, and American forces had landed on Mindoro at Luzon's southern tip. Yamashita could count on no help from the air on Luzon except for the suicide bombers—"the dread kamikazes," the army's history called them, the "divine wind"—pilots whose deadly attacks were inflicting real damage on American warships. But those ships seemed limitless in their number. There was little hope of fresh troops, trucks, and fuel, or of replacements for tanks and artillery, as long as the enemy ruled the seas and the air. Luzon would be defended on the ground, with whatever Yamashita had or could bring together, for as long as he could make it last.

His strategy, as it had been in Malaya, was uncomplicated. First, he would not attempt to defend Manila. The Americans could have it. He could not feed its million inhabitants with his threatened and diminishing resources, its urban core would require far more defenders than he had at his command, and its flat terrain, at the seaward edge of Luzon's central plain, was unsuited to the combat he needed to fight in a delaying action. What he did need to do, in Manila, was to carry the army and navy's supplies out of the city for his use and demolish its bridges and piers and whatever supplies he could not transport.

Second, he would remove his forces to strategic locations beyond Manila and wait for the Americans. As Leyte had shown, the Japanese were superb tacticians of the terrain, and Luzon offered many opportunities for his troops to dig in and hold off the enemy.

He divided his forces into three groups. He would himself command the largest, some 152,000 soldiers in four infantry and tank divisions, which he named Shobu Group. It would retreat to Baguio, the summer capital of the Philippines some 125 miles north of Manila, where it would control the rugged northern Luzon mountains and oppose the expected landing of the Americans at the beaches of Lingayen Gulf, on Luzon's northwest shoulder. He placed his trusted subordinate Lieutenant General Shizuo Yokoyama in charge of the second, the 70,000-man Shimbu Group, which would fall back to the area east and northeast of Manila to cover the evacuation of critical military supplies from the capital and delay the approach of the Americans to the city after they had passed out of the Shobu Group's tactical area. The third and at 40,000 soldiers the smallest, Kembu Group, would occupy an area northwest of Manila, to deny to the enemy as long as possible the mammoth Clark Airfield; it would then fall back into the western mountains to carry on a delaying action (see the map on page 194).

The primary reason behind this strategy was to take advantage of the mountainous terrain and thick vegetation that was so hospitable to defenders and so daunting to the attackers. But another important consideration—and one that was to be a significant issue at his trial—was simple communication. With the imminent landing of the Americans, communication throughout his forces, never reliable, was sure to become much worse. Smaller groups fighting independently might at least be able to pass orders and reports internally.

Communication was no small matter. For Yamashita's army, as throughout the Japanese forces, the primary means of long distance communication was not radio but telephone. The standard Japanese field unit was heavy, complex, and obsolescent, a hand-cranked 1932 model that was inferior in its construction and prone to dropped calls and noisy interference.

In addition, telephones needed wires strung between units, which took a lot of time, equipment, and manpower. Trained wiremen were in short supply to begin with, and moving from unit to unit, often through enemy-controlled areas, shortened their life expectancy considerably. Putting up telephone poles and wires was difficult, and keeping them up was just as hard. "Crucially, maintaining the wire system required ceaseless work," wrote one historian. "The miles of line were constantly being cut by artillery and mortar fire, enemy infiltrators and patrols, hostile civilians, weather damage (high winds, fallen trees, flooding) and—the worst culprit of all—friendly vehicle traffic."

The environment was decidedly hostile as well. In the jungle, moisture and humidity rotted the leather carrying cases, and ants ate the wires' insulation. And that was before the enemy landed. Throughout the Pacific, the Japanese had learned the difficulties of maintaining wire communications in the face of artillery, mortar, naval gunfire, and aircraft.

Radio was no better. Here too, the Japanese equipment was heavy, poorly designed, and aged. Radios consumed batteries voraciously; frequencies were unstable due to weather, terrain, and humidity; their waterproofing and insect-proofing was poor; dense jungle vegetation absorbed their waves; and they were easily jammed. The Japanese forces used radio only when telephones were unavailable, which they frequently were.

The 1944 U.S. Army field manual on operations summed up communications in the jungle concisely: "It is extremely difficult. Visual signaling is often impossible, the use of runners slow and frequently hazardous, the range of radio may be reduced greatly, and wire circuits hard to install and maintain." The manual suggested the use of pigeons for "important messages." Lacking pigeons, Yamashita was forced to rely on the oldest form of communication known to man—sending a messenger on foot to deliver it.

It therefore may have made some sense for Yamashita to break his army into three groups. But it may have backfired. Lieutenant Samuel Stratton, interrogating Yamashita (in Japanese) on military intelligence matters after his capture, was struck by how little information Yamashita had, and how little he actually knew about what his troops were doing. Stratton concluded that on Luzon, "American headquarters actually knew more about the whereabouts and composition of the Japanese defenders than their own commander. . . . By taking to the mountains Yamashita had avoided our motorized forward reconnaissance patrols, but only at the cost of close communication with and control over his own troops."

By late December, Yamashita had pulled his headquarters out of Fort McKinley, near Manila, where he had been since his arrival in October, and by January 6 he had relocated it to Baguio. The size of the force he commanded was growing: Tokyo had transferred the army's air arm to him on January 1, 1945, and Admiral Iwabuchi's men, now designated the Manila Naval Defense Force, were to come under his tactical command soon afterward.

Iwabuchi's force was no prize. A motley aggregation of construction and repair units, supply clerks, and hospital orderlies, its mission was to assist in the evacuation of supplies from Manila, to destroy docks and other harbor facilities, and then to retreat from the city. They were assigned to Yokoyama's Shimbu Group for purposes of tactical command, which meant that they remained administratively part of the navy but were, ostensibly, subject to Yokoyama's orders on where to go and what to do. Iwabuchi, however, would soon show that he had his own ideas as to whose orders he would take and what he would do.

The U.S. landing on Luzon came at Lingayen Gulf on the western coast, some 75 miles northwest of Manila, on January 9, 1945. It did not surprise Yamashita. What surprised MacArthur's Sixth Army, commanded by General Walter Krueger, was that Japanese resistance on shore was so light as to be almost absent altogether. As he had done at Leyte, Yamashita declined to repel the vast American forces on the beach. Without air or naval support, reliable communications, or oil and fuel, he ceded the central plains between Lingayen and Manila as well.

The American infantry and cavalry divisions regrouped at Lingayen and headed toward Manila, but MacArthur soon became impatient with Krueger's cautious advance. January 26 was MacArthur's birthday, and he wanted to celebrate it with a victorious parade down the broad boulevards of his beloved city. Lieutenant General Robert Eichelberger's Eighth Army, jumping off from

Mindoro, had landed south of the capital and was making its way north toward it. MacArthur urged Krueger to make haste.

But MacArthur had overestimated his forces' capabilities. Though they encountered no serious resistance on their march toward Manila, the Sixth Army's leading elements did not reach the outskirts of the city until February 3, 1945. And what they encountered there quickly ended any thoughts of a parade.

Yamashita's plan to abandon the city, leaving behind only enough soldiers to remove supplies to Baguio and to destroy harbor installations, was receiving little support from the navy. Yamashita had tasked Yokoyama's Shimbu Group with overseeing the evacuation of the city. But Okochi, the naval commander of the Philippines, put Iwabuchi and his Manila Naval Defense Force in charge of some 16,000 naval personnel, far more than were needed to carry out Yamashita's exit strategy. Having done that, Okochi departed with Yamashita to Baguio and transferred operational control, but not outright command, of Iwabuchi's forces to Yokoyama. To Iwabuchi and Okochi, this meant that Iwabuchi's forces would answer to Yokoyama (and thus to Yamashita) only if and when they were fighting with Yokoyama's army; otherwise they would take their orders from Okochi.

In combat, splintered and uncertain command is disastrous. The situation in Manila, the U.S. Army's history relates,

> mirrored a picture of disagreement and confusion existing among the lower-level headquarters under Yamashita's nominal control, and especially between the Army and Navy echelons of his command. Contrary to Yamashita's expressed desires, these conflicts led to a decision to give battle within the city—a development that was a cancerous growth on the 14th Area Army's plan for the defense of Luzon and that stemmed from a series of compromises among Japanese Army and Navy commanders in the Manila area.

Simply put, Iwabuchi did not recognize Yokoyama's authority over him, certainly not in any respect that would interfere with his mission, as he saw it, to remain in Manila and demolish its vast naval installations. Yokoyama, now well out of the city with his forces, was unpleasantly surprised to learn not only that Iwabuchi remained in the city, but that his 16,000 forces were four times larger than Yokoyama had expected. Lacking any authority to countermand the orders that Okochi had issued to Iwabuchi, Yokoyama reluctantly accepted a situation he could not change. Iwabuchi would remain in the city, but Yokoyama ordered him to withdraw once the Americans, now on their way, entered it.

Whether Iwabuchi would have obeyed that order became a moot point when the Sixth Army, approaching from the north, and the Eighth Army, approaching from the south, encircled Manila and everyone inside it. Iwabuchi instructed his forces: "You men must carry out effective suicide action as members of special attack units to turn the tide of battle by intercepting the attacking enemy at Manila."

Engaging the enemy in Manila was certainly not what Yamashita had wanted or ordered:

> Iwabuchi's plan for the defense of Manila was rather vague, promising only a suicidal fight to the death in place. By such a static defense he hoped to inflict heavy casualties upon Sixth Army and deny to the Allies for some time the facilities of Manila and Manila Bay. To help realize the latter objective, he planned extensive demolitions that ostensibly called for the destruction of purely military installations and whatever supplies were left in the city.

But for Iwabuchi, such "purely military installations" included not only docks and fuel dumps but the entire massive port area of Manila Bay, as well as bridges, transportation facilities, fresh water supplies, and electric power sources—all of which, of course, were vital to Manila's citizens. "Once started by a body of half-trained troops hastily organized into provisional units and whose only future is death in combat," the U.S. Army's history notes, "demolitions are impossible to control."

Manila was a magnificent city, the "Pearl of the Orient" in its day, with ancient universities, broad parks and boulevards, stadiums and cathedrals, and, as Americans soon learned, government buildings so magisterial in their marble thickness that they were virtually impervious to artillery and tanks. Iwabuchi turned the city into a battleground, barricading intersections with truck bodies and cement-filled oil drums, ripping up streetcar rails, stringing barbed wire along streets and sidewalks, planting land mines on thoroughfares, emplacing machine guns behind sandbags with fields of fire covering residential areas, even bringing in antiaircraft guns, cannons ripped from half-sunk ships, and hundreds of mortars, all of them manned by whatever untrained and undisciplined troops he could pull together. They were the raw materials of chaos.

By February 9, Filipino guerrillas had managed to cut all the telephone lines in the city, leaving the Japanese to rely on their radios. Soon afterward, Yamashita lost reliable radio communication with Yokoyama, and when he did manage to connect, voice traffic was often interrupted or lost altogether. "In addition," wrote historian Richard Lael, "the lack of batteries, replacement tubes, and heavy oil for the generators made long-distance communication exceedingly precarious, even early in the defense of northern Luzon."

As American forces battled their way into Manila block by block, Iwabuchi was providing Yokoyama, his ostensible superior in the Luzon foothills 50 miles away, with little information on what he was doing in Manila. And with landline communications down and radio contact unreliable at best, Yokoyama had no true picture of the situation in the city. Under the impression that the American forces numbered only a regiment or so (in fact, they were two divisions), he first ordered Iwabuchi to stand fast while Yokoyama's forces counterattacked to provide cover for Iwabuchi's evacuation. But on February 13, realizing the futility of a counterattack against overwhelming opposition, Yokoyama flatly ordered Iwabuchi to abandon Manila without delay. Two days later, on the fifteenth, Yamashita himself, first learning that Iwabuchi was still in the city and in command of troops, contrary to Yokoyama's earlier order, ordered Yokoyama to get all Japanese troops out of Manila, and to do so immediately. But with the city completely surrounded by the Americans, Yamashita and Yokoyama had no control over Manila.

Captured Japanese messages tell the story.

Yokoyama to Iwabuchi: "Shimbu Group has ordered your headquarters to move to [Fort] McKinley. In view of the increasing difficulty to effect a breakthrough, it is urgent that you move immediately, tonight (15th). Will the headquarters move?"

Iwabuchi replied, "The headquarters will not move."

To his true commander, Admiral Okochi, Iwabuchi sent a message: "Now with what strength remains, we will daringly engage the enemy. 'Banzai to the Emperor.' We are determined to fight to the last man."

Again on February 17, Iwabuchi radioed Yokoyama that he would not leave the city. It was no longer possible, he said. In any event, regardless of what Yokoyama and Yamashita had ordered, he told Yokoyama that he, Iwabuchi, considered the defense of Manila to be of "utmost importance"—an act of blatant insubordination and disobedience. On February 19 and again on February 21, Yokoyama ordered Iwabuchi to withdraw. Again, Iwabuchi refused. Indeed, by that time he could not. For Iwabuchi, the choice was to surrender or to fight to the death. For a Japanese soldier, whether private or admiral, that was no choice at all.

Iwabuchi's first two refusals were probably motivated by his obedience to his naval commander Okochi to stay in the city and destroy docks, by the limited tactical control that Okochi had passed to Yokoyama, and by the navy's misbegotten belief that Manila was defensible, all of which contributed to Iwabuchi's refusal to accept Yokoyama's superior authority. The last two refusals were a moot point—there was no way Iwabuchi could get out of Manila on those late dates, given the Americans' encirclement of the city.

On February 23, "all communication between [Yokoyama's] Shimbu Group and [Iwabuchi's] Manila Naval Defense Force ceased," the U.S. Army's history recounted. "Admiral Iwabuchi had made his bed, and he was to die in it." Three days later, on February 26, Iwabuchi and his staff officers committed suicide.

The battle of Manila, the only urban combat in the Pacific theater at any point in the war and the largest urban battle fought by U.S. troops anywhere, was a horror, not only for the citizens caught in its cross fire and victimized by the cruelties of Iwabuchi's forces—to which the trial of Yamashita would devote weeks—but also for the American soldiers fighting it. What began with plans for a parade, with Filipinos cheering as American soldiers marched by, soon became one of the most vicious, destructive, and deadly battles of World War II. The Japanese defenders had had plenty of time to dig in, not in caves and rock formations as on Leyte, but in hospitals, university buildings, and government offices. What began as street-to-street fighting soon became building-to-building and then room-to-room close combat.

Often when American soldiers knocked down barricaded doors to a building, Japanese soldiers on the roof dropped hand grenades through holes aligned in the floors and ceilings beneath. When mortars and howitzers proved ineffective in demolishing the buildings or driving the defenders out, the Americans used machine guns, bazookas (shoulder-mounted grenade launchers), flame throwers fueled by jellied gasoline, and sapper charges; they improvised a mixture of gasoline and oil that was poured into Japanese positions and ignited, roasting the defenders alive. Entreaties to surrender were futile; Japanese soldiers, relentlessly indoctrinated that surrender shamed their families, held their positions and fought until they were killed, or they killed themselves.

In university buildings, American soldiers found that the Japanese had built caves into the massive stone walls and had dug tunnels through walls and underground for evasion and maneuver. American infantry opened an attack on the New Police Station on February 13; after eight days of constant fighting, they took the building, in ruins. One field artillery unit fired over 2,000 high-explosive 105 mm shells into a hospital building where Japanese machine guns were emplaced.

Finally, on March 3, after three weeks of bitter and brutal combat, the battle of Manila came to an end. All of Iwabuchi's 16,000 soldiers were dead. In the fighting, 1,010 Americans had been killed; another 5,565 were wounded. Filipino deaths numbered in the tens of thousands, perhaps as many as 100,000.

"The devastation of Manila," wrote William Manchester, a Marine rifleman in the Pacific and a biographer of MacArthur, "was one of the great tragedies of World War II. Of Allied cities in those war years, only Warsaw suffered more. Seventy percent of the utilities, 75 percent of the factories, 80 percent of the southern residential district and 100 percent of the business district were razed."

MacArthur saw with his own eyes the destruction of his former home, a penthouse atop the Manila Hotel. "I watched, with indescribable feelings, the destruction of my fine military library, my souvenirs, my personal belongings of a lifetime," he wrote in his memoir. "Nothing was left but ashes. I was tasting to the last acid dregs the bitterness of a devastated and beloved home."

"The forces of MacArthur and Yamashita waged a bloody, devastating battle in Manila which neither had wanted nor anticipated," Lael wrote afterward. "The murky lines of authority between Rear Admiral Iwabuchi and Lieutenant General Yokoyama, the preexisting antagonism of the two rival services, and the rapidity of the American advance contributed to that clash. Ironically, the full responsibility for the city's destruction and the thousands of civilian deaths rested most heavily on the two who had sincerely wished to spare the capital."

The "triumph in the Philippines" (the title of the U.S. Army's official history volume of the campaign) was among the most brutal and lethal chapters of World War II. From the invasion of Leyte in October 1944 until Yamashita's surrender in September 1945, over 10,000 American soldiers gave their lives in combat, and 36,000 were wounded. But even these losses were dwarfed by Japanese casualties. From an initial strength of 380,000 (including some 38,000 Japanese civilians pressed into military service), 256,000, fully two out of every three, were killed or died of disease or starvation. Eighty percent of those were on Luzon. Only 11,000—3 percent of the forces—surrendered or were taken prisoner. Some 114,000 survived until the surrender at war's end.*

As brutal as the combat itself had been, the sufferings of tens of thousands of Filipino men, women, and children had been tragic, as a trial in Manila was soon to demonstrate.

---

* Many historians have characterized the Philippines campaign, in the six months after the recapture of Manila, as catastrophic and unnecessary. Japanese forces were isolated in the wilderness with no means of transport elsewhere, and the takeover of the Marianas in the summer of 1944 had already given the Americans airfields within striking distance of Japan. "The Filipino people whom MacArthur professed to love paid the price for his egomania in lost lives—perhaps half a million, including those who perished from famine and disease—and wrecked homes," wrote Max Hastings recently. "It was as great a misfortune for them as for the Allied war effort that neither President Roosevelt nor the U.S. chiefs of staff could contain MacArthur's ambitions within a smaller compass of folly. In 1944, America's advance to victory over Japan was inexorable, but three misjudgments of the Southwest Pacific supreme commander disfigured its achievement." Yet Hastings also acknowledges that this is "a perspective accessible only to posterity" because during the war itself there was no thought of halting operations. "The U.S. Marine Corps and Army divisions deployed in the Pacific expected to keep fighting, and so did their commanders and the nation at home. Once great peoples are committed to the business of killing, there is a bleak inevitability about the manner in which they continue to do so until their enemies are prostrate."

6

Military Commissions

The military commission that would sit in judgment of Tomoyuki Yamashita in 1945 would be the first tribunal to try anyone for war crimes following the end of World War II. But it had ancestors, and this commission in particular, through its charge and its verdict, would have descendants long after the deaths of the man who created it and the man who was judged by it.

For hundreds of years of warfare, commanders have been not only the leaders of their troops but their judges as well, handing out punishments for misbehavior and crimes, displacing the civil law and domestic judges. There are practical reasons for this. Armies are often far from sitting courts, beyond the borders that define their authority. It would be neither feasible nor particularly useful for armies to send soldiers home to face charges before judges unfamiliar with military matters and unable to summon witnesses to distant events. Moreover, civil law does not recognize purely military offenses: disobedience of an order, disrespect, desertion, and other offenses that only soldiers can commit. And above all, commanders are accountable for the good order and discipline of their troops. Punishment of the soldiers for a crime is not so different, in military terms, from discipline for laziness, cowardice, or incompetence—failings for which the commander must take corrective and sometimes punitive action.

Such plenary authority of commanders often led, not surprisingly, to harsh, summary, and often arbitrary punishments for the soldiers of European armies. But the American colonies at the time of the Revolution embraced the rule of law—the belief that the deprivation of life or liberty should be subject to law and not the whims of men—and believed in civilian control of the military. Together, these beliefs led the emerging Republic to give civilians authority to regulate the means by which military commanders could impose conviction and punishment. In 1775, the Provisional Congress of Massachusetts Bay enacted the first American code of military law, which was soon copied by the Continental Congress for the Continental Army. These legal codes, called Articles of War, were drawn up so that "Officers and Soldiers in the [Army] be fully acquainted with their duty, and that the Articles, Rules and Regulations thereof be made as plain as possible." Thus, "inhabitants of this Colony . . . will readily obey the Officers chosen by themselves, and will cheerfully do their duty when known, without any such severe Articles and Rules, (except in capital cases,) and cruel punishments as are usually practised in Standing Armies, and will submit to all such Rules and Regulations as are founded in reason, honour and virtue."

The Articles of War, which were to survive in one form or another until the middle of the twentieth century, defined the offenses for which soldiers could be tried and punished—disrespect of officers, refusal to obey an order, dueling, sleeping on post, mutiny, "profane cursing," and the like—and required that the more severe punishments be meted out not by the commanding officer but by military courts, known as courts-martial. Military officers made up the members of a court, sometimes as many as thirteen in a serious case. Charges were drawn up according to the legislature's articles; the accused soldier was informed of the charges against him and was allowed to present a defense, with the rudiments of due process: witnesses could be summoned and were to testify under oath; the accused was entitled to present witnesses on his own behalf and to be presumed innocent until proven guilty by the evidence. Under the American Articles of War, the members of the court-martial were bound by their oath to "well and truly try and determine" guilt or innocence according to the duly enacted articles, and to do so "without partiality, favor or affection, and if any doubt shall arise, which is not explained by said articles, according to your conscience, [to] the best of your understanding, and the custom of war in the like cases."

By 1787, when the Constitutional Convention convened in Philadelphia, both civilian control of the army and navy and the expectation of due process were firmly established. In Article I, the Constitution made the President Commander in Chief, but in Article II the drafters took care to include among the powers of the new Congress the authority "to make Rules for the Government and Regulation of the land and naval Forces"—Articles of War would rule.

Military courts thus have never been part of the federal court system created by Article III. No black-robed federal judges with lifetime appointments sit there. Military courts were different from civilian ones in many ways. There were no permanent courts; commanders convened courts-martial as and when needed, selected the members, preferred the charges, and reviewed the results, which led to chronic and often well-founded suspicion that they could also influence the outcomes. The members of the courts who passed judgment and sentence were seldom trained lawyers, nor were the prosecutors, who were known as judge advocates. Defense counsel were not routinely provided to the accused, and when they were they were not necessarily lawyers, either. And a fundamental principle of military justice was that it was a closed system: there was no appeal to civil courts, no judicial review by the black-robed judges. "The court-martial is only an instrumentality of the executive power, having no relation or connection in law with the judicial establishments of the country," according to the 1920 edition of William Winthrop's *Military Law and Precedents*, the leading military-justice treatise of its time. Still, it was a serviceable type of due process: the Articles of War were enacted by a democratic body for the use of the army and navy, with procedures that when properly administered enabled a court-martial to adjudicate guilt and innocence more or less fairly. "As a court of law," according to Winthrop's text, "it is bound, like any court, by the fundamental principles of law, and, in the absence of special provision on the subject in the military code, it observes in general the rules of evidence as adopted in the common-law courts."

But this system of courts-martial was limited in two important ways: the courts could adjudicate only those offenses defined in the Articles of War, which typically did not include murder, assault, rape, thievery, or other civilian ("common-law") crimes. And courts-martial had jurisdiction only over American soldiers and sailors, not over civilians or enemy soldiers.

These limitations presented a problem. Commanders in distant theaters of war, particularly in the South and Southwest during the expansion of the American empire in the nineteenth century, sometimes had need to bring civilians or, at times, enemy soldiers to answer for various crimes, and so they needed some sort of judicial process. With neither civil courts nor courts-martial available, field commanders made up their own process. They resorted to informal adjudications through ad hoc tribunals that became known as military "commissions," to distinguish them from courts-martial. In military commissions, the Articles of War were irrelevant, because the accused were not subject to them. Charges were whatever the commander decided they should be. And so were the procedures.

Commissions performed a judicial function, in the sense of adjudicating guilt or innocence, but they were not courts. They were a classic example of military expedience: when the tool for the job is not at hand, a tool is improvised. And so civilians were brought before commissions for crimes against the army: usually theft or assault, but sometimes vague offenses like overcharging for provisions. And enemy soldiers likewise, for spying, for war crimes such as mistreatment of civilians or assaults upon their guards if they had been taken prisoner. Commissions did not displace courts-martial; they coexisted with them, serving a different function. There was no law, no manual, no rules of procedure for commissions; they were just among the things commanders formed because they needed to, and no two commanders constituted them in quite the same way. Sometimes commanders adapted court-martial procedures for them; sometimes they did not bother. Back in Washington, no high-ranking officer or civilian overseer cared much how the process was done. Congress did not ordain or regulate them, but neither did it forbid them. Commissions were not unlawful; they just took place without much attention to the law.

Before the mid-nineteenth century, commissions had been rare in the United States. The first, denominated a "board of inquiry," was convened in 1780 by General George Washington to try John André, a British major who had conspired with Benedict Arnold to arrange the surrender of the fort at West Point, of which Arnold was then the commandant. Captured and tried as a spy before a tribunal of fourteen military officers appointed by Washington, he was convicted, and the commission recommended to Washington that "he ought to suffer death." André pleaded to Washington that he "be indulged a professional death" by being shot, rather than suffering the indignity of a "felon's death" by hanging. Washington was unmoved. André was a spy, and "the practice and usage of war . . . were against the indulgence" of a firing squad. He went to the gallows. (Benedict Arnold fared better; he fled to England.)

The true father of American military commissions, however, was General Winfield Scott, during the U.S. occupation of northern Mexico in 1846–1848. Scott was concerned, with good reason, that undisciplined American soldiers engaging in thievery and rape would enrage the Mexicans and make his task of pacification more difficult. But he discovered a significant gap in the Articles of War: they did not provide "any court for the trial or punishment of murder, rape, theft, &c., &c— no matter by whom, or on whom committed." He sought help from Congress, asking it to exercise its authority to regulate the armed forces by enacting additional articles for those civil offenses. A Senate chairman told him such would not be necessary—he already had all the authority he needed, because a commander's right to punish such crimes "necessarily resulted from the condition of things when an army is prosecuting hostilities in an enemy's country."

Thus assured, Scott issued a general order proclaiming martial law in occupied Mexico, applicable to Mexican civilians and American soldiers alike—a step he characterized as "an addition to the written military code, prescribed by Congress in the rules and articles of war." And he specified the crimes—murder, theft, poisoning, rape—that would henceforth come under the jurisdiction of military commissions that he would convene as necessary. But Scott was no martinet: if Congress would not give him the laws he thought he needed, he would conform as best he could to the laws he had. So he specified that these commissions should be governed "as nearly as practicable" by the existing Articles of War, so that the proceedings would be held "all, as near as may be, as in the cases of the proceedings and sentences of courts-martial."

There were 117 commission trials so held, most involving Americans but extending to Mexican soldiers and civilians as well. Scott later wrote that his order "worked like a charm"—"it conciliated Mexicans; intimidated the vicious of the several races, and being executed with impartial rigor, gave the highest moral deportment and discipline ever known in an invading army."

So commissions were created not because commanders were dissatisfied with the procedural restraints of courts-martial but because they filled a need that courts-martial could not meet, a void that no court occupied. And Scott's experience shows that commissions are not inherently unfair; indeed, being entirely malleable, they can be as fair or unfair as the commander chooses to make them.

During the Civil War, military commissions proliferated—over 4,000 proceedings in all. President Lincoln gave his commanders considerable authority to convene them, both in the rebellious states and in Union territories, to try citizens who expressed sympathy for the Southern cause or dissatisfaction with Lincoln's administration. Lincoln considered such men rebels, traitors, and disloyalists. American citizens convicted by such tribunals sought recourse to the federal courts through a means that Yamashita would later pursue, that of habeas corpus—the right to have the legality of one's imprisonment reviewed by a federal court. Lincoln responded by suspending habeas corpus.

Union commanders, however, did not limit the commissions to civilian dissidents. General Henry Halleck, commander of the Union armies, a lawyer himself, and a noted authority on international law, ordered that commissions be convened to try "insurgents and marauding predatory and guerilla bands," who were "by the laws of war regarded as no more nor less than murderers, robbers and thieves" destroying railroads, burning bridges, and torching farms and homes—in short, war criminals.

By "laws of war," Halleck meant not the Articles of War or any other written code or formal law but, rather, customary international law: those vaguely defined standards of conduct—expectations of conduct, really—that had originated in medieval Europe and accumulated over the centuries, "the rules and principles, almost wholly unwritten, which regulate the intercourse and acts of individuals during the carrying on of war between hostile nations or peoples," as Winthrop described them. Chief among these "rules and principles" is that armies should fight armies and not civilians, and that civilians in turn should leave the fighting to armies and not engage in it themselves. To Halleck, as a nineteenth-century international lawyer, Confederate sympathizers who raided Union camps or ammunition storehouses, with no uniform, commander, or accountability to the Confederate Army, were no less war criminals than were soldiers who stole jewelry from homes as they marched through the countryside.

"Persons acting independently," wrote Winthrop, "who engaged in the killing, disabling and robbing of peaceable citizens or soldiers, in plunder and pillage, and even in the sacking of towns, from motives mostly of personal profit or revenge" are not protected by the laws of war but, rather, are "treated as criminals and outlaws, not entitled upon capture to be held as prisoners of war, but liable to be shot, imprisoned, or banished, either summarily where their guilt was clear or upon trial and conviction by military commission." And there were dozens of such cases during the Civil War, for homicide and destruction of property.

Most of those tried were civilians, though many of them claimed that they were in fact operating under the authority of the Confederate Army—that they were not war criminals but soldiers waging war. Pillaging a town or torching a farmer's barn would be crimes no matter who committed them, but raiding an ammunition storehouse or demolishing a bridge to disrupt an army's advance would be legitimate acts of war if carried out by soldiers or by those operating under military authority, usually known as "partisans" or "raiders."

Often the defendant's claim of military status was left unresolved or dismissed as fantasy; few defendants appear to have been acquitted on those grounds, but in any event the commissions paid little mind to whether the defendant stood accused as a civilian war criminal or a member of the enemy army. Henry Wirz, the commandant of the Confederate prisoner-of-war camp at Andersonville, was charged with conspiracy "in violation of the laws of war, to impair and injure the health, and to destroy the lives, by subjecting to torture and great suffering, by confining in unhealthy and unwholesome quarters . . . And by furnishing insufficient and unwholesome food, of . . . thirty thousand soldiers in the military service of the United States of America held as prisoners of war." He was convicted by the commission and hanged.

The proliferation of commissions during the Civil War led Congress to exercise its constitutional authority to regulate the armed forces by bringing commissions under the law for the first time, although to a very limited extent. Adopting Winfield Scott's request of fifteen years earlier, it brought common crimes within the jurisdiction of courts-martial and, almost as an afterthought, of military commissions as well. Spies against the United States were made triable by commission as well as by court-martial. The duties of the army's Judge Advocate General were extended to include reviewing the proceedings of military commissions as well as of courts-martial. And although commissions were to be convened only for cases that could not be tried by a court-martial or by a regular sitting civilian court, still they "should be regulated by the rules governing courts-martial so far as they may be applicable."

The last was an important point. Although Congress did not give commissions their own standard procedures, neither were they any longer to be subject only to a commander's whim or his ad hoc rules. The familiar principles of court-martial procedure were to be followed as much as practicable. According to a Union general order of 1862, commissions were to be "constituted in a similar manner and their proceedings . . . conducted according to the same general rules as courts-martial in order to prevent abuses which might otherwise arise." It was a foresighted order, one that MacArthur some eighty-three years later declined to adopt.

Although the legacy of the nineteenth century was that military commissions need not inevitably be legally unrestrained exercises of executive power, there were certainly occasions of overreaching and abuse. "Prisoners were sometimes taken on trivial charges, such as 'being a noisy secessionist,' 'giving sympathy to the "rebels,"' 'selling Confederate "mottoes and devices,"' or 'hurrahing for Jeff Davis.'" An Episcopal minister in Alexandria, Virginia, was arrested for "habitually omitting the prayer for the President of the United States as required by the church service." Military commissions sometimes acquitted a noisy sympathizer or a sly priest of such flimsy charges. When they did not, the Judge Advocate General, the General in Chief of the Union Army, even the President himself could do so, because Congress, although declining to regulate commissions as strictly as courts-martial, did require them to keep records of their proceedings and to send them up the chain of command for review. "Trials by military commissions restrained United States forces in the Civil War mainly by imposing systematic record-keeping and an atmosphere of legality on the army's dealings with a hostile populace," wrote historian Mark Neely. "Military commissions played a role in preventing martial law from degenerating into . . . 'the will of the general.' . . . Military commissions dictated not only record-keeping but also system, regularity, review and some safeguards for defendants' rights."

But these safeguards had to be sought in the executive branch, not the courts. Lincoln's suspension of habeas corpus effectively placed arrests by executive order—including arrests of civilians on order of military officers—beyond judicial review. Although the Constitution specifies in Article I, section 9, that "the Privilege of the Writ of Habeas Corpus shall not be suspended, unless when in Cases of Rebellion or Invasion the public Safety may require it," the clause does not specify whether the power of suspension lay with the President or with the Congress. Lincoln arrogated that power to himself. Congress averted a showdown on the issue by legalizing his suspension, but the question of whether he could legally do what he did without congressional approval was to remain controversial throughout the war. Congress again sidestepped the issue when in 1863 it authorized the President to suspend habeas "whenever, in his judgment, the public safety may require it"—thus precluding the courts from exercising their traditional authority to determine the legality of detention by the executive.

In 1863 the Supreme Court announced a critical development in military law, one that was to confront Yamashita eight decades later. Clement L. Vallandigham, a former congressman from Ohio, gave a speech in that state that was harshly critical of President Lincoln. He was arrested by Union military authorities and charged with "disloyal sentiments and opinions." Haled before a military commission, he sought dismissal of the charge, arguing that, not being in the armed forces, he was subject not to a military trial but to a regular civilian one, with a jury. He also argued that "the offence of which he is charged is not known to the Constitution of the United States, nor to any law thereof; that they were words spoken to the people of Ohio, in an open and public political meeting, lawfully and peaceably assembled under the Constitution."

The commission rejected both his challenge to its jurisdiction and his free-speech defense and convicted him. He sought a writ of habeas corpus from the Supreme Court, but it declined to act. It professed to search high and low in the Constitution and the laws creating federal courts for an affirmative grant to "review or pronounce any opinion upon the proceedings of a military commission." It found none. Its conclusion was clear: as far as courts were concerned, commissions were simply exercises of discipline by the military. A soldier might as well ask a court to overturn his failure to be promoted or his orders to a distant post. Trial and punishment by a commission (or for that matter a court-martial) was just the military taking care of business, and not a matter for courts to meddle in.

After the war was over, however, and the threat of a confrontation between the President and the Supreme Court receded, the Court, in the *Milligan* case, crafted an exception to this hands-off-military-commissions principle: courts of the United States, it ruled, could inquire as to whether a tribunal had been lawfully convened in the first place, and whether it was properly exercising its jurisdiction when it placed a defendant on trial. In this limited inquiry, the sufficiency of the evidence and the fairness of the procedure were beside the point; the only question was whether the military had the right to try the defendant before its officers. If it did, the court's job was done, and the verdict, whatever it was, stood.

After the Civil War and Reconstruction, commissions lapsed into disuse for the simple reason that there was no need of them. During the U.S. occupation of the Philippines in 1900–1902, when U.S. forces occupied those islands to beat back the uprising of Filipinos after the United States wrested the islands from Spain, commissions were resurrected by American authorities, who used them much as Scott had done half a century earlier, both to discipline American soldiers and to punish Filipino marauders.

Commissions were not used at all during or after World War I in the United States, nor were they to reappear until 1943. But they had become a familiar aspect of U.S. military law. In the words of Winthrop's 1920 edition:

> In the absence of any statute or regulation governing the proceedings of military commissions, the same are commonly conducted according to the rules and forms governing courts-martial. These war-courts [commissions]

are indeed more summary in their action than are the courts held under the Articles of war [courts-martial], and, as their powers are not defined by law, their proceedings . . . will not be rendered illegal by the omission of details required upon trials by courts-martial, such, for example, as the administering of a specific oath to the members. . . . But, as a general rule, and as the only quite safe and satisfactory course for the rendering of justice to both parties, a military commission will—like a court-martial . . . ordinarily and properly be governed, upon all important questions, by the established rules and principles of law and evidence. Where essential, indeed, to a full investigation or to the doing of justice, these rules and principles will be liberally construed and applied.

A quarter century later, however, General MacArthur's idea of what was safe and satisfactory, ordinary and proper was to diverge quite sharply from that description.

7

The Charge
The Accountability of Command

For a month after his surrender in September 1945, Yamashita languished in New Bilibid Prison, surely wondering what the U.S. Army had in store for him. His cell had a cot, a table, and two chairs, and two barred windows. But he was not alone. With him were Muto, his chief of staff during the Philippine campaign, his assistant chief of staff Major General Naokata Utsunomiya, and his personal interpreter, a thirty-nine-year-old officer named Masakatsu Hamamoto.

Hamamoto was hardly a typical Japanese army officer. A cum laude graduate of Harvard College in 1927, he returned to Japan and joined General Motors, where he rose through the ranks to become head of its office in Peking (Beijing) and later its representative in Manchukuo, Japanese-occupied Manchuria. He had spent the war in the Philippines as the deputy commandant of a POW camp and as an assistant to Philippine President José Laurel in the Japanese occupation government. He was to remain constantly at Yamashita's side throughout the trial.

Outside the walls of the prison, preparation of the case against Yamashita was well under way. Army lawyers, photographers, and intelligence officers had spread out through the Philippines, interviewing victims of Japanese brutality, taking statements, snapping photos, and preparing affidavits for signature. Army lawyers in Manila and Washington were researching international law for use at a trial that had yet to be officially authorized or announced.

Presiding over the preparations—and all other American affairs in Japan and throughout the Pacific—was MacArthur. Appointed at the end of August as Supreme Commander of the Allied Powers, he was in effect the dictator of Japan, the man whose word was, literally, law in that country. He had installed, as his commander in the Philippines, Lieutenant General Wilhelm Styer, a stateside engineer and staff officer, as Commanding General, U.S. Army Forces Western Pacific. MacArthur's responsibilities were vast, and he undertook them with typical bravado: meeting with the emperor, now compliantly subordinate,

59

and promulgating laws for the conduct of life in Japan, including controls on the press. But in all of this, the Philippines, as always, were never far from his heart or attention. They had been his father's command, his boyhood home, and his first duty station. He had been "field marshal" of the Philippine Army in the 1930s and the commander who had escaped on that dark night in 1942, leaving Americans and Filipinos to surrender and suffer the death march and three years of wretched imprisonment. The Philippines were the islands that he had passionately told FDR and Marshall the United States had a moral obligation to liberate, the place where he had waded ashore in October 1944 and triumphantly summoned Filipinos to arms. For MacArthur, with no American hometown, the Philippines were not his second home, but his first.

MacArthur made two decisions touching the Philippines in the final weeks of the war: there would be trials for General Homma, the leader of Japanese troops at the time of the Bataan death march, and for General Yamashita, the Japanese leader who had fought MacArthur's forces so doggedly in the final year of the war. There was no shortage of other Japanese military leaders—those at Guadalcanal and New Britain, Tarawa and Peleliu, Okinawa and Iwo Jima—but Homma and Yamashita were different: they had been in the Philippines; their troops had brutalized American and Filipino prisoners. The War and State Departments, focused on the impending trial of Nazi war criminals at Nuremberg, had given MacArthur complete free rein to formulate whatever war crimes policy in the Pacific he thought best—just the kind of supervision MacArthur liked. He was already making preparations for the trial of major Japanese militarists at an international tribunal to be held in Tokyo, but in the fall of 1945 that was still seven months away. For Homma and Yamashita, MacArthur would not wait. He sent his deputy chief of staff to tell Colonel Alva C. Carpenter, his war crimes chief, to try Yamashita first. And, he noted pointedly, "speed is of the essence."

What motivated MacArthur? Unfortunately for history, he did not explain his decision in any surviving memorandum nor share his thoughts with any member of his staff. And D. Clayton James, in his exhaustive three-volume biography of MacArthur, could find no evidence that would reveal his "real motives or feelings" on the matter. Those close to MacArthur speculated to James that perhaps he was yielding to the demands of the Philippines' new leaders, but they had been hand-picked by MacArthur from a coterie of exiles and were unlikely to be demanding anything of him. It could as well have been vengeance for Yamashita's successful campaign to impede the American attack, or for the atrocities of Japanese soldiers, or it could have been to deliver a swift and public blow to the Japanese military without awaiting a multidefendant trial that was months away. Perhaps MacArthur was simply motivated by impatience: he could not wait to see Yamashita and Homma executed.

Whatever his thinking, MacArthur "wanted justice meted out swiftly," recalled Lieutenant Stratton, who had interrogated Yamashita before the trial. "Manila had been ravaged, and the man in top command would have to stand trial." MacArthur was also eager to see the trial widely publicized, and he urged newspapers to send reporters, chief prosecutor Robert Kerr recalled some years after the trial. According to Kerr, MacArthur wanted the trial to serve as a "public disclosure . . . of what actually happened in the Philippines during the Japanese occupation."

On September 24, 1945, MacArthur issued three orders. The first laid out "rules and regulations" for what seemed to be an anticipated array of military trials in Japan and the Pacific—international military commissions composed of representatives of many nations, to try "offenses against two (2) or more nations"; and lesser tribunals composed of U.S. or other military officers to try "offenses against any one or more of such service branches, or any other offenses." The tribunals were to try not only the crimes of murder or atrocities against prisoners and civilians but the crimes of conspiracy, "initiating or waging a war of aggression," and many more. The list of crimes tracked the language of the charter of the International Military Tribunal at Nuremberg, which had been promulgated six weeks earlier, but it also contemplated a variety of lesser offenses tried in more modest tribunals.

The second order directed Styer, commander of U.S. forces in the Philippines, "to appoint military commissions for the trial of such persons accused of war crimes as may hereafter be designated by this headquarters." The third order made clear what MacArthur had in mind. Entitled "Trial of General Tomoyuki Yamashita," addressed to Styer, and signed by Carpenter, MacArthur's staff judge advocate and war crimes chief, it read: "It is desired that you proceed immediately with the trial of General Tomoyuki Yamashita, now in your custody, for the crimes indicated in the attached charge."

This order contained the specific—and only—charge that was to confront Yamashita. It was to be one of the most controversial aspects of the Yamashita case—in the trial, before the U.S. Supreme Court, and for decades afterward. In its entirety, it read:

> Tomoyuki Yamashita, General Imperial Japanese Army, between 9 October 1944 and 2 September 1945, at Manila and at other places in the Philippine Islands, while commander of armed forces of Japan at war with the United States of America and its allies, unlawfully disregarded and failed to discharge his duty as commander to control the operations of the members of his command, permitting them to commit brutal atrocities and other high crimes against people of the United States and of its allies and dependencies, particularly the Philippines; and he, General Tomoyuki Yamashita, thereby violated the laws of war.

It was a perfectly ambiguous accusation. It was true enough that Yamashita had been commander of Japanese forces in the Philippines from October 9, 1944, to September 2, 1945,* and it was certainly true that brutal atrocities had been perpetrated on Filipinos and on Americans who were prisoners of war and internees during that time. But what was the meaning of "permitting"? Did it mean that Yamashita had given his troops permission to commit atrocities? Or did it mean simply that his failure to control his troops had given rise to circumstances in which those troops were able to, and did, commit atrocities?

The difference between the two readings is crucial. If the former, then the prosecution would need to introduce evidence that Yamashita had ordered atrocities, or had affirmatively given permission for his troops to commit them, or at the very least, perhaps, that he had stood aside and let the troops rampage, not exercising his authority to intervene. It would give Yamashita a fighting chance to win acquittal if the prosecutors could not show such knowing and personal involvement.

But if MacArthur's charge meant that Yamashita had simply failed to control his troops—that he had taken no steps to control them, or had been unsuccessful in whatever steps he had taken—and that this failure resulted in brutal atrocities being committed by the uncontrolled troops, atrocities that a commander's control would have prevented, then the picture was considerably darker for him. Indeed, the failure to control his troops was obvious. Their savage acts in Manila and throughout the islands were ample evidence of that. If proof of those acts was itself sufficient to prove the failure to control his forces, and if that failure was a "violat[ion] of the laws of war," then it was hard to imagine that Yamashita had any defense whatever to MacArthur's charge.

A critically important point of law was concealed in the terse language of the charge. There would have been little that was new or startling in a charge that a commander who ordered his troops to commit crimes against civilians or prisoners should be held criminally accountable for his actions. But there had never in any military been any recorded instance of an officer being charged even with simply acquiescing in atrocities, much less with failing to control troops, a failure that permitted atrocities to happen. The charge against Yamashita thrust the principle of responsibility into the realm of criminal accountability.

Responsibility is the very DNA of the military. Armies are the epitome of hierarchical organizations, small units answering to larger ones, lieutenants answering to captains who answer to colonels, and so on. Each officer is responsible

---

* As noted in chapters 4 and 5, not all forces were under his command on his arrival in October 1944; some elements were not transferred to him until months later, and his command of naval forces was limited to tactical matters. But as a general matter the statement is substantially accurate.

for the unit under his command: its success is his success; its failure, his failure. And responsibility travels up the chain of command, with each successively higher echelon answerable for the performance of each unit beneath it. The Chinese strategist Sun Tzu wrote, twenty-four centuries ago, "When troops flee, are insubordinate, distressed, collapse in disorder or are routed, it is the fault of the general. None of these disorders can be attributed to natural causes."

But in 1945, this responsibility had never been equated to criminal accountability. No superior officer had ever been charged with the crime of a subordinate merely because he was the superior officer, without some affirmative act. The reason is both theoretical and intensely practical. It is a cardinal principle of criminal responsibility that no one be charged except for some action or omission on his part—what he does or fails to do. Generals command thousands of soldiers, and it would be absurd to think that when an ordinary soldier commits a crime, everyone in his chain of command up to the most senior generals should be held accountable for it.

By the same token, it is a familiar principle of military justice, and has been for centuries, that an officer who orders a subordinate to commit a crime can be punished as a participant in the crime—"a principal," in the language of the law. Because an officer has the lawful authority of command over a subordinate, his order cannot be dismissed as an offhand remark, or mere words of encouragement or support, or even an incitement from one soldier to another. It is a misuse of lawful authority that implicates the commander in the crime itself, and so he can be charged, convicted, and punished as a participant, just as if he assisted or aided or abetted the commission of the crime, which in a real sense, of course, he has. The Uniform Code of Military Justice, the federal criminal law to which all U.S. service members are subject, makes this explicit: Article 77 provides that anyone who "aids, abets, counsels, commands or procures" the commission of a crime "is a principal."

From this point it should be a short step to the sensible proposition that the same principles of accountability should apply to an officer who does not explicitly order the commission of a crime but who acquiesces in it, knowing that it is about to happen and taking no action to intervene, despite having both the authority and the means to do so. Personal knowledge is critical, of course: a commander cannot evade accountability by silence when he should speak, by inaction when he should act. In the military context, an officer who looks on with implicit approval as a crime takes shape is as much a participant as an officer who explicitly issues the order to commit it.

In addition, a commander who discovers that one of his troops has committed a crime, even without his knowledge or approval, is obliged to take appropriate steps to bring the perpetrator to justice, by punishing him or by reporting the event to higher authority, who can take the appropriate steps. In fact, one of the earliest U.S. laws on this subject made precisely this point. The Articles of War for colonial Massachusetts in 1775 provided that "Every Officer commanding . . . shall keep good order, and to the utmost of his power, redress all such abuses or disorders which may be committed by any Officer or Soldier under his command; if upon complaint made to him of Officers or Soldiers beating or otherwise ill-treating any person, or committing any kind of riots to the disquieting of the inhabitants of this Continent, he the said commander, who shall refuse or omit to see Justice done to the offender or offenders . . . [shall] be punished . . . in such manner as if he himself had committed the crimes or disorders complained of." It appears to be the only provision, prior to the twentieth century, that even suggests a commander's accountability for "crimes and disorders" that he neither committed nor ordered—but it depends upon a "complaint [being] made to him," thus providing the critical element of personal knowledge.*

In each of these three conventional cases—the commander who orders the crime, who allows it to go forward despite being able to stop it, or who comes upon it later but ignores it—the commander has made an affirmative decision that implicates him in the commission of the crime or its concealment. Prior to 1945, however, there were but few cases of prosecution of a commander who ordered a crime, and apparently no recorded cases of prosecution for simply allowing a crime to take place or for not reporting one afterward. There were from time to time trials of officers for mistreatment of POWs and abuses of civilians (including, in the Philippines, two 1902 cases in which U.S. officers were tried by U.S. court-martial for using waterboarding to torture prisoners and detainees). But no commander had ever been arraigned for crimes of his troops that he had neither ordered nor taken part in.

So as MacArthur and his staff and prosecutors well knew, the charge against Yamashita presented an unprecedented issue in command accountability—the issue of whether and to what extent a commander may be charged and convicted for a crime committed *entirely by others*, without the commander's participation and perhaps even without his knowledge.

At first, it may seem unfair to hold commanders liable for crimes that they do not order, take part in, or even know about. But this is the military; commanders are responsible for the actions of their troops. That presents the question of whether an officer who does not know about such crimes might be thought accountable if he is at fault for not knowing. In short, what if an officer does not know, but *should* have known?

---

* Although this provision was subsequently adopted after independence in the American Articles of War of 1776, it does not appear to have survived beyond that. If anyone was ever prosecuted under this article, there is no available record of it.

Even here, one can imagine scenarios of accountability—for example, if a commander orders subordinates not to inform him of malfeasance by his troops. He lacks actual knowledge of the crime, but only because he has affirmatively evaded the duties of a responsible commander. The same might be said of a commander who, though not affirmatively directing subordinates to keep him in the dark, is so irresponsible or inept that he does not take the ordinary and necessary steps to establish lines of communication within his command so that he is informed of pertinent developments, or who does not read what is put on his desk, or who is drunk every night. In the first case, the commander evades knowledge, and in the second, he negligently fails to acquire it. In both cases, one can say that he should have known the facts and would have known them had he been acting responsibly.

Over the centuries, incompetent or irresponsible officers were sacked, but in 1945 there had never been a prosecution of any commander for a crime of subordinates that he *should* have known about. Indeed, in 1945 there had never been any suggestion of such a proposition.

When the Supreme Court took up Yamashita's case in 1946, however, it professed to find legal precedent for exactly such criminal accountability, in the Fourth Hague Convention of 1907. That treaty, ratified by the United States and Japan and almost every other nation, provided that in order to be "qualified belligerents"—what today we call "lawful combatants"—fighting units must be "commanded by a person responsible for his subordinates."* Because the Court's decision upholding Yamashita's conviction depended so heavily on that provision and on the Court's interpretation of "responsible," it is worth getting a little ahead of the story to examine its analysis here.

The fact is that this "person responsible" language in the 1907 Convention had nothing to do with the accountability of commanders for the crimes of their troops, which was still an unknown concept in 1907. It arose, rather, from concerns during the U.S. Civil War over bands of "rangers" or "raiders"—sometimes also called partisans or guerrillas—who were only loosely affiliated with the armies of the Confederacy and whose casual attitude toward discipline and proper military conduct and whose readiness to attack civilians and civilian property alarmed opposing commanders. In 1862, General Ulysses S. Grant ordered, "Persons acting as guerillas without organization and without uniform to distinguish them from private citizens are not entitled to treatment as prisoners of war when caught and will not receive such treatment."

Confederate guerrillas were not above sacking and looting the South's own

---

* The other requirements are that combatants must wear uniforms or other insignia visible at a distance, carry their arms openly, and "conduct their operations in accordance with the laws and customs of war."

landowners, and in 1863 military authorities, dismayed at the "inefficient officers" who supposedly led the raiders, disbanded many of the units. General Robert E. Lee welcomed the decision: "Experience has convinced me that it is almost impossible under the best officers even, to have discipline in these bands of partisan rangers, or to prevent them from becoming an injury instead of a benefit to the service, and even where this is accomplished, the system gives license to many deserters and marauders who assume to belong to these authorized companies and commit depredations on friend and foe alike."

Disputes also arose, in both the United States and Europe, over militias—citizens voluntarily taking up arms to defend the country from an invading enemy. Militias were organized military units, but they were not part of the regular army, and their status raised questions as to whether, if captured, militia men were to be treated as prisoners of war or mere bandits and outlaws. In the words of a contemporary jurist,

> The root of this indisposition to admit militia to be legitimate combatants was rather in military pride than in any doubt as to the sufficiency of the guarantees which they present. Through prejudice inherited from feudal times and the era of mercenaries, soldiers thought a militia unworthy to share in privileges which were looked upon as the sign of the honourable character of the military calling, because its members were neither soldiers by profession, nor able to share in the larger operations of war which were the peculiar business of the latter.

The underlying issue was whether such volunteers, if captured, were to be given the privileges due a prisoner of war—humane confinement for the duration of the war and safe return home afterward—or whether they were common criminals, subject to prosecution and imprisonment (or death) at the hands of their captors.

The United States was the first to declare its position, in the Lieber Code of 1863, the first codification of the laws of war, promulgated by President Lincoln for the Union Army.* That code held that militias "are now treated as public enemies, and if captured, are prisoners of war." ("Public enemies" in this context is a good thing—as combatants organized and authorized to fight for their state they were "public," and thus were accorded the privileges of a POW upon capture.)

France adopted this position as well, but Germany rejected it, declaring that in order for a French fighter to be treated as a prisoner of war, he must be a member of a regular military unit and must prove it by showing "an order

---

* See chapter 1.

emanating from the legal authority and addressed to him personally." Those who could not produce such a document were shot. This disagreement was taken up by a convocation of jurists in Brussels in 1874, which approved the U.S. view and declared that, to receive POW treatment, it was sufficient for captured volunteers to "have at their head a person responsible for his subordinates" and to wear a uniform or other distinguishing insignia marking them as legitimate soldiers. Such leadership would bring a military discipline to the units, and the uniform would sufficiently separate them from gangs of armed civilians and enable the opposing army to know who was a combatant and who was not, and thus whom they could lawfully attack and who could lawfully attack them. True civilians would be spared, but those taking up arms without being in an organized and uniformed unit would upon capture be treated as criminals and outlaws, not military prisoners.

In the thinking of the time, the responsible chief need not even be a soldier: a mayor or other public official would do. A "responsible person" could "cause the laws of war to be observed" and "punish isolated infractions of them if necessary," but this discussion treated subordination to such a commander entirely as a matter of organization; there was no talk of criminal liability. The Brussels declaration was later adopted without much discussion by the more influential Hague Peace Conferences of 1899 and 1907.

The two Hague Conventions were the culmination of the late-nineteenth-century movement toward codifying the law of war, mitigating the savagery of warfare (by, for example, outlawing weapons that inflicted "grievous wounds"), and confining lethal warfare to soldiers on the battlefield, safeguarding civilians. In nearly twenty-five years, there was never the slightest reference to any idea that commanders should be legally responsible for the misconduct of their troops. The responsibility of capable leaders, rather, was to instill discipline and good order in their units, desirable for its own sake and for the protection of noncombatants. "When once it is recognized that War is the most serious of all pursuits in which man can ever presume to engage, and calls for the contribution of all that legislative science and educated habits of self-restraint can yield," an international scholar of the day proclaimed, reflecting a hopefulness typical of the period, "the field is at least partially cleared for the natural play of those orderly instincts which belong to conditions of Peace. It is in disorder, irregularity, hurry, and confusion that what is truly bellicose, ferocious and purely animal in man can best range at large."

The question of a commander's responsibility and accountability for war crimes did not emerge until 1919, at the Paris Peace Conference, a gathering of the victorious nations of World War I. The conference would culminate in the Treaty of Versailles, but first the delegates had to deal with a myriad of political, diplomatic, and military issues, from the redrawing of European borders to the creation of a League of Nations. Some sixty commissions were created to study and report on various matters, and one of them was chaired by the American Secretary of State Robert Lansing and included James Brown Scott, an eminent American international law scholar. It was given a broad mandate: to report to the conference on "the responsibility of the authors of the war" and on the enforcement of penalties. Who should be charged, and with what, and in what forum?

Lansing's commission addressed some tough and unprecedented questions. Investigations by many (victorious) nations had documented "abundant evidence of outrages of every description, committed on land, at sea, and in the air, against the laws and customs of war and of the laws of humanity. In spite of the explicit regulations [of the Hague Conventions], of established customs, and of the clear dictates of humanity, Germany and her allies have piled outrage upon outrage. Additions are daily and continually being made."

But the Americans and the rest of the commission did not agree on some important matters. On the question of "personal responsibility," for these "outrages of every description," the commission's majority reported, "There is no reason why rank, however exalted, should in any circumstances protect the holder of it from responsibility when that responsibility has been established before a properly constituted tribunal. This extends even to the case of heads of states"—by which the commission meant, most prominently, Kaiser Wilhelm. "There is little doubt," said the commission's report, "that the ex-Kaiser and others in high authority were cognizant of and could at least have mitigated the barbarities committed during the course of the war. A word from them would have brought about a different method in the action of their subordinates on land, at sea and in the air." The commission proposed that all high officials, including the kaiser, be brought before a twenty-two-member international criminal tribunal to face not only charges of "offences against the laws and customs of war" but also of offenses against "the laws of humanity."

That was too much for Lansing and Scott. Their dissenting statement, the official view of the United States, accompanied the commission's report to the conference. Their objections were several. First, while the laws and customs of war were a "standard certain," they wrote, the "laws and principles of humanity vary with the individual" and were unsuited to be judged in a court of law. Second, bringing a head of state before an international court would be highly improper, because he is responsible to his nation alone; an international trial would be "subordinating him to foreign jurisdictions to which neither he nor his country owes allegiance or obedience, thus denying the very conception of sovereignty."

The Americans also declared that they were "unalterably opposed" to the view that German military officers (and civil authorities as well) should be held criminally liable because they "abstained from preventing, putting an end to, or repressing [that is, punishing] violations of the laws or customs of war." It gave this concept the awkward name of "negative criminality," though a more ac-curate name might be passive criminality, and urged its rejection.

> It is one thing to punish a person who committed, or, possessing the au-thority, ordered others to commit an act constituting a crime; it is quite another thing to punish a person who failed to prevent, to put an end to, or to repress violations of the laws or customs of war. In one case the in-dividual acts or orders others to act, and in so doing commits a positive offence. In the other he is to be punished for the acts of others without proof being given that he knew of the commission of the acts in question or that, knowing them, he could have prevented their commission. To estab-lish responsibility in such cases *it is elementary that the individual sought to be punished should have knowledge of the commission of the acts of a criminal nature and that he should have possessed the power as well as the authority to prevent, to put an end to, or repress them.* Neither knowledge of commission nor ability to prevent is alone sufficient. The duty or obligation to act is essential. They must exist in conjunction, and a standard of liability which does not include them all is to be rejected. [Emphasis added.]

It was the first articulation in any international body of what would later come to be known as command responsibility—the first suggestion that criminal re-sponsibility should run up the chain of command and inculpate not only lead-ers who actually ordered war crimes but also those whose intentional inaction permitted them to happen—and the first time it had been raised in the context of criminal prosecution. What is noteworthy is that the difference between the majority's articulation of a commander's responsibility and the Americans' expression of the same concept was not very great. The majority had declared that criminal responsibility should attach to those leaders who "abstained from" preventing, ending, or punishing criminal acts. The American view was only that this standard was too loose, and that there must also be some showing that the defendant knew of the acts, had both the authority and the power (by which they meant the actual ability) to prevent, end, or punish them.

In fact, the commission as a whole did adopt the American qualification; its final report clearly states that charges should be brought against all authorities "who ordered, or, with knowledge thereof and with power to intervene, ab-stained" from intervening. But to the dismay of the American delegation, the report retained the recommendation that Kaiser Wilhelm be brought to trial and that the charges include "offences against the laws of humanity." Indeed, the idea of an international tribunal and the idea of indirect criminal responsibil-ity were closely linked, for only by invoking the latter could the international powers bring the kaiser before the former.

So the concession that the majority had made to the American view on command responsibility itself—adding the requirements of knowledge, authority, and power—mattered little in the end to the Americans. "The purpose of constituting a high tribunal for the trial of persons exercising sovereign rights was persisted in," the Americans said of the majority,

> and the abstention from preventing violations of the laws and customs of war and of humanity was insisted upon. It was frankly stated that the purpose was to bring before this tribunal the ex-Kaiser of Germany, and that the jurisdiction of the tribunals must be broad enough to include him even if he had not directly ordered the violations.
>
> To the unprecedented proposal of creating an international criminal tribunal and to the doctrine of negative criminality the American members refused to give their assent.

Without American support, the commission's proposal was dead on arrival at the Peace Conference. No tribunal was ever convened, the kaiser took refuge in the Netherlands, and the standard of command accountability, however carefully limited, was never applied to anyone. Germany conducted a few war crimes trials of its own soldiers to appease the victors, but these were strictly for show and did not unduly inconvenience the few who were convicted.* The world moved on.

The issue did not arise again until 1944, when an early draft of war crimes principles by the U.S. Army reportedly suggested that German officers might be held liable for refusing to prevent a war crime "when he knows of, or is on notice as to their commission or contemplated commission and is in a position to prevent them," but this never became official. A 1944 French law provided that superior officers of a defendant could be charged as accomplices if they had "tolerated" the crimes, and some Canadian regulations seemed to be to the same effect, but there is no evidence that anyone was actually charged under these fragmentary laws.

Even the Charter of the International Military Tribunal at Nuremberg, which was promulgated two months before Yamashita was formally charged, contains no mention of any notion that superior officers are chargeable with offenses committed by their subordinates—a remarkable omission, considering that the defendants at Nuremberg included several German flag officers.†

---

* See chapter 1.

† Article 7 of the Nuremberg charter provided that "the official position of defendants, whether as Heads of State or responsible officials in Government Departments, shall not be considered as freeing them from responsibility or mitigating punishment." The effect of this

So if MacArthur's charge against Yamashita had been that he "knew or should have known" about the atrocities committed by Japanese troops and did nothing to prevent or punish them though he had the ability to do so, it would have been an unprecedented, though justifiable, extension of the law, essentially adopting the formulation of the Lansing-Scott committee at the Paris Peace Conference. But the charge did not allege that Yamashita knew. It did not allege that he should have known, nor that he could have prevented or punished any crime. It alleged something new and quite different, eliminating altogether the issues of personal knowledge and ability to prevent or punish. It simply alleged that he "unlawfully disregarded and failed to discharge his duty" to control his troops, "permitting" them to commit the atrocities they did.

That is why the ambiguity of "permitting" was so fraught with consequences. If it was intended to mean only that Yamashita looked on while the crimes occurred, acquiescing in what he had the means and ability to interdict, thereby permitting those crimes, then it would have been a novel allegation but one rooted in the established doctrine of commanders held accountable for ordering crimes. It simply would have substituted implicit permission for explicit order. And it would have allowed Yamashita a defense if the prosecution could not prove that Yamashita did in fact know what horrors were taking place in Manila when he was not there. But it was soon to become clear that the prosecution did not intend that meaning at all.

The prosecution of General Yamashita began on October 2, 1945, when an army lawyer came to Yamashita's cell at Bilibid Prison south of Manila and handed him a document titled "United States of America vs Tomoyuki Yamashita." On the document, translated into Japanese, was the charge drafted by Carpenter, MacArthur's chief lawyer, who signed under oath that he had "investigated the matters set forth in the charge, and that it is true in fact, to the best of his knowledge and belief."

MacArthur's "Regulations" for war crimes trials did accord Yamashita some rights of due process. The accused was to have "in advance of trial, a copy of the charges and specifications, so worded as clearly to apprise the accused of each offense charged" and "translated when he is unable otherwise to understand them." He was also accorded the right "to be represented prior to and during trial by counsel of his own choice" and to have his counsel "present relevant evidence at the trial in support of his defense, and cross-examine each adverse witness who personally appears before the commission."

---

provision was not to fix accountability but to strip senior officials of any sovereign immunity that, at least in earlier days, would have been a shield against criminal prosecution altogether.

Had he been given the opportunity, which he was not, to name defense counsel "of his own choice," Yamashita could not have assembled a more dedicated team than the one that was assigned to him. But that team, put together hurriedly while the prosecution was serving the charge in Bilibid prison, gave little early indication of its promise. General Styer, the Philippines commander delegated by MacArthur to organize the trial, turned to his own staff judge advocate, Colonel Bud Young, and told him to find defense counsel for Yamashita. There were to be six prosecutors, and so Young looked around for six lawyers for Yamashita's side.

He did not ask for volunteers. As the senior member of the defense, he appointed Colonel Harry E. Clarke of Altoona, Pennsylvania, who was the supervisor of the disciplinary barracks in Manila, the warden for American soldiers convicted in courts-martial there. Clarke, a World War I veteran who had returned to active duty prior to Pearl Harbor and had fought the Japanese in the brutal campaigns of the Pacific, was to be the oldest member of the team and the only one with combat experience. Young also drafted Lieutenant Colonel Walter C. Hendrix of Atlanta, Georgia, the legal adviser to the U.S. military police command in Manila. From his own staff, Young sent Lieutenant Colonel James G. Feldhaus of South Dakota, a tax lawyer.

Short of eligible names, Young turned to the army's Claims Service in Manila, the office responsible for handling Filipinos' compensation for property commandeered by American forces. It was not that the Claims Service was notable for the quality of its criminal defense counsel—it didn't have any—but it was the largest legal office in town. Young took Major George Guy of Cheyenne, Wyoming, and Lieutenant Colonel Leigh Clark, who had been a judge back home in Alabama.

One more was needed. Captain A. Frank Reel (the *A* was for "Adolf," a name he did not use), a labor lawyer from Boston, Massachusetts, heard what was going around and moved quickly. "Don't put me on that case," he told his Claims Service boss. "I'm only a captain and I'll be darned if I want to carry anybody's briefcase for the next six weeks." I understand, said his boss. I don't blame you.

After Reel departed, his boss wrote down his name as the final, and most junior, member of the defense team.

There was one glitch. When Clark heard of his appointment, he hit the roof. How could he possibly be reelected as a judge in Alabama, he griped to some fellow lawyers that night, if he defended a Japanese war criminal? His opponents back home would have a field day. His career on the bench would be over.

Most of the lawyers listening to him commiserated, but one—Captain Milton Sandberg of New York City, a lawyer in the state comptroller's office before the war—suggested that defending an accused general in a publicized trial might not be such a bad thing for a lawyer in uniform, even in Alabama.

New York was a long way from Birmingham. The next day, Clark called on Young and demanded that he be removed from the defense detail. Young acquiesced. In Clark's place, Young named Sandberg.

This pickup team of six Manila-based army lawyers—tax expert, labor lawyer, small-town practitioners, none of whom were criminal defense counsel or even had much experience in any courtroom—sat down together for the first time on October 4, 1945, four days before Yamashita was to be arraigned before a military commission, and reviewed the charge and the legal paperwork that had brought them together. Section 20 of MacArthur's rules and regulations for military commissions addressed sentencing with stark simplicity. "The commission may sentence an accused, on conviction, to death by hanging or shooting, imprisonment for life or for any less term, fine, or such other punishment as the commission shall determine to be proper."

In four days, their new client would be on trial for his life. They agreed that their first order of business really should be to meet him.

Before that happened, Reel had dinner with a friend, a lawyer from MacArthur's legal office, familiar with the charge. "Yamashita is being tried as a war criminal because his men violated the laws of war," he told Reel. "They have nothing on him at all. They're trying to establish a new theory—that a commanding officer is responsible if his troops violate the laws of war, regardless of whether he ordered the violations or even knew of them. Under such a principle, I suppose even MacArthur should be tried. It is bad law."

Monday, October 8, 1945, was no ordinary day in Manila. "FIRST JAP WAR TRIAL TODAY!" the *Chicago Daily Tribune* announced in bold caps. "Noose Tightens around Tiger's Neck as Yamashita Crimes Bared" was the headline on the front page of the *Manila Times*. ("Tiger"—from Yamashita's sobriquet as "the Tiger of Malaya"—and "Jap" were to prove popular shorthand in news accounts.) Americans and Filipinos; soldiers, sailors, and civilians; men, women, and children crowded around ice-cream and cold-drink vendors as they jostled for a glimpse of the savage Jap Tiger whose troops had caused so much destruction, death, and heartbreak in the city and throughout the islands. "Yamashita was already convicted in the eyes of the world, and certainly in the eyes of the Filipinos, even before a shred of evidence had been introduced against him," defense counsel Guy noted afterward.

Yamashita himself was unfazed, or at least he put up a good front. In an interview with an American newspaper reporter on the eve of trial, speaking through Hamamoto, he expressed some degree of bravado. "I don't see how I can be convicted," he said. "Any more than the United States President or General MacArthur could be if American troops had committed atrocities. How can I be convicted of crimes I didn't even know about?" Smiling, he noted wryly, "I recognize more than ever the American spirit of fair play, which I had not previously realized would work in my favor."

This first day was not to be the trial proper, but the arraignment—the formal presentation of the charges, Yamashita's plea of guilty or not guilty, and the setting of a trial date that would allow both the prosecution and the defense time to prepare. The prosecution had the burden of assembling evidence to prove guilt and had been at this task since Yamashita's capture more than a month earlier; the defense counsel had barely had a weekend to get ready for this day.

The venue for the trial was a large airy ballroom in the High Commissioner's Residence in Manila, amid the rubble and debris from which the Filipinos had only begun to dig out. The mansion, once the residence of the American representative in the Philippines, had served as the Japanese embassy in Manila during the war and had been itself damaged in the fighting of February. On opening day, seventy-five U.S. military policemen surrounded the building and lined the interior. The ballroom, the scene of many a diplomatic reception in its better days, had seven curved, floor-to-ceiling doors opening out to the broad lawn, with a magnificent view of Manila Bay just beyond. The commissioners were to be seated in leather-backed chairs behind a table on a foot-high platform, their backs to the doors, which were covered by gauzy curtains but were often kept open to allow ocean breezes into the hot and humid room.

In front of the commissioners' table were chairs and small tables for the interpreters, the court reporters at their stenotype machines, and witnesses called to testify, and longer tables for the accused and his lawyers to the commissioners' right and for the prosecutors to their left. Camera crews from the U.S. Army Signal Corps set up their equipment side by side with newsreel cameramen and radio broadcasters. One observer counted seventy-two reporters in the room. There were 300 folding chairs for spectators: VIPs up front, soldiers and anyone else lucky enough to snare a spot toward the rear. Klieg lights lined the room, their bright glare adding to the stifling heat, the curtains on the French doors only occasionally stirring in the still air. By two o'clock, when the proceedings were to start, every seat was filled, and more spectators mingled with reporters in the balconies overlooking the room. The wife of Philippines President Sergio Osmeña was there, as was General Styer himself.

The day's agenda would be brief. The prosecutor would read the charge against Yamashita, and Yamashita would enter his plea of not guilty. That done, the commissioners would ask the attorneys on each side how much time they would need to prepare for trial and then set the date and adjourn until then.

Promptly at two, five generals stepped from the lawn through the French doors into the room and took their seats in swivel chairs at the table. As flashbulbs popped and newsreel cameras whirred, Major General Russel B. Reynolds, the senior officer and thus the presiding member, took the middle seat.

MacArthur's rules and regulations for military commissions had stated, "If feasible, one or more members of a commission should have had legal training." Evidently it was not feasible to find any army officers with legal training, for none of the commissioners had any. As far as their records show, none of them had participated in any court-martial or other legal proceeding during their thirty years or so of army service.

Reynolds, two stars pinned on each lapel of his open-necked khaki shirt, was not a combat officer but a member of the army's General Staff Corps. He had progressed to flag rank not as a commander but as an administrator and had spent much of World War II as a director of military personnel in the U.S. Midwest, his duty station downtown Chicago.

The other members of the commission—Major General Leo Donovan, Major General James A. Lester, Brigadier General Morris C. Handwerk, and Brigadier General Egbert F. Bullene—had much in common. All were between the ages of fifty and fifty-four; none but Lester had combat experience in World War II (Bullene and Donovan had served briefly in World War I). They were stationed throughout the war in the United States in various training and administrative assignments, and all were posted to the Philippines only in the final few weeks of the war. Lester had been an artillery officer in the Pacific from 1942, landing with the Sixth Army on Luzon and advancing to Manila.

General Yamashita entered with his lawyers, in a worn but neatly pressed green uniform, his jacket over an open white shirt, and wearing a cavalryman's high boots, complete with spurs, and four rows of decorations and ribbons. Yamashita was, as he was to be throughout the trial, quiet and reserved and a bit distant, as if he were watching the proceedings from afar. "Yamashita was the consistent stoic," Reel wrote later. "A man of dignity and poise." Though quick to smile, "his features never betrayed emotion. Whatever else might be thought of him, General Yamashita personified dignity and serenity. Victor or vanquished, commander or captive, he carried himself like a man."

Reel's co-counsel George Guy had a similar impression at their first meeting:

He stood about 5′7″ tall and was clad in the gray-green Japanese field uniform. He was a large man for a Japanese but his clothes hung in folds on his body, he having lost a very considerable amount of weight as a result of the reduced diet upon which Japanese troops had been subsisting during the last months of the Philippine Campaign. . . . His figure was erect but not stiff and he acknowledged each introduction with a little bow and in a rather solemn manner, although there were traces of a smile about the corners of his large mouth and his large brown eyes brightened perceptibly as they rested in turn on each of us. His head seemed to be unusually large, particularly so for a Japanese, and the face was marked with heavy lines. . . . The eyes were deep and expressive. . . . His forthright manner, his candor and his strength of character made a distinct impression on me.

He impressed others as well. U.S. Navy Lieutenant George Mountz, the custodian of documents for the prosecution team, whose letters home during the trial provide a candid account of daily events, wrote that when Yamashita entered, "he hesitated, bowed slightly with respect but not servitude, and sat down. He carried himself with all the poise and dignity a man could possibly have. Personally, I think he nearly stole the show and even knowing the terrible things he ordered—or at least permitted to occur—you had to admire him as he stood before a U.S. Commission sworn to give him justice."

Reporters at the arraignment, perhaps anticipating snarling ferocity from a man known as "Tiger of Malaya"—pretrial news reports had described him as "swaggering" and "arrogant"—were taken aback. "Yamashita maintained a calm exterior throughout, cocking his ear now and then to catch the words of the court interpreter," reported the *Manila Times*, adding, "Yamashita appeared hale and hearty" and "self-confident throughout." Others were less impressed. "The arraignment was carried out in Hollywood-like atmosphere, with flash bulbs lighting the room intermittently, reporters scribbling constantly and news-reel cameras grinding away," reported the Associated Press, "but Yamashita regarded them with a bored expression." Robert Cromie, who covered every day of the trial for the *Chicago Daily Tribune*, noted that Yamashita was "plump and potbellied" and that his face was "sad but intelligent."

Yamashita's demeanor was to change little throughout the trial. He had a remarkable ability to convey a sense of warmth while remaining quiet and exceedingly calm. "I have never run across an American soldier who had had a chance to know Yamashita who was not attracted to him personally," Reel wrote after the trial. But as the trial went on, others were to take his unchanging expression as a sign of detachment or stoniness as victim after victim told their stories of horror at Japanese hands.

Reynolds called the proceedings to order. "This military commission has been appointed by Lieutenant General W. D. Styer," he intoned as the official interpreters repeated his words in Japanese, "by direction of General Douglas MacArthur, Commander-in-Chief, to conduct the trial of General Tomoyuki Yamashita, Imperial Japanese Army. Its duties are to hear the evidence of the prosecution and the defense, to arrive at a finding as to the guilt or innocence of the accused, and if he is found guilty, to determine an appropriate sentence.

The proceedings will be conducted in a fair and impartial manner, which is traditional American justice."*

Clarke, the chief defense counsel, stood and asked permission for Yamashita to have his personal interpreter, Masakatsu Hamamoto, sit by his side during the trial and interpret quietly for him. General Yamashita, Clarke explained, was having difficulty understanding the official, American-born interpreters. Reynolds granted the request.

"This was a tour de force of stupendous proportions," Reel later recalled, "shortening the proceedings by many weeks." Even witnesses testifying in English would have been required to pause while their words were translated into Japanese for Yamashita. Allowing Hamamoto to whisper his simultaneous translation into Yamashita's ear eliminated such delays. But still, as witnesses testified in Japanese or Tagalog, the necessity of interpretation—particularly between Japanese and English, no easy job under any circumstances—was to prove a challenge throughout the trial. The official interpreters were American servicemen of two quite different backgrounds. The U.S.–born Nisei, second-generation Japanese Americans, were thought to be quite good in "elementary expressions," Reel noted, but not sophisticated in English. The U.S. Navy and Marine Corps officers who had studied Japanese at a military school in Colorado "required constant use of translation dictionaries." Both prosecution and defense also had, at their tables, their own interpreters who would whisper perceived inaccuracies as the official interpreters spoke, which occasionally brought counsel to their feet to ask for a review or correction, necessitating extended dialogue among interpreter, counsel, and the commissioners.

The first snag arose a few minutes later when Reynolds routinely recited that, as required by MacArthur's order, "the charge and specifications" had been

---

* In the account of the trial that follows, the words appearing within quotation marks are taken verbatim from the official transcript of the trial. I have from time to time, and without the formality of showing an ellipsis, omitted sentences that are repetitive or off-topic, but I have introduced nothing into quotations unless shown in [brackets]. Testimony or argument not within quotation marks is my summary of what was said. I have also removed the court reporters' military capitalization ("Charge" and "Defense," for example) and occasionally changed punctuation, generally by adding commas in the longer sentences. Considering the length and complexity of the trial, the crowded room and open windows, and the frequent interpretation to and from English of Japanese, Tagalog, Spanish, and other languages spoken by witnesses, the transcript is an admirably professional product. Two court reporters, enlisted soldiers identified only as E. D. Conklin and L. H. Winter, worked eighteen hours a day in tandem to produce each day's transcript by 8:00 a.m. the following morning. In over 4,000 pages, I noticed but two typographical errors.

When quoting from the letters of Lieutenant Mountz, I have corrected the occasional misspellings and typos.

duly served on the accused. Yamashita himself stood, and through the official interpreter, he said that he had received the charge, but not the specifications.

Major Robert M. Kerr, the chief prosecutor, took the opportunity to explain to presiding officer Reynolds what a charge and specification were—the equivalent of having to explain to a judge what an indictment was. In court-martial practice, he said, the charge was the statement of the offense: for example, "murder, in violation of the 86th Article of War." The specification was the details of what the accused had allegedly done: the time, the place, the victim, and so on. Here, explained Kerr, the charge contained the specifications within itself.

It was a curious argument, because the document was titled "Charge," not "Charge and Specification," and stated only that Yamashita had failed to control his troops, permitting them to commit atrocities in violation of the "laws of war." It contained no details of what these atrocities were, or where or when they were alleged to have taken place, nor what "laws of war" were violated, nor for that matter what the prosecution was alleging that Yamashita actually did by way of "permitting" the unspecified atrocities. Kerr had a facile explanation: this was not a court-martial. "Since court-martial procedure is much more strict and not as liberal with respect to pleadings or procedure as a military commission's procedure," said Kerr, "certainly this charge does include the elements of both the charge and specifications as those terms are used in [MacArthur's September 24] order."

But there were none of the details that constitute an actual specification. Yamashita spoke up again: "There is no specification," he said. "There is only a charge."

Kerr grew impatient. "If the commission please, I ask the commission to rule that the charge and specifications have been served upon the accused within the meaning of those terms used in this order."

Reynolds had no answer, perhaps still trying to fix the distinction between charge and specification, which Kerr's explanation had done nothing to clarify. Was this brief charge also an adequate specification?

Clarke took Reynolds off the hook. He rose from the defense table and announced, "We are agreeable, sir."

"On that basis," the presiding general said, "the commission rules that the charge and specifications have been properly served upon the accused." He looked over the room. "We will proceed."

With Clarke's acquiescence, Kerr had sidestepped a potential problem. Tall and rail-thin, with dark hair and a Clark Gable mustache, the thirty-nine-year-old Kerr, chief prosecutor on the case, cut an impressive figure. The son of the president of Oregon State University, Kerr had enlisted in the Army Reserve in the 1920s and was given a commission in the Judge Advocate General's

Department (JAG) upon his graduation from law school at the University of Michigan. After Pearl Harbor, he volunteered for active duty but, he told army brass, not as a lawyer. He wanted to be an infantry officer and fight the enemy. Sorry, he was told. You're a JAG officer and they don't lead troops in combat.

Kerr had an astonishing response. He promptly resigned his commission and enlisted in the army as a private. He went to basic training with green recruits, then went to Officer Candidate School, where he earned a commission again, this time in the infantry. Kerr clearly was not a man easily diverted from his goal.

Kerr had fought in the Pacific, and in 1945 his legal training brought him an assignment to the war crimes investigation unit in Manila, under Colonel Carpenter, chief of MacArthur's War Crimes Branch and, as the acting theater judge advocate, MacArthur's top lawyer. There, Kerr and a colleague, Captain Manning Webster, wrote the memo that briefed Carpenter on the law and policy of war crimes trials.

Kerr's practice in Oregon had consisted chiefly of advising agricultural co-operatives. He had never tried a case in his life, but a colleague noted that he was "smart as a whip and can think like lightning on his feet, and knows the law and rules." Styer's headquarters had assigned him four captains as assistant pros-ecutors, each recommended by Carpenter at MacArthur's headquarters: Kerr's erstwhile colleague Manning Webster, Delmas C. Hill, William N. Calyer, and Jack M. Pace. This made the prosecution team equal in number to the defense team, but there was a difference: the assistant prosecutors had been district at-torneys or assistant district attorneys in civilian life and had considerable expe-rience in the courtroom. They were skilled in the preparation of cases, in the cross-examination of defendants and defense witnesses, and in persuading juries to convict. "I never want to meet any better prosecutors," Reel noted ruefully. A sixth lawyer, a Filipino, was also named to the prosecution staff as a "special as-sistant prosecutor," but he quickly showed himself not in the same class as the American district attorneys and did not play a significant role in the trial.

On paper at least, the prosecution lawyers clearly outmatched their defense counterparts, and the defense was not helped when Feldhaus, the tax lawyer, needed emergency surgery and missed the first month of the trial. The defense table was reduced to four when Clarke dispatched Guy to Japan for a month to find, interview, and bring back witnesses who could testify to Yamashita's good character: an important part of the defense strategy to show that Yamashita was not a man to permit atrocities.

In addition, the prosecution section was supervising a sizable contingent of investigators who had been interviewing witnesses before and after the arraign-ment, as well as some twenty to thirty translators of Japanese documents that the prosecution would introduce into evidence. There were dozens of typists, file clerks, and assistants who worked behind the scenes to prepare hundreds of documents for orderly submission to the commissioners. "I am as near bushed as I have ever been," wrote Mountz the day before the trial opened. "In fact I think I have worked harder in the last three weeks than at any time in my life." Each prosecution document required at least seven copies: one for each of the commissioners, one for the defense, one for the witness or the court reporter, all made on a large Photostat machine that produced a negative—in about three minutes per page.

With the charge-and-specification business out of the way, Reynolds resumed the opening formalities. Was Yamashita satisfied with his defense counsel? Yamashita stood and bowed slightly to the generals. Speaking through the official interpreter, he said, "I am happy to accept the choice of the commission as to my counsel. I am highly honored to have been given such distinguished persons to represent me."

But he had an additional request. "I should like to have my Chief of Staff, Lieutenant General Muto, and my Assistant Chief of Staff, Major General Utsunomiya, as additional counsel. There are a number of records and facts with which they alone are conversant. I need their advice and assistance."

His chief of staff and assistant chief of staff as defense counsel? It was an odd request—they were not even lawyers. But the night before the arraignment, when the commissioners and lawyers had gathered in the reception hall for a walk-through of who would stand where and in what order the formalities would be taken up, defense counsel Clarke had asked prosecutor Kerr if he would have any objection to Muto and Utsunomiya sitting at the defense table. Yamashita relied on those men for information about the events of the past year in the Philippines, Clarke explained.

Kerr certainly did object. If he had anything to say about it, Yamashita would have no one with him but his lawyers.

Reynolds, overhearing the conversation, had a suggestion. MacArthur's order allowed Yamashita to choose his own defense counsel, so why not just designate Muto and Utsunomiya as defense counsel?

It was an idea only a nonlawyer could come up with. But at the hearing and on the record, Kerr objected. Are either of those men to be called as witnesses for the defense?

Yes, said Clarke.

"That rules them out entirely," Kerr told the commissioners. "In a criminal proceeding it would be entirely irregular if a witness for the defense should also represent the accused as counsel."

In this he was correct; defense lawyers cannot testify in their clients' trials. More to the point, defense witnesses are normally barred from the courtroom until they testify, lest their testimony be shaped by what they learn of the prosecution's case. Kerr, who had a few minutes earlier told the commission that the charge should not be held to the strict standard of a court-martial, now urged them to follow the strict standards of criminal proceedings.

Reynolds declined. "The accused has stated his belief that he needs Lieutenant General Muto and Major General Utsunomiya in his defense. He has asked that they be appointed associate defense counsel. It is the desire of this commission to conduct a fair trial; accordingly, subject to objection by any member of the commission, the request of the defense is granted."

Kerr got in the last word. "The prosecution does not and will not recognize the men named as Chief of Staff or Deputy or Assistant Chief of Staff. We maintain, sir, that the day when Yamashita had his Chief of Staff or Assistant Chief of Staff is over!"

The matter is closed, said Reynolds. Move on.

Kerr read aloud the charge. Reynolds asked if Yamashita was ready to enter his plea.

At this point Clarke stood up and launched the defense of his client. "The accused respectfully moves that the charge now in hearing be stricken, on the ground that it fails to state a violation, in so far as General Yamashita is concerned, of the laws of war."

It was a terse statement, with no briefing or argument or citation of legal authority or discourse on the laws of war, but the defense had been on the job only a few days, and had had little time to research and prepare. But the effort had to be made, and made before the trial began. The charge, he said, should be dismissed and the trial terminated, because there is no such charge as failing to control one's troops in violation of the "laws of war."

Kerr's response was equally terse. "This commission has been ordered to try General Yamashita. There is no provision in the commission's procedure for a motion such as defense counsel now interposes."

Clarke insisted. "The charge and specifications alleged therein do not state an offense under the laws of war as to General Yamashita."

Reynolds needed no briefing, no extended argument, no discourse on legal matters. "The objection of counsel for the defense is not sustained," he ruled.

As a matter of law, Clarke was correct, considering that in the centuries-old collection of trials, treatises, orders, and treaties that together comprise the body of international authority known as the laws of war, there was scant reference to criminal accountability of commanders. Clarke was inviting these five nonlawyers to tell MacArthur and his lawyers that they agreed with Yamashita's lawyer that the charge was invalid under international law and that they therefore had decided to terminate the trial before it began.

There was no chance of that, as Clarke must surely have realized. MacArthur had ordered the generals to try Yamashita, and try him they would. If Clarke wanted to argue that the charge did not actually allege a violation of the law, he could take it up with MacArthur's lawyers when the verdict had been given and the matter was before MacArthur for review.

Clarke had another motion, again focused on the vagueness of the charge. He moved for a "more definite and certain" statement of the details, specifying "the time, place and dates wherein the accused disregarded and failed to discharge his duty as commander to control the operations of members of his command, as alleged. And particularizing as to time, place, dates and details of the alleged atrocities and other high crimes."

Kerr, having a few minutes earlier urged the commission to follow the standards of a criminal proceeding on defense witnesses, now switched field again. "Such a motion would be appropriate in a court of law, perhaps, but certainly not in this proceeding. We certainly do object to apply in the proceedings of this commission the technical objections and rules of evidence, pleadings and procedure which might apply in a court of law."

It was all something of a fencing match, because Kerr's staff had in fact already drawn up a detailed statement of the charge, specifying the time and place of atrocities that he was prepared to file, and Clarke knew it. It was captioned a "bill of particulars," a term unknown in military law but familiar to civilian practitioners as a detailed statement of the circumstances of the defendant's alleged crime, accompanying a grand jury's indictment. It was, essentially, the specifications that the defense had argued were missing from the charge sheet itself. "We are glad to supply defense counsel with such a bill of particulars," Kerr told the commission.

Just "one condition," said Kerr: "that the prosecution at a later date has the privilege of serving and filing a supplemental bill of particulars. We have certain new information just recently received which we have not had an opportunity so far to incorporate in the bill of particulars. If we may have assurance that later we may file a supplemental bill of particulars, we are willing to proceed on the basis which I have suggested; otherwise not."

Intentionally or not, Kerr's condition bordered on the insolent: threatening to withhold the already-prepared statement of particulars unless the commission agreed to let him file a supplemental bill later on. But Reynolds appeared not to notice. He told Kerr to file the bill of particulars, and to file a supplemental bill when it was ready.

The bill of particulars was a remarkable document. It began with a brief introduction: "Between 9 October 1944 and 2 September 1945, at Manila and other places in the Philippine Islands, members of Armed Forces of Japan under the command of the Accused committed the following:"

There followed, in sixty-four numbered paragraphs over nineteen pages, a list of appalling atrocities committed by Japanese troops in the Philippines. The great majority of the crimes took place in February and March 1945—the height of the battle for Manila—and none were alleged to have occurred after May 1, 1945.

Some of the allegations were painstakingly specific:

> 17. During the period from 7 February 1945 to 14 February 1945, both dates inclusive, at and in the vicinity of De La Salle College, 1501 Taft Avenue, Manila, brutally killing, without cause or trial, Judge Jose R. Carlos and Brother Xavier, Rector of that College, both of whom were unarmed noncombatant civilians; brutally killing, without cause or trial, Antonio Carlos, Ricardo Bartolome, Dr. Antonio Cojuangco, and 38 other men, women and children, all unarmed noncombatant civilians; brutally mistreating, wounding, maiming and attempting to kill, without cause or trial, Father Francis J. Cosgrave, Dionisia Carlos, Servillano Aquino, and fourteen (14) other unarmed noncombatant civilians; rape of two female civilians; attempted rape of one female civilian; and attempt to have carnal intercourse with the body of one dead female civilian.

Other allegations were broad and sweeping:

> 5. During November 1944, in northern Cebu Province, massacre, without cause or trial, of more than 1000 unarmed noncombatant civilians.
> 55. On or about 12 February 1945, at Calamba, Laguna Province, massacre, without cause or trial, of more than 7000 unarmed noncombatant civilians, and rape of 37 civilian women.

Crimes against Americans were singled out in several allegations:

> 4. On or about 30 October 1944, at Carigara, Leyte, cruelly mistreating, torturing, mutilating and subsequently executing and, without cause or trial, killing Private Wade E. Gensemer, a member of the Armed Forces of the United States of America, then in captivity of the Armed Forces of Japan as a prisoner of war.
> 13. On about 28 January 1945, at Los Banos Internment Camp, Laguna Province, brutally mistreating and then summarily executing, and, without cause or trial, killing George James Louis, an unarmed noncombatant civilian subject of the United States of America, then interned and held captive by Armed Forces of Japan.

Other paragraphs alleged dozens of crimes:

64. During the period from 6 February 1945 to 23 February 1945, both
dates inclusive, in and in the vicinity of St. Augustine Church and Convent, Intramuros, Manila, brutally abusing, raping and attempting to rape
numerous women and female children; wounding, killing and attempting to kill, without cause or trial, unarmed noncombatant civilians;
pilfering, stealing and looting personal property of civilians confined
therein, including watches, money, clothing, food, medical supplies,
jewelry, and other personal belongings; installing, maintaining and operating, in and on the premises of the Church and Convent, military
weapons and other military objectives, despite the exclusively religious
purpose and nonmilitary use of those buildings; and deliberately and
wantonly, without military necessity, devastating, burning and destroying the Convent and damaging the Church, together with the furniture,
fixtures, religious library and other properties therein.

Over and over, the bill of particulars recited: "unarmed noncombatant civilians," "brutally mistreating, wounding and killing," "without cause or trial,"
"deliberately and wantonly burning and destroying." Forty-seven of the sixty-
four allegations concerned Manila and the surrounding area in southern Luzon; the rest were in Cebu, Palawan, and other outlying islands.

The specifications in the bill of particulars listed crimes, locales, and victims
so extensive that proof of all of them would have taken many months, perhaps
years. Indeed, Kerr had boasted to American reporters that his evidence made
"such a fat file that it would take the reviewing authorities a year to read it."
Yet Yamashita's name appeared nowhere except in the introductory paragraph
asserting that the atrocities were committed by troops "under the command of
the Accused." There was no assertion that Yamashita had committed any of the
crimes, had ordered any of the crimes, or had acquiesced in any of the crimes;
indeed, there was no allegation that he knew about any of the crimes.

With the bill of particulars in hand, the accused was ready to enter his plea.
Yamashita stood and spoke in a strong, clear voice. The translator repeated: "My
plea is not guilty."

It was time to set a date for trial. Kerr stood. "Sir, the prosecution defers to
the desires of defense counsel in that particular. We are agreeable to the defense
having a reasonable time in which to prepare their case."

Clarke responded: "Sir, we believe that two weeks will be sufficient time."

Kerr was aghast. "How long?"

"Two weeks."

Kerr turned to the commission. "I would like to request three weeks. I am
not sure that we can be ready in two weeks. Frankly, I am surprised that the
defense believes they can properly prepare a defense in this case in two weeks."

Very well, said Reynolds. Three weeks it is.

The trial would begin on October 29, at eight o'clock in the morning, in the High Commissioner's Residence overlooking Manila Bay.

The lawyers and the generals gathered up their papers, and the audience slowly filtered out, back to the streets of Manila.

"It was a wonderful show," noted Lieutenant Mountz. "And if it can be permanently established as our main principle that a commanding officer is personally and criminally responsible for the conduct of his troops, then it has been well worth while and a big step taken toward insuring peace in the future."

Over the next three weeks, the defense attorneys—now effectively reduced to Clarke, Hendrix, Reel, and Sandberg—met daily with Yamashita, going over the long list of atrocities in the bill of particulars, probing what he knew, what he had and had not done over the course of his Philippine campaign and particularly over the course of the battle in Manila, the focus of the accusations. Yamashita was unequivocal: "If those crimes were committed, I positively and categorically confirm that they were against my wishes and in direct contravention to all my expressed orders, and, further, if they were committed, they occurred at a place and a time of which I had no knowledge whatsoever."

If they were committed? His lawyers were at first incredulous. "We cut him short," Reel later wrote. "There was no doubt about it. The atrocities could certainly be proved. What we were concerned about was the question of any connection that the general might have had with them. What we wanted to know, first, was how in the world so many brutalities could be committed and he not know about them?"

As they talked, they came to understand, and to accept, his explanation. And they realized that Yamashita would have to testify and be his own best advocate. Clarke and Reel and the lawyers could argue the law, that no one had ever in the history of the United States, or any military as far as could be determined, been charged or convicted of crimes based exclusively on a failure to control his troops. For those purposes, it would have been sufficient for Yamashita to acknowledge that yes, he heard that terrible crimes were taking place far away from his command post, and that, however much he disapproved, he was powerless to stop them. But Yamashita was setting himself a higher bar by insisting he did not even know about them.

As Reel explained it, Yamashita's account of his ten months in the Philippines "was the story of a man with a mission to perform, a man who was beset by overwhelming difficulties and harassed by overpowering forces, a man who was entirely unable to carry out the ordinary functions of a 'desk' commander in a rear echelon, whose ability to communicate with his troops was destroyed, and who was finally isolated and crushed by the superior power of his opponents."

The defense of the Philippines had been doomed well before he was given command in October 1944, Yamashita explained. Neither his predecessor nor his superior commander, Marshal Terauchi, nor the Imperial General Staff in Tokyo had a coherent plan for the defense of the islands. The soldiers were poorly trained and dispirited. Critical supplies, especially rice and gasoline, were at dangerously low levels. The command was splintered, with Yamashita controlling none of the navy or air force, with whom there was very little communication and less coordination. Americans ruled the skies and, after the disastrous Battle of Leyte Gulf soon after his arrival, the seas as well. Transport of troops and supplies from Japan was haphazard, with more lost to American submarines, planes, and battleships than ever made it to the Philippines. He had virtually no staff, no knowledge of the tactical situation, not even his own transportation. He had been ordered, over his objection, to send precious troops and material to Leyte—a decision that he knew would cripple his defense of Luzon.

The order to defend Leyte in a hopeless effort to turn back the Americans seemed to rankle him most. "I was naturally unprepared for the sudden change in our overall defense plans and experienced tremendous difficulty in the successful execution of this new order," he told his lawyers.

> The problem of assembling the widely dispersed units originally intended for the defense of Luzon, the drawing up and execution of new disposition of troops, the reconcentration and rearrangement of war-material depots, the mobilization of transport facilities, the consultation and arrangement with the navy and the air force command for convoy and aerial protection, and other complex problems connected with having to organize and transfer a large army composed of units under diversified command to a new battlefield were multifarious and difficult to solve, and, in spite of my anxiety for quick action, progress was slow and far from meeting requirements. The transports which were massed through admirable efforts on the part of my subordinates were, with a few exceptions, practically all sunk or damaged by the American air force en route, and it was my misfortune to receive discouraging reports of these disasters day after day. However, my orders were such that I was obliged to draw up new shipping plans to meet the critical situation in Leyte. I was so occupied with these difficult problems that I had hardly time to turn my attention to other business.
>
> In view of the Leyte operations I realized that a decisive battle was impossible. Therefore, I decided on a delaying action to divert American forces in Luzon so as to keep them from attacking Japan as long as possible. In my experience with the Leyte operations I realized that the American air forces and navy were exceedingly superior to ours and also the fire power of the ground forces was superior and very mobile. Therefore I knew that I could

not conduct warfare on flat land. So I decided to employ a delaying action in the mountains.

And what about Manila, then?

"I decided to put Manila outside the battle area. I ordered my troops out of Manila. I decided to abandon it without a battle."

Why?

"First, the population of Manila is approximately one million; therefore, it is impossible to feed them. The second reason is that the buildings are very inflammable. The third reason is that because it is flat land it requires tremendous strength to defend it."

Pausing now and then to confer with Muto and Utsunomiya about details, Yamashita continued the explanation to his defense counsel. "The Japanese army had moved out. There were only fifteen or sixteen hundred army troops left in the city, and their essential mission was to guard those military supplies that had not yet been removed. But there were approximately twenty thousand Japanese naval troops who did not move out, and they were the ones who fought the Americans." It was Admiral Iwabuchi who was in command of the troops in Manila, the ones who committed the atrocities in February 1945, the ones who were killed to a man as the Americans seized the city. Communications between Yamashita's headquarters in the hills of Baguio and the elements in Manila had been cut off soon after the Sixth Army under General Krueger landed at Lingayen. In fact, said Yamashita, although the Americans entered the outskirts of Manila on February 4, Yamashita did not learn until February 13 that Japanese forces were still there. He ordered General Yokoyama at the Shimbu Group to get the remaining Japanese troops out of Manila, but at that point there was no way Yokoyama could penetrate American lines to do anything in the city.

"Thus we saw revealed," Reel wrote,

> the picture of Yamashita's insurmountable difficulties upon his arrival in the island, the blueprint of a situation that began with such a welter of impossible tasks that there simply was no time for training procedures or even inspection trips and that ended with the general's virtual isolation from the diverse elements of a scattered command. The state of his communications was such that he could not know of atrocities which we said Japanese troops had committed in Manila and Batangas and in other islands of the archipelago.

It was a credible explanation, and, as lawyers sometimes wryly note, it had the additional advantage of being true. "There were no secrets, no discrepancies, no loopholes," Reel said. "For over two months we were to discuss this narrative and explore into hundreds of ramifications and details. Never once would we find that these men had lied, concealed, or invented. Yamashita and his staff officers were telling the truth." Sandberg recalled years later that, before meeting Yamashita, his lawyers "didn't, in the slightest, think there was any possibility that he was innocent because we had heard rumors of the atrocities. It didn't take long after we began preparing the case—you can't argue with the facts—before we became aware of the fact that we were defending an innocent man."

About two weeks before trial, two American army psychiatrists asked if they could question Yamashita. Yamashita was willing, and Clarke gave his permission. The psychiatrists' questions were pointless and inept—Had he wet the bed as a child? Was his marriage a happy one? What did Yamashita think of the sneak attack on Pearl Harbor?—but Yamashita, speaking through the ever-present Hamamoto, answered them patiently, to the surprise of the doctors, who had evidently been expecting a snarling beast. "The general appears more as a benign, aging Japanese officer than the formidable 'Tiger of Malaya,'" they reported. "He was, throughout the interview, alert, interested, courteous, and cooperative."

The emergence of the Tiger as an honest, candid, and sincere military leader who had a coherent and credible account of his inability to prevent the atrocities of Japanese troops might have impressed the psychiatrists and motivated his lawyers, but it was not in MacArthur's script. On October 29, the prosecution would begin putting on its case before the cameras in the High Commissioner's Residence, and the bill of particulars provided the gruesome story line of what that case would be. There was no role for a benign Japanese officer.

At that point, Clarke could have approached Kerr with a simple proposition. "Look," he could have said, "We will stipulate that every one of the sixty-four episodes in the bill of particulars did in fact take place. We acknowledge that Japanese troops did commit those crimes. There is no need to bring these poor people before the commission and the press and the cameras to relive the horrors of the atrocities that were inflicted on them, how they saw their children and husbands and mothers murdered, how their homes and their city and their lives were destroyed at the hands of brutes. Let us confine this trial to what truly matters: the factual question of what, if anything, Yamashita ordered, or approved, or permitted, or knew about; and the legal question of whether, in light of that evidence, what he did or did not do was a violation of the laws of war."

Had he made such a proposal, Kerr certainly would have rejected it. The rape of Manila was not going to be written out of the trial with a simple acknowledgment that it had indeed occurred. Sometimes a trial is more than the process of reaching a verdict. Sometimes it is theater and spectacle, catharsis and redemption. The people of the Philippines, and most certainly MacArthur, wanted a full and public exposition of these crimes in all their grim and tragic details. The victims were demanding their day in court, and Yamashita, that swaggering, arrogant leader of this army of savages, was going to sit there and listen to every word of it. And five American generals, who would decide whether Yamashita would live or die, would listen to every word of it too.

8

The Prosecution
The Hearsay Problem

After the October 8 arraignment, the defense team made the most of the three weeks allotted for preparation for trial. They met daily with their client in prison, listening to his account of his eleven months commanding the Fourteenth Area Army, probing him with questions: Why had he done this? Why had he not done that? What did he know of this? Who was in charge of that?

Then, on Friday, October 26, 1945, late in the afternoon, they had an unpleasant surprise. Major Kerr delivered a "supplemental bill of particulars," as he had suggested at the arraignment that he might do. This "supplemental" bill listed fifty-nine new episodes of crime in the Philippines, now added to the sixty-four specified in the original bill. With the trial scheduled to begin the following Monday morning, the defense lawyers were outraged at this last-minute maneuver.

When the commission convened for trial on Monday the twenty-ninth—the streets again thronged with spectators, the lights and cameras and reporters again poised to record the events—Captain Reel stood to object to the new listing of crimes, arguing that it was "unconscionable in a case of this type to practically double in the last minute the list of offenses charged." Moreover, he claimed, the new particulars presented "an entirely different theory of the prosecution of this case" because the original bill alleged that Japanese soldiers "committed" the acts that followed but these new charges claimed that the soldiers "were permitted to commit" the newly named crimes. But nowhere in the bill, argued Reel, were there any details of this alleged permission. "The new theory, the different theory is not that acts were 'committed' by members of the command, but that somebody—we do not know who and somebody presumably connected with the accused or the accused himself—permitted these acts."

Kerr was unruffled. He reminded the commission that it had given him permission three weeks earlier to file a supplemental bill of particulars, and "as to the difference in the wording of the prefatory portion," he said, "that really has no significance one way or the other. Whether the bill of particulars says 'permitted' or that these acts were 'committed' by members of the command of the accused is immaterial."

Reel, in rebuttal, persisted. "When my brother* says there is absolutely no difference between somebody 'committing' an act and that act being 'permitted' by superior authority, it seems to me that he is going beyond the bound of reason. The very essence of this case," said Reel, "is whether or not an offense against the laws of war is stated (1) simply by saying that somebody did an act who was under the command of a certain general, or (2)—and now we take another step—whether somebody permitted those acts. Then we can go further steps and say (3) whether somebody authorized those acts or (4) whether somebody ordered them. But those are fundamental distinctions here."

It was an instructive point, foretelling what the defense intended to develop over the course of the trial. An experienced judge would have handled the matter easily. "Mr. Prosecutor," he would have said, "since you say there is no significance to the addition of 'permitted' in the supplemental bill, please redraft that bill to track the language of the original one, and we will move on." But Reynolds simply announced that the defense objection was "not sustained."

Reel had more. Since the supplemental bill was now filed, he requested "particulars as to each case as to who granted the alleged permission to commit the alleged offenses, to whom such permission was granted, the form of expression of the permission, and the times, places and dates of the permission."

Kerr waved off the request. "It was the accused who permitted these acts to be committed," he told the commission. "The charge so states." He went on to argue that what the defense really wanted was a look at the prosecution's evidence: what Yamashita had said or done to constitute "permission." In this, he was exactly right. But "an accused in a criminal proceeding," he said, switching back to the criminal-proceeding model, "is not entitled to a revelation of the details of evidence upon which the prosecution bases its case." Said Kerr, "the accused has no rights under the Constitution of the United States. He is an enemy alien. The Constitution does not apply to him."

Reel challenged him. "The Fifth Amendment of the Constitution of the United States says 'any person,' not 'any citizen.'" This was a reference to the Due Process Clause—"No person shall be . . . deprived of life, liberty, or property, without due process of law." But just what the matter of constitutional rights had to do with the bill of particulars was becoming obscure, and if the commission was following this discussion, it gave no indication. Reynolds denied the request.

---

* Meaning, "my brother at the bar," a genteel reference to the lawyer for the opposing party, once in common use in Boston courtrooms. It is heard less often today, perhaps because one's adversary is as likely to be a sister.

Reel had one more request: a further two-week extension of the trial so the defense could prepare its case on the new allegations. Reel reminded the court that at the October 8 arraignment the defense had asked for two weeks and Kerr had said he was surprised they thought that would be enough. "I do not think they can now object to two weeks," Reel said, somewhat slyly, "to prepare a defense for a similar number of specifications based on new facts, new places, new names and a new theory of the case."

Reel pointed to MacArthur's own rules and regulations for such trials, entitling the accused to a statement of the charges and specifications "in advance of trial." "This phrase obviously means sufficiently in advance of trial to allow the defense to prepare itself," Reel argued. Furthermore, "this commission should not deviate from a fundamental American concept of fairness, decency and justice, which dictate that an accused has a right to defend himself. And that means a right to have time in which to prepare himself."

Kerr did not object to the request. "Defense counsel is much better prepared to judge the difficulties of preparing the defense than am I."

Reynolds recessed the proceedings, and the five generals stepped through the French doors, making their way around the back of the building to their private office near the ballroom. They returned to announce that the request for a continuance was "not sustained." "However," said Reynolds, "at the end of the presentation by the prosecution of evidence concerning the [original] bill of particulars dated 1 October 1945, as presented during the arraignment, the commission will consider such a motion."

It was a curious ruling, because it assumed that the prosecution was going to present all of its evidence on the original sixty-four crimes before it presented any of its case on the fifty-nine new ones. But the prosecution had given no indication that it would proceed in that order, and the commission had said nothing requiring it to do so.

Here again, an experienced judge would have had a different response. "Major Kerr," he would have said, "you have alleged the brutalization and killing of thousands of victims by Japanese troops, which you have aggregated into sixty-four more or less specific allegations. What does it add to this case to raise the number of crimes to 123—except, of course, to extend this trial by many weeks or months?"

It is hard to imagine a satisfactory answer, or what the prosecution hoped to prove by the new allegations that it could not prove with the original ones, other than to demonstrate in lengthy detail what everyone in the room—indeed, everyone in the Philippines—already knew: that extensive and horrific crimes had been committed by Japanese soldiers on civilians and prisoners of war. There was not much difference in the nature of the crimes laid out in the two bills. Some of the allegations even overlapped. Did the prosecution really fear that they might go 0 for 64 on the crimes originally alleged, but that twice as many might bring a different outcome? Did they believe that the commission might acquit on the first sixty-four massacres, but not the new fifty-nine?

The commission's rejection of two more weeks of preparation was easier to understand. Time was passing. MacArthur wanted to get on with the trial and the guilty verdict, as the five generals well knew. Two more weeks of delay, no matter how busy the defense might be, would not go down well with MacArthur.

His continuance denied, Colonel Clarke rose to argue, as he had at the arraignment three weeks earlier, that the charge should be dismissed because it did not validly allege any crime on the part of General Yamashita. His argument at the arraignment had been somewhat extemporaneous, the defense counsel not yet having seen a bill of particulars. Since then, the defense lawyers had sharpened and polished the argument. Despite the commission's earlier denial of the motion, Reynolds let Clarke argue it again.

"The bill of particulars," Clarke began,

> details sixty four instances in which members of the accused's command are alleged to have committed war crimes. In no instance is it alleged that the accused committed or aided in the commission of a crime or crimes. In no instance is it alleged that the accused issued an order, expressly or impliedly, for the commission of the crime or crimes. Nor is it alleged that the accused authorized the crimes prior to their commission or condoned them thereafter. The bill of particulars sets forth no instance of neglect of duty by the accused. Nor does it set forth any acts of commission or omission by the accused as amounting to a "permitting" of the crimes in question.

Clarke was energized. "The accused is not charged with having done something or having failed to do something, but solely with having been something. For the gravamen of the charge [is] that the accused was the commander of the Japanese forces, and, by virtue of that fact alone is guilty of every crime committed by every soldier assigned to his command."

"American jurisprudence recognizes no such principle so far as its own military personnel is concerned," Clarke continued.

> The Articles of War denounce and punish improper conduct by military personnel, but they do not hold a commanding officer responsible for the crimes committed by his subordinates. Neither the laws of war nor the conscience of the world upon which they are founded will countenance the support of any such charge. It is the basic premise of all civilized criminal justice that it punishes not according to status but according to fault, and that one man is not held to answer for the crime of another.

Clarke was correct, as far as he went: the charge had no precedent in the law. But his analysis gave the prosecution an opportunity to argue a powerful point: the law can change, and it does and should change to meet changing circumstances. What was at the heart of this case was not the formal and unchanging words of a treaty but the centuries-long evolution of customary international law. The most devastating war in history had barely come to an end; atrocities against civilians, not only in the Pacific but throughout Nazi-occupied Europe, had reached unprecedented levels, in numbers as well as in horror. Perhaps it was time for the common law of war to advance, to begin to elucidate the accountability of commanders for the crimes of their troops: what must they know or fail to know, do or fail to do, to create the circumstances under which the law should hold them answerable? Perhaps this was the trial to start the law down that path.

But Kerr did not go there. As he had three weeks earlier, he declined to engage in any discussion at all of whether the charge validly stated a violation of law. The commission, said Kerr, "is under direct orders" to conduct a trial on the charge drawn up by MacArthur's headquarters. "The contentions of defense counsel might more appropriately be addressed to the Commanding General, Army Forces, Pacific"—that would be MacArthur—and "not to this commission." In short, the charge was a given; its validity was none of the commission's concern.

As he was to do throughout the trial, Kerr had deftly targeted his argument to the generals. Kerr surely knew that, in one sense, Clarke was right. There had never been a case charging that a commander violated the law of war by failing to control his troops or failing to prevent war crimes. But Kerr was right, too: these generals had been ordered by their commander—all five stars of him, if they needed any reminder of that—to hold a trial on the charge he had given them. If that charge was unprecedented, or unauthorized by law, or unconstitutional, or faulty in any other respect, then the defense's recourse was to save their arguments until the trial was over and the verdict was announced and the case went up the chain of command for review by MacArthur's lawyers and by the general himself.

A careful listener to the argument might have noticed another point: nowhere in his reply had Kerr said, in effect, "Members of the commission, this point will soon become moot: when all our evidence is in, you will have adequate proof that General Yamashita did in fact order, authorize, condone and permit these crimes of his soldiers." It was a telling omission, and the defense lawyers must surely have noticed it.

Reynolds gave the defense the courtesy of taking a recess to consider the motion to dismiss the case. But when the commission members returned, Reynolds gave the only answer he could: "The motion is not sustained." After some further skirmishing on legal points, Reynolds grew impatient. "In view of the direction of the Commander in Chief, Army Forces, Pacific, to proceed with this trial," he announced, "the prosecution will make its opening statement." The trial was, at last, under way.

How long would it take? Reynolds was clearly intent on its taking as little time as possible. He had met with Kerr—but not, apparently, with defense counsel—five days earlier to discuss the point. Assistant prosecutor Mountz described the outcome.

> About 4:30 [that day, October 23] the blow fell. Kerr came back from a conference with Gen. Reynolds and the General stated we had to introduce all our evidence in *10* days [emphasis in the original]. In the first place who ever heard of such a thing, and in the second place, the most important war criminal in the Pacific and expect [sic] to put in the evidence of over 100 separate atrocities which took place in all parts of the Philippines in that time. I told Kerr I was ready to pack up and go home—let alone try to get all the documents copied and translated in that time.

"The more I see and hear generals," he wrote later, "I am thankful that I am nothing but a lieutenant." Reynolds later relented on his unrealistic deadline, but except for Sundays, one Saturday, and the afternoon of Thanksgiving Day, there were to be no days off for the next five weeks.

Kerr began his opening argument, wasting little time in telling the commission what they were about to see.

> We make no effort to present to the commission in this proceeding all, or even a substantial part, of the evidence on the general subject of atrocities in the Philippine Islands, nor do we select the instances on the basis that they are the most horrible, the most nauseatingly horrible that might be presented to the commission. If we bring before the commission a witness in a stretcher, permanently mutilated, physically ruined for life, it is not because we are endeavoring to impress the commission through the use of shocking evidence; it is simply because that witness on the stretcher has a story of factual information which the commission should hear. If the commission finds the evidence unpleasant, as I am sure it will in many instances, it is simply because those are the facts. That is the type of case we are trying, gentlemen; it is not a pleasant proceeding.

"We will show," Kerr went on,

> that various elements, individuals, units, organizations [and] officers, being a part of those forces under the command of the accused, did commit a wide

pattern of widespread, notorious, repeated, constant atrocities of the most violent character. They were so notorious and so flagrant and so enormous, both as to the scope of their operation and as to the inhumanity, the bestiality involved, that they must have been known to the accused if he were making any effort whatever to meet the responsibilities of his command or his position; and that if he did not know of those acts—notorious, widespread, repeated, constant, as they were—it was simply because he took affirmative action not to know. That is our case.

In revealing the theory of the prosecution's case, Kerr had also telegraphed its vulnerability: the atrocities were so numerous and widespread that Yamashita must have known of them, and thus the commission could overlook the absence of any evidence that he actually did know of them. Yet Kerr had acknowledged at least the possibility that Yamashita did not know of them, despite their extent and duration. That possibility required Kerr to urge on the commissioners a new theory of command responsibility—that if Yamashita did not know, he must have taken "affirmative action not to know," which the prosecution evidently meant to be the equivalent of actual knowledge. But the charge had not alleged anything about knowledge at all, whether actual (he did know, because under the circumstances he must have known) or constructive (if he did not know, he will be treated as having known anyway, because he took affirmative steps not to know). The charge alleged only that Yamashita had failed in his "duty as commander to control the operations of the members of his command, permitting them" to commit atrocities. Kerr's theory did not address that aspect at all, nor did it address the question of whether Yamashita, whatever he knew, was in any position to prevent or halt the atrocities.

But Kerr's explanation did suggest why he had added fifty-nine new counts: the more widespread and numerous he could prove the crimes to be, the more easily the commission could conclude that indeed Yamashita must have known about them. Kerr left untouched the question of how the commission was to cross the gap between what if anything Yamashita knew and what he permitted.

Kerr moved on to the rules by which the commission was to proceed. The commission, he reminded its members, was not bound by technical rules of evidence appropriate in a court of law, nor was it bound by the Articles of War—the laws passed by Congress to govern procedures in courts-martial. "This commission is not a judicial body; it is an executive tribunal" created to advise MacArthur "as to the punishment, in the event that the commission finds the charge to be sustained. It is an executive body, not a judicial body."

The five generals needed no reminder that they were uniformed officers assigned to get a job done and not black-robed judges learned in the law, but Kerr was delivering the message anyway. "We are cognizant of the commission's desire that this proceeding be expedited as much as possible. That, likewise, is our desire. Military justice, we realize, is expeditious; it brooks of no unreasonable delays. It does not tolerate the tortuous technicalities which characterize criminal procedure in the law courts of the States."

"We must support the charge with adequate, clear, convincing proof," he acknowledged in his conclusion. "We seek to establish as quickly as possible, with as many uses of labor or time-saving procedures as possible, the establishment of a clear and a convincing and a complete case."

Kerr's first step was to submit into evidence several translations of captured Japanese documents showing that Yamashita was indeed the Commanding General of the Fourteenth Area Army in the Philippines. The defense objected because the Japanese documents themselves had not been made available to them. Reynolds allowed the translations in, but a few hours later a more serious dispute arose, one that was to have serious consequences for the evidence and for the trial itself.

In the eight weeks since Yamashita's surrender, investigators from MacArthur's war crimes unit, working with the prosecutors but not with defense counsel, had taken statements from a great many Japanese soldiers, including those on Yamashita's staff. Among them was Naokata Utsunomiya, the assistant chief of staff whom Reynolds was allowing to sit with Yamashita during the trial as one of his chosen "counsel." Kerr now submitted the transcript of an interview of Utsunomiya, taken at the Bilibid Prison the week before the arraignment. In the interview, Utsunomiya had said that when Yamashita had arrived in the Philippines in October 1944, the navy troops on the island were not under his command but that on January 6, 1945, Yamashita was given "tactical command" over navy units fighting on land. Kerr wanted to establish early on that, at the time of the greatest atrocities in Manila in February 1945, many of them involving naval troops, Yamashita was indeed the commander of those troops.

The defense was not going to dispute the point—Yamashita himself would later testify that indeed he did assume tactical command over the navy in January 1945—but they wanted to take a stand opposing the use of out-of-court statements as evidence against their client. It was the plainest form of hearsay.

Their effort was doomed before it began, and they knew it. The regulations governing the trial—issued by MacArthur, drafted by his staff lawyers—placed no restriction on what testimony, documents, photographs, or other evidence the commission could consider. The regulations directed that the commission "shall admit such evidence as in its opinion would be of assistance in proving or disproving the charge, or such as in the commission's opinion would have probative value in the mind of a reasonable man."

The regulations went on to specify in sweeping terms that the commission could accept—without any need to establish its authenticity—"any document which appears to the commission to have been signed or issued officially by any officer, department, agency, or member of the armed forces of any government"; "any report . . . which appears to the commission to have been signed or issued by . . . An investigator or intelligence officer . . . or by any other person whom the commission finds to have been acting in the course of his duty when making the report"; and any "affidavits, depositions or other statements taken by an officer detailed for that purpose." And if there was a piece of paper that was not an official-looking document, or a report from an investigator, or a statement taken by an officer, then that could come in, too, because the regulations authorized the commission to consider "any diary, letter or other document appearing to the commission to contain information relating to the charge." And if the writing itself was not available, no matter: the commission could accept any "secondary evidence" of the contents of any letter or diary or other paper, "if the commission believes that the original is not available or cannot be produced without undue delay." Under this last catchall, a witness could testify, "I saw a document that said . . . " without having to produce the document itself, and the commission could proceed as if the document itself were before it and said what the witness said it said.

In short, MacArthur had made it quite clear that no rules of evidence whatever were to apply. Anything the commission wanted to consider—anything it thought might "be of assistance" or have "probative value" or "information relating to the charge"—it could consider.

This may strike some as a welcome release from the constraints of rules of evidence—what Kerr had called "the tortuous technicalities" of the criminal law—but the regulations allowed the introduction of hearsay in terms so limitless that no judge in an American courtroom would entertain them for a minute. Rules of evidence may appear technical to a layman, and many of them certainly are, but they are designed, however imperfectly, to ensure that only reliable evidence is admitted, to allow the accused to test that reliability by cross-examining the witness who presents it, and to allow the judge and jury to see and hear the witness testify, in order to judge his credibility. In the hands of military officers unfamiliar with the law, the absence of rules was to become a free-for-all, a release only from concerns of reliability, accuracy, and the value of confrontation.

Hearsay, especially, is suspect, and for good reason. Hearsay is a statement made outside of court that is related or repeated in the trial for the purpose of proving the truth of the statement. In a murder trial, a prosecution witness who took the stand and testified, "My friend Joe told me that the defendant shot the victim," would be giving hearsay. Joe, who made the statement, is not in court; the witness is only repeating what Joe told him.

Hearsay has traditionally been excluded from trials for several reasons. First, the out-of-court statement is almost never given under oath, and for those who believe, as American law does, that witnesses are more likely to tell the truth under oath, its absence can cast doubt on the veracity of the statement. Second, regardless of an oath, the accuracy and reliability of the statement is suspect. What one person tells another can be misheard, misunderstood, or misremembered on its way to the courtroom. Third, American law proceeds on the belief that judges and juries are better able to determine the truth of a statement if they see and hear the person who is making it. With hearsay, the real witness— the one who made the statement in the first place—is not present. The jury has no way of judging whether he seems sincere, honest, and credible and has a decent memory of events, or whether he is a furtive and suspicious character, or a biased one, or one whose memory seems vague or faulty.

Finally and perhaps most importantly, allowing a witness to testify as to what someone else told him deprives the defendant of the right to examine the true witness against him. The defendant's lawyer cannot ask the real witness— the absent one—the relevant questions: Did he actually see the shooting, or is he just repeating what he heard from someone else? How does he know the shooter is the defendant? Did he know the defendant beforehand and recognize him? Where was he when he saw the shooting? How far away? How was the light? What was the victim doing when the shot was fired (perhaps aiming a gun at the defendant)? Did the shooter say anything? Didn't you tell the police a contrary story? The witness on the stand has no firsthand answers to these important questions; he is only repeating what he heard, or what he thinks he remembers he heard.

These threats to reliability are no different in a military trial than in a civilian one. Two hundred years ago, one of the earliest American treatises on military law treated it as "a settled rule of law" that "no evidence can be received against a prisoner but in his presence; therefore, it is agreed that what a stranger has been heard to say, is in strictness no manner of evidence, either for or against the prisoner." A 1945 army manual, published for the use of nonlawyers detailed to courts-martial, was equally clear on the point: "The 'hearsay' rule means simply that a fact cannot be proved by having a witness testify as to statements made by someone else or by introducing in evidence a book, document, report or other paper in which statements are made. . . . Hearsay is literally no evidence at all. It cannot be considered by the court, and if the only evidence to support a finding is hearsay, the finding cannot be upheld."

This warning—which MacArthur's rules and regulations had simply ignored—drew on a long legal history. By 1789, when the Constitution was drafted, the requirement of confrontation was solidly established in criminal cases in England, and in writing the Bill of Rights, Congress included in the

Sixth Amendment the guarantee that "in all criminal prosecutions, the accused shall enjoy the right . . . to be confronted with the witnesses against him."

Confrontation thus is not a "technicality"; the Supreme Court has repeatedly reversed convictions where this "bedrock procedural guarantee" has been denied to the defendant. "The principal evil at which the Confrontation Clause was directed," said the Supreme Court in 2004, was the "use of *ex parte* examinations as evidence against the accused"—statements taken in the absence of the defendant and put into evidence against him in the absence of the declarant. "Our cases have thus remained faithful to the Framers' understanding: Testimonial statements of witnesses absent from trial have been admitted only where the declarant is unavailable, and only where the defendant has had a prior opportunity to cross-examine."

And the problem is not in any way cured by allowing judges—even real judges—to admit out-of-court testimony that they conclude is "reliable" or, in the words of MacArthur's regulations, has "probative value in the mind of a reasonable man." "Admitting statements deemed reliable by a judge," said Justice Antonin Scalia, writing for the Supreme Court in the 2004 case, "is fundamentally at odds with the right of confrontation." The Confrontation Clause "commands . . . that reliability be assessed in a particular manner: by testing in the crucible of cross-examination." Allowing a judge to substitute his or her own view of reliability for the crucible of cross-examination "replaces the constitutionally prescribed method of assessing reliability with a wholly foreign one." Nor can the signature or seal of a government official or an investigator on a document be an acceptable substitute. "Dispensing with confrontation because testimony is obviously reliable," said the Supreme Court, "is akin to dispensing with jury trial because a defendant is obviously guilty."

To say, as Kerr had, that an enemy alien soldier on trial in the Philippines in 1945 had no "constitutional rights" thus misses the point. The right to question the prosecution witnesses is not solely a constitutional protection like the ban on cruel and unusual punishment, nor a civil liberty like free speech, nor a mere aspiration. It is the most effective means of ensuring the reliability of evidence and thus the integrity of the trial and its verdict. It serves a profound responsibility of the government itself: to see that no defendant is wrongfully convicted.

Hearsay gains no particular reliability by being written into a document. A police report of a murder might state that the victim had been shot eight times, but handing up the report to the judge and jury to prove that fact is nothing more than repeating the words of the absent policeman. If he were present in court, he could be asked whether he saw the victim's body and counted the bullet wounds or whether he is guessing, or repeating what someone else said.

The ban on hearsay is loosened by well-defined exceptions. For example, a service record showing that a soldier was posted to a particular place on a particular date could be admitted, on the presumption that such official records are accurate. A newspaper report might be accepted to show what the temperature was on a given day, on the presumption that newspapers traditionally come by that information reliably and so there is little chance of error. But that applies only to routine entries made without regard to the controversy in court. There is no blanket exception for "official records" as such. MacArthur created such an exception and then extended it to virtually every piece of paper the prosecution had, whatever its content, however it was created, wherever it was found.

Depositions are a special case. A deposition is an interrogation before trial, in which the testimony of a prospective witness is taken, under oath and in the presence of the defendant's lawyer, who may cross-examine the deponent-witness. If, at trial, the deponent is not available to testify, because of death or illness or absence, the deposition is almost always allowed into evidence, because the accused has already had the opportunity to confront and cross-examine a witness testifying under oath against him. The judge and jury read the transcript of the deposition, or the statement signed by the deponent, as if it had been given in the courtroom. True, they do not see and hear the deponent actually testify, but that shortcoming, in the law's eyes, is preferable to losing the testimony of an absent witness altogether.*

If hearsay is suspect, double hearsay is worse. "Joe told me that Dick had told him that the defendant shot the victim" introduces the weaknesses not only in Joe's reliability but also in Dick's and then compounds the risk that statements passed along from one person to another might become corrupted. And triple hearsay? "Joe told me that he had heard from Dick that Dick's uncle knew that the defendant shot the victim." Enough said.

So, to say, as MacArthur's regulation did, that the commission could receive evidence that "in its opinion would be of assistance in proving or disproving the charge, or . . . have probative value in the mind of a reasonable man" jettisons the hearsay rule but does not replace it with any reliable standard. In fact, "assistance in proving or disproving the charge" and "probative value" are not, as the order implies, alternative standards but the same thing. They both mean any evidence the commission thinks is relevant.

But to say that an out-of-court statement appears *relevant* says nothing about whether it is *reliable*. "Joe told me that the defendant shot the victim" might seem quite relevant to the ultimate question of guilt. But the commission is in

---

* Lawyers have argued for years as to whether a deposition is even hearsay at all, or whether it is an exception to the rule against hearsay. But there is no disagreement that, however characterized, its reliability is as close as one can get to actual testimony in the courtroom.

no position to accurately gauge its reliability. To be sure, MacArthur's regulations did not require the commission to accept anything and everything that was offered—it could reject any evidence, including hearsay, that would not in its view be helpful or probative. So it could have done just what real judges, including courts-martial judges, do: follow the "bedrock principle" that hearsay is presumptively unreliable, unhelpful, and unprobative and exclude it.

Ruling on hearsay objections is often a challenge for real judges, let alone for those who have not studied law or at least had some concentrated training in the hearsay rule and why it exists and what its dangers and exceptions are. There was no chance the commission was going to wade into those waters. Over the five weeks of trial, it would repeatedly accept proffered evidence—almost all of it from the prosecution—"for whatever probative value it might have," without ever then or later disclosing what probative value that might be. It was surely easier to let everything in for whatever it may be worth than to come up with a reason for keeping it out. And the appointing order, as all members were abundantly aware, was signed by the Supreme Commander of the Allies in the Pacific, to whom they all were subordinate. His word was, literally, the law.

So when Captain Sandberg for the defense stood up to object to the prosecution's introduction of the Utsunomiya interview, he had to have known that there was little chance the commissioners would agree. But he was holding a trump card, or at least he thought he was.

The Articles of War—the statutes enacted by Congress to define offenses under military law and to set out the procedures for charging and trying those accused of such offenses—had made a very specific rule for the use of depositions. Article 25 provided:

> A duly authenticated deposition taken upon reasonable notice to the opposite party may be read in evidence before any military court or commission *in any case not capital* . . . when it appears to the satisfaction of the court, commission, board, or appointing authority that the witness, by reason of age, sickness, bodily infirmity, imprisonment, or other reasonable cause, is unable to appear and testify in person at the place of trial or hearing: Provided, That testimony by deposition may be adduced for the defense in capital cases. [Emphasis added.]

The inclusion of military commissions in Article 25 was atypical for the Articles of War, which dealt primarily with courts-martial. The rules of commissions were determined not by Congress but by whatever officer was convening them. The Yamashita commission was firmly in this tradition. But Congress had explicitly included commissions within the prohibition of Article 25, and not even MacArthur could overrule an act of Congress. And the meaning of

Article 25 seemed plain to anyone: in a case where the military commission could impose the death penalty, a deposition could not be submitted as evidence by the prosecution. The implication seemed equally clear: if a deposition with all its safeguards of notice, oath, and cross-examination by the defense could not be used against a defendant in a capital case, surely ordinary hearsay, lacking all those safeguards, could not, either.

But MacArthur and his lawyers had anticipated this problem, and they meant to evade it. They went to Major General Myron C. Cramer, Judge Advocate General of the Army—the army's highest-ranking lawyer—and secured an official opinion, titled "Applicability of Articles of War to Trials of War Criminals by Military Commissions," and provided it to the prosecution. For those who believe that lawyers can argue that black is white, Cramer's memorandum is hard to top.

Cramer's six-page typewritten memo started out by noting, correctly, that military commissions have traditionally been used to try enemy belligerents for violations of the laws of war. But they have also been used, said Cramer, to try "our own nationals either in time of war or under martial rule, and [they] have power to try members of our own forces." That was true only to a very limited extent: except for Lincoln's attempts to try Northerners who were Confederate sympathizers, there were precious few instances of commissions trying U.S. nationals, much less members of the U.S. Armed forces, and none since the Civil War and Reconstruction. And the Supreme Court had struck down even Lincoln's commissions as unconstitutional, where civilian courts were open and operating.

Cramer acknowledged that when Congress enacted the most recent version of the Articles of War in 1916, several articles, including Article 25, imposed rules that explicitly applied to military commissions as well as to courts-martial. But, he said, "none of these Articles of War are of any help in attempting to ascertain whether the protections embodied therein were intended to apply to military commissions *trying alleged war criminals*" (emphasis added).

The gentlest thing to be said about this conclusion is that it is beside the point; in legal terms, a non sequitur. The articles set rules for "military courts and commissions" without any distinction based on who the accused might be, alleged war criminal or anyone else. Cramer's conclusion was flatly inconsistent with the most elementary principle of interpreting statutes: that statutes mean just what they say—no more, no less. If a statute refers to military commissions, without qualification, it means military commissions, without qualification. To say, as Cramer did, that Congress gave no clue as to whether "military commissions" included military-commissions-trying-alleged-war-criminals is pure sophistry, approaching (some might say crossing) the line of honesty. What

Cramer had done was to characterize military commissions as primarily vehicles to try U.S. citizens and U.S. soldiers, which they were not, and then to conclude that when specifying commissions without qualification, Congress was silently excluding commissions trying enemy soldiers.

In fact, Cramer's conclusion contradicted the army's own interpretation of the law of war. The manual *Rules of Land Warfare*—issued by Cramer's predecessor in 1940—authorized punishment of "captured individual offenders" for offenses including "ill-treatment of prisoners of war" and "ill-treatment of inhabitants in occupied territory"—the very crimes alleged to have been committed by Yamashita's troops. Such punishment necessarily had to come from commissions, because enemy soldiers were not subject to the U.S. Articles of War and thus were beyond the jurisdiction of courts-martial, and because trials in civilian courts were both unprecedented and impractical. A commission was the only alternative. The army's manual acknowledged as much: "No individual should be punished for an offense against the laws of war unless pursuant to a sentence imposed after trial and conviction by a military court or commission or some other tribunal of competent jurisdiction designated by the belligerent [that is, the United States, in this case]." This was not new: the prior edition of the manual, published in 1934, had said the same thing. So Cramer's distinction between military commissions trying U.S. soldiers and military commissions trying alleged war criminals was not only imaginary but contrary to both the law enacted by Congress and the regulations issued by his own office.*

Beyond that, his conclusion made little sense anyway. Why would one expect Congress to draw distinctions between commissions trying alleged war criminals and commissions trying U.S. nationals or members of the U.S. Armed forces, particularly when the great majority of commissions—and virtually all of those whose legality had been upheld by the courts—*did* try alleged war criminals? In enacting Article 25, Congress was clearly concerned that prosecutors seeking the death penalty before a military court or commission not rely on out-of-court depositions that might be accepted in lesser cases.

Cramer went on to bolster his conclusion by noting that in the committee hearings and debates as Congress considered the revision of the Articles of War, "there is a complete absence of factual statements . . . indicating that it was the intent of Congress that the safeguards of the Articles of War should apply to

---

* Cramer's conclusion also contradicted an official ruling of the army JAG in 1921: "The offenses denounced by A.W. [Articles of War] 75, 76, 77, 78, 81, and 82 [generally, misbehavior before the enemy, aiding the enemy, and spying] are made punishable by death. . . . Therefore, depositions may not be introduced by the prosecution in a case arising under any one of these articles." And Articles 81 and 82, like Article 25 and its no-deposition rule, were explicitly applicable to military commissions.

military commissions trying alleged war criminals." In effect, Cramer used that "absence" of discussion to conjure up a category of commissions that Congress itself did not and then concluded that Congress must have intended to exclude the war criminal category of commissions. The natural reading of Article 25, however, is simply that Congress intended to treat all death penalty cases alike, regardless of whether the defendant was charged with war crimes or some other capital offense.

Cramer noted that under American law, "enemy belligerents are without the protection of constitutional guarantees"—a defensible proposition in 1945. From that he concluded, "It is therefore improbable that Congress intended . . . that alleged war criminals should receive . . . the right to be confronted with the witnesses against him." Here again, Cramer was drawing a distinction that, by its silence, Congress had not. Congress had not remotely dealt with the question of whether the Constitution extended to alleged war criminals. Article 25 was simply a rule of evidence addressing the use of depositions before commissions. Cramer did not acknowledge the obvious: that Congress had barred the use of depositions in capital cases, not out of any constitutional considerations but because the verdicts of courts or commissions of any kind, no matter whom they were trying, should not rest on out-of-court testimony, even formal depositions, when a life was at stake. That this safeguard was also enshrined in the Confrontation Clause of the Sixth Amendment in no way inhibited Congress from inserting it into the rules of procedure for military commissions, nor does it justify any inference that doing so would somehow extend constitutional rights to war criminals.

"For the reasons given," Cramer's memo concludes, "I am of the opinion that Congress did not intend the Articles of War to apply to military commissions trying enemy belligerents or civilians for war crimes."

As legal reasoning goes, it was atrocious, so eccentric in its analysis that one is hard put to avoid the conclusion that MacArthur, perhaps through his staff judge advocate Alva Carpenter, had demanded that Cramer deliver an official opinion allowing the prosecution to use depositions in the Yamashita case, no matter what the Articles of War might say. But five nonlawyer generals were certainly not going to take the official opinion of the Judge Advocate General of the Army as anything but the final word on the matter. Indeed, that seems the whole point of taking the extraordinary step of going to the JAG beforehand for a formal opinion rather than leaving the admissibility of depositions to be argued by Kerr as any other evidentiary question would have been. That would have opened up the possibility that General Reynolds might say, "Mr. Prosecutor, I'm no lawyer, but I can read, and Article 25 says that depositions can only be used against the accused in a military commission in a case 'not capital.' This case is capital. No depositions."

Technically, the Utsunomiya statement that Kerr was seeking to put before the commissioners was not even a deposition, since it had been taken without the participation of Yamashita's lawyers. So the defense objection to the statement had a much larger point: that the inevitable effect of Article 25 was that no hearsay *at all* was to be used in capital cases before military commissions. After all, if Congress prohibited the use of statements that had been taken in the presence of the accused's lawyer and with opportunity for cross-examination and transcribed verbatim or nearly so, it surely could not have intended to allow the "Joe told me" statements that came without any of those safeguards.

The defense arguments were in vain. Reynolds ruled the objection "not sustained" and accepted the Utsunomiya statement into evidence. Unlike the motion to dismiss the charges altogether, which the defense could not have had any realistic hope of winning, this ruling seemed to leave Sandberg truly perplexed: "The defense requests instructions from the commission as to whether or not Articles of War 25 is deemed inapplicable to this entire proceeding."

Reynolds declined to answer. "The commission considered all matters that were presented, and other matters, and refuses to elaborate on the reasons for its conclusions," he said. The message was clear: move on.

Sandberg tried once more, asking the commission to order that the investigating officer who had interrogated Utsunomiya be brought in "for the purpose of examination with respect to this deposition."

Kerr gave no ground. "We are not required in any way to produce the testimony of the officer who questioned the witness. That exhibit is complete in and of itself."

Sandberg protested. "The defense was afforded no opportunity to cross-examine the witness questioned under the deposition," he argued. "The defense was never given the opportunity to cross-examine the officer who conducted the interrogations for the prosecution."

Sandberg's exasperation was plain, if a bit misplaced in this instance. Utsunomiya was sitting at the defense table; the defense team could talk to him all they wanted and could call him as a witness in their case, if they wished. But the fight was not about Utsunomiya; it was about the intention of the prosecution to offer statement after statement taken out of court and presented with no opportunity for the defense to question the declarant or even the investigator who had interrogated him and who may have written the statement himself from his notes, and with no opportunity for the declarant to read it or have it read to him in his own language. The defense team had suffered an important defeat.

9

The Prosecution

The Victims

Its legal offensives rejected, the defense sat down and Major Kerr took over. The preliminaries were done with; it was at last time for witnesses to come forward, and the prosecution started with a flourish when it called its first to the witness chair. "My name is Patrocinio Abad," she said. "My screen name is Corazon Noble."

Corazon Noble needed no introduction to Filipinos. She was the nation's biggest movie star—the "queen of tearjerkers," a Manila newspaper recalled in 2006, five years after her death. Dressed in black, her arm in a white cloth sling, "the lovely 26-year-old brunette," as the *New York Times* recounted, "with tears in her eyes and a catch in her low, slightly accented voice, told simply a story of horror."

On February 10, 1945, she had gone with her infant daughter to the Manila headquarters of the Philippine Red Cross, which was being used as a hospital and refugee center. Four Japanese sailors—she recognized the naval uniform—came by in the morning and gave the children candy, but they returned that evening, barging into the building without warning, and in the space of an hour brought carnage, shooting and stabbing all those they found inside, most of whom were women, children, and nurses. She herself was shot in the elbow and was bayoneted nine times, "here, and here, and here," she testified, pointing to her chest, ribs, abdomen, leg, and back. The killers bayoneted her daughter as she held her in her arms—three times, and she was dead. Twenty-five others were killed in similarly brutal fashion. Captain D. C. Hill, an assistant district attorney from Kansas, showed the commission photographs of her stab wounds. When she concluded her testimony, the commission broke for lunch.

It was a brilliant start for the prosecution. It was opening day. All the news organizations were there, though many of them would leave after a few days. The nation was riveted, the courtroom was filled to capacity, the streets were thronged, the Tiger was in his seat, and the prosecutors had put on a movie star who testified—clearly, and in English—to her nightmare at the hands of the

Japanese. Kerr had promised the commission and the press that he would prove the most horrible atrocities, and if anyone had any doubt about his intent, it did not survive the morning. The actress had "made a very good witness," Lieutenant Mountz wrote that day. "We had murder and pathos and everything."

The afternoon brought more pathos in testimony about the massacre at the Red Cross building. A nurse testified that she told the Japanese "that that was a Red Cross building and that I was a nurse and that nobody was inside except refugees. This Japanese who had a fixed bayonet and gun turned to his officer behind him, and before I knew it he turned back to me and stabbed me with the bayonet, on the left chest above the heart region." Then, she said, "I went to the other side of the building where the Jews were hiding and then I heard a Japanese say something to the Jews. [The Japanese] were saying, 'Americans! Americans!' and all I heard was shots and the women were screaming, and then no more." The Jews, later testimony revealed, were in fact about two dozen refugees from Germany who had fled to the Philippines in 1939, but the fact that the Japanese thought they were killing Americans was doubtless not lost on the commission.

Another nurse was called to the stand; she testified to much the same effect, recounting the slaughter and identifying photographs of her bayonet wounds but adding little to the overall picture. A German Jew, the sole survivor of the group, told the story of the rampaging Japanese that day too, and a man who lived next door to the Red Cross center recalled what he saw from the outside.

The testimony had become cumulative, but at one point the Manila neighbor mentioned that several months before the massacre, a Japanese officer whom he had met had told him "that the Orient should be for the Orientals, that there should be no mixed blood."

Renewing the hearsay battle, Colonel Hendrix for the defense objected that this hearsay should be stricken. Technically, it was not hearsay, for it was not being introduced to prove that the Orient should be for Orientals. It only demonstrated the anonymous Japanese officer's state of mind, whatever the point of that was, and Hendrix's objection should properly have been that the statement was simply irrelevant. But Kerr took Hendrix on: "This is a very important question," he told the commission.

> During the course of this trial we will offer to the commission a considerable quantity of hearsay evidence. I advert once again to the regulations which provide that this commission shall receive such evidence as it believes to have probative value. You gentlemen are certainly in a position to evaluate hearsay, or any other type of evidence that may be of value to you. And I most earnestly submit, sir, that the commission will deny itself some extremely illuminating, trustworthy, and helpful evidence, which certainly would have probative value in the mind of any reasonable man.

"Furthermore," Kerr went on with considerable exaggeration, "there are about 57 different varieties of exceptions to the so-called hearsay rule, and if the commission has to get into that maze of legal technicalities as to what is and what is not admissible as hearsay, we will be here for months."

Again, Kerr's arguments were aimed at the five generals, pitting legal technicalities against good old common sense. Hendrix, in reply, seemed to be arguing more for the benefit of the headquarters lawyers who would be reviewing a conviction for MacArthur. He pointed out that Article 38 of the Articles of War required that the rules of procedure and evidence for courts-martial and military commissions be the rules "generally recognized in the trial of criminal cases" in federal courts, unless the President issued additional or different rules for the court-martial or commission to follow.

Here, said Hendrix, the President had not provided any such rules. Only MacArthur had. His regulations did of course radically depart from U.S. criminal trial rules, and so "this entire letter," Hendrix said, holding up MacArthur's order, "is null and void; General MacArthur, in preparing this letter, did not have authority from Congress to make any rules or procedures of a military commission. The only man in the world that has such power from Congress is the President, and he has not done anything about prescribing any rules." He looked at the commission. "Apparently the commission will have to decide whether we are going to decide the evidence [based] on what Congress has passed, or whether we will go by a letter that has been prepared by General MacArthur and which has directed General Styer to carry on this trial."

Put *that* way, the commission did not even go through the motions of recessing to consider the objection. "The objection of counsel for the defense," said Reynolds tersely, "is not sustained."

The witness closed his testimony on a note of pathos. On the evening of the Red Cross massacre, he recovered the body of his daughter and her ten-day-old baby. "I could not recover any more excepting the bones of the rest of the family," he said. To underscore the point, the prosecution displayed a photograph of the grave of his infant grandchild.

The afternoon had grown late, and the testimony of cruelty and carnage had certainly been enough for one day. But the commission meant to keep to its scheduled hours of 8:30 to 5:00, with an hour and a half for lunch, and so the prosecution turned to its next case: a slaughter at the Dy-Pac Lumber Yard, on February 4, 1945, a week before the Red Cross murders.

Here the prosecution ran into its first headwind from the generals. The Dy-Pac incident was identified in paragraph number 16 in the bill of particulars ("On about 4 February, 1945, at the Dy-Pac Lumber Yard in Manila, brutally mistreating and killing two hundred noncombatant male civilians"), and also in number 93 in the supplemental bill, alleging another slaughter that had occurred on January 14. Without prompting from the defense, Reynolds interrupted Kerr. "The commission will not listen to testimony or discussion of [supplemental] bill of particulars number 93."

Kerr seemed taken aback. Not on any allegations of the supplemental bill?

"That was the ruling made this morning, to permit the defense to have time to prepare itself on the supplementary bill of particulars," said Reynolds.

Kerr protested. "It will be necessary, then, to recall the same witnesses to testify to the balance of this particular incident."

"So be it," said Reynolds.

But the defense, said Kerr, "has had full notice on that particular case, at least, because it was named in the original bill of particulars."

The solution at this point would have been simply to strike supplemental charge 93 and move on to the Dy-Pac events, but Captain Reel for the defense saw an opportunity to make clear what had been left uncertain that morning. "We understood this morning," said Reel, "that after the prosecution's case was in on the 64 [original] particulars, that then we would be given some time to prepare on [the supplemental allegations]."

"That is correct," Reynolds answered, though he had said that morning only that the commission would consider such a request.

Reel pressed the advantage. "We will require two weeks to prepare ourselves on the 59 new ones."

"There is nothing further to say," Reynolds replied.

Had the commission just granted the defense a two-week continuation at the conclusion of the prosecution's case? Reynolds had seemed to say so.

Despite the commission's ruling, the prosecution's first witness testified that she had seen her husband tied up, with others, at the lumber yard on January 13—the event alleged in the supplemental bill—and that two days later she recovered his body, his throat slit and a bullet wound over his heart. The defense objected, accusing the prosecution of attempting to evade the commission's ruling on the supplemental bill. No, said the prosecutor, the January 13 event is actually covered in another part of the original bill, which, without specifying any details, alleged that "during the period from 1 January 1945 to 1 March, 1945," Japanese troops had engaged in "the extermination, massacre, and wanton, indiscriminate killing of large numbers of unarmed noncombatant men, women and children, inhabitants of the City of Manila."

In any American court, that tactic—introducing evidence of an event that the court had specifically forbidden—would have drawn a sharp rebuke from a judge and a warning that any such future attempt to evade the rulings of the court would find the prosecutor held in contempt. But Reynolds was showing himself to be an even-tempered chairman, and he ordered only that the prosecution discontinue all evidence of what happened at the lumber yard on either date "until the evidence can be presented in its full entirety." And with that, the commission adjourned until morning.

It had been a long day, but all in all it had not gone badly for the defense. They had lost their legal arguments to dismiss the charge, to bar the use of out-of-court statements, and to throw out the supplemental charges, but in each case, they were asking the commission to go against the orders of MacArthur, so they could hardly have been surprised at the commission's rulings. On the other hand, they had secured permission to have Yamashita's assistants and his personal interpreter sit at the defense table and a continuance to prepare for the prosecution's supplemental charges; plus, the commission had turned aside the prosecution's attempt to prove the lumber yard case. And several of the witnesses had identified the marauders as wearing navy uniforms, which was to fit with the defense that the worst of the atrocities were committed under the command of Admiral Iwabuchi, who, the evidence would show, had refused Yamashita's orders to abandon Manila.

But the image of Corazon Noble—"noble heart"—a sling on her arm, a catch in her voice, and a tear in her eye as she told of her infant savagely murdered in her arms, was the lead in every newspaper covering the trial; her close-up appeared in newsreels around the world. Through it all, Tomoyuki Yamashita had sat quietly, somberly, listening to the testimony, occasionally whispering a word or two to his lawyers, his eyes intent on the witnesses but his face otherwise largely expressionless at the first day's account of atrocities. Clearly, Kerr had not exaggerated: this was going to be a long and unpleasant trial.

The second day saw no movie stars; instead, the prosecution called a prominent Philippine general, Basilio Valdes, for what turned out to be a hearsay festival in the ballroom of the High Commissioner's Residence. Valdes was the chief of staff of the Philippine Army, the indigenous force for whom MacArthur had been the field marshal prior to the Japanese attack in 1941; Valdes had been with MacArthur at Bataan and had rejoined him in Australia. But while MacArthur regrouped and launched his counterattack up through the Pacific in 1943 and 1944, Valdes had gone to the United States—"on a mission" that he did not otherwise explain but no doubt was part of a Filipino delegation to shore up American support for its beleaguered territorial ally. Valdes had returned to wade ashore with MacArthur at Leyte in October 1944 and had watched MacArthur raise the Philippine flag over the presidential palace in Manila four months later. Valdes was a big deal.

In Manila, Valdes had gone looking for his brother Alejo, a local police officer who had been taken away by Japanese sailors in early February 1942. To deflect any inference that Alejo might have been a collaborator, evacuated by his sponsors, the prosecutor asked Basilio if he knew what his brother had done "during the Japanese time"—when the witness had been nowhere near the Philippines.

"In my investigations," said Valdes calmly, "I discovered that Colonel Alejo Valdes had been consistently loyal to his oath as an officer and a gentleman, and had not served in any capacity, form or manner, either with the Japanese or with the puppet government." It was rank hearsay, from unidentified sources, but the witness went on. "When the Japanese came in, I was informed he was arrested, and he was thrown in jail, and there was kept for several days subjected to inhuman tortures and bodily harm, during which period they tried to obtain from him information as to the strength of the Philippine Army, position of troops, and what-not."

That was too much for the defense. Captain Sandberg objected that not only was the testimony "pure hearsay," but it related to a period more than two years before Yamashita had even come to the Philippines.

Kerr had a ready answer. "This portion of the testimony is entirely in accord with the special procedure"—MacArthur's regulations—"under which any evidence that might be of probative value in the minds of the commission may be admitted by the commission. This is very important, because this evidence will give you the whole picture of the situation under the Japanese regime, especially as to those persons who had the misfortune of staying in the Philippines during that time"—all this, from a witness who had been in the United States "during that time."

It was too much for Reynolds as well. He ordered stricken from the record all of Valdes's testimony about what had happened in 1942.

Valdes went on to testify that on his return to Manila in 1945 he went to a field near a paper factory and found the shallow grave of his brother and his brother's son, their hands tied behind their backs, their bodies burned.* Then the commission was plunged back into the hearsay thicket again. The prosecution offered into evidence several documents prepared by unnamed "Filipino guerrillas," ostensibly under the supervision of a Philippine army investigator, purporting to record the alleged confessions of several Filipino collaborators—referred to as "spies"—who, Valdes assured the commission, "were responsible for the arrest and execution of my brother." A statement written by an unnamed "guerrilla" of what an unnamed "spy" had confessed to? Anonymous double hearsay was enough to concern even Reynolds.

Is the spy available as a witness? he asked.

---

* A few weeks later, Valdes was appointed president of a military commission to try seven Japanese soldiers on charges of murdering seven U.S. And Filipino prisoners of war on the island of Cebu in March 1945. General Handwerk, on the Yamashita commission, was named a member of that commission too. Valdes also was a member of the commission that tried General Homma, the Japanese army commander during the Bataan death march. General Donovan, from Yamashita's commission, was the presiding officer at Homma's trial.

"He is supposed to be dead," said the prosecutor, apparently not intending irony.

And the guerrilla who took the statement?

"Very ill," said the prosecutor.

And the investigating officer?

"In the United States."

And, said the prosecutor, we have five other statements where these came from, and in all of them, neither the speaker nor the author nor the investigator is available to testify.

Would you repeat that? asked Reynolds, obviously perplexed.

Kerr would probably have been wiser to abandon the spies-and-guerrillas statements—after all, was there any doubt that it would have been the Japanese or their collaborators who had committed such obvious murders? But he was unfazed, and evidently determined to press the anything-goes evidentiary rules to their limits, if they had any. The statements were admissible as evidence, he told the commission, because the regulations allowed "statements taken by an officer detailed for that purpose by military authority," thus elevating the anonymous Filipino guerrillas to the status of official investigators.

Reynolds drew the line. "The exhibit is excluded. Should the prosecution be able to establish the authenticity of the circumstances surrounding the taking of the document to a greater extent, the commission will consider the matter further at that time."

Now it was Kerr's turn to be perplexed. The commission had excluded a document, yet any document was permitted under the rules if the commission found it "probative" and "of assistance," which Reynolds had evidently found this daisy chain not to be. "May I inquire whether or not that means that in the future we may not offer an affidavit without testimony as to the circumstances under which it was taken?" Kerr asked.

Reynolds was noncommittal. "The commission will rule on each case as it is presented, depending on the circumstances."

The question was soon answered. After the testimony of another Filipino resident who had seen Japanese soldiers leading the soon-to-be-murdered victims away from their homes, the prosecutor announced that the "oral evidence" on the matter was concluded. Then, holding up a sheaf of papers, he announced, "I am just going to introduce now in evidence statements of witnesses who were not called to the stand. The purpose of presenting this evidence is to establish the fact that there were three groups of Filipino civilians taken to the open field in front of the Japanese paper factory [where Valdes had found the bodies]; that these civilians were blindfolded and shot by the Japanese." He offered the first statement into evidence.

"Is this witness available to testify before the commission?" Reynolds asked.

"Yes, sir," said the prosecutor.

The defense objected. "The deponent is available and may be brought before this proceeding." On what possible ground could a written statement be introduced under those circumstances?

"Now, sir," said Kerr, addressing Reynolds, "if we are to be required, in each case where we propose to offer into evidence sworn statements, to produce the oral testimony of that witness in lieu of the sworn statement, it merely means that we will unduly extend the period of the trial. The purpose of the regulations authorizing the acceptance of a statement of this sort certainly is to avoid that necessity. I see no reason why the commission should hesitate to accept these sworn statements."

Other than the fact that the commission had no assurance of their accuracy, and the fact that the defendant would have no opportunity to cross-examine, and the fact that the witnesses were nearby and available to come before the panel to be heard and examined, there probably was no reason the commission should hesitate.

And Reynolds did not. "The document will be accepted in evidence," he said. With that, the prosecution handed four written statements to the generals.

The next witness was Father Cosgrave, who told the ghastly story of the invasion of the boys' school by Japanese soldiers, followed by two more teachers at the school, all of whom identified photographs of their murdered colleagues. The defense did not cross-examine. As the afternoon wore on, several local residents who had seen what had happened at the school, or who knew the victims, were called to the stand to recount bits and pieces of the story and to identify photographs of the deceased. The massacre became a story of who went to what room, and what they saw when they went downstairs or upstairs, and whose cousin was whose. Except for a chilling mention of the attempted rape of a dead girl, none of it added anything significant to the story that Father Cosgrave and others had related.

That case done, the prosecutors moved on to the murder of a justice of the Philippine Supreme Court and his family and called four witnesses to establish that the judge and his family had indeed been killed by Japanese soldiers. The testimony was grim:

> The soldiers were forming a semi-circle around the group, and then before we knew it a machine gun, which was placed right at the very center of that semi-circle broke loose—rather, fired—then everybody fell, those who were hit by the machine gun and those who were not, both, so as not to expose themselves to the fire. Then there was moaning, screaming and crying; then the soldiers closed in with their bayonets, including the officers,

who drew their broad swords, and then the officers hacked right and left, up and down the line. They struck with their sabers, sir, and the soldiers joined in with their bayonets and with their iron pointed poles, sir; kept on thrusting up and down the line. When the broad sword went down, I was able to swerve to the left, and it missed me. Then the officers stopped striking with their sabers and wiped them on the backs of the dead, and then put them in their—put their sabers back in their sheaths.

The prosecution concluded the day by offering into evidence the statements of eleven people about the event. The defense objected, to no avail.

The next day, October 31, only the second full day of testimony, though it must have seemed like more, brought further evidence of killing, this time at the National Psychopathic Hospital in early February 1945. The administrative officer for the hospital took the stand and testified that a group of Japanese, wearing the naval service uniform, entered the hospital and killed some seventeen patients and staff. Then the chief psychiatrist was called, essentially to repeat the story and to identify by name each of the dead. Then a ward attendant was summoned to tell what she saw. A nurse took the stand to name two nurses who had been killed.

The prosecution turned then to another massacre on the same day, in Manila. Japanese soldiers stormed into a neighborhood, setting fire to the houses and slaughtering the inhabitants. The city undertaker was called to testify that he took away some hundred bodies from the scene of the massacre, noting that one was "a lady whose breast had been completely chopped off, and also we found a lady whose genital organs had apparently been ripped off with a bayonet."

In these first days, the defense was tentative in its cross-examination of the victims on the stand—understandably, because they had never spoken to them and had no idea of what their testimony might be. The core of the victims' testimony was unassailable; the defense could hope at best to nibble at the margins. So for most witnesses, they prudently declined to cross-examine at all, and when they did venture in, they did little good. One line of questioning, soon abandoned, explored whether there was any nearby combat between Japanese and Americans, to plant the suggestion that some of the deaths might have been caused by battle rather than by marauding soldiers. Another explored whether the victims had been supporters of the Filipino guerrillas, perhaps to imply that they were legitimate targets, an ill-conceived theory that was likewise soon dropped. Except for establishing at several points that the marauders wore naval uniforms, cross-examination accomplished little. Clearly, the day belonged to the witnesses and to the prosecution.

Through the afternoon of October 31, the prosecution returned to the murder of priests, calling several witnesses who described killings at the San

Marcellino Church. Hearsay was rife ("I made some inquiries to know the fate of our fathers and they told me the story they knew"; an apparent reference to "some Chinese," otherwise unidentified). Another case dealt with the murder of nuns, staff, and students at St. Paul's College in Manila—800 by one witness's estimate, though another said 500, and another said 250, for which the prosecution called no fewer than seven witnesses. For most witnesses, the prosecution had sheaves of photographs and maps, to allow witnesses to explain their movements and escape attempts or the vantage point from which they had witnessed the atrocities. The testimony was appalling by any measure. One survivor testified that the Japanese placed boxes of candy in some chandeliers in the church; as the famished captives crowded around, the Japanese detonated bombs hidden in the chandeliers. "Bonbons Used for Massacre Bait by Japs," read the next day's headlines in U.S. newspapers.

The defense occasionally got a witness to acknowledge on cross-examination that he or she had not actually seen all the details testified to, but in the context of the atrocities these slipups were minor. The survivors had clearly been through hell, and they were not making it up. There were repeated notes of pathos ("There was a terrific fire, and afterwards I carried my small child with me to the chapel, and then at 12 o'clock she died, and I wrapped her in a mantle, put her on the altar") and of horror ("I saw a baby of about a week being carried and then thrown up into the ceiling [by] a Japanese soldier. He grabbed him by the arm and he just threw him as one throws a ball. And another Japanese with a fixed bayonet came in and just thrust his bayonet." She demonstrated for the commissioners. "I saw the baby dangling with the bayonet still in his stomach.")

Throughout the testimony, the members of the commission were almost entirely silent save for Reynolds's terse rulings on evidence or other administrative matters. At one point during a cross-examination, prosecutor Kerr objected that defense counsel Reel was eliciting "only such portions of the answer that might be in his favor, and is extremely anxious to avoid such part of the truth as may be adverse to his client." It was hardly a shocking charge against a defense attorney, but Reel shot back, "If these remarks are directed at me, I personally resent them and consider them untrue." Reynolds intervened. "Cease this unseemly bickering," he directed both men. It had been a long and wearying day, and it was only the third of the trial.

Later in the day, Reynolds called all the lawyers into the commission's office for a lecture. According to Reel, Reynolds told them, "You men aren't knights in armor jousting with one another. You are officers of the Army and of this court [*sic*], and you are detailed to help us find the facts here—that's all." It showed a naive misunderstanding of the role of counsel, particularly defense counsel. In the civilian world and in courts-martial, counsel are officers of the court and are bound to act honestly and ethically. But they are not a judge's assistants; they are advocates. The defense answer to Reynolds's scolding was blunt: "As officers of the United States Army, and as lawyers appointed to defend the accused, defense counsel are charged with a duty to the accused, to the Army, and to the people of the United States to pursue all proper legal remedies open to the defense."

Reynolds looked directly at the defense lawyers. "You fellows should talk to us, not to the record. You'll get along better."

The testimony the next day was no less gruesome than that of the first three. It centered on an orgy of rape, and at the prosecution's request the public was barred from the proceedings while victim after victim took the stand. The first woman, twenty-four years old, testified that she was rounded up with about twenty-five other girls and young women and taken to a room in the Bay View Hotel where Japanese soldiers ripped off her clothes and underwear, raped her, and left her for other soldiers to abuse throughout the night. This went on for three nights. Her anguish obvious, she had to be asked several times to speak up so the commissioners could hear. After she finished, her sixteen-year-old sister was brought to the stand, where she gave the same account of her ordeal. And after she finished, their fourteen-year-old sister was brought in, and she told an almost identical story.

After the third sister had stepped down, Reynolds addressed Kerr. "Is the testimony of the remaining witnesses merely corroborative or have you some new episodes of a similar nature?"

There will be five or six more witnesses, said Kerr, and all of them "have somewhat different testimony." The difference, he explained, was that each of them could name a somewhat different group of other neighborhood girls and women who endured the same savagery. And not all of them had been raped in the Bay View Hotel, Kerr pointed out.

Reynolds, evidently uncomfortable at the graphic testimony of such young victims, cut Kerr off. "The commission will forego listening to further witnesses with respect to the Bay View Hotel." Kerr, undeterred and apparently oblivious to Reynolds's concerns or the triviality of the difference, called five more rape victims. Each of them, tearfully whispering the story of their humiliation and pain to a roomful of uniformed men, recounted nearly identical episodes of savagery in five different hotels—all of which, it emerged, were on the same block as the Bay View.

"The case is progressing nicely, much as any lawsuit does," assistant prosecutor Mountz wrote in his letter home. "We are introducing from three to eight separate cases each day, some with good witnesses and some with poor witnesses. Yamashita sits through it all with little or no expression on his face—occasionally he frowns. His interpreter gives him a running account of the evidence as it goes along."

The rest of the day was taken up with victims of several different episodes of Japanese brutality in early February in Manila, almost all of them testifying as to the deaths of family members, servants, or neighbors before their eyes. Then, at the end of the day, Reynolds did something unexpected, and, for the prosecution, certainly unwelcome.

Captain Hill, one of the assistant district attorneys on the prosecutor's staff, was introducing a written statement of a witness to prove the killing of three men by the Japanese, in an incident that the prosecution did not intend to call any live witnesses to prove.

"The commission is unwilling to accept affidavits as the sole proof of an item in the bill of particulars," said Reynolds. "Therefore, unless you have witnesses to introduce, this exhibit is rejected by the commission. Is there some reason why the witness cannot appear personally?"

Hill was not expecting this. "We thought, sir," he said, "that we could cut down, possibly, the time that it would take to present all of these matters by presenting some of them this way."

No, said Reynolds, evidently now starting to appreciate the shortcomings of hearsay evidence. "I think the prosecution should consider the desirability of striking certain items [from the two bills of particulars]. The commission feels that there must be witnesses introduced on each of the specifications or items. It has no objection to considering affidavits, but it is unwilling to form an opinion of a particular item based solely on an affidavit. Therefore, until evidence is introduced, these particular exhibits are rejected."

Kerr's consternation was apparent. "The balance of our cases for today would have been presented purely through documentary evidence. That will be true, sir, as to quite a large number of the particulars in the two bills of particulars. It has been our understanding that under the regulations prescribed by General MacArthur, statements would be admissible, and we had assumed that the commission would receive them."

Reynolds did not answer. He adjourned the day's proceedings, leaving the prosecution to wonder whether, without live witnesses, it could still make its case for the "quite a large number" of remaining atrocities.

Friday, November 2, the fifth day, saw the trial's most tragic and grotesque testimony. Five witnesses described an attack by Japanese troops on civilians in Manila in early February, and then a depraved attack on a thirteen-year-old girl, gang-raped by twenty soldiers who mutilated her afterward. "I couldn't see how anybody, at their worst—I hadn't heard, in the worst of horror stories or horror pictures or books, anything like that. It couldn't be possible," said Francisco Lopez, an eyewitness. He testified that he saw still more grotesque cruelty—men emasculated, their testicles stuffed in their mouths; women decapitated and then raped; children burned alive; children speared with pikes. Gripping the arms of his chair and staring at Yamashita, he cried, "Like sadists, they enjoyed it and they made fun of it! That is one thing that I can never understand and never forgive!"*

"Try to live," Lopez testified that a dying neighbor told him, "just to tell whoever gets to this side from the Americans to tell them what has been done to us." It was a "story rivaling in horror the sufferings of the damned in Dante's 'Inferno,'" wrote Robert Cromie for the *Chicago Daily Tribune*, "laid bare by a master story teller. Not even the wholesale butchery of the Belsen prison camp in Germany was more revolting than the testimony of Francisco Lopez."

There was no cross-examination. Yamashita listened to the testimony with his head bent and his hand over his eyes. "The imperturbable Jap commander," Cromie wrote, "sits unmoved thru [*sic*] all this testimony."

Later in the day, a thirty-eight-year-old Chinese woman, "sitting quietly in a Chinese high-necked dress with a slit skirt," according to the *Sydney Morning Herald*, testified that her entire family had been killed, her baby bayoneted as she held him. Finishing her testimony, she leapt from the witness chair and charged the defense table, crying out, in Chinese, "'I would like to kill that short-legged Jap. Those Japanese were to blame for everything. He's got to be killed." She was led out of the room, still calling out between sobs, 'Kill that Jap.'" "So everyone took pictures and lots of color," Mountz wrote. Cromie reported that "Yamashita, seemingly ignorant of the cause of her outburst, just sat and looked at her until court attaches led her away." Yamashita sat "calm and apparently unconcerned," concluded the *Manila Times* reporter.

Indeed, Yamashita had no friends in the press. "He looked incredibly tame and safe," *Time* magazine wrote in its summation of the testimony to date:

A froglike man in a green uniform who sat shaven-headed, sleepy-eyed, almost motionless at a long table. Occasionally he smiled. As witnesses talked from the stand, the nerves of many a spectator ached for the sound of a scream. As the testimony wore on, formality lent the proceedings the curious improbability of a bad horror play. The five U.S. generals of the trial commission, conducting the first U.S. war-crimes trial, were thus setting a precedent; they proceeded with the utmost caution.

---

* Exclamation points are in the transcript.

Yamashita, *Time* continued, "would be given every legal courtesy—by men who devoutly hoped to see him face a firing squad."

All of the day's testimony concerned events alleged in the supplemental bill of particulars, the fifty-nine add-ons for which the defense had vigorously sought more time to prepare, yet now those allegations were being introduced into evidence with no defense objection. Reynolds raised an eyebrow. "Is the defense prepared to proceed" with the supplemental charges? Yes, said Clarke. Kerr volunteered the apparent reason: "Sir, our practice has been, and will be, to notify defense counsel in advance of the cases in the supplemental bill which we desire to take up the following day."

The defense had resigned itself to going along on such short notice, probably because it had realized, by the end of the week, that there was little difference between the two lists of atrocities—both of them alleged massacre after massacre, many of them in and around Manila during the terrible month of February 1945, all of them the subject of survivors testifying about the loss of their mother and father, or son and daughter, or brother and sister. A week's worth of testimony had shown that no amount of preparation time would have aided the defense or muted the agony of the witnesses.

The defense never objected that the evidence was cumulative, repetitious, and needlessly heartrending, or that the massacres were becoming almost indistinguishable from one another, or that the witnesses were being made to recount experiences of unfathomable tragedy and sadness, or that the translations into English from the Tagalog spoken by many witnesses was halting and time-consuming, or that not one witness had remotely connected any of this to Yamashita, whose name had yet to be mentioned in the week's testimony.

It was obvious that the prosecution was not particularly concerned, just yet, in drawing any direct links to Yamashita. It was presenting a theater of the wretchedness and cruelty inflicted by the Japanese on the residents of the city and country in which the trial was being held. The only feasible course for the defense was to wait until the prosecution was done with them all. Cross-examination had all but abated, defense counsel rising from time to time only to question a witness about the Japanese uniform, to establish that many of the marauders wore the dark green uniform and anchor-insignia caps of the Japanese Naval Landing Forces.

Reynolds, having earlier ruled that hearsay statements alone would not suffice to prove atrocity episodes, was becoming less patient with them even when accompanied by live testimony. At one point, without being prompted by the defense, he excluded an affidavit in which a witness had described in detail a roundup of civilians but added, "I did not see this because I was sleeping." At another point a witness testified that she had gone from house to house in her neighborhood to compile a list of the dead after a bloody Japanese intrusion.

She had the list, and read the names of the deceased, all seventy-five of them. The defense objected: the list is "pure hearsay," said Sandberg, quite correctly. The prosecution had a facile explanation: "This witness of her own volition obtained this information from the persons in the neighborhood." Surely it was easier to get the names into the record this way than to call all seventy-five survivors to testify about their dead, he urged. "Under the rules, the Commission may accept such testimony if it sees fit." Reynolds evidently did not see fit and sustained the defense objection.

Yet just a few minutes later he admitted into evidence, over defense objection, a fourteen-page report, prepared by a U.S. Army war crimes investigating team, describing the murder of 400 Filipinos in Manila on February 10, 1945, carried out "principally by members of the Imperial Japanese Navy aided by some members of the Army." The report concluded, "A more brutal and cold blooded series of murders can hardly be imagined." The investigators recommended that "the Imperial Japanese Government be held responsible." The report was double or triple hearsay, because it recounted what the victims interviewed had been told by others. In that sense, it was less reliable than the list of seventy-five dead neighbors. But this report had the signatures of three army officers and that of Carpenter, the chief of MacArthur's War Crimes Branch. It was very official. Reynolds accepted it.

The problem was not that the report was devastating to the defense—it was, in essence, just another account of another massacre by Japanese troops in Manila. In fact, parts of the report were helpful to the defense, as when the investigators noted that those interviewed described the perpetrators as wearing "green uniforms with an anchor on their collars and hats." According to one witness, "During that time the army had all gone and left the navy in charge."

Nor was the problem that Reynolds's rulings on evidence invariably favored the prosecution. He sustained defense objections from time to time, and his ban on victims' accounts in uncorroborated affidavits had been a significant setback for the prosecution. But despite that ruling, he had just accepted a report from an absent investigator summarizing the accounts of absent victims. The problem was that the rulings were inconsistent, unpredictable, and usually unexplained, leaving prosecutors and defense counsel alike guessing.

Then, four days after his ruling that the commission would exclude affidavits that were uncorroborated by the testimony of live witnesses, he abruptly overturned that decision. He said only, "After further consideration, the commission reverses that ruling and affirms its prerogative of receiving and considering affidavits or depositions, if it chooses to do so, for whatever probative value the commission believes they may have, without regard to the presentation of some partially corroborative oral testimony." Nothing in the record explains the reversal, but the verbatim transcripts of each day's proceedings were being flown daily to MacArthur's headquarters for review by staff lawyers and perhaps Mac-Arthur himself. It seems almost certain that a message from those headquarters had set Reynolds straight on what was expected of his commission.

The long trial days were already taking a toll on the lawyers, particularly the prosecutors, who had to present one day's cases and prepare the next day's simultaneously, routinely working late into the night. Kerr met privately with the commissioners to ask that no sessions be held on Saturdays. Reynolds answered that he was seriously considering holding them on Sundays too. Kerr managed to talk him out of that, but the Saturday sessions remained. Kerr was "fed up on the whole situation," in the words of his assistant Mountz. Carpenter was "insisting that all charges be proved, and the commission keeps insisting that we hurry up and complete the case in a few days."

The anguish of the testimony was at times tangible. "An orgy of murder, torture and rape of 1,200 to 1,500 civilians," wrote Robert Trumbull of the *New York Times* about one witness's story, in words that could have described the testimony of many. "His account of the sadistic frenzy of the Japanese, of rape, mutilation and killing, electrified the trial commissioners. At several points of the incredibly gruesome recital the spectators gasped audibly." Yet the next day Trumbull wrote that "the usual pattern of such atrocities" had become "so familiar after five days that some dozed in their seats while the massacre of entire families was being described."

On the sixth day of trial, several witnesses who had been taken to Japanese military police headquarters described an experience that they called the "water cure," today called waterboarding. A Filipino who had worked for the Japanese military police described it: "They tie up the person to be questioned, lay him flat on his back, put a piece of cloth over his mouth and nose, and pour water, usually from a water hose. I saw about 30 of them."

One victim: "They tied my mouth with a piece of towel, then three or four, maybe about six of them were on top of me, and they pitcher or—they just pour water in my mouth and my nose. I surely cannot breathe, and they are holding your hands and standing over you."

Another: "They began to pour me water with a bottle of, I think, one liter. I think up to 12 or 13 bottles they poured in me. And then I cannot resist because my heart was beating very, very fast, and I cannot resist that water, because I was drowning. So I told them that I will tell the truth. And then they pour me three more bottles, and after a while I told them lie."

Several witnesses were asked on cross-examination if they had ever aided or been affiliated with the Filipino guerrillas, those self-organized fighters against the Japanese who were not affiliated with a military unit and thus under international law were unlawful combatants and war criminals themselves. Under international law at the time, they were civilians who could be executed for engaging the enemy, and the defense questions were suggesting that some of the murders might have been executions of guerrillas, or of those who had aided them or at least sympathized with them, the last of which would have included most Filipinos. The commission grew increasingly impatient with this line of questioning, and when the defense raised it with a witness who had testified he had been tortured, Reynolds had the better of the argument:

> [Reynolds:] The commission grants that in the eyes of the rules of land warfare and international law, guerrillas, if captured, can be tried and sentenced, but under no condition can they be tortured. Unless the defense is suggesting to the commission that torture and third degree is a proper defense of the accused in this case, which I am sure you do not mean to do, why, still it would be immaterial to the presentation of this case.
>
> [Hendrix for the defense:] In view of the fact that the witness was arrested, as we see it, because he indirectly aided the guerrillas, we take the view that this mistreatment was probably by virtue of the fact that he had been arrested.
>
> [Reynolds:] The commission accepts all that. The only point at issue is the propriety of torture, which for centuries back has been condemned by civilized nations, and, hence, could not be a defense. The arrest may indeed have been well founded and the questioning well founded. I believed the defense understands that. We appreciate your zeal and effort to inform the commission of the facts.
>
> [Hendrix:] Yes, sir.

The witness who had worked for the Japanese and witnessed the "water cure" mentioned another matter. One day in December 1944, the military police garrison commander had called everyone together to read them "a word of commendation from General Yamashita on the work that they had done in suppressing guerrilla activities." It was the sixth day of testimony, and the first mention of the defendant's name.

But this routine letter to a military unit for its good work in fighting the enemy seemed to signal a shift in the wind. The next prosecution witness was not a Filipino victim testifying about yet more Japanese atrocities but a man whose testimony, if it was true, was very damaging indeed to Yamashita.

10

The Prosecution
The Defense Scores

Narciso Lapus was a sixty-year-old Filipino man, incarcerated at New Bilibid Prison as a suspected collaborator with the Japanese. He said he had been the "private secretary" to Artemio Ricarte, a longtime Filipino nationalist who had come to some prominence in the insurrection of 1900 against the United States. When the insurrection was put down in 1902, Ricarte, rather than take an oath of allegiance to the United States, had gone into self-imposed exile in Japan, where he earned a living running a tea house in his home and teaching Spanish on the side. In 1942, shortly after the Japanese invasion, Ricarte had returned to the Philippines under Japanese sponsorship. He was seventy-six years old at the time. According to Lapus, Ricarte had been personally chosen by Prime Minister Tojo to be the new Philippine head of state under the independence promised by Japan.

Lapus testified that Ricarte had met several times with General Yamashita, with a Japanese staff officer acting as interpreter (Ricarte, despite his long stay in Japan, was evidently unable to converse in Japanese). Lapus was not present. Each time, said Lapus, Ricarte returned home in anguish to tell Lapus that Yamashita had told him, Ricarte, that he, Yamashita, had ordered every Filipino in Manila and throughout the islands to be killed when the Americans invaded. "There is a general order issued by General Yamashita all over the commanders of the military posts in the Philippine Islands," Lapus testified that Ricarte told him about what Yamashita allegedly said, "to wipe out the whole Philippines, if possible." "We take the Filipinos 100 percent as our enemies," Lapus said that Ricarte said that Yamashita said, "because all of them, directly or indirectly, they are guerrillas, or helping the guerrillas." He went on, "Ricarte revealed to me, sir, that the order of Yamashita was this, to all the commanders of the military posts all over the Philippines: that whenever the Americans succeeded in landing at certain points, and the population gives signs of pro-American movement or actions, the whole population of that part or place or town or barrio should be wiped out."

Lapus said that Ricarte had told him that he had pleaded with Yamashita to rescind his order, but to no avail. "He was in tears, sir. He told me, 'Lapus, I am very, very sorry.' He said, 'I fail because Yamashita was very determined not to change his order of massacre.'" At a later meeting, said Lapus, channeling Ricarte, "'I talked it over again, but Yamashita told me he could do nothing; that the order was given and he was sorry.' [Yamashita] said, 'War is war, and the enemy should not be given quarters [*sic*].'" According to Lapus, Ricarte had said, "I did everything. I appealed to the heart of this man, but he has no heart. He would not listen. The order was given and he could not change it."

It was all hearsay upon hearsay, but Reynolds overruled Reel's repeated objections, allowing Lapus to testify without restriction. At one point Reynolds, still grappling with the implications of hearsay, asked Reel, "There have been so many objections from the defense under the hearsay rule that the commission is impelled to inquire whether defense contends that all hearsay evidence, regardless of its nature, is normally excluded from any court of law."

Reynolds's unfamiliarity with such an elementary concept took both prosecutors and defense counsel by surprise. ("Imagine the judge asking the defense counsel what the law is," Mountz wrote in his letter home.) Reel answered that hearsay is indeed excluded, though there are certain exceptions. But this, he said, is double hearsay, "and we certainly do object to having it enter here." The prosecutor, not willing to risk an adverse ruling, withdrew the question.

The defense caught a break when, at the conclusion of Lapus's direct testimony, Reynolds uncharacteristically adjourned the proceedings in midafternoon so that the defense could have Sunday to prepare its cross-examination. The prosecutors were jubilant. "Yesterday was, in my opinion, the top day for the prosecution," Mountz wrote the next day. "We are beginning to string the rope around the neck."

Colonel Clarke, who would do the cross-examination, was clearly under the gun, facing for the first time in the trial a witness who was actually tying Yamashita to the Japanese crimes. If the commission believed Lapus, the game was over for Yamashita: not only had he "permitted" the atrocities, but he had ordered them, and no novel theory of command accountability would be needed to send him to the gallows for that.

But Lapus's story was also highly suspect. For one thing, Ricarte was dead, succumbing to illness and old age in August 1945 in the mountains of Luzon as he accompanied Yamashita, the man who had supposedly ordered the deaths of all his countrymen. Lapus had asserted that no one else had been present during his conversations with Ricarte, conveniently leaving him as the only one to tell the tale. And although Lapus had painted a heroic picture of Ricarte as "the Number 1 Filipino" in the eyes of the Japanese, a man who had received a sealed and beribboned warrant signed by Tojo himself to become the ruler of the Japanese-liberated Philippines, he in fact was a decidedly minor figure by this time. The idea that Tojo would look to him to lead a puppet regime in the Philippines seemed absurd.

Moreover, the alleged orders on their face were fantastic—wait until the Americans landed, and *then* kill all Filipinos? When would the Japanese fight the Americans? And just how many years of unrestrained mayhem would it take for Japanese soldiers to kill several million Filipinos? Yet Lapus had insisted the alleged "orders" were not hyperbole: "There will come to Manila the Japanese forces, and there will not be a single Filipino living in the city of Manila."

Beyond that, although Yamashita had supposedly sent the order to all his subordinate commanders in the Philippines, there was no corroboration of it at all—no American unit had intercepted any such communication, no record of it had been found in any captured Japanese documents, no Japanese officer or soldier in U.S. custody had said anything about it. And why, for that matter, would Yamashita confide such ghastly plans to a supposedly prominent Filipino leader in the first place?

On Monday morning, November 5, Clarke devoted little attention to these obvious questions. He began a three-hour cross-examination that wandered through a mass of collateral details—Lapus's political background, his writings, his views on America, his son's difficulties with the police—all having nothing to do with his tale of Yamashita's orders. After a while, the prosecution stood to object that all this was irrelevant, but Reynolds overruled the objection, giving Clarke wide latitude to go where he wanted in his questioning.

Nudged back to the important facts, Clarke committed the mistake a cross-examiner most needs to avoid: he let the witness repeat his whole story, more or less as he had told it on direct. His questions let Lapus reinforce it ("Are you sure of that?" "He believed what he told you?" "And General Ricarte told you that?"). He framed questions that supported Lapus's credibility by assuming that his story was established fact ("When did you first learn of the existence of this order?" "So that in every spot in which the Americans had control, the Filipinos then were to be massacred by the Japanese soldiers?" "What do you think they discussed at the second meeting?" "Didn't the order direct that the Filipinos would be wiped out after American forces arrived in that particular area?")

Clarke's only significant impeachment of the witness was to establish that he had been imprisoned since February 1945 for collaboration and that, having told no one the story of Yamashita's orders from February to October, he had then taken it on himself to write to Reynolds after the arraignment, offering to come and testify about it. But Lapus stoutly denied that he had made any deal for leniency with the prosecutors, and there was no evidence that he had.

But Lapus also testified that he had talked to no one about his testimony. That was a lie, and the prosecution knew it. "He did not do so well on cross examination," wrote Mountz that evening, "first because he was very dumb, and second he fell for the old trick of saying he had not talked to anyone about the case or his evidence, and Capt. Pace and I had been out to see him last night, which is another story." Mountz's letter gives no further details. The prosecution let the lie—it was no "trick"—go uncorrected.

When Clarke finished his cross examination, the prosecutor stood up to begin redirect examination, the point of which is to rehabilitate the damage done on cross. Reynolds soon interjected: "We will accord the prosecution a very few moments" for its redirect—usually a sign that little rehabilitation is necessary. But the real question was whether the commissioners actually believed Lapus. They gave no indication.

The prosecution then called another witness to tell a similar tale. Joaquin Galang, like Lapus, was at that time imprisoned as a collaborator. He was a friend of Ricarte's, he said, and in December 1944 he was visiting Ricarte at his home, in the presence of Ricarte's wife and twelve-year-old grandson, who had been born in Japan during his grandfather's long residency there and had come to the Philippines with him two years earlier. While they were sitting and talking, who should arrive at the house but Yamashita himself. Because Ricarte could not speak Japanese, he summoned his grandson, who could, to serve as an interpreter between the two.

According to Galang, "The child told me that General Yamashita said that 'All Filipinos are guerrillas and even the people who are supposed to be under Ricarte.'" Ricarte through his grandson supposedly then told Yamashita, according to Galang, "'I would like to take this occasion to ask you again for you to revoke your order to kill all the Filipinos and to destroy all the city.' He [Yamashita] stood. He was very angry. He was frowning. You could see it in his face and his hands were clinched, and he said, 'An order is an order. And because of that it should not be broken or disobeyed. It ought to be consumed [*sic*], happen what may happen.' And then he left and he was accompanied by General Ricarte to the stairs." Asked who was present during this conversation, Galang answered, "General Ricarte, General Yamashita, myself and the child."

This was bad news for the defense. Galang had corroborated Lapus (though they were talking about different alleged meetings with Yamashita), and, unlike Lapus, he was testifying as to what he said he himself had heard, not what Ricarte had told him after the event. Ricarte was dead, and his grandson was God knew where. On cross-examination, Captain Sandberg got Galang to admit that he knew Lapus (they were in fact fellow inmates at Bilibid Prison) and that he had never told this story to anyone until the previous night, after talking to Lapus about his testimony, which had also been widely reported in local papers.

How Galang got to the investigators and then the witness stand so quickly was not clear from his testimony, but he was there, and he had added a distinctly valuable piece to the jigsaw puzzle the prosecution was assembling. Whether that piece was true or false was the question.

With that question hanging in the air, the prosecution returned the next day to the horrors of February 1945 in Manila. The *New York Times* recounted the testimony in its daily dispatch:

> Manila, Tuesday, Nov. 6—Big tears streaming down her little brown face, 11-year-old Rosalinda Andoy, testifying today in the war-crimes trial of Gen. Tomoyuki Yamashita, told the story of the slaying of her father and mother by the Japanese last February.
>
> In a tiny, quavering voice the child said her parents were bayoneted to death, her father in Fort Santiago and her mother at her side in Santo Domingo Church where the Andoy family took refuge inside Manila's walled city of Intramuros after the Japanese had burned their home.
>
> The girl herself was bayoneted thirty-eight times. She lifted her short pink frock to her neck and showed the scars on her chest and back to the military commission hearing the case of the top Japanese commander in the Philippines.
>
> Testifying in Tagalog through an interpreter, the Andoy girl bravely stifled sobs and related how Japanese soldiers tossed grenades at the Filipino refugees as they made their way to the church.
>
> The girl's feet were dangling in wooden Filipino slippers that kept slipping off as she sat in the witness chair. She gravely repeated her dying mother's last words to her, "Always be good."
>
> American generals on the trial board wiped their eyes during the child's testimony. Many GI's crowded into the courtroom were visibly affected by her pitiful story.

Time magazine added details:

> As she testified Rosalinda began to cry, and the tears ran down her cheeks and fell on the pink dress. She turned toward the five U.S. generals sitting as commissioners, and showed them her left arm. There were ten scars. There were four more on her right arm. She stood up and pulled her dress up above her brown bloomers, showing 18 scars on her chest and stomach, one on her back. The marks of five wounds showed on her legs.
>
> With her homely little face twisted with weeping, Rosalinda said she had stayed close to her mother on the bloody church floor. Her mother had whispered, "I am dying." Then, said the girl, she told me "always to be good." Rosalinda had not left her mother's body until dawn. Then she

had crawled away—slowly, because her intestines were coming out of a wound—and had reached Santa Rosa College, where nuns took her in.

While Rosalinda testified, the Japanese general Yamashita stared coldly at the table before him. In the audience many people wept.

After the little girl told her pitiful story and left the witness stand, the prosecution announced it would continue with another massacre, this one at Fort Santiago. Much of it would be from the supplemental bill of particulars. Clarke stood with a plaintive plea. "I don't know whether you realize or not," he told the commissioners. "We have been working on this night and day. We don't have time to do anything. If we were given a certain amount of time we would be ready and prepared to go through the entire testimony at that time, sir."

Reynolds was not unsympathetic. "The commission will insist that counsel have adequate time to prepare the defense and we are most eager to proceed expeditiously." Turning to Kerr, he asked, "Do you have other witnesses with which you can proceed?"

Yes, said Kerr. But, he asked, when will the defense be ready to take on Fort Santiago? He added, "Frankly, sir, it took the war crimes [investigators] some three months to investigate these matters and I cannot conceive of the defense undertaking a similar investigation with any less period of time."

It was a candid and curious statement. Kerr surely knew there was no chance the commission would recess for three months. Yet his statement seemed to acknowledge that the defense was being forced to go on without adequate preparation.

"Let the commission answer that," said Reynolds. "We realize the tremendous task which we placed upon the defense and with which they are faced and it is our determination to give them the time they require. We ask that no time be wasted and we feel confident that you will not waste any, and we will see to it that you get time to prepare your defense. Therefore the prosecution is directed to proceed with other items."

And with that, testimony resumed, confined to atrocities inflicted on POWs and civilians at Fort Santiago, which had been among the original particulars. As the Americans approached, the prison was set on fire, with hundreds of men inside; men were killed in front of their children; men were beheaded ("I saw heads on the pavement," one witness recounted. "Fallen heads. Some of the heads were dangling from their bodies"); young girls were raped in the church where they had sought refuge.

A priest testified about a group of seventy confined to an air-raid shelter:

We were then praying and preparing for our souls because we knew more or less what would happen next, and in half an hour, while we were talking inside, hand grenades fell inside the shelter. The confusion inside was terrible and we were colliding [with] each other inside, each one trying to escape. But a group of Japanese were waiting for us outside with their guns and bayonets and all those who intended to escape were [on] the spot fired.

November 7, the ninth day of the trial, continued the prosecution's emphasis on atrocities against priests and nuns and their pupils and on the desecration of churches, with the commission allowing the witnesses to recount the anti-American statements of anonymous Japanese soldiers. Much of the testimony was cumulative, as one witness after another recounted the same events. After the flurry of testimony a few days earlier about what Yamashita had supposedly said about killing all Filipinos, he and his name went unmentioned again. Cross-examination was desultory; the defense stuck to its tactic of trying to establish that the marauders were wearing the uniforms of the naval landing forces, sometimes getting the answer they wanted from the witness, sometimes not. They also suggested repeatedly that the havoc in Manila during the month of February 1945 was caused by American bombers and artillery. While this was certainly true to some extent, none of it detracted from the gruesome horror the witnesses were called to recount.

Despite eight days of unremitting testimony on Japanese crimes, the commission showed no inclination to hasten the prosecution along to more evidence that would link Yamashita to any of it. At one point the prosecution called to the stand Henry Keys, a correspondent for the *London Daily Express* who had accompanied American forces into Manila on February 23, near the end of the battle for that city. Keys testified at length, without interruption, of the horrors he had seen, particularly in Intramuros, the oldest part of the city, its narrow streets and thick walls the last stand of the Japanese.

It was an almost unearthly vision: "I saw hundreds of refugees from Intramuros. They were ragged. Some of them were very shell-shocked. They bore what I could recognize as bayonet wounds and some were saber cuts. Others were very emaciated, starved, skin just hanging to their arms." He entered a church. "The first thing I saw was a dead girl. One of her feet was crushed to pulp and her mouth was broken and a lot of blood had come from it. On my right I saw a body of a little boy in a kneeling, crouching position with a bullet hole through the base of the skull." He followed an American lieutenant into the adjoining convent. "There was another lieutenant kneeling against a girl whose mouth had been shattered by blows with something. And she bore other wounds on her body and was barely breathing. The lieutenant gently patted her lips and was dropping water into her mouth. There weren't enough medics or anybody around with any experience to do anything for these people other than to give them what little relief was possible with virtually nothing." In a nearby room "was a beautiful Filipina girl lying on her back and a soldier called me over and he said, 'Look at this!' He said, 'She told us that a Jap hacked her feet off,' and he lifted a blanket that was lying over her feet. Her feet had been cut off and the stumps tied with what I took to be handkerchiefs."

He went on, "Crouched in some rubble and mortar was a girl, very emaciated, very thin, and you could hardly recognize it as a human being or that it lived. And only every so often, minutes perhaps, the whole body would convulsively shudder. Well, the flies were all over her as they were all over all these other wounded and dead. We brushed them away." Walking away, he saw the girl whose feet had been hacked off, carried out by litter bearers. "As they carried her out head first on the litter, shoulder high, she lifted her left hand with a 'V' sign—a very effective sight!" he concluded.

Later in the day, the prosecution shifted its focus, turning for the first time to the issue of the Japanese army's treatment of civilian internees at Santo Tomas University in the heart of Manila. Santo Tomas was no ordinary internment camp. It was the 53-acre campus of one of the world's oldest universities, founded in 1611, its distinguished schools of law, theology, medicine, and philosophy the alma mater of generations of Filipino elite. In early 1942, while the Japanese were still battling American and Filipino forces on Bataan, they commandeered the university and rounded up and confined on its fenced grounds nearly 4,000 civilians, three-quarters of them Americans and most of the rest British. Santo Tomas was by far the largest of the six civilian internment camps the Japanese set up in the Philippines, and it held the largest group of American civilians in history to have been held captive by an armed enemy. They were to remain there for over three years, until the American army liberated the camp in the battle of Manila in February 1945.

There were no military prisoners at Santo Tomas, and no Filipinos. These were teachers, businessmen, missionaries, engineers, and journalists; men, women, and children; most of them middle-class, many of them college graduates and longtime residents of the islands, many of them married into local families. With the reluctant cooperation of the Dominican fathers of the university and the International Committee of the Red Cross, the sprawling campus became a makeshift city within a city.

It was a stressful and unpleasant environment, but not an intolerable one, at least for the first two years. The internees formed for themselves a governing committee that dealt with the camp's Japanese administrators, who allowed them a good deal of autonomy to arrange living quarters in the dormitories and classrooms, distribute food and medical supplies, hand out work assignments, and conduct classes and games for the children and recreation and entertainment for the adults. Some internees were allowed to leave the grounds during the day to go into Manila and buy food, clothing, and other necessities from their own funds or from an account the camp administrators established for the purpose. There were seven American physicians, including surgeons, and some seventy-five nurses in the camp's population; Filipino doctors came and went; internees in need of more than basic medical care were transferred to Manila hospitals.

The inmates cultivated a large garden for greens, the yam-like camotes, and other vegetables. Local citizens could deliver food, packages of clothing, books, and other necessities to the front gate of the campus. In 1943 the American Red Cross delivered a 55-pound package of food to each internee (though many more Red Cross shipments were diverted by the Japanese). A study written in 1945 by an American doctor who had himself been interned at Santo Tomas concluded that the health of the internees "was not deleteriously influenced during 1942 and 1943, the first two years of imprisonment. The crude death rate was less than that of the Philippine civilians and not notably greater than that of an ordinary American community."

The Japanese warders kept a watchful eye on the internees but generally left them alone. There were no beatings, no torture, no overt mistreatment except when the occasional escapee was recaptured and roughed up as an example to others. The internees' committee evolved into a rather sophisticated self-government, with subcommittees and task forces, regular meetings with the Japanese administrators, and protracted negotiations over financial accounts, food deliveries, sanitation and living conditions, and communications with the outside world. The internees themselves were in charge of disciplining those who broke camp rules. Some of their fellows grumbled that this verged on collaboration, but others accepted it as preferable to leaving discipline to the Japanese. Sexual activity was formally forbidden, but the commandant's men could not be everywhere; seventy-five babies were born in the camp.

The whole purpose of the camp—just why the Japanese thought they needed to imprison and oversee 4,000 civilians for so long—remains something of a mystery. None of the prisoners were military, and few if any of them could have been considered security risks. Indeed, international law at the time did not allow the confinement of civilians who were not, at least indirectly, taking part in or supporting military action or who did not at least pose some tangible danger to the occupiers, but international treaties generally got little more than lip service from Tokyo. Just what the Japanese expected to gain by confining, feeding, housing, and maintaining such a teeming population for so long has never been clear.

By early 1944, conditions began to grow markedly worse at Santo Tomas. The war in the Pacific had turned with ominous strength against Japan, and in January, the camp was brought under military control. The camp's commandant curtailed the purchase of food on the open market and ended the package line of friendly Manileños at the front gate. All Filipinos, including food vendors and doctors who had been tending to the internees, were barred. Access to the Manila hospitals was ended; henceforth all medical procedures were to take place within the camp, with its primitive equipment and limited medicines.

Treatment of internees likewise took a harsh turn. Those who had engaged in illicit and secretive transactions with locals, usually to obtain food, were no longer turned over to the camp's internee committee for a few days of confinement; they were brutally interrogated by the Kempetai, the military police. Escapees were hunted down and executed summarily.

Most importantly, food deteriorated sharply in both quality and quantity. What the American doctor's study found to have been a limited but adequate quantity of food in the first two years of confinement decreased to about 1,300 calories per day by August 1944 and to fewer than 1,000 by the end of the year.* By early 1945, it had fallen to as little as 700 calories a day, and that usually as an unpalatable few ounces of boiled rice and corn, not counting whatever caloric value the worms and bugs that infested it might have added.

Japanese authorities later claimed that American ships and submarines were taking a heavy toll on Japanese merchant shipping, sinking food shipped from Japan for soldier and prisoner alike, and that when ships did make it to port, shortages of vehicles and gasoline made it hard to move food and supplies inland. This was only partly true, for there was no shortage of food in Manila. The commandants—there were four in 1944, each lasting about three months— simply refused to allow it through the gates to ease the increasing hunger of the men, women, and children inside, some of whom had plenty of money to pay for it. But money, even diamond rings, no longer had value; a "democracy of hunger and growing malnutrition" spread through the camp. By January 1945, the average man at Santo Tomas had lost 51 pounds over the course of his internment; the average woman, 32 pounds.

Malnutrition became a serious problem and the leading cause of death, though doctors were pressured to attribute deaths to "heart trouble" or "old age" rather than starvation. Edema and other illnesses caused by nutritional deficiencies became widespread. By the time of liberation in February 1945, some 394 of the 3,785 internees had died in captivity—a little more than 10 percent—and most of these deaths occurred in those final few agonizing months. Conditions were dire indeed by the time American tanks broke through the fences; had they arrived much later, they would have found corpses of hundreds of Americans who had starved to death. As it was, photos of the liberated

---

* For comparison, according to the Academy of Nutrition and Dietetics, moderately active American men consume 2,000–2,800 calories per day; moderately active women, 1,800–2,200.

civilians in February 1945 bear a striking resemblance to those of Nazi death camp survivors: prominent ribs, sunken eyes, spindly legs as thin as arms, some already past the point of recovery.

The prosecution's task at trial, of course, was to connect all of this in some way to Yamashita. This was a challenge for several reasons: Yamashita had not set foot in the Philippines until mid-October 1944, eight or nine months into the new and harsher regimen, so clearly he had not instigated it. He had not ameliorated it, either; there was no indication that he had done anything to make it better *or* worse. There was no evidence that he had ever been to Saint Tomas at all or had paid any attention to conditions there, either, in the few days before the American landings on Leyte or afterward. One former internee testified that he had often seen a black Cadillac there, with a Japanese army driver, and "which I am told belonged to General Yamashita." Defense counsel promptly objected to this hearsay, and Reynolds properly sustained the objection, ending the prosecution's only attempt to connect Yamashita to the camp.

The other problem was that, beyond the commandant, the chain of command overseeing civilian internment camps was uncertain, to say the least. "Neither a POW camp nor a temporary transit camp, the internment camps almost defied official classification," wrote one scholar recently, and it is "even more difficult to define the nature of that camp's proper administration." Each commandant, typically a colonel or lieutenant colonel, had virtually unchecked authority to run the camp as he wished, under "a loose, poorly defined state of administrative regulation that made, in essence, every commandant his own rule book." Some were unremittingly harsh; some were reasonably humane; at least one, the commandant of the camp at Baguio, was so esteemed by the internees that he was the guest of honor at their reunion in San Francisco in 1977.

The camps were in fact under civilian control, however ill-defined, until January 1944, when they were transferred to the War Prisoners Department, a Tokyo-based office of the Japanese army's staff, which had responsibility for prisoner-of-war camps and a reputation as a perch for undistinguished officers. There was a significant difference under international law between POWs and civilian internees: POWs were enemy soldiers who could be detained for the duration of the war, but civilians could be interned only for their own safety, and then only until it was safe to release them, or because they posed some security risk to their captors. Neither reason justified the years-long detention at Santo Tomas and the other civilian camps in the Philippines, but that mattered little to Tokyo.

Because the camp commandant was part of the War Ministry, not the Imperial Japanese Army, the role of the army field commander, such as Yamashita, in whose territory the camp sat remained vague; if the commandant of the camp did not raise matters with the field commander (and they seldom did), the commander seldom took notice. There was no independent channel of communication that would enable the commander to determine whether the local commandants were doing their jobs well or poorly or to determine whether the internees were being treated humanely or harshly. Commanders, charged as they were with defeating the enemy, seldom showed any interest in unarmed and confined civilians. Inspections of internment camps were rare; when they did take place (as one did at the Los Baños camp in 1943, 1944, and 1945 and at Santo Tomas in June 1944), protocol called for the local commander to be driven through the area, seldom stopping, then to speak briefly to the commandant before departing.

So when Yamashita took command of army forces on his arrival in October 1944, Santo Tomas and the other civilian camps may or may not have been under even his nominal command; by the time all Japanese forces were administratively transferred to his authority in early January 1945, he had already quit Manila for Baguio. It is not clear whether his order to abandon Manila ever reached the commandant at Santo Tomas, though if it did, he disregarded it. In fact, if there was ever any communication at all between Yamashita and Santo Tomas during the four months between Yamashita's arrival in the Philippines in October and the liberation of Santo Tomas in February, there is no record of it.

Survivors of Santo Tomas, including a dietitian and the camp's in-house historian, described for the commission the increasingly wretched conditions there—diminishing rations, the spread of malnutrition, the scraping of the ground for grass and roots, the abolition of the internees' governing committees, excessive beatings as punishments for infractions. What the five generals heard, as in the preceding days of testimony from Manila survivors, was a compelling picture of suffering and cruelty, but nothing that could illuminate any role of Yamashita.

There was, however, one critical distinction between the tales of suffering at Santo Tomas and the atrocities in the streets and churches of Manila that had occupied the commission for its first two weeks. It was unremarked by the prosecution at the time, but it was unlikely to have been missed by the commissioners. While Yamashita could (and would) plausibly contend that the crimes in Manila during February 1945 had taken place while he was isolated and incommunicado 125 miles away in the hilly forest country at Baguio, he could not say the same for Santo Tomas. He had arrived in Manila on October 7, 1944, and set up his headquarters at Fort McKinley, not far from the Santo Tomas campus, and he remained there until he left for Baguio at the end of December. During those three months, nothing prevented him from visiting Santo Tomas to see for himself the wretched conditions there. Whatever the niceties of the chain of command, it would have been a small matter for the Commanding General of the Fourteenth Area Army to lift the crushing restrictions and restore the relatively free flow of food into the camp. Tokyo would barely have noticed, or cared. Whatever the reason, Yamashita did not do that.

The next day, November 8, was the tenth day of the trial and Yamashita's sixtieth birthday. When Mountz approached him during a recess and asked if he could take some pictures, Yamashita genially complied and Mountz snapped away.

That day and the next, the focus of the trial shifted from Manila down to Batangas, a province about 65 miles south of the capital, as one survivor after another took the stand to tell their story. The suffering at the hands of Japanese soldiers in the spring of 1945 was as real as any suffered in Manila, but the accounts were repetitive and less gripping. The witnesses tended to give short answers to specific questions, rather than engaging the courtroom with dramatic accounts of cruelty and survival as their urban predecessors had. "We are getting our evidence of atrocities in the provinces in," Mountz wrote, "however, they definitely indicate the lack of preparation, especially when compared to the Manila cases where we had time to talk to witnesses and have everything in order. Just another example of why this case was put to trial too soon."

In addition, many of the witnesses testified in Tagalog, which meant everything had to be interpreted, a process aggravated by the official interpreters' unfamiliarity with the Batangas dialect. The defense counsel had a Tagalog speaker at their table and were particularly attuned to mistranslations. There was much ado over a translation of "east" that should have been "west" and over "grassy" rendered as "dirty," all punctuated by sniping among the lawyers over whether the defense was impugning the integrity of the interpreters, some of whom were civilian volunteers who were doing their best to keep up with the lawyers' questions, some of which were hard enough to follow in English.

"Language problems dogged the trial from the start," U.S. Marine major Eugene Boardman, one of the official interpreters, recalled shortly afterward. "No less than eleven languages or dialects were used in the course of the trial. English, Spanish, and dialects of Chinese and Tagalog were heard during the presentation of the case of the prosecution, whereas almost all the witnesses for the defense used Japanese." This presented real problems. "The correct rendering of meanings into understandable Japanese or English was at best a slow and painstaking job," Boardman recalled. "Speed was necessarily a secondary consideration. Even for an educated native, Japanese is a vague language, ill-suited to the niceties and verbosities of legal phraseology. After painful experience with long, involved questions, the trial lawyers learned to use short questions and simple terms."

The commissioners were visibly exasperated by all this—Reynolds said the alleged inaccuracies were all immaterial, which was true enough—but when

Sandberg for the defense pleaded that in a capital case any mistranslation was a serious matter, Reynolds granted his request that a second Filipino interpreter stand by in the courtroom in case future questions arose on the accuracy of translations to or from Tagalog. Tempers cooled, and testimony resumed.

The commission heard from twenty-five witnesses that Friday, the eleventh day of trial in the twelve days since the trial had begun. It took a rare day off on Saturday, November 10, to allow the beleaguered and backlogged court reporters to bring the official transcript up to date. No doubt every actor on the stage welcomed the luxury of a two-day weekend. Yamashita, as always, sat calmly and quietly throughout, listening intently, the all-but-forgotten man in the dramatis personae, on trial for his life.

Robert Trumbull, who was covering the trial for the *New York Times*, took advantage of the off day to file an overview of the legal issues in the trial. "While high Japanese officers such as Gen. Tomoyuki Yamashita, supreme commander in the Philippines for the last eleven months of the war, whose war crimes trial is now in progress, may not themselves have participated in atrocities, they are being held personally accountable," he wrote in the November 11, 1945, edition. "The fundamental theory behind the prosecution of such persons as Yamashita is that the commander is responsible for the actions of troop [*sic*] under his command."

"The trial of General Yamashita," he continued,

> marks the first time a military man has ever been brought before the bar of justice to answer for atrocities committed by his troops in war. This case doubtless is being watched closely by all nations contemplating similar war criminal prosecutions. Interest among students of international law, and of American military law too, is most intense, for the board hearing the Yamashita case is setting precedents for all times.
>
> All precedents in law have been thrown out the window in the Yamashita case, because this trial itself is without precedent. There are no regulations governing the [commission] except those it makes for itself, and it has made very few.
>
> War criminal trials in the Pacific so far are entirely in General MacArthur's hands.
>
> General MacArthur wanted no assistance—or would he call it meddling?—by the War Department's Commission trying the Nazis [a reference to the International Military Tribunal at Nuremberg, then under way]. That point decided, it was apparent to him that the Articles of War do not apply to the Japanese, for they are not members of the United States Armed Forces. Rules governing courts-martial are out—this is not a court-martial. Not even the United States Constitution applies, because the defendants are, of course, enemy aliens.

MacArthur, Trumbull wrote, had issued his "six and a quarter page document [that] contains twenty-two brief, simply phrased regulations, which are the only rules governing the conduct of these trials. The defendant has a right to make his case before the judges [*sic*], who are told they must be impartial. Other rules concern mostly the mechanics of the court."

"The rule of evidence set forth in General MacArthur's directive," Trumbull concluded, "can be boiled down to two words: anything goes."

As the trial headed into its third week, any observer might ask just how many murders, how many rapes and bayonet slashings and burnings, how many demolished homes and churches and convents, how many marauding gangs of Japanese troops the prosecution felt it had to present to prove its case. One might also wonder just when, if ever, Reynolds might lean over the table and ask Kerr, "This is all very tragic, but when are you going to bring the defendant into the picture? When are we going to hear evidence of what General Yamashita did, or did not do, or knew, or permitted, while all this was going on?"

Indeed, aside from the accounts of Lapus and Galang, the prisoners who had Yamashita killing all Filipinos, no evidence had established any discernible connection between Yamashita and the atrocities. No light had yet been shed on just how Yamashita had failed to control his troops, thereby "permitting" the crimes revealed in such horrific detail in the past two weeks. And yet, if one stepped back from the day-to-day parade of witnesses reliving the nightmare of Manila and Batangas, one might perceive that the prosecution's objective was taking shape just as Kerr had promised in his opening statement. Without having presented any evidence, so far, that Yamashita actually knew that any of this was going on, the prosecution was nonetheless painting a picture of havoc so widespread, so horrendous, and so unremitting as to raise the question, could anyone *not* know that this was going on? The prosecution's strategy, it seemed, was to persuade the commission that Yamashita must have known of all this, or even some of this, so it could then point to his failure to stop it—and, self-evidently, he *had* failed to stop it, because it did happen—and from there, to persuade the commission that Yamashita had necessarily "permitted" it to happen.

But that path—"setting precedents for all times," as Trumbull had put it in the *New York Times*—had obstacles. First is the question of knowledge itself. Suppose the prosecution could *not* prove, for whatever reason, that Yamashita "must have known" that these crimes were taking place—perhaps because he was too isolated, or communications were disrupted, or he was under unrelenting attack, or subordinates in Manila were not reporting fully, or all of these. Could he be found guilty for failing to prevent something he did not know was happening? Or could the commission get around that by ruling that he *should* have known what was happening, and therefore would be deemed to have known—treated as if he did know, whether he did or not? Yet could one conclude that he should have known, if there was no evidence that he was somehow at fault for not knowing? Or could one simply say that every commander should *always* know what his troops are doing, and therefore it matters not whether he was negligent in failing to know? None of these questions was being raised, much less discussed, by prosecutors, defense counsel, or the commissioners.

Beyond knowledge, there is also the question of power, or ability. As commanding general, Yamashita had the authority to issue orders to his troops, but after his departure from Manila at the end of December 1944 and until his surrender on September 3, 1945, did he have the actual ability to do so? Suppose that Yamashita did know what was happening in Manila and Batangas and elsewhere. Would the prosecution have to show that he would have been able to stop it—that, for example, he had functioning staff support, adequate radios, intact telephone lines, and at least a minimal chain of command and understanding of the tactical situation, so that he was actually able to communicate orders had he chosen to do so? And what if he had issued clear and explicit orders that if obeyed would have prevented or terminated the criminal activity—was he to be held accountable nonetheless if those orders were not passed on, or were even countermanded, by subordinate commanders?

These questions, too, went unremarked in the trial, as the prosecution churned into its third week.

Testimony resumed on the Batangas events, as the five generals heard survivors describe a ghastly episode in which Japanese soldiers shoved some 400 men beneath a large house, then dynamited it, then poured kerosene on the writhing bodies, and set them ablaze. The prosecution followed this with a massacre of some fifty villagers in Rosario on March 13, 1945; as to that, prosecutor Pace offered into evidence "the official report of the investigators of the War Crimes Branch for [the Pacific] theater, also supported by the statements of witnesses." And that was to be the sole evidence the prosecution intended to present on that episode—no witnesses would be called.

The defense objected, advancing a new perspective on out-of-court statements. Not only did basing the entire Rosario case on a written report deprive the accused of any opportunity to cross-examine, it also deprived the commission of its ability to carry out *its* responsibilities. "This is a report of the War Crimes Branch," Sandberg pointed out. "It is a self-serving document of the prosecution. It is full of conclusions, both of fact and of law. It, in effect, amounts to a usurpation by the prosecution of the functions of the commission to make the findings of fact in this case, and to make the conclusions of law."

It was a fair point: how could the commissioners determine the accuracy or the thoroughness of the investigators' report? How could they assess the credibility of those who were interviewed? How could they know if there was more to the story than what the investigators chose to put in their report? If the prosecution considered the Rosario crimes worth proving, why should it not call witnesses? Sandberg could even have gone a step further: the procedure not only usurped the commission's function but showed a certain disdain for it: "Here's the report," the prosecution seemed to say—"it's true because it comes from the prosecution's own investigators; you don't need to know anything else."

Kerr responded in a decidedly curious way. He pulled out the "Royal Warrant Given at the Court of St. James this 14th day of June, 1945, the Ninth Year of Our Reign by His Majesty's command"—the regulations governing British war crimes trials. He read from them at length, to show the commissioners that "these regulations are far broader than the regulations which have been prescribed by [MacArthur] for the regulation of this and other American military commissions in this theater."

The point was a dubious one—MacArthur's regulations allowed the commission to consider anything under the sun, and the British regulations could hardly be broader than that—but Kerr emphasized, oddly, that "hearsay of the most flagrant type is admissible before the British commissions." That likewise was not true—the British regulations allowed out-of-court statements "in particular if [the] witness is dead or unable to attend," a condition that MacArthur's rules omitted. Yet Kerr went on to argue that the British rule "refutes the frequent innuendoes and charges by defense counsel that the regulations covering this commission are unreasonable, unconscionable, and far broader than any other civilized government would prescribe"—a characterization that exaggerated the actual defense contention, which was that the regulations were unfair and inconsistent with American judicial standards. "It is well known," Kerr went on in another dubious assertion, "that the British government is very particular about its method of administering justice, and its standards are extremely high in that regard, and yet we find that, for the same and obvious reasons as govern here, they have seen fit to prescribe an even broader standard of evidence, an even broader set of regulations than this commission is governed by."

Reynolds, who had made it abundantly clear that the commission intended to follow the regulations that it had been given and who had not heretofore expressed the slightest curiosity about what His Majesty the King might be doing, politely noted that "we have been favored by lengthy arguments on this matter from the beginning of the trial" and that the investigators' report would be received in evidence for—as usual—"such probative value as the commission may decide to award to it."

The twelfth day's testimony of the horrors in Batangas plodded on throughout the morning. When the commission returned after lunch, Reynolds made an announcement that seemed to come out of the blue. "The commission wishes to introduce the following statement," he began, and then went on:

> The commission will grant a continuance only for the most urgent and unavoidable reasons. The trial has now consumed two weeks of time. The prosecution indicates that this week will be required to finish its presentation. Early in the trial the commission invited senior defense counsel to apply for additional assistants in such numbers as necessary to avoid the necessity for a continuance. The commission is still willing to ask that additional counsel be provided, for we do not wish to entertain a request for a continuance. The commission questions either the necessity or desirability for all members of counsel being present during all of the presentation of the case for the prosecution. We feel that one or two members of the defense staff in the courtroom is adequate and that the remaining member or members should be out of the courtroom performing specific missions for senior counsel. It directs both prosecution and defense to so organize and direct the preparation and presentation of their cases, including the use of assistants, to the end that need to request a continuance may not arise.
>
> As a further means of saving time, both prosecution and defense are directed to institute procedures by which the commission is provided essential facts without a mass of nonessentials and immaterial details. We want to know, one, what was done, two, where it was done, three, when it was done, four, who was involved. Go swiftly and directly to the target so the commission can obtain a clear-cut and accurate understanding of essential facts. Cross-examination must be limited to essentials and avoid useless repetition of questions and answers already before the commission. We are not interested in trivialities or minutiae of events or opinions. Except in unusual or extremely important matters the commission will itself determine the credibility of witnesses. Extended cross-examinations which savor of fishing expeditions to determine possible attacks upon the credibility of witnesses serve no useful purpose and will be avoided.

"The purpose of this statement by the commission," Reynolds concluded, "is to inform both prosecution and defense of our wishes and to direct prompt and effective steps to be taken to carry them into effect."

The edict had not come out of the blue, exactly. It had come out of Tokyo. MacArthur had directed Carpenter, his war crimes chief, theater judge advocate, and overseer of the trial, to allow no continuation that would give the defense more time to prepare. His deputy chief of staff, speaking for MacArthur, sent word to Manila that the Supreme Commander was "disturbed by reports of [a] possible recess" and doubted that the defense needed more time. He reiterated, as if anyone in Manila needed reminding, that MacArthur "desires proceedings completed earliest practicable date." Carpenter too had weighed in, emphasizing that MacArthur was opposed to any continuance. He wanted all trials in the Pacific theater to be "pushed to prompt conclusions, regardless [of] whether [the] first conviction [*sic*]" was of Yamashita or some "small fry."

Reynolds never acknowledged that this ruling and perhaps others were being dictated by MacArthur, but his announcement was nonetheless peculiar, for it seemed to place the blame for the prolongation of the trial on defense counsel, though the entire two weeks of trial had been organized and presented by the prosecution, which had lined up over 100 different accusations in its two bills of particulars and had frequently called four or five witnesses to testify to the same event. It was true that much of the cross-examination had been unfocused and at times repetitive, but the defense lawyers had never seen the witnesses before they took their seats, had never heard their stories, had never spoken to them to find out what else they might know or not know. Cross-examination was their first and only chance to address them. If the cross-examination sometimes "savor[ed] of fishing expeditions," it was because defense counsel had been allowed no earlier opportunity to test the waters.

The jab at the number of defense lawyers in the room was also below the belt: there were no more of them than there were prosecutors, and, as with the prosecutors, each member of the defense team had been responsible for preparing particular parts of the case and undertaking the questioning of those witnesses. To date, the prosecutors, with the benefit of several months of interviews and teams of criminal investigators, had presented their case on some forty specifications; to expect "one or two members" of the defense team, who had neither investigators nor preparation time, to handle all that themselves was unreasonable and unrealistic. Preparation is the most detailed, exacting, and time-consuming responsibility a trial lawyer faces; a death penalty case increases exponentially the importance of preparation. To undertake a complex, fact-intensive, six-week trial, eight hours a day, six days a week, three weeks after being appointed, given no investigators, is a staggering task; no sane lawyer would do it voluntarily, even if the case were not capital, and even if the legal principles were well settled, which in this case they assuredly were not.

The offer of additional defense counsel was a hollow one. It had been hard enough to draft the original six lawyers, one of whom, George Guy, had in fact been in Japan for the past several weeks, trying to locate and interview possible character witnesses to testify on Yamashita's behalf. Bringing in new lawyers midway through the trial, even if they could be found, would have required a significant investment of time in educating them, assigning tasks to them, coordinating them, and communicating with them, and time was the defense's scarcest resource.

But the sharpest blow was the commission's announcement that there would be no continuance—no opportunity for defense counsel to prepare their case after the prosecutors had presented theirs. On the first day of trial, when Reel had requested a two-week continuance so the defense could respond to the last-minute supplemental bill of particulars, he had pointed to MacArthur's regulations, which gave the accused the right to have a statement of the charges and specifications "in advance of trial." "This phrase obviously means sufficiently in advance of trial to allow the defense to prepare itself," Reel had argued, rightly enough. The commission had denied the request at that point. "However," Reynolds had said in doing so, "at the end of the presentation by the prosecution of evidence concerning [the original bill of particulars], the commission will consider such a motion."

Indeed, as recently as six days earlier, on the eighth day of trial, when Clarke had pleaded an inability to prepare fully for each day, Reynolds had assured him that the commission understood the "tremendous task which we placed upon the defense" and promised, "We will see to it that you get time to prepare your defense."

Reynolds had just tossed that promise out the window. The prosecution's case was going slowly, so the defense would lose its continuance. Nowhere in his admonition had Reynolds urged the prosecution to wind up its case expeditiously, to cut back on the number of repetitive witnesses, or perhaps to relate at least some of the evidence to Yamashita. Also curious was Reynolds's statement that the commission would determine the credibility of witnesses "except in unusual or extremely important matters." Of course, the commission's responsibility is always to determine the credibility of witnesses, *especially* in "important matters"; it is inherently part of the adjudicative function. Reynolds might have meant that except in "important matters" it did not wish to take time to hear cross-examination attacking the credibility of a witness, but that would be exceedingly irresponsible: no judge can disregard the issue of whether or not a witness is telling the truth.

In any case, Reynolds's directive evidently had little impact on the prosecution; when he had concluded, it called a witness to testify to murders in the same Batangas village that four witnesses in the morning had described, and it followed with four written statements of other villagers there, pertinent parts of which it read aloud—all without any eliciting any show of impatience on the part of the commissioners.

The rest of the day was taken up with seven more witnesses, most of whom testified as to executions and rapes, particularly against an extended ethnic Chinese family, in the province of Laguna, some 35 miles southeast of Manila. "Ang Kim Ling, the youngest witness in the first twelve days of the trial [he was ten], came to the witness stand holding the hand of his eight-year old sister Alicia," reported Mac Johnson of the *New York Herald Tribune*.

Gripping the sides of the chair, he told his story while his sister stood behind him, fascinated by the whirling motion-picture cameras and the pop-
ping of flash-bulbs. Sometimes crying, sometimes biting his lips, Ang Kim
Ling, through his interpreter, described how four generations of his family
were killed by the Japanese last February at Los Banos, in Lagunas Province.

Little Alicia lifted her black dress and showed the court sixteen scars
from bayonet thrusts. The audience of American soldiers gasped as every
one wondered how the girl survived the wounds, nearly any one of which
could have proved fatal.

Of the eight witnesses the prosecution called after the commission's warning,
the defense did not cross-examine five at all; cross-examination of the other
three consumed less than four pages of transcript in the ninety pages of the
afternoon's work. Adjourning for the day, Reynolds was pleased. "The commission would like to observe that the rate of progress this afternoon was very
satisfactory, conducted very, very smoothly, and we wish to commend both the
prosecution and the defense accordingly."

The next day started off routinely enough, with the prosecution calling survivors of the civilian internment camp at Los Baños, south of Manila, a smaller
version of the camp at Santo Tomas. Food there was likewise in short supply in
1944 and 1945, but most of the testimony focused on the death of an American who was shot by guards as he was attempting to slip back into the camp
after making some forbidden food purchases in the nearby village. The internee
committee typed up formal letters of protest to the camp commandant, analyzing the Geneva Conventions to conclude, accurately enough, that although
an internee could lawfully be shot while attempting to escape from a camp,
Geneva made it unlawful to shoot him on his way back in. Just what, under any
theory, connected this fatal shot to Yamashita was, as usual, unexplained by the
prosecution and unexplored by the commission.

After the lunch recess, the defense dropped a bombshell. They asked to
put on a witness of their own, because he "may leave the Islands shortly." The
witness was a fourteen-year-old boy named Bislumino Romero. Testifying in
Japanese ("I can speak, read and write Japanese," he affirmed), he told the commission that he had come to the Philippines from Japan in 1942 to live with his
grandfather. "What is the name of your grandfather?" asked Sandberg.

"Artemio Ricarte," said the boy.

"Is that General Artemio Ricarte?"

"Yes."

This was the lad whom Galang had identified as the interpreter of Yamashita's vow to kill all the Filipinos.

Under questioning from Sandberg, young Bislumino testified that his grandfather did not speak Japanese and that he, the grandson, sometimes did interpret for him. He knew Galang—"my grandfather's friend"—and he had seen Yamashita, once, on the streets of Manila, recognizing him from his photograph.

"Is that the only time in your life that you have ever seen General Yamashita?" Sandberg asked.

"Aside from that I have never seen him," the boy replied.

"Did you ever see General Yamashita at your grandfather's house?"

"I have never seen such a thing."

"Did you ever interpret anything that General Yamashita said?"

"There is no such occasion."

Sandberg drove to the bull's-eye. "Joaquin Galang has told this commission that you interpreted a conversation with General Yamashita at your grandfather's house. Is that statement true or false?"

"That is a lie."

"Joaquin Galang has told this commission that you quoted General Yamashita as having said, 'All Filipinos are guerillas and even the people who are supposed to be under Ricarte.'"

"I have never had occasion to translate anything like that, even once."

"Did your grandfather ever say in your presence to General Yamashita, 'I would like to take this occasion to ask again for you to revoke your order to kill all the Filipinos and to destroy all the city?'"

"I have never heard anything like that."

"Did your grandfather ever tell you that General Yamashita had ordered the massacre of the Filipino people?"

"Nothing like that was said," the boy answered. "And I believe that if my grandfather knew that all the Filipinos were going to be killed that it would not be reasonable for him to leave me living in the city" when he left with Yamashita to go to Baguio in December 1944.

"And what," concluded Sandberg, "is your reason for telling this story to the commission?"

"I know that any talk that my grandfather and General Yamashita talked together is a lie, and I came here today hoping to prove that."

Sandberg turned to the prosecutor. "Your witness," he said.

Just like that, the momentum had shifted, and the prosecution knew it. Their witness Galang had just been blown up in their faces. Now it was they who faced the prospect of cross-examining a witness whom they had never seen before and whose testimony had been explicit and credible. They had been under the impression that the boy was dead—"a bad slip on our part in not checking it carefully," Mountz ruefully noted. "It was not a pleasant situation for the prosecution, and Kerr was disgusted and sick about it."

Captain Hill was an experienced prosecutor—he had been the U.S. Attorney in Kansas before the war—but he had no clue on how to cross-examine this witness, so he wisely avoided doing much at all. He did get the boy to acknowledge that he had once said that he wanted Japan to defeat the United States—hardly a surprising or damaging sentiment for a boy who had lived his first twelve years in Japan with his Japanophile grandfather.

The defense had scored by far its most significant blow of the trial, but the good fortune had not just fallen into their lap. Deeply troubled by the testimony of Galang and Lapus, however suspicious their stories may have been, defense attorneys Clarke, Reel, and Sandberg had gone the following day to New Bilibid Prison, the holding pen for Galang and Lapus and other suspected collaborators, and there they located another Filipino who had worked with Ricarte. He found the "kill all Filipinos" tale ludicrous when he was told of it, but more importantly he said that the grandson might still be alive and in the Philippines—a surprise to the defense lawyers, who had been told by the prosecutors that the boy had not survived.

The three lawyers took off with the aid of a local guide on "a devious journey afoot through rice paddies and carabao wallows" to "a small shack hidden behind the wreckage of some blasted school buildings," where they found the boy. The boy listened to the lawyers' questions and told them what he would later tell the commission. In ten minutes, the defense had obliterated the only evidence so far that, however dubiously, had actually linked Yamashita personally to the horrors that Japanese troops had committed.

In 1974, Kerr revealed that he had called Lapus and Galang "against my better judgment." Their testimony, he said, "was not a part of or in accordance with my general trial plans." He admitted that he had "uneasily acquiesced in the recommendation of one of the assistant prosecutors that they be permitted to testify," and "high Philippine government officials were most insistent" that he do so. Because the commission was rushing the trial, he explained, he put the two witnesses on "without having opportunity to follow our usual procedure of checking and verifying the testimony" of the prosecution's witnesses. Even so, he maintained twenty-nine years after the trial, "I am unable to form any strong opinion as to the truth or falsity" of their testimony.

Few others seemed to have such doubts. Bislumino's "unaffected, childlike spontaneity presented so brilliant a contrast to the appearance and manner of the two collaborators," recalled Reel afterward, "that not a soul in the courtroom could doubt his honesty." The boy's "alert appearance and obvious intelligence held the spectators' attention," noted Cromie of the *Chicago Daily Tribune*. "His story completely threw down the testimony of Joaquin Galang."

11

The Prosecution
The Conclusion

In the final week of its case, the prosecution was clearly showing signs of the punishing pace of the trial—thirteen full days of testimony with only four days off. What had been for the most part a compelling and organized presentation now faltered. After young Bislumino Romero left the stand, the prosecution called—as if more evidence of murder, rape, and carnage were needed—Leonardo Palicte, a young man from the island of Cebu, in the south central Philippines, some 400 miles from Manila. There, on March 27, 1945, shortly after the Americans had landed on that distant island—three months after Yamashita had abandoned Manila for the hills of northern Luzon—Palicte's family had been slaughtered by Japanese soldiers. He had been away from the house that day and returned to find, in the cellar, "the charred remains of the members of my family—eleven skulls, and the remains of my kid brother who was barely three months old."

Over the strenuous objections of defense counsel, the prosecutors submitted the transcript of a U.S. Army investigator's interrogation of a Japanese prisoner of war, given a few days before the trial had begun, in which he described conversations he had overheard one night between four soldiers who, he said, had inflicted the carnage on the Palicte family. It was a spectacular quadruple leap of hearsay—an absent investigator relating what he had heard from an interpreter relating an account of a Japanese soldier who had allegedly overheard four missing and presumably dead persons, for the purpose of proving what had happened at the Palicte home. It teemed with repellent details of rape. According to the statement of the investigator, the POW had said that the four soldiers "proudly" told of burning the house on the orders of a sergeant, and repeatedly raping four "beautiful girls" as young as thirteen years of age who "screamed" and "wept and [were] very pitiful" as each of the four raped each of the four girls.

It was an ugly account of a sickening day of crime that no one outside the village, much less a general on Luzon, could possibly have known about, but the commission took it all in with no sign of impatience and admitted the entire account of what the investigator said the interpreter said the POW said the soldiers said about the rapes.

That done, the prosecution's case returned to Manila and to one of its recurring themes: rape, murder, and desecration in a church. This time, the church was the Manila Metropolitan Cathedral-Basilica in Intramuros. There, on February 5, as American troops were pressing forward on the northern edge of the city, Japanese forces rounded up, according to the first witness, as many as 4,000 or 5,000 people, and then soldiers "went inside the cathedral and they were going around pulling girls outside of the cathedral, and I saw two Japanese raping those women right there in the cathedral, and one by my side, she is pregnant five months." She went on, "I have seen plenty of girls that they were taking outside of the cathedral, they are very young. 'No, don't! Mama, don't let them take me!' Those girls are shouting like that." The next day, "I have seen girls there that were shot by the Japanese. The next morning, they took all our men; they took my husband. That is the last time I have seen my husband." A second witness told a virtually identical story of rapes in the cathedral, including those of pregnant women, as the generals listened patiently.

The morning of the fourteenth day of the trial was taken up with a laborious effort by the prosecution to prove, through a chain of witnesses, that an American pilot, evidently shot down on Cebu, was executed by a squad of Japanese soldiers or military police under the command of a captain. In the afternoon, the prosecution swung the spotlight back to Batangas, the site of testimony a few days earlier, to bring forward two women who testified that they were raped by Japanese soldiers. That testimony was taken behind closed doors to spare them the recounting of their ordeal in public. When the doors were opened, a witness took the stand to testify about atrocities she had witnessed. "One of my sisters is pregnant," she testified, weeping. "And they slashed her stomach open and when the baby came out they cut its head off."

When she had finished, Reynolds turned to the defense table. "Is cross-examination of this witness considered essential?" he asked. No, said the defense. As to whether examination of this witness in the first place was essential, Reynolds said nothing.

The prosecution spent the rest of the day putting on testimony from several witnesses, including a nun, about the atrocities at Fort Santiago, about which the eleven-year-old Rosalinda Andoy had testified a few days earlier, and concluded the day with a sheaf of reports on the situation, compiled by army investigators, whose presence was not required. Reynolds admitted them "for such probative value as the commission may award to it."

When Clarke and his defense team went through the reports that night, they were astonished, and deeply concerned, at what they found in one of them. It was an eight-page report written by a U.S. Army colonel who had been sent out into Manila in the final climactic days of the carnage, on February 26, 1945, "to sort out fact from fancy in the many reports of mass atrocities against civilians in Intramuros committed by the Imperial Japanese Forces." In his report five weeks later, his conclusions were concise: "Some 2,000 Filipinos, mostly men, were murdered in Fort Santiago—starved, shot, bayoneted, or burned to death between 3 and 15 February 1945."

He limited his report, however, to three events. "Between 100 and 140 white men, principally Spaniards and including some 37 members of the Catholic clergy were buried alive" in Plaza McKinley. Second, "women were hunted and violated nightly in the Church of St. Augustin by prowling Japanese soldiers and laborers." Finally, patients were taken from hospitals and murdered, and Manila residents seeking refuge at Santa Rosa College were murdered. Only these three atrocities were covered, the investigator wrote,

in order that their magnitude may not be overshadowed by extraneous evidence of less wholesale examples of Japanese savagery. . . .

Every one who escaped can tell a tale of horror; some by factual coherent reports which amaze the hearer no less by their frightfulness than by the matter-of-fact, dispassionate recital of events; others can only babble disconnected incidents, some actual, some imagined or told to them by others, of 20 days which except for their emaciation, their wounds, the loss of family, friends and everything they owned, is to them more like a terrifying nightmare than a real chapter from their lives.

Volumes of evidence could be gathered and authenticated, evidence of wanton cruelty, bestiality and bloodthirstiness that stagger the imagination, but the facts documented in this report are amply convincing to the investigating officer that the destruction of Intramuros, the slaughter of most of its male inhabitants over 14 years of age and the fiendish abuse of its women was not only countenanced by the Japanese command, but planned in advance and diabolically carried out under supervision of officers. . . .

It is conceivable that a commander of a confined area like Intramuros might find his defense impeded by a mob of panic-stricken civilians and that casualties among them might be heavy during an intense action. No such extenuating circumstances can be discovered to lessen the guilt of the Japanese in this abominable crime. . . . The inescapable conclusion from the facts revealed by this investigation . . . is that the Japanese high command intends to fight this war without any regard for rules of warfare, civilized or otherwise; and that similar wholesale acts of fiendish inhumanity against

non-Japanese civilians, even nationals of neutral white nations, may be expected as our forces drive the Jap from territory he now occupies.

The report was pure hearsay, and largely double hearsay, and for all its anguished
prose it added little to the evidence of atrocities in Manila that the commission had been hearing for fourteen days. What alarmed the lawyers more than
the victims' accounts was a brief excerpt of a Japanese radio transmission, intercepted and translated by MacArthur's Allied Translator and Interpreter Section (ATIS), an Australian-American unit largely made up of American Nisei
soldiers, whose accounts of Japanese documents and transmissions was authoritative. According to the report, ATIS translated the transmission as: "The
Americans who have penetrated into Manila have about 1,000 artillery troops,
and there are several thousand Filipino guerrillas. Even women and children
have become guerillas. All people on the battlefield with the exception of Japanese military personnel, Japanese civilians and Special constructions (Ganaps
in the Filipino language) will be put to death."

The investigator characterized the order as an "extract from an order of the
Kobayashi group," and that characterization was critical to the issues of the trial.
Major General Takashi Kobayashi reported to Lieutenant General Shizuo Yokoyama—and Yokoyama answered directly to Yamashita. Kobayashi's force was
northeast of Manila, part of Yokoyama's Shimbu Group, and was charged with
delaying the American Sixth Army advance to Manila while Japanese forces
evacuated the city pursuant to Yamashita's order. But if the order was read as
directing that "all people" in Manila, even the "women and children [who]
have become guerrillas" were to be "put to death," it was troubling indeed for
the defense. The order might have come from Yamashita. At the least, Yamashita
might have known about it and not countermanded it.

But a careful reading of the report and the accompanying ATIS translation
revealed a gap: despite the investigator's assertion, nowhere had ATIS identified
the unit sending the message. ATIS concluded only that the message had been
"transmitted on a radio circuit to the Japanese forces," that it had been sent "on
the frequency of the Japanese radio circuit," and that "there is reasonable assurance that the message was received."

But who had sent it? "It is apparent, sir," said Reel to Reynolds, "that there
is no clear evidence that this particular order came from the Kobayashi group."
The objection seemed to give Reynolds some pause, but he admitted the report anyway for whatever it meant, as usual giving no hint as to what that might
be, but suggesting to Reel that he might want to file something in writing
specifying the parts he objected to.

That done, the prosecution called its next witness, a twenty-five-year-old
U.S. Army sergeant named Richard Sakakida, who had a most unusual story.

Born in Hawaii to Japanese parents, he had joined the army nine months before Pearl Harbor; he was stationed in the Philippines when the Japanese attacked, and he had been among those surrendered at Corregidor in the spring of 1942. Afraid that he might be put to death if the Japanese discovered he was a Nisei soldier in the U.S. Army, he passed himself off as a civilian interpreter and was sent to work in the court-martial section of the Fourteenth Area Army, in what became Yamashita's headquarters when Yamashita arrived in October 1944.

Thin and soft-spoken, his eyes behind dark aviator glasses, Sakakida sat motionless and emotionless as he described the Japanese court-martial procedure. It wasn't much. Whether the defendant was a Japanese soldier, a Filipino civilian, or, a few times, a captured American, the military police compiled a dossier and then met with the lawyers in the court-martial section to decide the charge, the verdict, and the sentence. That done, the court-martial was convened and the accused was brought in, for the first time. He could enter a plea, or not; it made no difference. The judge announced the verdict and sentence. No witnesses, no counsel, no appeal. The whole process took only a few minutes. If the prosecution's objective was to show that military justice in the Japanese army in the Philippines was a sham, they succeeded. The point was relevant to forestall any claim by the defense that alleged Filipino guerrillas received an actual trial before they were executed.

But Sakakida's testimony was misleading. He testified that he had been at Yamashita's headquarters when Yamashita had arrived, and he had moved with the headquarters to Baguio in December 1944. Asked by the prosecutor, "And then where did you go?" Sakakida answered, "From there we headed to Kiangan" in April 1945.

"Did you remain there until the surrender in September 1945?"

"Yes, sir," replied Sakakida.

But in his autobiography, published in 1995, Sakakida told a different story. When the headquarters moved to Kiangan in April, he pocketed a few pouches of rice and slipped away into the jungle, looking for the American lines. With no map or compass, he quickly became lost. Foraging on plants, he wandered aimlessly through the jungle for months, sick, hungry, and disoriented, until he stumbled on an American patrol searching for Japanese stragglers. That's when he learned that the war was over. It had ended in August.

"I was momentarily stupefied," Sakakida wrote in his autobiography. "'What month is it now?' I asked in a somewhat embarrassed tone. 'It's September 1945' [the American soldiers] replied. I was shocked. I had been wandering around since April, delirious from hunger, illness, and my wounds and I had lost all track of time."

None of this came out at trial, and it is doubtful that the prosecution knew of it. The defense and the commissioners surely did not know. Why Sakakida

concealed it, even to the point of stating that he had gone to Kiangan and remained there, is a mystery, as is the absence in his autobiography of any mention
of the Yamashita trial. Because most of his testimony was focused on Japanese
courts-martial (or the pretense of same) in Manila prior to the December 1944
decampment to Baguio, it might be said that his lie about remaining with Yamashita's headquarters until September and his concealment of his escape in
April 1945 were immaterial.

But Sakakida made another point in his testimony. A few days earlier, he
said, he had been approached by his former boss, Colonel Hideo Nishiharu,
the head of the court-martial staff under Yamashita, now a prisoner in Bilibid
Prison. Nishiharu asked Sakakida if he were going to testify against Yamashita.
Sakakida said no one had asked him to. Then, he testified, Nishiharu said to
him, "Why, you better not, because the general—I have seen the general a
few days ago and we had a conversation about you, saying that the general
was pretty much worried if you should testify against him at the trial" because
Sakakida knew the activities of the Japanese army during the occupation.

Reel jumped to his feet and objected. This was hearsay, he argued, and besides, "General Yamashita has been in this building* and the person referred to
has not been here."

Kerr replied, "This is evidence that parties close to the accused were endeav-
oring to influence the prosecution's witnesses not to appear in the case." He did
not actually say that it was Yamashita himself who was allegedly trying to get to
witnesses, but the commissioners no doubt got the point.

Reynolds sustained Reel's objection and ordered the testimony stricken.
Undaunted, the prosecution attempted to work around the point with another
quadruple leap. It called a military police lieutenant, who testified that he had
been with Sakakida when he had spoken to Nishiharu—the conversation was in
Japanese—and that Sakakida had then related the conversation to him. As Reel
put it in his objection to the lieutenant's testimony: "The witness, who does not
understand what was said, is told by a second party [Sakakida] what a third party
[Nishiharu] told him that a fourth party said," the fourth party being Yamashita,
though neither Sakakida nor the lieutenant had actually attributed anything to
Yamashita, only to Nishiharu, and even that was more frets than threats.

In any event, Reynolds got it. The lieutenant's testimony was stricken, as
Sakakida's had been. The attempt to show witness tampering had failed.

That evening, one of the strangest scenes of the entire trial was played in the

---

* At the beginning of the trial, Yamashita had been moved from Old Bilibid Prison to
rooms in the High Commissioner's Residence so that he could meet with his attorneys and
need only walk downstairs each day to the trial. He was under twenty-four-hour surveillance, and only authorized visitors were allowed.

ballroom of the High Commissioner's Residence. The prosecution showed a thirty-minute Technicolor movie entitled *Orders from Tokyo*, produced by Warner Brothers Pictures and the Office of Strategic Services (OSS), the U.S. wartime intelligence agency, for the Philippine government.

The subject of the film, ostensibly, was the Battle of Manila in February 1945—"a flaming spectacle of Manila's death agony" in the reportage of the *New York Times*. And if there was any question about the film's objectivity, it did not last long. The film displayed its title in faux-Japanese script, dripping blood, against a brick wall showing the shadow of a gallows. The camera opened on Carlos Romulo, the Philippine resident commissioner in the United States, seated at a desk in a blue uniform. In a grave voice, Romulo told the audience that the film would show the "savage premeditated destruction of Manila" based on "orders from Tokyo." "We will inevitably bring to trial those responsible for this crime," Romulo promised, "the leaders of a nation devoid of all human decency. This film will be part of the evidence that will convict these criminals." He paused. "Manila is the price of Philippine loyalty to America."

An unidentified narrator then took over as the camera panned street scenes of a tranquil, prewar Manila—"the city we loved," said the narrator, "a city of happy people, free people, carefree people." There were long shots of Christmas shoppers in a department store, complete with Santa Claus, and a wedding in a cathedral. There followed home movies of a Christmas Eve scene at "the home of my friends [the narrator's, evidently] the Reyes family." A child played "Silent Night" on the piano as the family sat around, Dad reading the newspaper and Mother looking on fondly. Abruptly, bursting bombs interrupted the domestic scene. The narrator pinned the blame just where it belonged: "General Yamashita had requested orders from Tokyo. This was Tokyo's answer. Here was Japan's revenge for Philippine loyalty to America."

There was extensive footage of U.S. troops shelling the city, advancing through its streets with machine guns, rifles, mortars, and artillery, advancing "room by room, Jap by Jap." The National Assembly, City Hall, and the post office were "Jap fortresses." American soldiers were shown warily pushing over corpses of "fanatical" Japanese soldiers. "No one could be trusted," the narrator went on, "even in death."

Manila became a "chamber of horrors" as the "Japs pulled the city down in ruins." Civilians were shown frantically dashing for cover—"witnesses to the sack of the greatest Christian city in the Orient." One couple was forced to watch "a squad of Japs enter the Red Cross building and murder their children." The narrator went on, "There was no excuse for this suicide stand." MacArthur was shown, touring the devastation in a jeep.

But the kicker was yet to come. "Then the shocking discovery!" An American soldier approaches a corpse in the ruins of a church and crouches beside it.

He mops the sweat from his forehead and takes from the corpse's military jacket what appears to be a paperback book or journal about two inches thick. He fans the pages. The narrator explains: "On a Jap dead was found documented proof of orders from the Japanese Supreme Command for the systematic massacre of Manila's citizens and the complete destruction of the city."

The movie went on to show the nuns of St. Augustin, including "Mother Superior," being attended by U.S. soldiers. Women and children are shown being carried on stretchers. U.S. soldiers are shown exhausted from combat. "Here was Coventry, Rotterdam, Warsaw, Lidice"—all locales of Nazi devastation in Europe—"Here was Manila." Bodies of civilians are shown, mostly women and babies, some dismembered, some with hands tied behind their back. The camera lingers on those deceased who are wearing crucifixes.

Ruins of stately buildings, universities, stores ("No more Christmas shopping here," intones the narrator), and, especially, churches. "What kind of warfare is the shooting of children at prayer? What kind of warfare is the burning alive of men and women?" The camera pans over more grisly scenes of murder victims. "What kind of warfare is the cold-blooded murder of civilians with hands tied behind them?" Two bodies at the base of a statue outside a church. "What kind of warfare is a bayoneted mother and child at the feet of the Virgin Mary?"*

The movie ends with suitable melodrama. An emaciated boy is shown limping unsteadily down an empty street. "Look well at this evidence, young man, for it will hang the warlords of Japan." But because of the Filipinos' "unconquerable spirit and determination to rebuild the city the Japs destroyed—a pledge born in blood to freedom at long last fulfilled—a new nation is born in the Pacific." The camera pans over the steeple of a church in the sunset and "The Battle Hymn of the Republic" plays triumphantly as the movie fades to black.

There was nothing subtle about any of it. The sack of Manila was an attack on Christianity itself. It was a premeditated campaign of atrocities, requested by Yamashita and ordered by "Tokyo." The Filipinos paid a high price for their loyalty to America.

The footage itself was genuine, and as anyone could attest who had spent a day in Manila in February 1945—or a day at the trial in the past two weeks— the atrocities were real and gruesome enough. But the film made no effort to describe the events in any logical order or documentary fashion. It was a mosaic of American soldiers, grateful Filipinos, dead bodies, destroyed buildings, desecrated churches, devastated monuments. There was no sense of time.

---

* Like many of the atrocities it dwelt upon, the film's religious focus may have reflected MacArthur's own fixation on the religion of the Filipinos. "A Christian nation, the Philippines stand as a mighty bulwark of Christianity in the Far East," he told Congress in 1951.

The atrocities, given the way scenes were spliced, might have all taken place on Christmas Day.

The "orders from Tokyo" were of course completely phony. Whatever the American soldier was thumbing through, it was not a plan "for the systematic massacre of Manila's citizens and the complete destruction of the city" or for anything else. There was never any such "order," never any "plan" for systematic massacre. The prosecution never produced anything resembling such an order from anyone, from Tokyo or anywhere else.

Though they had obtained the film a month before the trial, the prosecutors had never disclosed it to the defense, perhaps because they knew the "evidence" was fraudulent. Previewing the film before the trial began, Mountz wrote in a letter home that it was "a colored movie on the burning & destruction of Manila. There is a lot of propaganda in it but the scenes & destruction are real. It has little or no value as far as war crimes trials are concerned as most of the claimed evidence even including the *order* are unsubstantiated in fact" (emphasis in the original).

The film was a public-relations piece intended for a U.S. Audience, designed to boost the image of Filipinos as a long-suffering, freedom-loving Christian people who had endured much carnage in the war, and particularly in Manila, at the savage hands of America's enemy. That message was truthful enough.

But as evidence in a trial? To show that Yamashita had "requested" these "orders from Tokyo"? That he had ordered the "systematic massacre" of which the commissioners had heard so much? That these words of Hollywood screenwriters and OSS propagandists were to be submitted as actual evidence of Yamashita's guilt? The prosecution could not be serious.

The prosecution was very serious. When court opened the next morning, a shaken Captain Sandberg for the defense stood to address the generals. "If the commission please," he began,

> the defense realizes very keenly that no objection it can now make to the motion pictures [*sic*] shown last night will alter the fact that the commission has already seen and heard them. That is a fact which cannot be undone. But we must protest very strongly that the showing of this film, with its highly inflammatory commentary, was highly prejudicial to the accused, and is not at all conducive to the calm, dispassionate sifting of the facts which has always been the cornerstone of American justice.
>
> And we make this statement: If the United States forces have such an order as the film says they have, it is the duty of the prosecution to introduce the order into evidence, and if the United States forces do not have such an order it is most improper for the prosecution to introduce into evidence a film whose sound track says they do.

Kerr answered with his familiar attitude: what is the problem here?

> The commission is expressly authorized to accept into evidence such docu-
> mentary evidence or other evidence as it may deem to have probative value
> in the mind of a reasonable man, or which, in the commission's opinion,
> would serve the commission in determining the issues of this case. There-
> fore, on technical grounds the documentary evidence which was produced
> last night and offered to the commission is admissible.
>
> There is no question that the film shows scenes of the crimes which are
> covered by the charge in this case. And I ask the defense how the prosecu-
> tion could possibly present evidence of stronger probative value than the
> scenic representation of the situs of the crime and of the victims themselves
> coming out from the ruins of the churches, homes and the buildings where
> the crimes were committed.

"So far as 'Orders from Tokyo' are concerned," Kerr went on,

> we do not contend that our case rests upon orders from Tokyo or any other
> source. The charge is clear in and of itself, namely, that the accused permit-
> ted the widespread, continuing atrocities to be committed.
>
> This commission, I say again, is not a jury, and we feel sure it is fully com-
> petent to weigh that evidence, to give it such probative value as a reasonable
> man would give it, to exclude therefrom those portions which it believes are
> not of probative value, and to take into consideration those portions which it
> believes to be helpful in determining the issues in this case.

It was a brash performance, and a cagey one. Kerr was not saying, exactly, that
there were actually "orders from Tokyo" as depicted in the film—he knew
there were none—but neither was he acknowledging that the scene was fictitious, nor was he for that matter backing off anything that the film portrayed.
The commission could sort out what was "probative in the mind of a reasonable man" and what was not, because they were, after all, reasonable men.

Perhaps he was right; perhaps the commissioners saw the "orders" for the
fiction they were and disregarded the whole matter. But if so, it would have
been an easy matter for Reynolds to say so, by ordering the film, or at least the
accusatory sound track, stricken from the record. He did not. "The commission
directs that the entire film, including the sound track, be placed in the record
of this trial for such probative value, if any, as the commission may decide to
award to it." As usual, he gave no hint of what "value" might be "awarded" to
the evidence.

With the film safely received in evidence, the prosecution resumed its presentation on the sixteenth day of the trial with testimony that in Cavite, near

Manila, several Filipinos were rounded up and slain by Japanese soldiers, ostensibly because they were guerrillas. Six witnesses testified to that. Witnesses from Pilar, in the middle islands near Cebu, were next; one woman told a heartrending story of watching all seven of her children murdered before her eyes. But by now, even General Reynolds was wondering how long this would continue. As the afternoon wore on, he asked Kerr when the prosecution expected to finish its case. Tomorrow afternoon, Kerr replied. Very well then, said Reynolds. "Let us be sure to proceed swiftly to the meat of the situation and move as fast as we can." The "meat of the situation," one might infer, would be evidence of what Yamashita did or did not do, said or did not say, knew or did not know, could or could not do. But Reynolds did not elaborate.

At that point, the prosecution's case took a sharp turn. Taking a chance, and hoping perhaps to bring Yamashita into the picture through testimony from his own officers, Kerr called to the stand Vice Admiral Denshichi Okochi, who had taken command of all Japanese naval forces, at sea and on land, in the Philippines and the surrounding waters in November 1944, following the disastrous defeat in the Battle of Leyte Gulf. At that point, Yamashita was commanding the Fourteenth Area Army—the soldiers on land. The prosecution now focused on an important point: when did Yamashita take command of the naval forces? And in particular, was he in command of those forces during the Battle of Manila in February 1945, when, as many witnesses had testified, some of the worst atrocities were committed by men variously identified as "navy," "sailors," or "marines."

It was a simple question, but it did not have a simple answer, for two reasons. First, although the Americans often created joint commands of various services with a designated commander at its head—MacArthur, for example, commanded the Southwest Pacific Area, comprising ground divisions of the U.S. Army, an air wing, and the Third Fleet of the U.S. Navy—the Japanese did not. "Unity of command did not work with the Japanese," noted naval historian Samuel Eliot Morison. The Imperial Japanese Army and the Imperial Japanese Navy seldom cooperated in planning and executing operations: the one decided what it was going to do, and sometimes—only sometimes—informed the other.

Second, in the frantic days of late 1944 and early 1945 in the Philippines, MacArthur's army—and his navy—were pounding the Japanese from the air and the sea virtually at will; by January his Sixth and Eighth Armies were approaching Manila from the north and the south, and Yamashita had abandoned the capital for Baguio. Communications were disrupted, and the tactical situation was dire. If Japan did not do unity of command in the best of times, it certainly did not do it well on the run.

Still, it was important for the prosecution to prove, if it could, that every Japanese man in uniform in Manila was under Yamashita's command, and Okochi gave them something to work with. He testified that on January 5, 1945—weeks after Yamashita had decamped for Baguio, and as MacArthur's Sixth Army under General Walter Krueger was about to land at Lingayen Gulf in north Luzon to fight its way to the capital, he had transferred his naval forces to Yamashita.

But only sort of. Yamashita was given tactical command, but Okochi retained what he called "administration outside of naval operations—military operations," such as control of supply, personnel, and logistics. In other words, Yamashita could, on paper, tell the naval units on land where to fight, but Okochi remained responsible for them in all other respects.

It was far from a clear picture, and it became less clear because Okochi transferred his responsibilities to his subordinate, Rear Admiral Iwabuchi, who did not report to Yamashita. In fact, it was not clear who if anyone Iwabuchi reported to, because Okochi himself left Manila and joined Yamashita in Baguio, where there was little for a naval commander to do. So when Yamashita ordered Iwabuchi to abandon Manila—an order that was clearly within his authority as tactical commander—Iwabuchi ignored him. He remained in Manila, and the atrocities that took place there in February 1945 were carried out by troops that—whatever might have been the chain of command on paper—were under his control, and not Yamashita's. Iwabuchi, and virtually all his men, were killed in Manila.

Two members of the commission who had been almost entirely silent during the trial now spoke up, alert to the importance of Okochi's testimony. James Lester put Okochi on the spot: at any time during his time with Yamashita in Baguio, "did the question come up as to the control of the naval land forces in the Manila area?" No, said Okochi. He had "no relation" with Yamashita; they had met face to face only five or six times, and "did not go into detail about military operations." Okochi testified that he did receive reports from Iwabuchi "regarding the military situation" in Manila, but he did not remember the "details."

Leo Donovan took over. "Who commanded the marines in the Manila area?" he asked. "Rear Admiral Iwabuchi," replied Okochi. "They were also under the command of the army?" Donovan asked. "Yes, since the 5th of January," said Okochi. That shed little clarity. Then a few minutes later he remembered something. "I asked Yamashita's headquarters the advisability of evacuating the navy land forces from Manila immediately. However, it was that the army has already given orders to evacuate Manila. That is all."

Cross-examination initially did little to remove the confusion. Sandberg had Okochi acknowledge that, given the divided responsibilities, Yamashita had no authority to promote, transfer, or court-martial anyone in Iwabuchi's command. He could have removed Iwabuchi, but only "through me," said Okochi, and "as a matter of fact, it is impossible, because during that time there were no other commanders who could lead the navy land forces in Manila."

Okochi testified that although he did not know the details, Yamashita's plan was "to evacuate Manila as fast as possible and make a stand" in the mountains. "Since the army did not have a policy to defend Manila, I heard that the army desired to avoid conflict in Manila. I made a plan to evacuate the majority of the naval troops that were in Manila as soon as possible, but because of bombings by plane, the transportation facilities weren't as I expected. A considerable number of troops was left in Manila."

Sandberg asked, "And was it General Yamashita's plan that the fighting be in the mountain terrain?"

"I heard that; that is what I heard."

"And it was his intention that there be no street fighting in Manila?"

"That is what I believe. My staff, through the chief of staff, went to the army staff and suggested the early evacuation of Manila and was told that such orders had been issued."

Okochi's own chief of staff, he testified, also sent a radio message to Iwabuchi to evacuate the city, although he no longer actually had such tactical authority over Iwabuchi's troops. "It was General Yamashita's authority, in matters pertaining to operation; but in matters not pertaining to operations it was my responsibility."

That seemed to clear things up well enough for the commission, and Okochi stepped down, to be escorted back to his cell at Bilibid Prison. The prosecution counted it a good day. "I think we got enough in to support our claim still further," Mountz wrote. "If we can just tie Yamashita up as having full command of the Navy in Manila, we will really have a good case against him, and I think there will be no question of what the verdict will be."

With that, the sixteenth day of the trial came to an end. It had been a good day for the defense as well. It was now clear: Yamashita had ordered Iwabuchi's troops out of Manila. Iwabuchi had ignored that order, and the carnage had begun. Though no one mentioned it, a new issue was introduced to the trial: could a commander be held accountable for crimes committed by troops who had disobeyed orders?

For most of the next day, November 17, the trial focused on three American airmen who had been shot down in the South China Sea in November 1944 and had come ashore in a rubber raft on the tiny and remote island of Batan, 150 miles at sea north of Luzon. Japanese soldiers bayoneted them to death. In preparation, a Japanese officer ordered the first airman, a captain, blindfolded. A Filipino witness testified: "The captain refused. He said that he can face death without blinding him. He said that he can look at anybody and die." (Or, as the *New York Herald Tribune* put it, "I can face death with my eyes open.")

The next witness to the execution had more ominous testimony. He said that he had asked the Japanese captain why the Americans were to be killed.

The captain replied that there was a "telegram by General Yamashita to General Tajima [Tajima was the local garrison commander] to kill all the American prisoners in the Philippine Islands." Reel objected on grounds that this was hearsay three times removed: "a witness telling the statement of a second man who tells of the order of a third man to a fourth man." Reynolds let the testimony stand.

But on cross-examination, the witness admitted that the Japanese officer did not speak English or Tagalog, and the witness himself knew only a few Japanese words. The witness said two of his relatives heard the conversation. Reel asked their names. The witness began to name his relatives.

Reynolds interrupted. "What is the purpose of all this?"

"The purpose, sir, is to find out who was present."

"And once you have that information, what value would it have?"

"Well," said Reel, "we have had one experience in this case sir, where a witness testified to a somewhat similar conversation and mentioned one other person who was present whom he thought was dead," referring to Galang's testimony about Ricarte's grandson. "We found that he was alive and we brought him in and showed the commission that that testimony was not true."

"You propose to bring those witnesses here?" Reynolds asked. "Is that the purpose?"

"We may, sir. It is something that we would wish to consider."

"There was one name in process of presentation, and that name may be included."

Reel was mystified. "I beg your pardon, sir?"

"You may finish the one name the witness was giving at the time we interrupted him."

"Sir, I believe he said that there were two relatives and I was asking him the names of the two of them."

"You may finish the one name," Reynolds directed.

Reel then asked the witness to repeat, in Japanese, the words the officer allegedly spoke. The witness did so. The interpreter then noted that the words contained no reference to prisoners of war, but to "soldiers." It also turned out, after some discussion, that the Japanese officer pronounced the name "Ya-ma-*shee*-ta," which would have been incorrect; the name was "Ya-mash-ta."

Reynolds interrupted again. "In view of the circumstances attending the arrival of these prisoners of war on the island in question, the commission considers the discussion of details, language, location of other prisoner of war camps, to be irrelevant, and directs that the questioning of this witness on those subjects be terminated."

And that was the end of that. As usual, Reynolds's train of thought was well hidden. Did he believe that the account of the supposed "order" from Yamashita had been so thoroughly discredited that no further impeachment was needed? The defense might hope so. But Reynolds had also shown in his admonishment about the pace of the trial, earlier in the week, that the commission was impatient with defense efforts to undermine the credibility of witnesses. Who cared what the two relatives might say about the conversation with the Japanese officer about an order from Yamashita? This witness had testified to it. Move on.

That afternoon, the prosecution called a man it must have thought would be one of the star witnesses: Lieutenant General Shizuo Yokoyama, commander of the Shimbu Group, one of the three main army detachments in 1944–1945, who reported directly to Yamashita.

Yokoyama began by describing how Yamashita gave him command of the 45,000 soldiers in the newly formed Shimbu Group on January 2, 1945, and told him that when the Americans attacked, Yokoyama was "to offer token resistance and make a quick withdrawal" to join Yamashita in Baguio. But a few minutes into the testimony, Reynolds interrupted.

"The commission fails to see any reason to go completely into the command setup of the Shimbu Group, or to hear in detail the technical plans which were under consideration. The Commission will recess for approximately ten minutes and ask the prosecution to re-evaluate the information sought from this witness as to its direct application to the purpose for which we are assembled."

It was an astonishing instruction. If this was not relevant, what was? After sixteen days of hearing testimony of over 100 witnesses relating atrocities committed by Japanese troops throughout the islands, the commission now had before it a Japanese lieutenant general who had commanded several divisions and was responsible directly to Yamashita himself. Yet after ten minutes of his testimony, Reynolds was telling the prosecution that the commission was not interested in the "command setup" or the "technical plans" because it did not see what it had to do with the charges against Yamashita.

When the generals retook their seats, Reynolds brusquely directed the prosecution to "state the substance of the testimony expected to be developed from this witness, which they consider essential to their case."

Captain Pace for the prosecution was up to the task:

The purpose of calling this witness, sir, is to establish the command that Yamashita had over the Manila area, the date when it started, the naval troops which he commanded, the chain of command between Yamashita and the naval commander in Manila, the fact that Yamashita exercised that command, the fact that there was communication between Yamashita and that command up to a certain date, and the fact that Yamashita exercised command over the prisoner of war camps in the Philippines and over the air force in the Philippines.

That was pretty much the purpose for which the commission was assembled. Reynolds stifled his impatience. "You may proceed," he said.

Yokoyama traced on a map the boundaries of his command—an extensive area of southern Luzon including the entire Manila metropolitan area and down to the island of Mindoro in the central Philippines. He received an order from Yamashita that the two other generals were to take command of all land-based forces, including naval forces on land, which was effective on January 10, shortly after the U.S. Army had landed on Luzon. The land-based naval forces were under the command of Iwabuchi, who reported, ostensibly at least, to Yokoyama.

A few weeks later, on February 3, as the Americans were on the outskirts of Manila, Yokoyama ordered all troops in his group to withdraw "to the hills." This included Iwabuchi's "fifteen or sixteen thousand" men in Manila, Yokoyama testified. This order came from Yamashita, Yokoyama said, and he transmitted it to Iwabuchi and notified Yamashita that he had done so.

With Yokoyama the direct link between Yamashita and Iwabuchi, the next questions should have been obvious: what information had he received from Iwabuchi about what was happening in Manila, and what information did he pass on to Yamashita? In other words, what did Yamashita know about Manila, and when did he know it?

But inexplicably, Pace turned to the defense table. "You may cross-examine," he said.

Reynolds could not wait for that. He looked directly at Yokoyama.

"What orders were received by you for the killing of Filipino citizens?"

"I have never received such orders," Yokoyama answered. "I have been previously cautioned by General Yamashita to be fair in all my dealings with the Filipino people."

"What orders were received by you for the burning or demolition of property in Manila?"

"I did not receive any such orders, but aside from certain demolitions essential to military operations I received no such orders as you have described."

"What orders were issued by you for the killing of Filipino citizens in Manila, Batangas, and other parts of your area of command?"

"I have never issued orders for killing."

"What orders were issued by you for the burning or demolition of property in Manila?"

"I never issued any orders."

"By whose orders were Filipino citizens killed in large numbers in Manila, Batangas, and other parts of your area of command?"

"I have never received news of, nor can I consider that any unit commander would have issued orders to kill large numbers of people. I first learned of this situation after having come out of the mountains and arriving at New Bilibid Prison."

It was a very effective cross-examination of the witness, even if not by defense counsel. Yokoyama's answers were clear and unequivocal.

But then Reynolds changed course.

"After United States troops reached the Pasig River [on the approach to central Manila] did you as commanding general visit your own troops in contact [with the U.S. forces, that is, Iwabuchi's troops]?"

"I have not," said Yokoyama.

"During the same period were the Japanese units in contact visited by members of your general staff?"

"The attack came at such a totally unexpected time that no staff member from the group command made such a visit," Yokoyama answered.

Reynolds was incredulous. He turned to the interpreter. "Tell the witness that the commission understands from his statement that during the defense of Manila neither he nor any member of his general staff visited the Japanese troops in contact during the entire month of February, and ask him if that statement is correct."

The interpreter did so. "There is no mistake about that," said Yokoyama.

Reynolds evidently did not understand that, between Yokoyama's headquarters 10 miles east of Manila and Iwabuchi's troops in the western sector of the city, was a formidable barrier to discourage visits by Japanese generals: the U.S. Army.

"Is this a normal procedure in the Japanese Army, by which generals and general staff officers avoid the area of combat?"

"That is by no means the usual custom," Yokoyama answered, perhaps not understanding Reynolds's failure to understand. "I was distressed with a lack of sufficient staff officers. I had no other recourse excepting to be satisfied with the messages that came to me from Iwabuchi by radio and later by ground telephone and buzzer and runners."

Reynolds did not let go of the issue. "Tell the witness," he said to the interpreter, "that the commission understands from his statement that during all the month of February the press of other duties prevented him from joining and contacting his own troops in contact with United States forces, and ask him if that is correct."

"There is no mistake," Yokoyama answered.

The defense, now given its opportunity to cross-examine, had one point to make, and it made it. Yokoyama testified that Yamashita ordered Yokoyama and his Shimbu Group to establish his line of defense east of Manila and fight the Americans when they arrived, then withdraw "as quickly and as positively as possible," taking Iwabuchi and his naval forces with him. This was to be done as soon as Iwabuchi had finished demolishing the docks and naval supplies in the city to keep them out of the hands of the Americans and army troops had finished moving trucks and heavy munitions and other assets out of the city. "It was General Yamashita's desire that there be no fighting in the city of Manila and for that reason he wished to have the citizens of Manila remain calm and continue in their business"—in other words, to stay out of Yamashita's way while he withdrew his forces. Accordingly, said Yokoyama, he ordered Iwabuchi to leave the city on February 13. But Iwabuchi said he would stay. "This was neither in accordance with my ideas nor with the ideas of General Yamashita," said Yokoyama.

Reynolds did all but yawn. "The commission is not greatly interested in the breakdown of responsibility between his subordinate commands," he said.

Reel for the defense persisted. Did Yamashita want the naval troops out of Manila?

"It was my idea, and I am confident it was General Yamashita's idea, that all other naval forces should be withdrawn from the city before engaging."

Reynolds had had enough. "The commission interrupts," he said, "and directs the defense to proceed to other matters." The most important witness to testify in the trial to date, and one of the few other than Yamashita himself who could illuminate with any authority what Yamashita might have known, was hustled off the stand and back to his jail cell.

The commission did not hear from Yokoyama, or anyone else, that he had ordered Iwabuchi to get out of Manila no fewer than four times (see chapter 5). Because the commission was not interested, the point was surely lost that Yamashita's only communications link to Manila went through Yokoyama's headquarters. If, as Yokoyama testified without contradiction, he had received no information from Iwabuchi about the murderous actions of Iwabuchi's forces, then Yamashita did not know, indeed could not have known, of those actions.

The third week of trial, the eighteenth day of trial, began on Monday, November 19. The prosecution, evidently aiming to finish its case with a bang, brought up one of the most grotesque atrocities of the Pacific war: the murder of over 100 American prisoners on the remote island of Palawan, at a camp at Puerto Princesa. Unfortunately for the theatrics of the piece, all the survivors of that crime were in the United States and the prosecution's request that they be made available to come to Manila to testify had been denied. Kerr and his staff had to make do with affidavits given by the survivors in the States, which they read aloud to the commissioners.

The readings were grim enough. There were about 150 American soldiers, sailors, and Marines at Palawan, most of them survivors of Bataan, who were put to work building an airfield. In October 1944, when U.S. planes began strafing the airfield, they had dug three trenches as "air-raid shelters," 75 feet long and only deep enough for men to lie down in.

A Japanese officer named Sato, whom we called "The Buzzard," ordered everyone to get into the shelters. Shortly after we were inside the Japanese attacked the shelters and foxholes. They fired into the openings and threw in gasoline which they set on fire with burning torches and paper. The men tried to escape by running out, some on fire, and tried to get through the barbed wire fence surrounding the area. The Japs shot the men down with rifles and machine guns and bayoneted and clubbed others. Quite a number of the men succeeded in escaping down to the beach over a fairly high cliff, after having gotten through the fence. We had to keep hidden until dark when we succeeded in swimming the bay which was four to five miles wide. We were then found and cared for by the Filipinos who brought us to a guerrilla camp, from which we were evacuated by plane to Morotai. All the others at the camp were either burned in the shelters or shot down and killed by the Japs so far as we know.

Not all who made it into the sea were able to get away. A survivor hiding on the beach said:

Another Jap came up with some gasoline and a torch and I heard the American beg them to shoot him and not burn him. The Jap threw some gasoline on his foot and lit it and the other Japs laughed and poked him with their bayonets. Then they did the same thing to his other foot. They poured gasoline on his hands and lit that and at this point the man collapsed. The Japs then threw the whole bucket of gasoline over him and it burst into flames. I was unable to recognize who this man was because he was all covered with mud. He had apparently been shot in the water and dragged out through the mud.

That done, the prosecution shifted back to Manila, introducing the affidavit of an American grocery clerk who had come upon his grandmother's body lying in the street in February. He did not know who was responsible for the killing. But, he added, "They were Japanese soldiers. They apparently were acting under orders of the Japanese commanding officer to raze the city and rid the city of civilians. The commanding officer was General Tomoyuki Yamashita."

It was beyond hearsay; it was utter speculation from someone in no position to have the slightest knowledge of its source, much less of its truth. Unblinking, the prosecution offered it to the commission as evidence of Yamashita's guilt.

Reel objected. Kerr was unyielding. "If the Commission please, already in this case it has been intimated by the defense that they will attempt to show that General Yamashita was known or tried to make himself known as a benefactor of the city of Manila. This tends to prove that so far as the general impression of the residents of the city of Manila is concerned, the accused is anything but a benefactor of the city of Manila."

It "tended to prove" nothing of the kind. In past instances, Reynolds had frequently stricken those parts of affidavits that were most obviously and explicitly based on hearsay. Here, perhaps weary of the process, he did not. The defense objection was "noted," he said, and the affidavit was accepted, "for such probative value, if any, as it shall be held to possess."

The prosecution called another Japanese officer, regimental commander Masatoshi Fujishige—"a hard-boiled commander as he came on the stand, wearing an unpressed green uniform with P.W. [for "prisoner of war"] painted in a lighter green on the back of his blouse," but "skinny [and] sour-looking," according to the *Herald Tribune*. Showing him notes made by an unidentified person, presumably a Japanese soldier, the prosecution attempted to have him admit that he had ordered his troops to "kill Americans cruelly." Fujishige's regiment was in Batangas, and there had been little evidence of any Americans killed there, but that point evidently went unnoticed. Fujishige denied any such order. What he said, he testified, was that "unless each Japanese soldier killed 100 Americans and destroyed 10 tanks we would lose the war." Spectators snickered as they heard his explanation, but there was no way to resolve the discrepancy.

Toward the end of the day, however, the prosecution offered a document of considerably more significance. After the war had ended, the War Department had put several Japanese generals and admirals on a "liaison committee" to assist U.S. military intelligence in analyzing what the Japanese had done during the war. The committee had been called into play for the trial, to provide written answers to two questions that the prosecution now proffered.

"1. Did General Yamashita, Tomoyuki, command all Navy forces in Manila during January and February 1945?"

"2. Did Yamashita's command extend to actual control over Navy Forces in land action after commencement of hostilities in or near Manila?"

The committee, after noting that no written documentation on either question could be located, answered yes to the first question. "While not all of the Navy personnel on the land throughout the Philippines was [*sic*] under the command of General Yamashita during January and February, 1945, the Navy personnel on the land in the city of Manila during January and February, 1945, was under the command of General Yamashita."

Turning to the second question, the committee was equivocal: "The answer to the second question is not known. It is known that General Yamashita was in or around Baguio during January and February, 1945, and that if there was any communication between him and the Japanese forces in or near the city of Manila during the period in question the communication was very poor."

The sequence of events was critical. Yamashita had decamped from Manila to Baguio in December 1944; command of the naval land forces had been transferred to him on January 5, 1945. Before January 5, he had no occasion to speak to Iwabuchi, who answered up the naval chain of command. After that date, he had no ability to speak to him, except through a communications network that the Japanese liaison committee characterized as "very poor." This came as close as anything had to a critical but still unaddressed issue of the trial: was it enough that Yamashita was in fact the commander of the troops who had rampaged through Manila? Or was it more important that, whatever his authority, he in fact had no actual ability to control those troops, who indeed had disobeyed his order to leave the city? But the prosecution did not pursue it, and the commission was not interested.

With that, on the nineteenth day of trial, the prosecution rested its case.

12

The Defense
Setting the Stage

Colonel Harry Clarke, the chief defense counsel, had been quiet during most of the prosecution's case, letting his assistants raise objections and cross-examine witnesses. Now he stood to do what criminal defense counsel often do at the close of the prosecution's case: to test its evidence by asking the commission for a verdict of not guilty.

In American courts, the rule is fundamental: if at the conclusion of its case the prosecution has not introduced evidence that, if believed, would be sufficient to justify a verdict of guilty, the judge must acquit the defendant. The jury never gets the case; the ruling on the sufficiency of evidence is a matter of law.

The determination must be made count by count; a judge might find sufficient evidence to support a guilty verdict on a count of, say, receiving stolen goods, but insufficient evidence on a count of theft. If so, the judge must acquit on the theft count and proceed with the trial on what remains.

Here, the generals—Reynolds himself, really—were making the rulings that a judge would make, had there been one: whether the charge was valid, whether evidence was admissible, whether a continuation would be allowed. But they were also the jury, weighing the evidence to decide if Yamashita was guilty.

MacArthur's regulations for war crimes trials in the Pacific allowed the defense to move for a not-guilty finding at the close of the prosecution's case, with the commission to rule whether the evidence "supports the charges against the accused." But Clarke had to have realized that there was no chance the generals were going to tell MacArthur that they thought so little of his prosecutors' case that they had thrown it out without needing to hear the defense. Still, he dutifully pressed his argument. "For the past 18 days," he told the commissioners, "the prosecution has been introducing evidence of atrocities alleged to have been committed by the armed forces of Japan, some of which were under the command of the accused, and others of which were under the command of officers on the same level and not in any manner subject to the accused."

"In no instance," he contended, "has the prosecution presented any direct evidence to establish the allegation contained in the charge that the accused unlawfully disregarded and failed to discharge his duties as commanding general of the forces alleged to have committed the crimes" nor any evidence that "the accused permitted the perpetration of the atrocities as alleged."

"In fact, the only evidence presented by the prosecution remotely connecting the name of the accused with any knowledge of the commission of any of the alleged atrocities is the testimony of two self-confessed collaborators." That evidence, Clarke said, was worth nothing. Lapus was reciting alleged statements of a dead man who was in turn supposedly relating something he had heard from Yamashita, and Galang had been thoroughly discredited by Ricarte's grandson.

> Because of the fact that there is absolutely no evidence before this commission of any of the essentials of [the] charge, no evidence of any disregard of duty, no evidence of any failure to discharge a duty, and no evidence of any permission by the accused to anyone to commit any of the things listed in the charge and in the bill of particulars, we hereby move this commission to render a finding of not guilty as to the charge and specifications.

Major Kerr was emphatic in his rebuttal.

> Altogether, sir, we contend that it is an overwhelming, a clear, a convincing proof that the man who was in command of the armed forces of Japan in the Philippines did permit these unquestioned atrocities! . . . What more direct testimony, what more convincing proof could there be of the actual commission of these atrocities than the very victims who have sat in this chair and who have told the commission what happened and who did it! I submit, sir, that there is no question of the commission of these atrocities— absolutely no question whatever!*
>
> Furthermore, I submit that there is no question whatever that these atrocities were committed by Japanese members of the armed forces of Japan in this area. That is uncontroverted.

As to the grandson—"that little pro-Japanese unfortunate," Kerr called him— he "was so thoroughly indoctrinated with hatred of Americans and admiration for the Japanese military that even his testimony is suspect, we submit."

Warmed up, Kerr came to his main point: "Our case does not depend on any direct orders from the accused. It is sufficient that we show that the accused

---

★ The exclamation points appear in the official transcript of the trial.

'permitted' these atrocities. I repeat, sir: there can be no reasonable question whatever as to the commission of these atrocities. They are established."

The commission of the crimes, Kerr implied, proved the permission:

> I submit, sir, that it is conclusive at this stage of the proceedings that Yamashita commanded the naval ground forces in Manila at the time that the atrocities in Manila which we have established were committed. . . .
>
> Who permitted them? Obviously the man whose duty it was to prevent such an orgy of planned and obviously deliberate murder, rape and arson—the commander of those troops!
>
> Now, sir, we must distinguish in this case between an incident where a member of the armed forces on his own . . . commits certain excesses or violations of law or the laws of war. That is one thing. But when that same man or others with him embarked upon military operations under the command and control of commissioned officers, engaged with the enemy, commits those same acts as a military unit, commits those same violations of the law, the laws of humanity, the laws of war, then that definitely is the responsibility of the overall commander because he is using those troops for a military operation in accordance with his duty and he is responsible for what those people do in carrying out his mission.

The two lawyers were ships passing in the night. Clarke was right that there was no evidence worthy of the name showing that Yamashita had issued any orders for carnage; the only evidence of his orders, in fact, was that he had ordered Japanese troops out of Manila. And he was right in pointing out that there was no direct evidence showing that Yamashita even knew of these crimes. Clarke's argument rested on the implicit premise that Yamashita could only be guilty if he had a bad intent: if he had ordered these crimes, or at least stood by and "permitted' them to occur, or at the least had known of them and not made some attempt to stop them.

Kerr, on the other hand, though contending that there was evidence that Yamashita had ordered the crimes—he did not specify it—emphasized that Yamashita need not have ordered the crimes to be guilty of them. He did not address the question of whether Yamashita "must have known" of them—perhaps not willing to imply that knowledge was necessary for conviction in the first place. Yamashita had indeed "permitted" the crimes, Kerr argued, because he had failed in his duty to prevent them. And he was responsible for what the troops under his command did in carrying out "his mission"—the defense of the Philippines.

Neither man addressed the fact that there was no law, and never had been any law, in the United States or under international treaties or the customary laws of war, holding a commander responsible for the crimes of his troops when he had not ordered them or personally taken part in them. Kerr in fact had come very close to arguing that the command relationship alone was sufficient to convict the commander of marauding troops, because the crimes themselves were obvious proof that the commander had not prevented them.

Both men, in short, had failed to lay out for the commissioners any coherent legal theory of what the evidence must show in order to justify a conviction, including most notably the issues of whether the commander's knowledge, or his ability to actually prevent the crimes, had any significance in determining his guilt. But the responsibility to articulate a coherent standard rested more heavily on the prosecution, which had brought the charge, than on the man presumed innocent until proven guilty.

The commissioners retired for "deliberation," but their conclusion was foregone. When they returned, Reynolds announced, "The motion of defense counsel for a verdict of not guilty is denied."

In addition to the lack of clear standards, both sides in the case, and the commission itself, had overlooked a significant point. When the trial began, the commission had directed the prosecution, before introducing its evidence as to this or that incident, to identify the specific count in the bill of particulars to which that evidence would relate. The prosecution had done so diligently. "That concludes our evidence on paragraph 109 of the bill of particulars," one of the prosecutors would typically say as a concluding witness stepped down. "The next matter is covered in bill of particulars paragraph 60." Some of the counts took two days or more, the evidence related through a dozen witnesses; others were dispatched in a few minutes with the submission of affidavits.

There were 64 counts in the original bill of particulars, and 59 in the supplemental bill filed on the eve of trial, 123 in all. When the prosecution rested, it had introduced evidence on 53 of the original counts, and 40 of the supplemental ones. That left 30 counts—nearly one-quarter of the allegations against Yamashita—on which there had been no evidence at all, whether because the prosecution had no evidence or because it had decided for some reason not to pursue them. Without evidence, of course, a defendant cannot be convicted. By any standard, therefore, Yamashita was entitled to an acquittal on each of those 30 counts. But no one mentioned it. The case sailed into the defense phase as fully fitted out as it had been when the trial began.

Clarke tried once more for a continuance. "During the time this court [*sic*] has been in session," he told Reynolds, "the defense has been working day and night to keep up with that new bill of particulars. We have had no time whatsoever to prepare any affirmative defense." He asked for more time, not specifying how much he wanted.

No, said Reynolds. Forty-two days had passed since the arraignment, he pointed out—though he did not mention that twenty-four days had passed since the supplemental bill of particulars had doubled the specifications against

Yamashita or that eighteen of those days had been consumed by trial sessions that had lasted all day, and a few times into the night. "The commission feels that ample time has been provided counsel to prepare its defense."

It was 10:00 A.M. Could the proceeding at least recess until tomorrow morning, Clarke asked.

"The commission would be more willing to grant a recess until 1.30 this afternoon," said Reynolds.

"That will not suffice, sir," said a weary Clarke. "We haven't had time to prepare an opening statement."

Reynolds glared. "In view of the statement of counsel that they are completely unready to make their opening statement and to proceed, the commission will recess until 8.30 tomorrow morning."

The *Herald Tribune* reporter Mac Davis noted that "Reynolds was obviously displeased with the turn of events, as it is the commission's intention to press for a rapid conclusion of the war crimes trials."

Clarke and his team made the best of the truncated recess. First thing next morning, the twentieth day of the trial, Clarke delivered a focused, concise argument of the defense case.

"As we stated yesterday," he began,

> the prosecution has failed to prove that the accused has disregarded any duty, has failed to discharge any duty, or has permitted anyone to commit any atrocity. The defense will now show affirmatively that the accused has not disregarded any duty and that he carried out the duty of his command under indescribably difficult circumstances to the best of his ability, and that he never permitted anyone to commit any atrocities, and that he is not a war criminal.
>
> More specifically, [the] defense will show that the accused never ordered the commission of any crime or atrocity; that the accused never gave permission to anyone to commit any crimes or atrocities; that the accused had no knowledge of the commission of the alleged crimes or atrocities; that the accused had no actual control of the perpetrators of the atrocities at any time that they occurred, and that the accused did not then and does not now condone, excuse or justify any atrocities or violation of the laws of war.

Clarke had subtly moved the focus from Yamashita's command to his control. And "on the matter of control," he told the generals, the defense would focus on facts:

> 1. That widespread, devastating guerrilla activities created an atmosphere in which control of troops by high-ranking officers became difficult or impossible.

2. That guerrilla activities and American air and combat activities disrupted communications and in many areas destroyed them altogether, making control by the accused a meaningless concept. And

3. That in many of the atrocities alleged in the bill of particulars there was not even paper control; the chain of command did not channel through the accused at all.

"We shall also show," Clarke went on,

the general background and circumstances surrounding the accused's activities in the Philippines. We shall give you a true picture of the accused, not only through a number of character witnesses but through witnesses who will tell the story of the accused: a man who had never been in the Philippines until he arrived to take over an impossible task just nine days before the Leyte landing, who from the day that he arrived in this theater was under a state of siege by the enemy troops.

You will see the picture of a general working under terrific pressure and difficulty, subject to last-minute changes in tactical plans ordered by higher headquarters, and a man who when he arrived in Luzon actually had command over less than half of the ground troops in the Island.

In apparent reference to Reynolds's dismissive comment to General Yokoyama about his staff's failure to visit Japanese troops, Clarke concluded, "The picture will be quite different from that of a well-staffed commander who had his time to make frequent inspections and who could afford to go behind the reports of the officers upon whom he must and should rely."

As its first witness, the defense called Lieutenant General Akira Muto, Yamashita's chief of staff in the Philippines, the man who had arrived two days after the Americans had landed at Leyte, and had asked, "Where's Leyte?" Muto had been by Yamashita's side ever since, retreating with him into the hills, surrendering with him, and then sharing his cell and sitting next to him during the trial. No one in the Japanese army knew more about what Yamashita had done in the Philippines than Muto. Short, plump, and soft-spoken, wearing thick black glasses, Muto did not cut an imposing figure in his green army uniform as he took his seat by the American generals. Clarke began his questioning by taking Muto back to his arrival in the Philippines in October 1944.

Muto held out no false hopes back then. "The defense of Manila appeared to me to lead towards certain failure, and I felt great sympathy for General Yamashita in his new assignment," he said, speaking through an interpreter. "The assignment [of Yamashita] had been made six months too late. It was my opinion that Japan had been too slow in preparing [the] Philippine defense;

that this should have been done sooner. However, having been ordered to duty as his chief of staff, I prepared myself to perform that duty to the utmost of my ability and vigor."

But the picture was bleak. "The number of troops was extremely insufficient," Muto testified. Defensive preparations

> were practically nonexistent and they were obsolete and inadequate protection against American attack or bombardment. While there were considerable supplies in the Manila area, they were piled in an unsystematic or helter-skelter way. Of the shortages, the most acute were rice and gasoline. Because of the recent mass induction of new troops, Army standards had fallen physically, and because of the retreat and long service in the tropics not only were the troops physically below par, but their fighting spirit or morale was low. I was greatly surprised to discover that there were guerrillas not only between Manila and Fort McKinley [Yamashita's headquarters, south of Manila] but surrounding Fort McKinley itself. General Yamashita had just come to the Philippines, and of the 15 members of the staff only three were retained from those of General Kuroda's staff, the others having come from Manchuria or from other locations, and we were all extremely troubled by our lack of knowledge of conditions in the Philippines.

Solving these problems was difficult, Muto explained, because of the division of command. Yamashita reported to Field Marshal Terauchi, Supreme Commander of the Southern Army, which encompassed all of Japan's land forces south of the homeland and west into Burma, of which Yamashita's Fourteenth Area Army was a part. There was also a combined fleet naval commander, the counterpart to Terauchi, and a separate command for maritime shipping. Yamashita had command of ground troops in the islands, but not of any of the air, naval, or shipping units. "Of the 290,000 or 300,000 troops in Luzon, approximately 120,000 were under General Yamashita's command," Muto testified. "Therefore, although there were many undesirable conditions, it was not possible for General Yamashita to take them all in hand immediately and correct them."

The original defense plan was that if the Americans landed on Leyte, the Thirty-Fifth Army on nearby Cebu was to engage them, but no troops were to be sent from Luzon. Yet when the Americans did land, the Imperial General Staff in Tokyo changed the plan and ordered Terauchi to have Yamashita's Luzon forces make their way to Leyte and join the battle there. "Since this was a fundamental change in the defense plans for the Philippines," Muto explained, "it created very grave problems and difficulties."

The available ships were inadequate for the task, and Yamashita did not command the maritime transport anyway. Moreover, Yamashita's troops in Luzon were widely dispersed, "but at that time the Japanese Army was exceedingly short on both motor transport and gasoline." In addition, the plan would require "protection of the transports carrying reinforcements to Leyte, which had to be obtained from the 4th Air Army, which was not under General Yamashita's command," and "both the navy and the air force, having their own assignments, did not carry out all of General Yamashita's desires."

Meanwhile, Muto testified, American bombers and submarines attacked the transports that "with great effort General Yamashita was able to send from Manila towards Leyte, [and] practically every one of them was sunk en route." One infantry division reached Leyte more or less intact; two others were decimated. "And at this time there was [*sic*] always two or three representatives from the Imperial General Headquarters vehemently urging General Yamashita to more vigorous action." Even when the Americans were landing at Ormoc, on the western shore of Leyte, surrounding Yamashita's beleaguered forces, the Imperial General Staff "insisted on renewed activity in Leyte." But it was soon obvious, even in Tokyo, that Leyte was lost.

Luzon was surely MacArthur's next target. But "the first problem was to increase the number of troops to make up for the vacuum" caused by the diversion of some 50,000 troops to Leyte, few of whom returned. "The second problem was the tightening up and clarifying the chain of command under the single command of General Yamashita, and a great deal of effort was made to secure this result." Muto ticked off the steps that were put into place in November and December 1944. First, there were approximately 30,000 troops in Manila who were stranded because the ships to take them elsewhere in the South Pacific had been sunk, as well as sailors and others rescued from sinking ships, and still others who had been discharged from the hospital and had no place to go. They were all swept into Yamashita's command. The intent was for Yamashita "either to form new battalions or to use [them] as replacements in units sent from Japan," one-half to two-thirds of which had not survived the journey through seas controlled by U.S. Navy warships and submarines. Terauchi removed his headquarters from Manila to Saigon, leaving the maritime transport command to Yamashita. Tokyo told Yamashita to take over the air force as well, so that by the beginning of February 1945, Yamashita had, on paper, command of many of the troops in the islands, most of whom he still knew little about. "The conditions in Luzon, from the middle of November until into December were so precarious that if the Americans had made a serious attempt at that time they could have undoubtedly captured the whole island with one blow."

Muto outlined the Japanese strategy after the American army landed on Lingayen Gulf, on the northwest corner of the island, on January 9, 1945. "The impression at that time," he said, was that the Japanese campaign in the Philippines was not a victory and could not succeed. The Americans had completely effective naval and air forces and were in a position to make a landing at any point where they could choose. In addition to this, the American ground forces possessed far superior fire power and mobility. Comparing the Japanese forces to this, the defense positions on the shores were exceedingly inadequate. Fire power was inferior and mobility had practically disappeared. There would be no possibility of combating the American forces with arms. Although General Yamashita had been told to fight a decisive battle against the American troops on Luzon, it became clear that that plan would unavoidably have to be changed.

The new plan had little to do with any actual defense of the Philippines. It was "to occupy mountain positions in Luzon and engage American forces for as long as possible, in order to postpone as long as possible any fighting in Japan proper," Muto explained. To occupy the mountains, all troops had to abandon Manila. "Manila was the principal and cultural center of the Philippines, with a population of not less than one million, and of highly inflammable construction. To defend a highly inflammable city with one million inhabitants in it was considered not only impossible but disadvantageous. Moreover, General Yamashita considered that to invoke the hatred of the Philippine people would have a very disastrous effect upon his operations."

By the time the Americans landed at Lingayen, "most of the ground forces had been withdrawn from the city. With respect to supplies, however, only about one-third had been successfully removed. The primary reason was the lack of transportation of the Japanese troops." In addition, American air forces had Manila under unrelenting attack. And "there was reluctance on the part of many to leave the city of Manila. Among those who were not under General Yamashita's command, there were a number of officers who were opposed to his idea of withdrawing from Manila and leaving it outside of the area of operations." "None of [the unit commanders] shared the idea of the imminence of the American landing which General Yamashita had."

Yamashita deployed his ground troops in three groups: the Shimbu Group under Yokoyama took up positions in the mountains east of Manila; the Kembu Group straddled Luzon between Lingayen Gulf and Manila; and the Shobu Group retreated to Baguio in northern Luzon under Yamashita.

"Was any order given by General Yamashita to the commanding general of the Shimbu group [Yokoyama] relative to the evacuation of Manila?" Clarke asked.

"There was," said Muto. "Written orders were issued, at the end of December." Muto also met with the chief of staff of the air forces, now nominally under Yamashita's command, and "personally told him of General Yamashita's desires. Written orders were given."

Nonetheless, 1,500 to 1,600 soldiers remained in Manila, as did 16,000 naval troops, but, said Muto, Yamashita could not issue orders to their commander, Admiral Iwabuchi, who answered to his own naval chain of command. "I had talked with the chief of staff of the naval forces, and the naval commander [Iwabuchi] was well aware of General Yamashita's desire that all troops be taken from the city and the city eliminated from the battlefield."

Later, Yamashita was given operational control over Iwabuchi's forces, which should have made Yamashita's orders binding, but Iwabuchi simply refused to follow them. Muto suggested that Iwabuchi felt "that his principal mission had supersedence over all others and it was to conduct shore defense" in Manila.

Muto's account was an accurate one, but the complex and subtle distinctions of command may well have been lost on the five American generals, four of whom were career staff officers without substantial command experience, and all of whom came from a military establishment in which chains of command were well established. But the defense had made an important point: Yamashita had ordered Manila abandoned. Iwabuchi had refused. The soldiers and sailors in Manila during the ghastly month of February 1945, whatever their chain of command on paper, were there because Iwabuchi had defied Yamashita's orders.

Clarke then turned to a key question of the case: What had Yamashita known about atrocities in Manila? "Did you in your capacity as chief of staff," he asked Muto, "receive any reports from any subordinate commanders [of] General Yamashita of the mistreatment of civilians in Manila?"

"I have not received such a report," Muto replied. "I did receive reports during the battle for the city of Manila, but they concerned major phases of the battle, and I received no reports as to any small details." Small details? That could not have gone down well with the commissioners. Yet Muto was getting his reports not from Manila—army communications between Baguio and Manila went down on January 12, shortly after the U.S. landing at Lingayen and weeks before Manila erupted—but from Yokoyama's Shimbu Group, and Iwabuchi was giving Yokoyama little information himself. In any event, there were no reports of mistreatment of civilians in Manila. Muto said he did not hear of the annihilation of Iwabuchi's forces in Manila until "about the middle of March," some two weeks after the fact.

"Did General Yamashita at any time give any orders for the killing of noncombatant civilians in Manila?" asked Clarke.

"There is absolutely no such thing has ever occurred," Muto replied.

"Did you ever hear of any commander under General Yamashita issuing such orders?"

"I have not."

Clarke moved on. Who was in charge of prisoners of war in the Philippines? As of November 1944, Muto replied, "this command came directly and clearly" under Yamashita. But Yamashita had never issued any "special orders on these subjects."

"Did General Yamashita ever issue an order that all American prisoners of war should be killed?"

"There is nothing of the sort ever occurred."

What about his subordinate commanders?

"Such a thing is impossible and I have never heard of such an order being issued," said Muto. In fact, he had heard Yamashita "express a desire that, because the prisoners of war are in a somewhat helpless position, they should be treated with as much kindness as possible." But he acknowledged that neither he nor Yamashita had ever visited any POW camps. "After the landing at Leyte we were exceedingly busy. We received constant attacks, bombing during the daytime and had to do all of our work at night, and it was impossible to make inspection trips at night." Muto was emphatic: "I have always been with General Yamashita, and I know, I am very sure of my facts. He has never been to any such place." Yamashita did receive two or three reports from his POW chief, but they were "short, simple, routine reports," with no suggestion of anything out of the ordinary "excepting that there was a shortage of food for the inmates."

Shortages of food were endemic, he testified, because 85 percent of the transports from Tokyo, Bangkok, and Saigon never made it past American submarines and aircraft. Rations for Japanese soldiers were reduced to 400 grams a day, less than one pound. So naturally the POWs suffered too, even though "according to General Yamashita's orders, they were equal, they were the same." Just what order Muto had in mind was not clear, given his testimony a few minutes earlier that Yamashita had issued no "special orders" concerning prisoners. Muto was adamant that no reports of POW mistreatment had ever reached Yamashita's headquarters.

Did Muto know anything about the massacre of 150 American POWs at the airfield on the island of Palawan, on December 14, 1944? No, said Muto; that airfield was under the control of the Fourth Air Army, and that group was not transferred to Yamashita until New Year's Day of 1945. In fact, Muto testified, Yamashita's plan was to abandon American POWs to the "protecting power"* when the Americans landed at Lingayen in January, since it would be impossible to take them with his army when it retreated into the hills. But Tokyo had other ideas, said Muto. It wanted American POWs transported to Japan.

---

* Under the Geneva Conventions at the time, an army holding prisoners of war was required to provide information about them and their conditions to a neutral "protecting power," which would in turn relay the information to the International Red Cross and on to the prisoners' own army. In this case, the protecting power for Japan was Spain. The protecting power for the United States was Switzerland.

The POW "hell ships" were in fact one of the most scandalous atrocities of the war. American prisoners were herded into the overcrowded, dark, and unventilated holds of transport ships, with no sanitary facilities and very little food or water—and that lowered by buckets for the prisoners to fight over. The ships were not visibly marked as prisoner transports, making them easy targets for American fighter planes, who had no idea what was inside. Americans died in agony from suffocation, starvation, and attacks by their own forces.

Clarke moved on: what reports did Yamashita receive about guerrilla activity in the islands? "This was considered a very serious matter," Muto replied, "because reports from Leyte were to the effect that practically the entire Philippine population became guerrillas and rendered the Japanese position extremely precarious. We were paying a great deal of attention or interest to these guerrilla units at that time."

Clarke read to him the translation of an intercepted order from the Fourteenth Area Army dated October 11, 1944, a few days after Yamashita had arrived in the Philippines and taken command of that group: "In view of the special characteristics of the Philippine Operations, subversive activities of the residents and attacks in our rear by airborne raiding forces must be considered. In order to avoid mistakes in conducting the operations, take precautions against armed guerrillas, subjugate them quickly, and put a stop to their activities."

Clarke pointed out to the commissioners that the order specified "armed guerrillas," not all citizens or noncombatants. "Did General Yamashita ever issue any orders for the killing of noncombatant civilians?" he asked Muto.

"Absolutely not," the general replied. And his headquarters never received any reports that they were being killed. In fact, he went on, Yamashita was very concerned about "smirching the fair name of the Japanese Army with untoward and undisciplined acts." Yamashita had told President Laurel to let him know of any "incidents that should come to his attention," and "I heard him tell the commanding officer of the military police to be particularly careful to conduct himself fairly with respect to the Filipino people." Muto testified that Yamashita soon lost confidence in the military police's dealings with civilians, and he requested that Tokyo relieve its commander, which the Imperial Staff eventually did.

As the day's work came to an end, it was clear that Muto had been a good witness. "He really sang his song very well," Mountz noted grudgingly, "if you care to believe it."

The next day, the twenty-first of the trial, was Thanksgiving Day. Reynolds announced that the commission would sit only half a day, in observance.

Muto returned to the stand, and Clarke asked him to explain the division of authority between the army and the navy in the Philippines. Muto gave a lengthy but illuminating answer.

The chain of command in the Japanese Army and the Japanese Navy are absolutely separate and parallel chains of command. The Japanese Army was created prior to the junior service, the Navy, and in order to insure its independence there is a history of a very clear demarcation of chain of command from the very start between the two services.

And more recently, there has been revealed a strong tendency to jealously guard all of their rights and prerogatives by both services. As a result, it has been impossible to do as is done in the American forces, for Washington to issue an order whereby naval forces and army forces can be put together in a single chain of command.

"On the other hand," Muto went on,

there frequently occurs situations where the objective of operations is such that it is necessary for the two services to be welded together for operational purposes. For instance, the situation which existed here in Manila. Therefore, the Army portion of the Imperial General Headquarters, and the Navy section of the same headquarters, conferred and determined . . . that wherever naval forces were stationed ashore, where land operations, land battle, should develop, under those circumstances those naval forces should pass for operational control under the command of the army commander also stationed there.

Operational control meant that the navy would retain the responsibility for "training, punishment or discipline, personnel, and pay and supplies," and Yamashita's authority would be "confined to operations pertaining to a battle, such as 'forward march' or 'withdraw' or 'halt.'"

Reynolds was growing impatient with Muto. "From his prior testimony, it is unlikely that he was in a position to know much about the subject," he said—a curious observation to make of a general who was Yamashita's chief of staff.

Clarke, having completed his prepared examination, asked Muto if there was anything else he would like to say "to aid in the determination of the issue."

"Only one more thing," said Muto. "To me the idea of General Yamashita's being indicted as a war criminal is something the likes of which I have never seen in a dream. I was absolutely astounded when I learned about it."

"That is not pertinent to the issue," Reynolds interjected, and with that Clarke turned Muto over to the prosecution for cross-examination.

Captain Pace took on the task, but his questions seemed aimless and extemporaneous. He questioned Muto in detail about his military assignments in the 1930s, prompting Reynolds to interrupt. "We wish to know whether this is leading to something which is material to the issues for which we are assembled." Pace, chastened, tried to get Muto to admit that Iwabuchi's command in Manila in February 1945 was not a naval operation but an army one. Muto sidestepped the questions. "It is impossible to divide and create a clear line of division between the naval operation of defending the port and bay of Manila, and the land operation of defending the land portion of Manila. The two cannot be clearly divided." But he readily acknowledged that during February Iwabuchi was under Yokoyama's Shimbu Group, and therefore in Yamashita's chain of command.

"Did General Yamashita tell Yokoyama to have those troops cease their fighting street by street?" asked Pace.

"Yes," said Muto.

"Was the order obeyed?"

"It was not obeyed," said Muto. And then, seizing the opportunity, he resumed his defense of Yamashita on an important point.

> The order not to engage in street fighting had been revealed to the commander of the Shimbu Group [Yokoyama] towards the end of December. The fact that General Yamashita did not desire any street fighting in Manila had been explained to the naval forces [Iwabuchi] and they should have made preparations in accordance with those desires. Admiral Iwabuchi came under General Yokoyama's command on 6 January [1945], and both General Yokoyama and Admiral Iwabuchi were well aware of the necessity for withdrawing from Manila. On the 9th of January [as Americans were streaming ashore at Lingayen on Luzon] General Yamashita sent an urgent order to General Yokoyama asking, "Why is all this delay? Hurry up and get those troops out of the city!"

Pace, losing control of the witness, asked again, "Was the order obeyed?" and Muto said again, "I know that Admiral Iwabuchi received the order. It was not obeyed."

Reynolds interrupted again. Speaking to Pace, he said, "Find out what action was taken, if any, to prevent this mutinous act or chain of mutinous acts, and find out whether such things were part of the standards of the Japanese army and navy."

The prosecution had proven clearly what the defense on direct examination had been vigorously urging: that Iwabuchi had unequivocally rejected Yamashita's order to abandon the city. Reynolds took it a step further: Iwabuchi was not merely insubordinate—he was "mutinous." That was not quite correct: mutiny is the overthrow of lawful military authority; Iwabuchi was simply ignoring it. Still, Clarke had to be pleased with Reynolds's hyperbole.

And Reynolds's contemptuous question of whether mutiny was "part of the standards" of the Japanese military put Pace in a bind. First Muto had taken over his cross-examination, and now Reynolds had. Pace dutifully asked the question, and Muto answered that no, insubordination was not a tolerated practice in the Japanese army.

Reynolds was still not satisfied. "We know the order was issued, we know it was disobeyed. We would like a sharp, clear-cut answer to the question, 'What did General Yamashita do about it?'" Muto gave the obvious answer: Yamashita could do nothing about it. In fact, Manila was so surrounded by the American army that he never even knew about the disobedience until long afterward. "We never found out," said Muto.

Captain Sandberg for the defense raised a curious objection to Reynolds's question of what Yamashita had done about Iwabuchi's disobedience of his order. "Any inference that there was any willful disobedience of the order is improper," he told Reynolds. "The witness has not testified that there was any 'willful disobedience' [of] the order. He simply stated that the order was never fully complied with or was never fulfilled." Just why the defense wanted to avoid an inference of willful disobedience is not at all clear; the more willfully insubordinate Iwabuchi was, the better Yamashita looked.

Reynolds wanted to know when Manila had become so surrounded by Americans that Iwabuchi could not comply with the order to withdraw. Muto, who had been 125 miles away in Baguio at the time, again said he had no idea:

I received daily reports [evidently meaning reports from Yokoyama] principally concerned with the progress made on the north and the south [of Manila] by the American troops, but with respect to details of occurrences within the city proper, I received no reports whatever. The power, the efficiency of Japanese radio equipment was so low that American soldiers would scarcely believe the lack of efficiency that existed, and the Shimbu Group was exerting the utmost limit of possibility in getting signals through to us as it was.

At 11:30, Reynolds cut off further questioning. It was time for a Thanksgiving meal. "We ask the prosecution to go thoroughly into their plan and need for further cross examination," Reynolds cautioned Pace, "so that we may release this witness and proceed to other matters."

As the commission adjourned, the focus of the trial had changed noticeably, from Japanese atrocities to the strategic and tactical difficulties of a military command under unrelenting attack and of an army general fighting the Americans with one hand and, it seemed, his own navy with the other.

Thanksgiving over with, Muto returned to the stand for the third day, but the prosecution made little headway. Robert Cromie, covering the trial for the *Chicago Tribune*, summed it up:

Cross-examination of Lt. Gen. Akira Muto, who was on the stand for the third day, led exactly nowhere in this morning's hearing of Gen. Yamashita on war crime charges.

Capt. Jack Pace of New York City attempted to trip up the witness with notable lack of success. Sometimes the witness' answers were sharp and quick, sometimes he registered surprise—his moon face breaking into a smile, his eyes widening. On other times he leaned his head back, pursed his lips in thought, and answered slowly as tho [*sic*] making an effort to recall. But never did his answer in any way incriminate Gen. Yamashita, no matter how long or how thoroly [*sic*] Pace fished for such a reply.

All Pace was able to learn of interest was that in early January there were approximately 230,000 troops in Yamashita's 14th army on Luzon, that Yamashita had issued orders to exterminate armed guerrillas but not women, children or guerrilla sympathizers, and that Muto had no idea how many guerrillas had been killed—but certainly not the 60,000 figure offered by Pace.

When Muto stepped down, Sandberg for the defense had a pointed reminder for the commission. He pulled from the stack of exhibits the report of the post-war liaison committee of Japanese generals and admirals that the prosecution had tendered at the end of its case. Sandberg read the Japanese officers' conclusion: "It is known that General Yamashita was in or around Baguio during January and February 1945, and that if there was any communication between him and the Japanese forces in or near the city of Manila during the period in question the communication was very poor."

In this respect, the Japanese officers had impressive backup, though it did not come out at the trial. In his postwar memoir, General Robert Eichelberger, recalling combat on the large island of Negros, wrote: "To be sure, the enemy fought with tenacity in an inland mountain bastion for many weeks, but the outcome was never in doubt. The Negros campaign highlighted one glaring Japanese deficiency of which we were already cognizant. Enemy commanders rarely had an accurate picture of a battle situation. The reason became clear: their military communications system was primitive and untrustworthy and ridiculously inferior to our highly efficient network of field telephones and field radios."

The next day the defense called Major General Goichi Kira, then being held by the Americans, who had been the quartermaster for Yamashita's Fourteenth Area Army, the man in charge of finding enough food to feed 250,000 men—not only the Japanese troops, he testified, but the Americans being held prisoner as well.

It was not an easy job. Even before Yamashita arrived in the Philippines in October 1944, he said, American submarines and aircraft were devastating the shipments of food from Tokyo and Saigon. Food shortages in Luzon were made worse when soldiers were sent to Leyte, with rations being cut from the normal, or at least the official, 850 grams per day—nearly two pounds—of fish, rice, fruit, and vegetables down to about 600 grams per day, and then to 400 grams per day of rice alone, then to 300 grams, and then to a scant 100 grams (about 3.5 ounces). There was plenty of rice in the Cagayan Valley, he acknowledged, but that was in far northeastern Luzon, between two mountain ranges; there were no trucks to carry it, and no gas to fuel trucks had there been any.

Kira knew Yamashita well and had often spoken to him about the dire food situation, a matter of concern to both men. And what did Yamashita have to say about food for the prisoners of war and in the internment camps such as Santo Tomas? asked Captain Reel.

"General Yamashita often mentioned the food supply situation in internment camp[s] and in the PW camp[s], and seemed to have had much concern regarding the situation. And he said it wouldn't do if it were bad. He expressed his desire that internees and the PW's should be well taken care of. I have heard his desire that the food situation should not be allowed to be worse than that of the army." And shortly after he arrived in Luzon, Yamashita "issued an order regarding the forced requisition from the civilians, and included in that order was a clause forbidding pilfering from the civilians."

Reynolds was confused. At "28.3495 grams to an ounce," he said, was the witness correct in calculating that a shipment of 8,000 tons of rice would feed 250,000 soldiers and prisoners for thirty days? He asked the defense to check "the straight, simple arithmetic involved."

The answer, at 2 pounds per day, would have been yes, but neither the prosecution nor the defense bothered to solve this fourth-grade problem. After twenty-three days of trial in four weeks, six days a week, eight hours a day, their evenings spent preparing for trial the next morning, the lawyers on both sides were exhausted. The trial was becoming tedious. The Filipino witnesses with their heartrending tales of death and brutality were gone; the ballroom of the High Commissioner's Residence had empty seats; the newsreel crews found little to film when the lawyers recited documentary exhibits into the record.

Testimony of the Japanese officers, prisoners now, put on by the defense, slowed the proceedings by half, as each question and answer had to be interpreted. Rendering English into Japanese and vice versa is a challenge under the best of circumstances, and the American soldiers struggled to convey accurately the convoluted questions of the lawyers and the subtleties of the Japanese language. Testimony was regularly interrupted by requests for repeats and clarifications.

The dozen reporters covering the trial, most of them from American newspapers and wire services, diligently filed their daily stories, but they were shorter, and back home they no longer appeared on the front page. The occasional breeze that fluttered the curtains of the ballroom doors open behind the commissioners' table did little to relieve the oppressive air. Reynolds was becoming testy, prodding defense counsel to move along, to refrain from dwelling on matters of organization and logistics, though he frequently relented if counsel claimed to be laying the groundwork for significant testimony later on.

Through it all, the witness everyone seemed to be waiting for sat impassively at the defense table, listening carefully, showing little emotion, listening to his personal interpreter, occasionally whispering to his lawyers.

A key element of the prosecution's case was the treatment of prisoners of war, most of them Americans, held by the Japanese since the surrender of Corregidor in the spring of 1942, as well as the treatment endured by civilians interned at Santo Tomas and a few other locations. The prosecution had submitted into evidence a fifty-seven-page transcript of the interrogation of Lieutenant General Shiyoku Kou, the commanding general of POW and civilian internee camps in the Philippines beginning in March 1944. Kou, captured by Americans, had been interrogated the week before Yamashita's arraignment, but rather than call him as a witness the defense decided simply to read relevant portions of the interrogation transcript as part of its case, and no one objected to that. It was quicker, already translated, and guaranteed to contain none of the surprises of live testimony.

On the treatment of POWs, Kou gave an outrageous account. He received a copy of the Geneva Conventions from the War Ministry and he carried out its policies on the treatment of prisoners. Prisoners of war received the same rations as Japanese soldiers, and in fact at some of the camps they were able to eat "better than the Japanese soldiers" because they could raise livestock and cultivate gardens, and so they ate meat and vegetables. Prisoners were paid according to their rank; "if a P.W. is a captain, he receives the pay of a captain in the Japanese Army." No prisoner, and no civilian internee either, died of malnutrition or beriberi or any other similar disease, at least not on his watch. He saw to it that all prisoners sent to Japan "got new and warm clothing," and he himself requisitioned medicine from the army and delivered it to the camps so the prisoners could be adequately cared for. A prisoner who committed a serious offense would go before a court-martial, because the Japanese guards were not permitted "to beat the offending party," and any who did so "would be punished in accordance with his crime." Indeed, any physical maltreatment of prisoners, even a slap, would have been "intolerable, however serious might be the offense committed."

Not a word of it was true. Why the defense would even read it aloud in the trial is a mystery. The brutal and sadistic treatment of American prisoners during three years in the Philippines was common knowledge; many had starved to death, and none of them escaped beatings, disease, and malnutrition. While civilian internees did have some ability to grow gardens and, for a while, to receive food from Filipinos, prisoners of war had no such luxuries. Meat, vegetables, fish, and fruit were a dream; the reality was thin soup with a little rice and as often as not maggots and insects.

Reynolds remarked on none of this when the reading was done, but he did want to know whether Kou had done anything to actually inspect his POW camps, beyond asking the camp commandant "if everything was satisfactory." He told the prosecutors to summon Kou to the courtroom.

The next morning, Kou appeared—"an unimpressive little figure in a shabby uniform adorned with three rows of faded ribbons," wrote Cromie. He bowed to the commissioners and took his seat, "both hands gripping the chair arms firmly."

Reynolds told Captain Hill what the commission—or Reynolds himself at least—wanted to know:

> We wish to determine the extent of the actual inspections made by General Kou; whether he actually saw the food placed on the tables for prisoners of war and civilian internees, because that is the only place that the food would do any good. We want to know how long, how thoroughly he conducted these inspections. We want to know whether he made any allowance in increasing ration component to prisoners and civilian internees to compensate for the amount of food products which the Japanese soldier gained by confiscation of civilian products. We want also to know whether he was informed of the numerous written protests which were put into the camp commanders and what action, if any, he took upon them.

Why Reynolds should have been focused on these details is curious: Kou reported to the War Ministry in Tokyo, not to Yamashita, to whom he sent only a few routine dispatches that all was well in the POW camps.

But given the opportunity, Kou continued the fantasies of his interrogation the month before. At the Cabanatuan camp—verifiably the most brutal of all Japanese camps in the Philippines—he observed that the prisoners had "quite a bit more [food] than what we received in Manila": rice curry with sauce, meat and potatoes and vegetables. And that was lunch. And there were three meals a day. He spoke to some prisoners and heard no complaints from any of them. There was no mistreatment and no prisoner deaths; sanitary conditions were "quite good"; the hospital was "well equipped"; the patients were "well taken care of." Meals at Santo Tomas were just as filling and delectable: rice curry and "four or five pieces" of beef with bananas and vegetables.

Reynolds then took another curious turn. He directed the prosecutor to go into the matter of the *Oryoku Maru*, one of the most notorious hell-ship transports of the war. In December 1944, some 1,300 American POWs were loaded into the hold of this rust bucket, with no food, water, or sanitary facilities. The ship headed for Japan, but with no POW markings visible, it was soon attacked and sunk, with much loss of life, by American planes. It was an appalling episode, but Kou's testimony, uncontradicted, was that the ship was under the control of the maritime transport command, which at that time was not within Yamashita's command, and that he, Kou, was in charge of loading the prisoners, and he was not in Yamashita's army. So the *Oryoku Maru* was extraneous to Yamashita's guilt or innocence. That did not seem to have registered on Reynolds.

Nor did the truth register on Kou. The prisoners' "rooms" (there were no "rooms") were crowded, but they could come on deck to eat "meals" (there were no "meals") prepared in the mess hall or to go to the "sick bay" (there was no mess hall or sick bay, either). Kou went on about the prisoners exercising and taking "walks" and told other bizarre tales, and soon even Reynolds was content to move on. The defense had only one question. Where did the orders for this transport come from? From Tokyo, Kou replied.

The next defense witness needed no interpreter. He was Norman Sparnon, a U.S. Army captain in ATIS, the custodian of translations of all captured Japanese documents of any intelligence value from anywhere in the Philippines or elsewhere in the Southwest Pacific theater—"some hundreds of thousands," Sparnon estimated. Captured documents were sorted and resorted according to the importance of their content, the most significant were translated, and intelligence officers then decided which of the translations were important enough to be disseminated to Allied commanders. All of the several hundred thousand documents seized in the Philippines had gone through that process, Sparnon testified.

Sandberg crisply ticked off his questions:

"Now, have you ever seen among the captured documents an order signed by General Yamashita ordering the destruction of the entire city of Manila?"

"No."

"Have you ever seen an order of General Yamashita ordering the killing of noncombatant civilians in the Philippine Islands?"

"No sir, I have not."

"Have you ever seen an order of General Yamashita calling for the killing of prisoners of war?"

"No, I have not."

"Now, a film was shown before this commission in which a statement was made that the United States Army had captured an order from Tokyo for the destruction of Manila. Have you ever seen such an order among the captured documents?"

"No, I have not. I would like to say that if such an order was captured, the information would be of such high intelligence value that it would undoubtedly be translated and published."

Furthermore, Sparnon testified, any order from an army-sized unit, such as Yamashita's Fourteenth Area Army, would be issued over the name of the commanding general and disseminated to as many as twenty-five subordinate commands, most of which would disseminate it further within their units. The number of copies of the original order would thus be, as Sparnon put it, "considerable," and any one or more of them might find their way to ATIS.

"And would you say," Sandberg asked, "that you have never seen any orders of the types I have described? Do you mean that you have never seen any such order either in its form originating from the headquarters of General Yamashita, or in its form in any subordinate headquarters?"

"No," said Captain Sparnon. "I have not."

He acknowledged in a very brief cross-examination that he dealt only in written documents, including written confirmation of oral orders, but not communications that were sent solely by radio or telegraph. Still, his testimony on a key piece of the defense case had been unequivocal.

The defense then changed its course, and Major George Guy made his first appearance before the commission. Guy had spent weeks in Japan, locating character witnesses to testify on behalf of his client. MacArthur's orders governing the commission made no mention of character evidence, but it has long been accepted in criminal cases, the rationale being that evidence that the defendant is an upstanding, honest, and peaceable fellow may be taken into account in determining whether he is the sort of person who would have committed the crimes charged. Kerr raised no objection.

Guy's first witness was Keichoku Yoshida, a Tokyo lawyer who testified that he had known Yamashita personally for six or seven years, introduced by a mutual friend. "Our association has been very intimate," Yoshida said. "We were family friends, and my children visited his family quite often." It was an odd statement, because since the late thirties Yamashita had been stationed in China, then Malaya, then Manchuria, and finally the Philippines and had spent very little time in Japan. Since his embarkation for Malaya in 1941, in fact, Yamashita had stopped in Japan only twice, for a few days each, and would have had precious little time to socialize with anybody. The discrepancy went unremarked.

Yoshida testified that Yamashita had a wonderful reputation. "Among the people of Japan General Yamashita was highly respected for his high ideals and for his morals and deep sympathy towards each and every one and in his strict military discipline. Aside from his military activities General Yamashita was known for his friendship and for keeping his promises and for his high character—a man of the highest character."

When Guy asked Yoshida if the news of the trial in Japan had any adverse effect on Yamashita's reputation, Yoshida answered that it had not. "In fact, this publicity has had the opposite effect, and the people knowing [*sic*] General Yamashita to be a person of such high character that the public is in sympathy with General Yamashita." Indeed, said Yoshida, Yamashita had always been opposed to the war—in China, against the British, and against the Americans—and an opponent of Tojo's aggression. "General Tojo disliked General Yamashita extremely," Yoshida said. "General Yamashita always stated to me that war between the United States and Japan was undesirable." And when Yamashita learned he was to be sent to the Philippines, he asked Yoshida to introduce him to a Catholic priest because he knew the Filipinos were predominantly Catholic and "he had great concern for the religion of the Filipinos and he wanted to study on these matters."

Next up was Shigetaro Amakasu—"a very elderly-appearing officer," said the *New York Times*—a lieutenant general in the Imperial Japanese Army who had known Yamashita for forty years. Yamashita's reputation in the army was that of a man who "believed very greatly in righteousness. As a leader of troops, he was well disciplined. If the manner of the troops were not good, he would deal with them sternly, and if their behaviors were good he would praise them. His righteousness in dealing out discipline to the men is well known. While his disciplines are stern, he is very kind. And furthermore, he is a humanitarian."

Guy then introduced the written statement of a general from Yamashita's prefecture, who had known Yamashita since they were teenagers and later classmates at the military academy. Retired in 1941, the general had stayed in touch with Yamashita through the years:

His personal reputation is that of an upright, sedate and good citizen of a pleasant, kindly and human [*sic*] disposition and is a man of simple and complete honesty. He is particularly known for his friendly manner and for his ability to make and retain friends for many years. During his years as a poor young officer, he was known as having helped his family in a financial way. He is known to be of an even disposition and not quarrelsome or given to force and violence.

His kindly and human disposition has endeared him to all who have served with him and particularly to those who have served under him. He is known as a strict disciplinarian, requiring a high degree of conduct and performance from his subordinates but at the same time is an officer who has never misused privileges attending his high rank and position. Always he was known to make absolutely certain when any mistake had been made that upon reflection, he would determine whether he himself might have been at fault instead of the subordinate before taking action against that subordinate; but then taking action swiftly and surely. His reputation as a

combat general and tactician is well established. Knowing his personal character and his upright and honest nature I am sure for that reason, if for no
other, that he would always require a high degree of personal conduct from
those serving under him.

It was becoming apparent that these self-described friends and colleagues
of Yamashita were but the opening acts for the headliner. It is a common truth
that a major trial is as much theater as law. Both the prosecution and the defense have a story to tell, and presenting that story to those who hold the verdict in their hands is among the most important elements of trial strategy. A
lawyer must master the cast of witnesses, the script of the drama, the timing of
the action, and the reaction of the audience as skillfully as any director. The defense team was not nearly as experienced in courtroom theater as the assistant
district attorneys on Kerr's staff, but they were learning. Before introducing
the main character, they were showing the audience—the commissioners—just
who this man was who was about to take the stage. For much of the first four
weeks, his name had barely been mentioned. Soon he would be in the spotlight. Anticipation ran high on the next day, the twenty-sixth of the trial. After
days of lackluster attendance, the Manila mansion was packed with U.S. soldiers
and sailors, Filipino citizens, and newsreel cameras.

But there were more opening acts to go through. A twenty-five-year member of the Japanese Diet, who had known Yamashita as a lieutenant colonel
many years earlier, testified that there had been great celebrations in Japan after
the victory at Singapore, but that "General Yamashita said that at that time he
told his troops that, as the war was not over, it was not the correct time to celebrate, and furthermore, there were more than 100,000 allied prisoners. So it
was felt that it was not proper to celebrate the fall of Singapore at that time, and
so instead a ceremony for the more than 3000 [Japanese] dead or injured was
sponsored." A monument to the Japanese dead was erected, and "at that time
General Yamashita said that as there are [*sic*] no one here to commemorate the
English dead it is very proper to set up a similar monument for the English.
So a cross-shaped monument was put up at the very spot and it is still there.
This monument was in commemoration of both British and Australian troops."
About a month before he left Singapore, "General Yamashita attended or visited
these monuments and put flowers on them."*

---

*Yamashita did indeed order the building of such a monument. It was a 10-foot-high
wooden cross, simple and rough-hewn, apparently from two-by-fours, in a secluded, landscaped spot not far from the memorial to the Japanese dead, which was 40 feet high. A photo
appears on the Singapore National Archives' website Roll of Honour (http://www.roll-of-
honour.com/Overseas/SingaporeJapaneseInvasion.html).

Guy then read into the record some statements from Japanese generals, each emphasizing that Yamashita was considered a "moderate" in the Japanese military establishment, urging that Japan not go to war against the British and the Americans, and that he was respected, apolitical, and professional, and a man of excellent character. One general noted, "As an illustration of the kindly and gentle nature of the man I wish to point out an instance. When General Yamashita returned from Germany [after his inspection of German forces in 1941], he brought me a gift. One might have expected from such a soldier to receive a sword or some weapon indicative of the military profession. Instead of that he brought me a beautiful little statue of a little girl, sitting on a bench. He seemed to think that the statue was very pretty and [he] evidenced great pleasure in presenting it to me."

A colonel who had visited Yamashita in Singapore shortly after the fall of that city took the stand to relate a story of a noncommissioned officer who had assaulted a "native woman" during the campaign. "He court-martialed the noncommissioned officer who committed this crime. In addition, he reprimanded the immediate superior officer of this noncommissioned officer, [and] he published this fact throughout his subordinate units. The purpose of this posting of this notice was to warn the Japanese Army against such crime, so that it will not take place again."

Kerr saw his opening. "Is it customary in the Japanese Army to punish the officers of men who commit wrongful acts?" he asked on cross-examination.

"There is moral responsibility," the colonel replied. Asked to explain his answer, he said, "There are two types of punishment: first, by military court, or by law; and on the other hand, there is punishment for delinquency of supervisory responsibility."

"Under Japanese military law, is an officer held responsible for the wrongful acts of his men?"

The colonel may have seen the path he was being invited to walk. "Yes, a Japanese officer is responsible for the subordinate's acts," he said. "However, it is not legal responsibility, but it is a moral responsibility."

"And is he punishable by reason of that moral responsibility?" Kerr asked.

"Yes," said the colonel. "What I meant to say regarding this moral responsibility is that in some instances an officer is forced to resign from the service."

Nice try. But the defense had opened the door. Kerr:

In view of the fact that the defense has seen fit to put on testimony concerning the conduct of Yamashita's troops in Singapore, his disciplinary measures, his reputation and character by reason of those acts in Singapore, the prosecution will be prepared at the time of its rebuttal case to introduce competent testimony concerning the conduct of Yamashita's troops in

Singapore and during the Malayan campaign, as well as the acts or failures to act, of Yamashita.

It was a startling statement. Opening the trial to evidence of what had happened in Malaya and Singapore—a campaign MacArthur and the United States had had nothing to do with—would effectively create a second trial, with months of preparation and testimony, delaying indefinitely any execution. Reynolds was unruffled. "The comments of the prosecution are noted," he said.

The final two character witnesses took the stand. Like the others, they had nothing but good to say about Yamashita. ("Very fine and lofty character," said one. "Honest, straight and frank. Very kind, affectionate and sympathetic.")

With that, Clarke stood. "General Yamashita," he said.

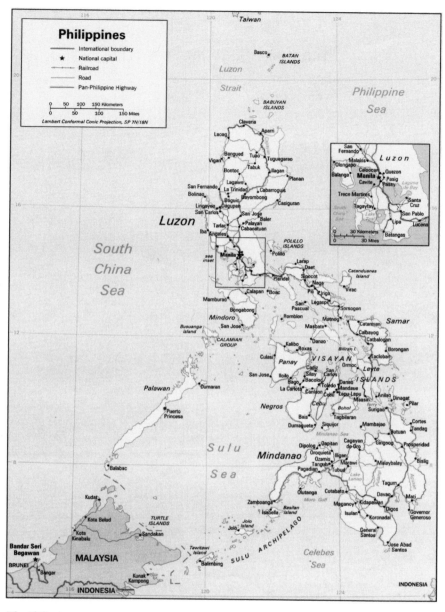

The Philippines.

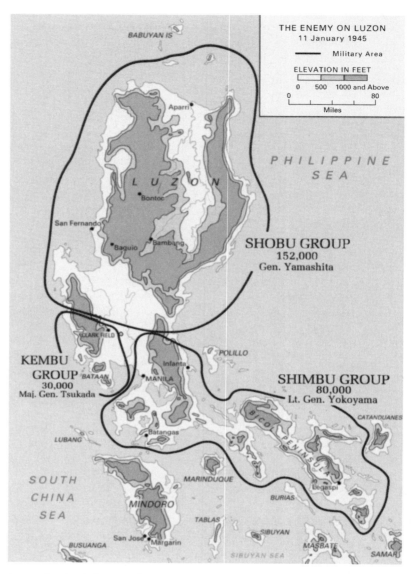

Luzon, showing deployment of Japanese forces in January 1945. Yamashita's command post was in Baguio. U.S. forces landed at Lingayen, south of San Fernando, and at Mindoro, and advanced to Manila.

General Tomoyuki Yamashita, in an official portrait following his promotion in 1942.

General Yamashita surrenders near Kiangan, northern Luzon, on September 2, 1945.

General of the Army Douglas MacArthur. Courtesy of the Library of Congress.

Yamashita arrives at the High Commissioner's Residence on October 8, 1945, to enter his plea of not guilty at his arraignment. On the right is Aubrey Saint Kenworthy, the military police chief.

The prosecution team. Seated from left, Captain Jack M. Pace; Captain Delmas C. Hill; Captain William N. Calyer; Lieutenant George E. Mountz, USN; Major Robert M. Kerr, chief prosecutor; Captain Manning Webster; Major Glicerio Opinion of the Philippine Army. The person in the rear is unidentified. Courtesy of the Allen County Library and the family of George E. Mountz.

The defense team. Seated from left, Lieutenant Colonel James G. Feldhaus; Colonel
Harry E. Clarke; chief defense counsel Lieutenant Colonel Walter C. Hendrix; standing, left
to right, Captain A. Frank Reel, Major George F. Guy, Captain Milton Sandberg. Courtesy
of the Allen County Library and the family of George E. Mountz.

The commissioners pose. Seated in the center is Major General Russel B. Reynolds; to
his right is Major General Leo Donovan, and to his left is Major General James Lester.
Standing are Brigadier General Morris Handwerk, left, and Brigadier General Egbert
Bullene, right. Courtesy of the Allen County Library and the family of George E. Mountz.
(Reynolds, a major general, appears to wear only one star on his left collar.)

The trial in progress, in the ballroom of the U.S. High Commissioner's Residence in Manila. The commissioners are in the center; General Yamashita and defense counsel to their right, behind the interpreters; prosecutors to their left. The witness is unidentified.

Chief prosecutor Major Robert M. Kerr. Courtesy of the Allen County Library and the family of George E. Mountz.

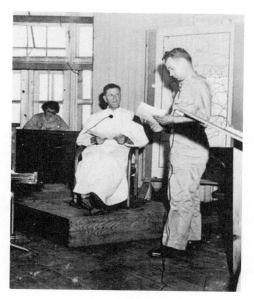

Captain Calyer examines Father Cosgrave.

The defense team listens to testimony. At rear of table: Masakatsu Hamamoto, Yamashita's interpreter; General Yamashita; General Muto; and Lieutenant Colonel Feldhaus. At front of table: Colonel Clarke, Captain Sandberg, Captain Reel, Lieutenant Colonel Hendrix, and T/4 Lea (Walker) Wood, secretary to the defense team. In front of the defense table, Major Harry Pratt, USMC, the chief interpreter, sits with a U.S. Army interpreter.

Captains Sandberg (foreground) and Reel (right) flank their client.

Yamashita testifies.

Reynolds (behind microphones) pronounces sentence on Yamashita, December 7, 1945. Colonel Clarke and Mr. Hamamoto look on; Major Pratt is to Yamashita's left. The prosecution team stands at its table. (Lieutenant Mountz has identified himself.) Courtesy of the Allen County Library and the family of George E. Mountz.

The Supreme Court of the United States, 1945–1946. Seated from left, Stanley Reed, Owen J. Roberts, Chief Justice Harlan Fiske Stone, Hugo L. Black, Felix Frankfurter. Standing from left, Robert H. Jackson (on leave 1945–1946), William O. Douglas, Frank Murphy, Wiley Rutledge. Justice Roberts retired shortly before the Yamashita case was argued and was replaced by Harold Burton, but no new photograph was taken. Courtesy of the Supreme Court of the United States.

13

The Defense

Yamashita Testifies

General Yamashita had thought he would be called as a witness by the prosecution. When his lawyers told him that he would testify in his own behalf, he was hesitant. "In America, is it considered proper for a man to testify in his own defense? In Japan it is not done. It is not considered dignified for an accused person to say anything in justification of himself. The Japanese leave that to heaven—the Omniscient knows the truth and will make the final judgment."

"I told the general," Captain Reel noted dryly, "that we Americans did not trust heaven to that extent."

Yamashita stood at the counsel table and walked forward. Thinner now than when he had surrendered nearly three months earlier, he was still an imposing figure, tall and completely bald, wearing his green uniform with campaign ribbons on the breast, an open-necked white shirt, and leather boots with spurs. Flashbulbs popped as he strode to the witness chair and raised his right hand and swore his oath. A Nisei American sergeant interpreted.

"Please state your name," Colonel Clarke said.

"Tomoyuki Yamashita."

"What was your assignment prior to the surrender?"

"Commanding General of the 14th Area Army."

"When did you first assume command of the 14th Area Army?"

"9th of October, 1944."

Yamashita spoke in clear, measured tones, his hands on the arms of the desk chair, his eyes fixed on Clarke, all other eyes in the room fixed on him.

"Will you describe the general state of affairs which existed in the 14th Area Army group at the time you assumed command?"

"They were in an unsatisfactory condition. For example, the chief of staff of the headquarters was sick in bed. Among the old staff members there were only three left, and the new staff officers were not familiar with the conditions in the Philippine Islands. The strength was insufficient. We needed about five more divisions."

205

"Were there sufficient military supplies for the defense?"

"No. We needed food, gasoline and transportation facilities particularly. All supplies were deficient."

"Were you the supreme commander in the Philippines?"

"I was not the supreme commander," Yamashita answered. Field Marshal Terauchi, commander of the Southern Army, was. "I was under the command of Terauchi until the 30th of August of 1945," a few days before his surrender.

"Was the 4th Air Army under your command?"

"No."

"Was the 3rd Maritime Transport Command under you?"

"No." And in addition, Yamashita said, "there were approximately 30,000 men who were directly under the command of Imperial Headquarters and the Southern Army."

The commission broke for lunch. Clarke and Yamashita were off to a good start: precise questions, direct answers. And Yamashita was still a general. During the break, he approached the interpreter and asked him not to start reciting his answers until Yamashita was done.

After lunch, the subject was Leyte. The original plan, Yamashita testified, was for the navy and the air army to take the lead, coordinating with the army units stationed there. But the orders were changed, on October 22, shortly after the landing. "According to this new plan the greatest troop strength possible will be sent from Luzon to Leyte to assist in the decisive battle. It was a basic change on the Luzon plan so myself and the members of my headquarters were busy day and night and even at that we were short of time."

Under Clarke's questioning, Yamashita described the hopelessness of the situation. "I sent approximately 50,000 troops to Leyte, but due to the air attacks and attacks from the submarines only half of the troops actually arrived at Leyte."

"When did it become apparent to you that the battle of Leyte had been lost?"

"That was about the 7th of December when the Americans landed on Ormoc Bay," on the west coast of Leyte.

"What was your next problem?"

"It was the defense of Luzon." Terauchi sent three divisions in December, but a third to a half of those troops were lost to air and submarine attacks. Yamashita asked Terauchi that the Fourth Air Army, the Southern Army troops, and the Maritime Transport Command be transferred to his command, and gradually from December until mid-February they were. "The navy never came under my command," Yamashita testified. "But the navy land units which were stationed in Manila came under my command as of the 6th of January for tactical purposes."

What was the strategy for the defense of Luzon? asked Clarke.

Yamashita laid out his plan. "Taking advantage of the mountain terrain, my plan was to establish three strongpoints: in the north a strongpoint at Baguio and Balete Pass [Shobu Group, and Yamashita's headquarters]; the second strongpoint was west of Clark Field [Kembu Group]; the third strongpoint in mountains east of Manila [Yokoyama's Shimbu Group]. These plans were to carry out a delaying action."

Why a delaying action?

"In view of the Leyte operations, I realized that decisive battle was impossible. Therefore I decided on a delaying action to divert American forces in Luzon so as to keep them from attacking Japan, as much as possible. I realized the American air forces and navy were exceedingly superior to ours, and also the firepower of the ground forces were superior and very mobile. I could not conduct warfare on flat land. Therefore I employed a delaying action in the mountains."

"Where did Manila City fit into this picture?"

"I decided to put Manila outside the battle area," Yamashita answered. There were three reasons for this: "First, the population of Manila is approximately one million; therefore it is impossible to feed them. The second reason is that the buildings are very inflammable. The third reason is that because it is a flat land it requires tremendous number of strength [*sic*] to defend it."

"The army units evacuated Manila gradually in accordance with my orders," he went on, by the middle of December. Some 1,500 or 1,600 were left behind "to guard military supplies, to protect the military supply route, and to obtain oil."

And the navy?

"On or about the 13th of February"—this would have been ten days after the Americans crossed the Pasig River in the city itself—"I received a report to the effect that, while just an element of the Navy had evacuated the city, the majority still remained in Manila."

"What did you do upon learning that a large part of the Navy had remained in Manila?"

"I immediately sent an order to the Shimbu [Group, Yokoyama]. The order was to the effect that, in accordance with our original plan, to evacuate immediately all the navy troops from Manila."

Yamashita testified that when the Shimbu Group was organized in late December, he personally told Yokoyama that Manila was to be evacuated. "I fully instructed him as to the Manila situation. And the Shimbu Group fully informed Admiral Iwabuchi of these plans, and he should have been fully cognizant of them." When he learned in mid-February that Iwabuchi and his naval forces were still in Manila, he told Yokoyama to order the navy to "withdraw from Manila immediately."

Clarke might have done well to remain there, asking follow-up questions to make sure the commissioners were getting the point, but instead he cut to the chase. "During the period of your command of the 14th Army Group [*sic*], between the dates of 9 October 1944 and the date of your surrender, did you know of any mistreatment of the civilian population in Manila?"

Yamashita spoke deliberately. "I knew nothing about mistreatment of civilians in Manila." Only in early April, he said, did he receive any report, and that was from Tokyo, to the effect that the government of Spain had lodged a protest about Spanish citizens in Manila—their mistreatment, presumably—"and I was ordered to investigate this matter, so I sent a message to the Shimbu Group telling them to conduct an investigation and report it to me immediately." About a week later Shimbu Group reported that they had been unable to find out anything. Though Yamashita did not say so, Shimbu Group was in no position to make inquiries about anything in Manila, the city being firmly in control of the American army at that point. That was the extent of his knowledge of what was happening to civilians in Manila.

"Did you issue any instructions or orders for the destruction of buildings and other property in the city of Manila?" Clarke asked.

"I never issued such an order, but I did order the destruction of the militarily important bridges on the road from Lingayen to [Manila] and in between Manila and Batangas"—two bridges the Americans would have to cross on their advance on the city, Krueger's Sixth Army from the north after their landing at Lingayen, and Eichelberger's Eighth Army from the south after coming ashore in Batangas.

"Did you receive any report from any source whatsoever to the effect that buildings and other property was [*sic*] being destroyed in the city of Manila?"

"No, I absolutely did not receive such reports."

"Did you at any time issue any orders directing the killing of noncombatant civilians?"

"Absolutely not."

"Did you receive a report from any source whatsoever to the effect that noncombatant civilians were being killed or raped by Japanese troops in the city of Manila?"

"I never received such a report."

"Did you know or did you receive a report to the effect that any of your subordinate commanders had issued any orders directing the killing of noncombatant civilians in the city of Manila?"

"I have never heard of it."

"Did you at any time issue an order directing the execution of American prisoners of war?"

Yamashita raised his voice. "Absolutely not."

"Did you receive any reports to the effect that your subordinate officers had issued any orders of that kind?"

"No."

"Did you receive any report from any source whatsoever that Japanese soldiers had or were killing American prisoners of war?"

"No."

Yamashita acknowledged that he had never visited any POW or civilian internment camps in the Philippines. "I was absorbed day and night in planning for the defense of Luzon. I had to concentrate on tactical matters and consequently I had no spare time to look into anything else."

Clarke asked what Yamashita's "policy" was with respect to POWs.

"My policy was that they should be treated exactly the same as officers, noncommissioned officers and enlisted men of the Japanese armed forces." He heard nothing different from General Kou, the War Ministry's staff officer in charge of POW matters. Kou filed routine reports twice, and twice spoke to Yamashita personally, but the only irregularity he brought up was the growing shortage of food. "There was a definite deficiency of food," Yamashita said, contradicting Kou's fairy tale, but Yamashita had ordered that the portions allotted to the POWs should be the same in quality and quantity as that given to Japanese soldiers, "and I never received any reports to the contrary."

To alleviate the food shortage as much as he could, Yamashita said, he repeatedly requested shipments from the Southern Army, "but they were always attacked on the way by American airplanes or submarines." His staff bought rice on the market, but because of the lack of transportation, little could get through. "It was unavoidable but the situation became increasingly worse."

Clarke returned to the subject of American prisoners of war, but only briefly, asking Yamashita when the Maritime Transport Command had been transferred to him. Yamashita replied that it happened in the middle of January. The natural next step would have been a statement in the form of a question: "So in December 1944, when the notorious hell-ship *Oryoku Maru* departed from Japan and was attacked with much American loss of life, was maritime transport under your command?" But Clarke moved on.

"Did you receive any instructions concerning the disposition of civilian internees?"

Perhaps due to the translation, Yamashita answered as to prisoners of war, not internees. He said he had received orders from Tokyo, through Terauchi's Southern Army, that "if the enemy approaches and the conditions become unavoidable," he was to release the prisoners. The order that he in turn issued, Yamashita said, was somewhat different. "My instructions were that if the United States troops *landed*," he testified (emphasis added), "a roster of all the prisoners was to be made up and turned over to a third power, a neutral power, and that one month's supply of rations should be prepared to be left with the prisoners. Since the time element in the two orders was different, I was reprimanded by the Southern Army."

Yamashita said that "prisoners were released in accordance with my instructions—not exactly as my instructions stated, but generally speaking they followed that plan." The difference was that "the camp commander was supposed to turn over the list of prisoners to the protecting power, and he thought that the protecting power of the United States was the Swiss, and he asked the ambassador about it, but he was unable to contact the Swiss government." In fact, Kou had tried to contact the American protecting power, Switzerland, instead of Japan's protecting power, Spain, and as a result the release plan was never actually implemented. But Yamashita's assertion that the prisoners were "released in accordance with my instructions," even if inexactly so, was clearly wrong. The biggest POW camp, at Cabanatuan, was liberated by a daring and stealthy assault led by U.S. Army Rangers in late January 1945, some three weeks after the landing at Lingayen. There was no "release" of any kind, there or at any other POW camp.

Clarke turned to the matter of Filipino guerrillas. What reports had Yamashita received?

"After the American landings on Leyte, the guerrilla attacks increased more and more, and they interfered with military operations at quite a few places," Yamashita answered. On October 11, two days after his arrival in the Philippines, "at a conference with the chief of staff, we discussed this matter, and I said that armed guerrillas, those guerrillas carrying weapons, must be suppressed by means of military action. I issued an order for the suppression of armed bandits."

Major Harry Pratt, a U.S. Marine acting as a supervisory interpreter, interjected. "If the commission please, the witness has made a specific point of using this term of 'armed bandits' in contrast to the word adopted in Japanese as 'guerrilla.' I don't know just why he has, but he has made a specific point of adopting this word."

"Very well," General Reynolds responded. "We think the meaning is clear."

Clarke pulled out the operations order issued on October 11, which the prosecution had introduced in its case, and read, "In view of the special characteristics of the Philippine operation, subversive activities of the residents and attacks in our rear by airborne raiding forces must be considered. In order to avoid mistakes in conducting the operations, take precautions against armed guerrillas, subjugate them quickly, and put a stop to their activities."

Yes, said Yamashita. That was my order.

And with that the day ended. It had been a vigorous performance. Yamashita's knowledge of English was apparently greater than many had assumed. "Staring at his interpreters, Yamashita frequently shook his finger like a lecturing schoolmaster," the Associated Press reported. "He repeated remarks for the young

Nisei interpreters, nodding benignly when they translated to his satisfaction." "Booted, spurred, beribboned and self-possessed," wrote Robert Cromie in the *Chicago Daily Tribune*, "the burly general filled the witness chair and tapped his leg with his fingers as he spoke. He peered intently at the ceiling between questions" and "nodded his huge head to emphasize his answers and spoke in a firm, decisive voice."

The accuracy of the interpreters continued to raise questions. "One could sense that Yamashita felt that some of the information he gave was not reaching the American Military Commission in the form he wanted," wrote Mac Johnson, covering the trial daily for the *New York Herald Tribune*.

Across the courtroom his personal interpreter, Japan-born, Harvard-educated Hamamoto, would stir uneasily and grimace, informing the courtroom in pantomime what he could not say in court—that questions put to his boss were improperly worded or that the "Tiger's" answers were not properly interpreted. Defense counsel, however, said that nothing important had been mistranslated or misinterpreted during the afternoon. The five generals on the commission seemed to agree that the job of hurdling the language barrier was satisfactory and fair to Yamashita.

Yamashita returned to the stand the next morning, November 29, the twenty-seventh day of trial, this time with Major Pratt as the interpreter. Clarke took his client over some of the same ground that had been plowed the day before, his questions drawing distinctions between what Yamashita had ordered and what he knew.

"Did you issue any order or did you authorize the killing of noncombatant civilians?"

"Absolutely not."

"Did you receive a report from any source to the effect that noncombatant civilians were being killed by Japanese forces?"

"I never received such a report from anyplace."

"What was your policy regarding the relationship that should be carried out between the Japanese troops and Filipino civilians?"

"Since we were allied with the Philippines," he began—an assertion most Filipinos would have spat upon—"I said that we should maintain close relationships with them and cooperate with them." Meeting with his subordinate commanders and chiefs of staff, "I told them to think this matter over and to handle the Filipinos carefully, to cooperate with them and to get as much cooperation as possible from the Filipino people."

"Did you order or did you authorize the military police to employ methods of torture in order to extract information from any persons?"

"Absolutely not."

"Did you receive any reports from any source whatsoever that the military police were using methods of torture for this purpose?"

"I did not receive such a report from anywhere."

"Did you ever order or authorize the military police to execute suspected guerrillas?"

"Absolutely not."

"Did you ever receive a report from any source whatsoever that the military police were executing suspected guerrillas?"

"No."

Clarke returned to the subject of General Ricarte, recalling the testimony of the two Filipino collaborators claiming that they had been told that Yamashita had ordered the slaughter of all Filipinos. He had met Ricarte three times, Yamashita said, none of which were at his home.

"Did you, during these three occasions on which you met General Ricarte, tell General Ricarte that you had issued orders, or that you intended to issue orders, for the extermination of the Philippine population?"

"I definitely did not say anything to General Ricarte about killing the Philippine population, and if you consider it from a common sense point of view, the killing of thirty million Filipinos is an unthinkable matter. I have never issued such an order."

Clarke was nearly done, and he ended emphatically. "Did you ever issue any order directing that any of these atrocities be committed?"

"I definitely did not order these things."

"Did you ever receive any reports, from any source whatsoever, that any of these atrocities had been committed?"

"No. The first time that I heard about them was when I got the charges [in the bill of particulars] at New Bilibid Prison, and I was very surprised."

Clarke paused. "Having heard the testimony relating to these atrocities in this trial, have you anything further to say with reference to that testimony?"

"I have a word to say," Yamashita answered deliberately. "The matters which are referred to in the charges, I have known for the first time from the testimony of the witnesses before this court. And if such acts were committed by my subordinates, they are in complete disagreement with my own ideas. And if such did occur, I feel that they occurred at such a time and place that I could not have known of it beforehand."

Yamashita turned to the American generals. "I have never ordered such things, and I have never condoned such actions, nor have I ever recognized such actions, and if I had known of them in advance, I would have taken every possible means to have caused them to stop. And if I had found out about them afterwards, I would have punished them to the fullest extent of military law."

Clarke knew a good final line when he heard one. "You may examine," he said to Kerr. But Reynolds apparently sensed the drama of the moment as well. He called a recess of twenty minutes, twice the usual midmorning length.

The direct examination had been Clarke's finest performance of the trial. It was less than three hours long, total—less time than had been spent on some of the episodes in the prosecution's case—and Clarke had forsaken every extraneous detail in order to focus repeatedly on what Yamashita had known and what he had ordered, on what difficulties he had faced, and on why he had done what he did. Yamashita's answers had been simple and wholly unequivocal—his voice "steady as a chant," one reporter noted. If the verdict was to turn on his orders, his knowledge, or his intentions, and not just his status as commanding general, he had made a powerful case for his acquittal.

Still, he had next to deal with Major Kerr, who had shown himself a skilled advocate when presenting his own case. When the commissioners filed back in, Kerr began the most important cross-examination of the trial.

He started in 1909 and had Yamashita recount thirty-five years of military service prior to his assumption of command in the Philippines. Yamashita had risen steadily through the officer ranks, rotating between command and staff positions: battalion commander, attaché in Germany and Switzerland, War College, regimental commander, War Ministry, brigade commander, chief of staff of an army, division commander, inspector general of the air force, commander of the Twenty-Fifth Area Army in Malaya and Singapore—then Manchuria, then to the Philippines as commander of the Fourteenth Area Army. Kerr asked him about his duties at each step along the way, pausing at Yamashita's service as a brigade commander in China in 1937, the opening of the war between Japan and China, and the year of the notorious Rape of Nanking, when the Japanese army had brutalized the Chinese unmercifully.

"Did you hear of any cases of mistreatment of civilians in China by Japanese troops?"

"I didn't hear anything about that. The Chinese people were fully cooperative," Yamashita replied—a characterization that few Chinese would have agreed with.

"Did you ever hear of the so-called Rape of Nanking?"

"At that time I was in Peiping [Beijing] and I didn't hear about anything in that area."

Kerr moved on, asking Yamashita about his actions against guerrillas in China. Yamashita was unruffled: guerrillas were not a particular problem in his area; their victims were primarily civilians. Weren't guerrillas a problem in Malaya and Singapore? No, said Yamashita. There was no contact with guerrillas. "Things were extremely quiet."

Kerr moved on to the Philippines, letting Yamashita repeat the limitations of his command when he arrived in October 1944, much as he had done on direct. Kerr elicited little that was new.

"Do you know that it was a requirement of the Japanese military in Manila that civilians bow to Japanese sentries?"

"That was a matter of free will with the Filipinos,"Yamashita countered. It was not; Filipinos were humiliated at the requirement. But Kerr did not dwell on the point.

"Did you see civilians being arrested on the streets of Manila?"

"No."

Did Yamashita ever visit any POW camps in the Philippines?

"No, I did not. Since I was extremely busy with my operational command and future plans, I did not have the time to do this."

What was the attitude of civilians toward the Japanese? Kerr asked.

"They maintained an anti-Japanese attitude,"Yamashita acknowledged."As the Americans approached, the people in those areas gradually became more hostile."

"What did you do about that hostility?"

"There was nothing I could do about this attitude."

Kerr moved quickly, seldom pausing to press Yamashita on his answers, questioning him about organization, officers, channels of communications, reports. If there was a pattern to his cross-examination, it was difficult to discern.

Why did Yamashita leave antiguerrilla matters to his subordinate commanders?

"Since the operations against the American forces were the most important matter at hand, anything concerning the guerrillas was merely a minor matter along with other things."

"As military commander in this area, in the Philippines, was it not your duty to see to it that the civilian population was protected?"

"It was one of my duties,"Yamashita replied carefully. "But after operational commands—I was absorbed completely by these operations."

"Was it your responsibility to protect civilians against the wrongful acts of Japanese troops?"

"If the Japanese forces did these things and if I knew about it, it would be my duty to stop it."

Kerr went into several questions about when and where Yamashita moved his troops after the attack on Leyte, and then about his efforts to obtain food, giving Yamashita an opening to repeat much of what he had said on the subject during his direct examination.

"Were all of the prisoner of war camps in the Philippines under your command?"

"Yes."

"Were the civilian internment camps under your control?"

"Yes."

"You testified that it was a policy from Tokyo that in the event of land fighting, naval troops on land would come under your command?"

Food supplies, POWs, civilian internees, command of naval forces, all in four questions—Kerr seemed unwilling to stay with any subject, or to press Yamashita on anything. To be sure, Yamashita was giving him little to work with: his answers were responsive, but brief and consistent.

Kerr's frustrations began to show. Did the military police—the Kempetai—have as one of their duties the investigation of persons suspected of being anti-Japanese?

"It would depend upon the extent to which they were anti-Japanese, and this would include the guerrillas."

"What if they were not guerrillas but merely pro-American?"

"That is something that is in their mind only and we can't possibly know it."

"Are people who assist guerrillas by giving them food or shelter treated as guerrillas by the Japanese Army?"

"We recognize only those armed bandits as guerrillas, and I have [issued] orders to that effect."

"Then a person who was found to have given food or shelter to a guerrilla was not considered a guerrilla, is that correct?"

"No, they are not."

"What in your opinion would be required to justify a death sentence" for guerrillas?

"It would be an extremely serious crime."

"Would being the wife of a guerrilla be such a crime?"

"That is not a serious crime."

"Would being a child of a guerrilla be such a crime?"

"Absolutely not."

"Or being a brother or other relative of a guerrilla?"

"Being a relative of a guerrilla is not a serious crime."

Kerr asked if it was "customary" for Japanese soldiers "to slap or cuff another below his rank"—a well-known practice in the Japanese army, but Yamashita denied it was so, and moreover said that he had never seen it happen. Its relevance was dubious, as was the denial.

It was getting late in the day, and Kerr had not laid a glove on Yamashita. At 4:30, Reynolds interrupted him in the middle of a question to announce that the trial would recess until the morning.

"Three hours of searching cross-examination by Major Robert M. Kerr, chief prosecutor," the *New York Herald Tribune* reported, "failed to wring a single contradictory or damaging statement" from Yamashita. "The best the prosecution could do was cast doubt on his credibility as a witness. Yamashita testified that he had never heard of and knew nothing about the 'rape of Nanking,' and that he had never seen a Japanese officer slap, cuff or beat a subordinate." (In fact, Yamashita testified only that he did not know of the Rape of Nanking at the time it had happened, in 1937; he did not testify that he had not heard of it since.)

Kerr resumed the next morning, focusing on several incidents in which American prisoners had been mistreated or executed by Japanese soldiers on islands distant from Luzon. Yamashita repeatedly testified that he did not know of these events, and Kerr moved on to details of the destruction of the bridges to slow the American advance on Manila, an action that must have been recognized by everyone in the room as a legitimate military tactic. Yamashita answered patiently: "These bridges were a part of the communications system between Manila, Batangas, and Lingayen and it was done in order to cut these lines of communication so that the United States forces could not move along these lines at will."

"Did you receive any instructions from the Southern Army that in the event of the loss of Manila, its use to the enemy will be hampered by cutting off its water supply and by other such measures?"

"No, I haven't."

"Are you sure?" Kerr asked. "Is that correct?"

"Yes."

Whatever Kerr's skills as a presenter of evidence, his inexperience in cross-examination showed. Undermining the credibility of this defendant was proving to be a far more challenging task than letting victims tell their stories, and Kerr was making no discernible progress. To be fair, he had not interrogated Yamashita before the trial—though it is not clear why he did not—and so he was flying by the seat of his pants, as the defense had during the prosecution's case, but the stakes were much higher here, and Yamashita was giving Kerr nothing to work with. He was not contradicting himself; there was nothing to catch him up on.

Kerr resorted to sarcasm. Yamashita testified, as he had on direct, to the dates of his three brief meetings with Ricarte. "Since you were such a busy man that you did not have time even to inspect the Fort McKinley prisoner of war camp, how do you account for your clear recollection of the dates of these visits?"

"There are some things that I do not recall and there are some things that I recall sufficiently well."

"If you did issue an order for the killing of Filipino civilians who showed hostility towards Japanese forces, would that be a highly secret order?"

"I neither issued such an order secretly or officially."

"If you had issued such an order, would it have been classified as highly secret?"

"I didn't issue such an order and I don't know about that."

In the afternoon session, Kerr hit upon a nugget that had not come out in Yamashita's questioning by Clarke. "Do you recall how many death sentences by courts-martial assessed against persons charged as guerrillas were approved by you in the Philippines?"

"I recall reviewing about 40 of the sentences concerning guerrillas from military tribunals," Yamashita replied. And "approximately four military court-martials."

"Then the only death sentences for guerrillas which you approved in the Philippine Islands totaled not more than 44; is that correct?"

"It was 44 cases. Forty cases involved the death sentence and some cases only involved one person and others involved five or six."

"A death sentence for a guerrilla could not be effected without your approval, is that correct?"

"Yes."

Because the Hague Convention of 1907 requires that those who take up arms in combat against the enemy be in an organized unit commanded by a person responsible for them, freelancing civilians, sometimes called bandits, who are not in such units are committing crimes of war and can be executed, after a trial. Some Filipinos were in organized units; others were not. Kerr did not draw Yamashita out on the difference or on the process of review that Yamashita said he undertook in the forty-four cases; nor did he press him on Sergeant Sakakida's testimony that the trials in the judge advocate's office were little more than formalistic orders of execution. His questions began to verge on the rhetorical; at one point Kerr asked Yamashita if the killing of 25,000 people in Batangas would be considered murder. Yamashita said he did not understand the question, and Kerr withdrew it and moved on.

Kerr began to question Yamashita on his understanding of the duties of a military commander, and the verbal fencing match that followed showed the prosecutor to be gaining some traction in his cross-examination, but the general to have a firm understanding of the law of command responsibility.

"Is it a recognized duty among soldiers of a commanding officer to control his troops so that they do not commit wrongful acts?"

"It is a recognized duty," Yamashita replied.

"Is it a wrongful act for soldiers to commit rape?"

"Not only for soldiers, is that a wrongful act."

"Is it a wrongful act for soldiers to kill unarmed civilians without trial?"

"Yes."

"Is it a wrongful act for soldiers to execute guerrillas?"

"Without trial, it cannot be done."

Kerr turned to a more subtle point. "Is it a wrongful act to execute a prisoner of war merely because he attempted to escape?"

"That would depend upon the circumstances," Yamashita answered.

"Under what circumstances would it be proper to execute a prisoner of war merely because he attempted to escape?"

"If the prisoner goes beyond the fixed limits of the [POW] area, and if there is no other means of stopping him, it falls within the duty of the guard to shoot him."

"I am referring to a prisoner who has attempted to escape and has been recaptured."

"In that case it cannot be done."

It was an exactly correct statement of international law.*

Kerr paused and consulted his notes. "You acknowledged that it is a recognized duty of a commanding officer to control his troops so that they do not commit atrocities?"

"It is his duty."

"Does the responsibility of a commanding officer stop when he takes action to punish his men for wrongful acts?"

"This would depend on the nature of the offense, and the offender will be legally punished, and if the offender's superiors have condoned or permitted or ordered the offenses, then they, too, would be punished. However, if the commanding officer has taken the necessary precautions and means to prevent it, then he is subject only to administrative reprimand."

Yamashita paused for the translation, then went on. "This is an extremely important point, and I wish there to be no mistake about the meaning of my words. I wish there to be no mistake in translation."

Reynolds spoke up. "The accused is offered an opportunity, if he wishes to do so, to reduce that statement to writing and have it translated by the interpreters and read to the commission. We wish to be sure that the accused has every opportunity to express himself." You can do so at the lunch recess, Reynolds said.

Kerr resumed his cross-examination. "If a commanding officer fails to take proper action to control his troops, under what circumstances would the responsibility be criminal responsibility?"

"In the case when a commanding officer should order murder or other such actions, or in the case when he orders it, permits it or condones it, that would be criminal responsibility."

---

* Because POWs are lawfully confined in military facilities, they are required to observe the limits of their internment. Prisoners attempting to escape may be shot in the act if warnings are ineffective. But if they make good their escape and are later recaptured, they may not be subject to punishment for the escape, though they may be put under "special surveillance."

"If a commanding officer, knowing that his troops might commit wrongful acts, took no action to prevent them, would he be criminally responsible?"

"Acts such as this must be stopped, but the location of the commanding officer and the time and the circumstances must also be taken into consideration."

"If, despite everything he did to prevent the acts, his troops committed wrongful acts, would the commanding officer be administratively responsible?"

"Even though he takes all the available means in order to prevent these acts, the location and the time and circumstances must be taken into consideration. However, if he has taken all possible means to stop them and still finds it impossible to prevent them he is subject to administrative responsibility. However, if the conditions are such that it is utterly impossible for him to take any action, then he would not even be administratively responsible."

"Under administrative responsibility might that officer be dismissed from the service?"

"It would depend upon the investigations and the decision of the superior officer as to whether he would be dismissed from the service or forced to resign."

Yamashita had given Kerr, and the commissioners, a clear line between criminal accountability and administrative responsibility. A commander (and if appropriate his superiors) would be criminally accountable for ordering, permitting, or condoning crimes. He would face administrative responsibility if he had simply failed to prevent those crimes, after location, time, and circumstances were taken into account. If it was "utterly impossible" for him to have prevented them, he would be exonerated. Otherwise, he would face administrative punishment ranging from reprimand to dismissal. It was a skillful comparison of legal accountability and military responsibility that in 1945 no lawyer could improve upon and no military officer, it would seem, could dispute. Yamashita had guided Kerr and the commission to exactly where he wanted them.

Kerr wanted no more of that. He turned and pointed dramatically to a map of the Philippines on the wall, marked with red pins and discs, representing the sites of the atrocities the commission had spent weeks hearing about. "Each red pin or disc represents a major violation of the laws of war, which according to testimony in this case was committed by your troops." He paused for effect. "According to the evidence," he continued, "approximately 60,000 unarmed men, women and children were killed in the Philippine Islands by men under your command. Do you deny to this commission that you knew of or ever heard of any of those killings?"

Yamashita was calm. "I never heard of it nor did I know of these events."

"Can you explain to the commission how all of those murders could have been committed from one end of the Philippine Islands to the other for a period of over seven months without your ever having heard of it?"

"I absolutely know nothing about it,"Yamashita replied.

Kerr paused, pointed his finger at Yamashita, and shouted, "This is your opportunity to explain to this commission, if you care to do so, how you could have failed to know about these killings."

Yamashita could not have asked for a better question, or a more opportune chance to state his defense. And he did so quietly, comprehensively, and at length. He leaned forward, gripping the arms of the witness chair, and turned to face the commission. He spoke slowly and precisely, pausing frequently for the interpreter, for forty-five minutes.

"The facts are," he began,

that I was constantly under attack by large American forces, and I have been under pressure day and night. Under these circumstances I had to plan, study and carry out plans of how to combat superior American forces, and it took all of my time and effort.

At the time of my arrival I was unfamiliar with the Philippine situation, and nine days after my arrival I was confronted with a superior American force. Another thing was that I was not able to make a personal inspection and to coordinate the units under my command. As a result of the inefficiency of the Japanese system, Japanese Army system, it was impossible to unify my command, and my duties were extremely complicated.

Another matter was that the troops were scattered about a great deal, and the communications would of necessity have to be good, but the Japanese communications were very poor and therefore the communications were not all they should have been.

Reorganization of the military force takes quite a while, and these various troops, which were not under my command, such as the air force, and the Third Maritime [Transport] Command, and the Navy, were gradually entering the command one at a time, and it created a very complicated situation. The source of command and coordination within a command is, or lies in, trusting in your subordinate commanders. Under the circumstances I was forced to confront the superior U.S. forces with subordinates whom I did not know and with whose character and ability I was unfamiliar.

Besides this, I put all my efforts to get the maximum efficiency and the best methods in the training of troops and the maintaining of discipline, and even during combat I demanded training and maintenance of discipline. However, they were inferior troops and there simply wasn't enough time to bring them up to my expectations. These were insufficiently trained troops, and for a long time they had been under the influence of a tropical climate, and due to the lowering of morale my plan became even more difficult.

I wished to augment my inefficient communications system by the use of airplanes, but when they came under my command they proved to be all useless. I tried to dispatch staff officers and various people to the outlying units, but the situation was such that they would be attacked by guerrillas en route and would be cut off. Consequently, it became very difficult to know the situation in these separated groups. When the Americans landed on Leyte, Mindoro and Luzon, the situation came to a point where our communications were completely disrupted.

And under conditions like this and with both the communication equipment and personnel of low efficiency and old type, we managed to maintain some liaison, but it was gradually cut off, and I found myself completely out of touch with the situation.

I believe that under the foregoing conditions I did the best possible job I could have done. However, due to the above circumstances, my plans and my strength were not sufficient to the situation, and if these things happened they were absolutely unavoidable. They were beyond anything that I could have expected. If I could have foreseen these things I would have concentrated all my efforts toward preventing it. If the present situation permits it, I will punish these people to the fullest extent of military law. Certain testimony has been given that I ordered the massacre of all the Filipinos, and I wish to say that I absolutely did not order this, nor did I receive the order to do this from any superior authority, nor did I ever permit such a thing, or if I had known of it would I have condoned such a thing, and I will swear to heaven and earth concerning these points.

Yamashita paused. "That is all I have to say."

The room was silent. Kerr hesitated, then stood up to resume his questioning.

"The commission interrupts," Reynolds said. He called a recess.

It had been "a dramatic forty-five-minute oration," Robert Trumbull of the *New York Times* wrote, "the simple eloquence of which shone even in the interpreter's version of his words. With his large shaven head thrust forward and his eyes narrowed to brown slits that glinted under the floodlights, the 'Tiger of Malaya' . . . [was] obviously aware that his life might well depend on his words."

When the commissioners came back in, Kerr tried to pick apart Yamashita's statement.

"These difficult conditions you describe became apparent to you soon after you came to the Philippines, did they not?

"Yes, immediately after my arrival."

"In view of your realization of those difficult conditions did you make any special effort to maintain control of your troops?"

"Yes, I took every possible opportunity and all possible methods to instruct the subordinate units in accordance with my instructions."

"Did you ever personally visit the battlefield?"

"At Fort McKinley we were constantly being bombed and at Baguio we were under shellfire all the time and my headquarters were just the same as the front lines."

"Can you as a soldier and as the commanding officer of the troops who committed those acts explain to the commission how it came about that those terrible things would be done in the Philippines during your command?"

"The reasons are the same as in the testimony I gave previously."

Kerr raised his voice. "You have no explanation to make concerning that conduct by your troops, is that correct? You desire to lay the blame and responsibility for these wrongs entirely upon subordinate officers and men, is that correct?"

Yamashita spoke quietly. "The persons who perpetrated these crimes should be punished and the immediate superior units should be subject to investigation and upon the findings they should receive either criminal punishment or administrative punishment."

"You admit, do you, that you failed to control your troops in the Philippines?"

"I have put forth my maximum effort in order to control the troops, and if this was not sufficient, then somehow I should have done more. Other people might have been able to do more, but I feel that I have done my very best."

Kerr, his voice raised still: "Did you fail to control your troops? Please answer yes or no."

"I believe that I did control my troops," Yamashita answered.

And with that Kerr sat down. "That is all, sir," he told the commission.

It was, by all the reviews, a formidable performance. "Major Kerr repeatedly attempted to make Yamashita contradict himself but never succeeded," Trumbull noted. "If his speech had not been broken at the end of each sentence for a translation," reported Mac Johnson of the *New York Herald Tribune*, "it would have been a dramatic oration. His booming voice held the attention of the commission and the spectators, although his words were understandable only to the interpreters."

Time magazine summed up the turn the trial had taken:

In their misery during the Japanese defense of Manila, Filipinos spoke the name of General Tomoyuki Yamashita as if it were blasphemous. When peace came and the "Tiger of Malaya" was brought to trial, they crowded the courtroom to stare. As they had expected, he looked like an ogre—a squat, shaven-headed simian figure in a green uniform. When prosecution witnesses told of the raping, killing and burning which Manila had endured at Japanese hands, many in the audience guessed that the verdict would be quick and harsh.

But [this] week, as the Japanese general rose to defend himself, spectators began to experience an uneasy perplexity. The chunky Japanese neither cringed nor swaggered. He bowed politely to the five U.S. generals sitting as judges. With ponderous dignity he instructed the Nisei interpreter: "Yamashita wants no mistakes. On long sentences I will repeat them twice. Listen carefully." Then he seated himself in the witness chair, [and] denied that he had ever known of Philippine atrocities, much less condoned or ordered them.

In ensuing hours of cross-examination he was never trapped into contradiction. Yamashita simply waited, without anger, through the prosecutor's periods of elaborate sarcasm, then licked his lips and answered in unhesitant Japanese.

He gave shrewd emphasis to a point few military men could consider without sympathy: he had arrived in the Philippines only nine days before the U.S. landings on Leyte, had been unfamiliar with the country, the people and even his own officers; thereafter he had been involved in the nerve-racking confusion of losing battles. "I was under constant attack by superior American forces," he said.

Slowly, almost passionately, he made his plea for understanding. . . . When the defense rested, the task of the trial commission no longer seemed simple. Yamashita's spirited defense had suddenly emphasized the lack of precedent for war crimes trials, the vagueness of the charges—violations of the rules of war. The commission had other problems. What was Yamashita—a consummate liar or a victim of circumstances? What was to be his fate? The rope or the firing squad? Prison? Freedom? Manila waited for the answer.

The twenty-eighth day was over, but not the trial. Manila would have to keep waiting for the answer. Yamashita had taken advantage of Reynolds's suggestion that he write out exactly his answer to Kerr's question on the responsibility of a commanding officer for the wrongful acts of his men. It was in Japanese, and the interpreter read it into the record, a somewhat more formal version of his answer, but not a different one.

The prosecution now had its chance for rebuttal, bringing evidence to respond to what the defense had presented. Reynolds reiterated his desire to see things wrapped up. "The commission anticipates with confidence that the trial will be brought to an early conclusion, other than the final arguments of counsel and the prosecution," he said, his words meant for Kerr.

But no prosecutor wants to see the curtain fall on the evidence while the words of an articulate and perhaps unexpectedly sympathetic defendant hang in the air. These five generals may have been handpicked by General MacArthur, but the prosecution staff would have been foolish to be overconfident, to assume that the verdict was a foregone conclusion, and fools they were not. Apart from General Reynolds, only General Donovan and General Lester had spoken during the proceedings, and then only to ask a few questions of a few witnesses. Reading a jury while the trial is underway, most trial lawyers would admit if pressed, is a crapshoot.

So Kerr had a lineup of witnesses waiting in the wings, and he called them one by one to the stage. Most of them were not very interesting, at this point in the trial. Two aid workers testified that there were difficulties delivering food to the internees at Santo Tomas, but most of their testimony was focused on a time before Yamashita had arrived in the Philippines. The city health inspector and the director of public markets were each called to testify that there was a shortage of food in Manila during the months preceding the arrival of the Americans and the battle in the city, and great difficulty in bringing down rice from the uplands or from abroad, which seemed, if anything, to corroborate Yamashita's account of the difficulties he faced.

When the prosecution called its next witness "to show the rice situation as it existed in the provinces and in Manila" during this time, Reynolds wearily objected. "Unless the prosecution has something entirely new, the commission feels it is fully informed about the rice situation." Captain Calyer said that the testimony would be brief; it turned out to be an extended lesson in the bureaucratic organization of the Philippine Rice and Corn Administration. When defense counsel took up an extended cross-examination, Reynolds had had enough. "The commission interrupts," he said. "We feel the point is being tortured." At this point, clearly, the commission was no longer interested, if it ever was, in such details.

The next prosecution witness, an attorney, testified that, contrary to Yamashita's testimony, the requirement that Filipinos bow when passing a Japanese sentry was no voluntary matter. "I saw people slapped by sentries, that did not bow, and we were even instructed through the press as to the manner of how to bow to these sentries"—these "gorillas," he called them. "We never did that before!" What followed was ironic. The defense objected to the testimony as not proper rebuttal—an unfounded objection, because the attorney was refuting Yamashita's testimony on the point.

But Kerr's answer was even more surprising. "Sir, this goes to the credibility of the accused, and in addition to that, it shows how little he knew about affairs in Manila."

Yamashita had spent nearly three days explaining why it was that he knew so little about "affairs in Manila." After twenty-nine full-day trial sessions in thirty-four days, both sides were close to exhaustion.

But Kerr had one more card to play. He called Colonel Hideo Nishiharu, now a prisoner but in Yamashita's headquarters the head of the judge advocate section, and as such the overseer of legal matters, including courts-martial and what he called "military tribunal" cases, reviewing the proceedings before sentences were carried out. The prosecutor's purpose was to show that Yamashita had at least once approved the immediate execution of many suspected Filipino guerrillas, without any trial.

Under Captain Webster's questioning, Nishiharu recalled that in December 1944 a "large number"—he later estimated 600—of guerrillas had been arrested by the military police. At that time, Nishiharu and the rest of Yamashita's headquarters were hurriedly preparing to head up to the hills of Baguio, and so, he testified, there simply was not time to hold trials.

"Did you discuss that matter with General Yamashita?" Webster asked.

"Yes, I spoke to the general, and I told him that a large number of guerrillas were in custody, but to try them in court would be impossible due to lack of time, and therefore the officer of the military tribunal, after an investigation, would cooperate with the military police in the handling of these prisoners"—the clear implication being that "cooperation" and "handling" meant execution, though Webster did not press him on the point.

"What action did General Yamashita take on your suggestion?"

"General Yamashita offered no suggestions. He just nodded."

"Did you take that nod as the approval of proceeding?"

"He didn't have any particular opinion to offer, so I accepted it."

"Is it true that those persons who were executed were without a proper trial or court-martial?"

"In theory, I cannot say that they were legally or officially tried."

"Did General Yamashita approve of all of the death sentences?"

"I did not understand that to be General Yamashita's idea or opinion."

"Did General Yamashita act upon all the sentences of death in December of 1944?"

"I do not know myself in detail how the general handled the matter."

Reynolds interjected. "What we are seeking is a clear cut picture of what he has to say, and we do not seem to have it. I would like to know more about what happened after he had the discussion with General Yamashita. It would be interesting to know how much time elapsed after the conversation with General Yamashita and the execution of these people."

Nishiharu had a surprising answer. The "conversation" with Yamashita—his nod of the head—had taken place on December 14 or 15. Over the next ten or eleven days, until December 25, the military police interrogated the suspected guerrillas at Bilibid Prison. This sequence of events would seem to have undercut the prosecution's theory—never fully articulated, but hanging in the air—that Yamashita's nod had been his assent to execution of the prisoners. Had it been, there would seem to have been no need for ten or eleven days of interrogation. Nishiharu was not asked how many of the 600 prisoners were executed, or whether any had been spared.

"Did you inform General Yamashita as to what happened to those suspected guerrillas?"

"Since I did not know fully myself, I couldn't report this to General Yamashita."

"Did General Yamashita ever ask you what was done with those suspected guerrillas?"

"No," said Nishiharu.

What had begun as ominous testimony that Yamashita had approved, by a nod, the execution of guerrillas without trial in December 1944 had degenerated to uncertainty over what had actually happened; who was executed; when; who, if anyone, was released; and by whose decision. Nishiharu stepped down, "leaving everyone thoroughly confused by his winding testimony," wrote Trumbull of the *New York Times*.

Nishiharu returned to the stand the next day, and Reel led him through a long, and far from clear, explanation of how court-martial and tribunal sentences were reviewed and approved in Yamashita's army. Some of the confusion, as the interpreters pointed out, arose from the fact that a term Nishiharu used could be translated as "policeman," "investigator," or "judicial officer." Reynolds expressed increasing frustration at the lack of clarity.

But when Reel finally brought the subject back to what Nishiharu had actually said to Yamashita in the head-nodding meeting, he got an answer different from the one Nishiharu had given the day before.

"Well, just what did you say to General Yamashita?" Reel asked.

"I expressed my opinion to General Yamashita as follows," said Nishiharu. "There is absolutely no time to judge [the detainees] in a formal court. They should be investigated by the officers of the military tribunal, and then in liaison with the Kempetai those who should be released should be released, and those that were to be punished should be punished, according to my opinion."

"And General Yamashita said nothing at all, is that right?"

"He said nothing. He only nodded."

That was quite a change from his testimony that he had told Yamashita that the military police would "cooperate in the handling" of the prisoners. In this version, Yamashita was simply being presented with a routine recommendation that the actual guerrillas should be punished and the rest released—a recommendation met with a dismissive nod. It was impossible to tell whether Nishiharu was changing his answer, or just rephrasing it, or whether the difference arose from a change in interpreters.

Whatever it was, Reynolds either was not listening or failed to appreciate the difference. "We have heard this story now four times," Reynolds said. Or so it seemed, anyway.

Nishiharu "had confused both prosecution and defense by his statements on Yamashita's responsibility for executing Filipino guerrillas," said the Associated Press dispatch.

The commission sat from 8:00 until nearly 10:30 that night, because Reynolds recalled Yamashita to the witness chair and questioned him at considerable length on who had authority to convene courts-martial, to review the verdicts, and to order that sentences be carried out, particularly death sentences. He seemed particularly concerned that Yamashita had testified that approval of death sentences was his responsibility and that he never delegated it. Nishiharu had testified, according to Reynolds's understanding anyway, that in fact several other general officers in the Philippines had authority to approve death sentences. Only after much questioning about the minutiae of court-martial procedure in the Japanese army did Yamashita understand the uncertainty over what he had testified to. He then explained that other commanding generals had such authority by virtue of their commands. It was not something he delegated to them.

He might have wondered why Reynolds was now focused on such a narrow point that seemed so far afield from the crimes he was charged with. At one point, when Reynolds asked whether the commanding general of Shimbu Group could "direct the execution of American prisoners of war or civilian internees, without obtaining the approval of General Yamashita," Yamashita explained: "He has the authority, but it must be in accordance with international law and the Geneva Convention. But this matter did not arise. He had this authority but in actual fact the situation never arose."

As he had in his earlier testimony, Yamashita showed a firm command of international law: the 1929 Geneva Convention on POWs did provide that they were subject to the laws in force for the army that had captured them, and a prisoner who committed a crime while a prisoner was subject to the same penalties as those prescribed for similar acts by members of that army, including death, provided that he had received a trial on the matter.

The questioning at last finished, Yamashita stepped down, having spent eighteen hours on the witness stand. His second stint lacked the drama of his testimony earlier in the week, but neither Kerr nor Reynolds had been able to establish any inconsistency in his testimony.

The trial was over, save for the closing arguments and the verdict. Reynolds, who had been relentless in scheduling trial sessions—thirty of them, including on Thanksgiving and several nights, in thirty-six days, save only Sundays—now announced that they would not sit the following day, so that counsel could prepare their closing arguments, which would be heard on Wednesday, December 5. "The commission anticipates with confidence that the findings will be announced on Friday, very likely in the afternoon," Reynolds announced.

It was Monday, December 3, 1945. Friday would be the fourth anniversary of the Japanese attack on Pearl Harbor.

It was an odd statement. How could Reynolds, or anyone, predict that, after thirty days of trial, producing a transcript of 3,900 pages and several hundred documentary exhibits, the judgment against the accused on 123 separate charges, and the sentence as well were he convicted, would be reached in less than forty-eight hours—and make such a prediction "with confidence"? MacArthur's regulations required that two-thirds of the commissioners concur on both the judgment and the sentence; that meant that four of the five generals must agree. Reynolds was the chairman, but each vote was equal: who was he to, in effect, speak for the other four about how long they would want, or need, to deliberate?

Unless, of course, he knew something. In civilian trials, judges routinely instruct jurors at the outset to keep an open mind until all the evidence is in and not to discuss the evidence among themselves until deliberations begin. Here, there was no judge to give those instructions, and MacArthur's regulations were silent on the point, although they did require that when all the evidence was in, the commission was to "consider the case in closed session," and so by implication not before.

But one of the dangers in a trial with the same five generals taking the roles of both judge and jury is that they must discuss the case among themselves as it is going on in order to make rulings on objections to evidence and on motions on a variety of subjects—to dismiss the charge, to require a bill of particulars, to allow a continuance.

There is no indication in the record, or from any other source available today, of the extent to which the five generals discussed the trial, the charges, the evidence, MacArthur's orders, the credibility of witnesses, the accused, the victims, or other aspects of the proceedings prior to their formal deliberations. But they had been together, virtually without interruption, for all their waking hours, at least six days a week for over five weeks. They were not only fellow officers but general officers, with a single common assignment that required them to work cooperatively together to reach a joint decision. It is hard to imagine that they had not been discussing Yamashita's guilt or innocence among themselves throughout the trial.

Before sending the lawyers off for their day of preparation, Reynolds had a request for them. "The commission desires to have presented by both prosecution and defense a factual, accurate, objective, dispassionate analysis of the matters before us which will be of help in arriving at a decision as to the guilt or innocence of the accused," he told them.

The procedure now was set. After oral arguments to conclude the case, the commission would deliberate and then in open court "deliver its judgment, and in the event of a conviction shall pronounce sentence," according to Mac-Arthur's regulations. "The commission may sentence an accused, upon conviction, to death by hanging or shooting, imprisonment for life or for any less term, fine, or such other punishment as the commission shall determine to be proper."

The commission's judgment would not be the end of the matter. No sentence would be final until it was "approved by the officer who convened the commission," in this case, General Wilhelm Styer, the U.S. Army's commander in the Philippines, who could reduce or suspend the commission's sentence but not increase it. And "no sentence of death shall be carried into effect until confirmed by the Commander-in-Chief, United States Army Forces, Pacific"— General of the Army Douglas MacArthur. Other than that, "the judgment and sentence of a commission shall be final and not subject to review." And that certainly meant no review by an actual court, with real judges, in the United States.

14

The Verdict

Popular impression sometimes to the contrary, closing argument is not a time for soaring rhetoric and dramatic appeals. The best closings, particularly in a trial as long and fact-filled as this had been, marshal the facts and mold them into a cohesive and coherent story, leading the jury to see the case as the prosecution or the defense wants it to be seen. The best arguments lead the jury to say not, "What a brilliant argument," but rather, "Yes, that's how it happened. That makes sense. I believe it."

Apart from his request for objective and dispassionate argument—a request that stood no chance with either side—General Reynolds had not put any limits on the length of closing argument, and the defense went first, taking all morning, three hours without interruption.

Lieutenant Colonel James Feldhaus, who had missed much of the trial in the hospital, took the opening and least contentious aspect, tracing General Yamashita's career before coming to the Philippines, much as Yamashita and his character witnesses and fellow officers had related it from the stand. Yamashita was never a warmonger in the Japanese army, Feldhaus began; he was in fact an apolitical moderate who saw no sense in going to war against the United States. His opposition to Minister of War and Prime Minister Tojo led to his exile in Manchuria (no mention of Malaya and Singapore, because there had been no testimony about it). When Yamashita was sent to the Philippines on October 9, 1944, he was given command of only 120,000 of 300,000 troops. He faced a shortage of food, gasoline, and transportation and had a new and unfamiliar staff; he was five divisions short of the troops he needed, and those he had were unfit and poorly trained. The Filipinos strongly opposed the Japanese, the defenses were in bad shape, and morale was poor.

Then the Americans landed. Tokyo forced him to spend precious resources on the lost cause of Leyte and finally gave him command of all the troops in the Philippines except the naval land forces, over whom he had only tactical command. His plan for the defense of Luzon was tactically sound: abandon Manila and fight a delaying action from the hills.

After the American victory on Leyte, the Japanese situation on Luzon became extremely precarious. The American blockade became more and more effective, the shortage of food became critical. The American air force continually strafed and bombed the Japanese transportation facilities and military positions. General Yamashita, charged specifically with the duty of defending the Philippines, a task that called for the best in men and equipment, of which he had neither, continued to resist our army from 9 October to 2 September of this year, at which time he surrendered on orders from Tokyo.

Feldhaus paused, and then concluded. "The history of General Yamashita's command in the Philippines is one of preoccupation and harassment from the beginning to the end."

Captain Sandberg next addressed the commission. "No one will ever know the complete story of what happened in Manila in those bloody days of February 1945," he began. "The Japanese who participated cannot tell because undoubtedly they are all dead. But if there is one fact which emerges clear and unmistakable from the welter of conflicting reports, rumor and gossip, it is that General Yamashita did not want fighting in the city of Manila, and that what happened occurred not only against his judgment and his wishes, but against his express orders."

His decision to abandon Manila was sound, and "borne out by what happened. The Japanese forces caught here were crushed between the bay and the river, and with no natural defenses and no escape route, were demolished to the last man."

As a result of these orders, Sandberg argued, the evacuation of the Japanese was orderly and effective, leaving only 1,500 to 1,800 soldiers to guard supplies that could not be moved and the military facilities that remained. They, and Admiral Iwabuchi's navy.

Given all these moves, why did General Yamashita's plan fail? Why did the navy stay behind? We know that they were ordered to leave. Even before the navy came under his tactical control, General Yamashita had instructed the Shimbu Army to inform the naval commander of his wishes. And when the navy came under Shimbu on January 6th, it came under the direct compulsion of the direct order to evacuate. On February 13th, General Yamashita learned for the first time that there had not been substantial compliance with his order—that the bulk of the navy troops were still in the city. Very much concerned, General Yamashita sent an urgent order to Shimbu that the navy must withdraw immediately in accordance with previous orders. But the navy did not withdraw and the battle of Manila ensued.

Sandberg laid responsibility for the atrocities that followed squarely on Iwabuchi and his troops:

> We submit that it is very doubtful indeed whether under any definition of
> the term these navy troops were under General Yamashita's command. It is
> true that they passed to his command on paper, but it is also true that the
> only important order he gave them—the order to evacuate—they failed
> to carry out. How can the man possibly be held accountable for the ac-
> tion of troops which had passed into his command only one month before,
> at a time when he was 150 miles away—troops which he had never seen,
> trained, or inspected, whose commanding officers he could not change or
> designate, and over whose actions he has only the most nominal control?

There was no plan to these atrocities, Sandberg continued. "We see only wild,
unaccountable looting, murder and rape. Trapped in the doomed city, knowing that they had only a few days at best to live, the Japanese went berserk,
unloosed their pent up fears and passions in one last orgy of abandon." Did
Yamashita order this? Sandberg recalled the testimony of Captain Sparnon,
the translation custodian, "who stated that nowhere among all the hundreds of
thousands of documents captured by the United States was such an order to
be found."

Sandberg pointed out at some length that Yamashita's acts were entirely consistent with his stated if hopeless desire to maintain good relations with the
Filipinos. He invited President Laurel to let him know of any misbehavior by
Japanese troops, and when Laurel complained that the military police were
overzealous in their arrests of supposed guerrillas, Yamashita had the police
commander removed from his post.

> The defense has maintained from the very beginning that the explana-
> tion of much of the matter covered by the bill of particulars is contained
> in the history of the guerrilla movement in the Philippines. As Americans
> we know only too well what we owe the Filipino guerrillas. They spied for
> us on Japanese military installations and troop movements. They harassed
> Japanese supply lines, damaged bridges, ambushed Japanese detachments and
> assassinated Japanese soldiers and officers. One thing we must concede: that
> however much we admire these staunch and fearless fighters, they were, in
> Japanese eyes, criminals, and the Japanese had every right under interna-
> tional law to try and execute them as such.

The Japanese method of trials and procedure for accused criminals was "foreign to and repugnant to American standards of justice," Sandberg went on, but

as the American sergeant Sakakida had testified, those methods were applied to guerrillas and Japanese soldiers alike. He dissected and dismissed Nishiharu's vague and contradictory testimony on Yamashita's "nod," concluding that "we cannot believe that the commission, after listening to General Yamashita on the stand for 19 hours, will accept this story" over Yamashita's "definite and forthright statements." The military tribunals bore no relation to American courts, Sandberg acknowledged, but "in no event are Japanese methods of trial provided by Japanese law the fault or responsibility of the accused in this case."

In the course of an hour, he had delivered a closely reasoned account of the evidence that put his client in the best possible light—not ignoring discrepancies in the evidence, but not letting them overwhelm the larger point: that Yamashita's actions spoke louder than vague or conflicting or mysterious words of others.

It was left to Captain Reel to take on the most disturbing aspects of the trial: the atrocities inflicted on the Filipino people, particularly during the awful month of February 1945, and the brutal treatment of prisoners of war, including Americans.

He began with the prisoners of war, dealing first with the testimony on several incidents in which POWs were killed. The Palawan slaughter occurred at an air force base at a time when the air force was not under Yamashita's command. There had been testimony about the killings of individual prisoners at Santo Tomas and Los Baños camps, but "no evidence whatsoever that General Yamashita knew about this, condoned it, excused it, ordered it or had any connection with it whatsoever." In these isolated incidents, "soldiers took the law into their own hands and naturally there was no report made to the commanding general." Moreover, the evidence was often hearsay, in some cases third- or fourth-hand hearsay. As to the hell ships, and particularly the wretched *Oryoku Maru*, "it is clear that General Yamashita and his chain of command had no connection with the Third Maritime Transport command that operated this vessel and was responsible for its operation at this time." Moreover, said Reel, "there is no evidence on this matter that anything in connection with it was brought to General Yamashita's attention, that he knew about it, approved it, condoned it, permitted it, justified it or excused it any way."

As to treatment of POWs in the camps, Reel acknowledged that food was indeed scarce, but it was scarce throughout the Philippines, and American submarines had effectively cut off shipments from outside. Even Sergeant Sakakida, who was in Yamashita's headquarters—"a place where, if anywhere, we would expect the food situation to be at its best in the Japanese Army"—agreed that rations were skimpy in Manila and got worse at Baguio, Reel argued.

"Finally, and this is very important, we come to the question of the orders of General Yamashita for the freeing of prisoners of war and civilian internees. Far from ordering all American prisoners of war executed, or ordering any prisoners of war executed, General Yamashita's orders were to turn them over to the American forces at the earliest available time"—an order that went unexecuted because of confusion over which protecting power was to be notified of it.

As to atrocities that took place outside Manila, "throughout this trial the defense has made a point of bringing up the matter of guerrilla activity, not in justification of torture or in justification of execution of persons who were not guerrillas, but in explanation of the circumstances surrounding the entire bloody picture." After the Leyte landings that followed days after Yamashita's arrival, guerrilla actions intensified and included attacks against Filipinos suspected of pro-Japanese sympathies. That could explain many of the unwitnessed murders in the outlands, Reel said. "To us the guerrillas were patriots and heroes, and rightly so, but to the Japanese forces they were war criminals, and rightly so. They were the most dangerous form of war criminal: treacherous, ruthless, and effective." Once the American and Filipino armies had surrendered to the Japanese in 1942, freelancing guerrillas were no longer lawful combatants. Had the situation been reversed, Reel told the commission, "would we consider them honorable combatants entitled to the privileges of prisoners of war, or would we turn to the Hague regulations, and take the correct position that they would be subject to execution and that we would have the right to use stern methods to exterminate them? I don't think there can be much question about this."

Again he emphasized:

There has been no testimony that General Yamashita ever ordered or permitted or condoned or justified or excused in any way these atrocities.
We submit that General Yamashita did precisely what he should have done under those circumstances. He issued an order in which he directed action against armed guerrillas—[he] was careful to say "armed"—and "to handle the Filipinos carefully, to cooperate with them and to get as much cooperation as possible from the Filipino people."

Reel then turned to the question of knowledge:

The prosecution will undoubtedly point out and claim that there were so many of these atrocities, that they covered so large a territory, that General Yamashita must have known about them. In the first place, a man is not convicted on the basis of what somebody thinks he must have known. It must be proven beyond a reasonable doubt that he did know; the test known to criminal law is not negligence but intent. And in the second place we submit that General Yamashita did not know and that he could not have known, and that it is entirely unreasonable to expect that he did know about any of these atrocities.

Yamashita did not know, Reel argued, because lines of communication were disrupted and destroyed by American forces, and subordinate commanders would not report such atrocities to higher headquarters anyway, particularly when they took place in violation of the headquarters' orders.

Reel quoted Yamashita's testimony at length, and concluded his summation. "When we judge him, sir, we must put ourselves in his place, and I say that unless we are ready to plead guilty before the world to a charge of hypocrisy, to a charge that supinely succumb[s] to a mob's desire for revenge, then we must find General Yamashita not guilty of these charges!"

As the commission took a break, Yamashita approached Reel. Visibly moved, he held Reel by both shoulders, and said—in English—"Thank you. Thank you."

It was a powerful and detailed argument, though not without its vulnerabilities. Reel had characterized the mistreatment of POWs as a matter of food shortages, but the cruelty had extended far beyond skimpy rations. Reel had suggested that some of the killings in the provinces might have been committed by guerrillas against pro-Japanese Filipino sympathizers; while this was possible in some cases, it could certainly not explain the widespread atrocities that so many witnesses had recounted. He had fully acknowledged the horror and extent of the atrocities while suggesting that some of what the commission had heard was too vague and uncertain to be credited. True, but a great deal of what they had heard was not. His argument that Yamashita did not know of these atrocities, and that they had occurred against his orders, did not elaborate on the significance of knowledge in the legal determination of whether a commander was accountable for atrocities. Reel clearly wanted the commissioners to accept Yamashita's lack of knowledge as a defense, or at least part of a defense, but the truth was he did not know what the legal consequence of knowledge, or its lack, was; nor did anyone else in the room. The charge had said nothing about it, nor had any court, any case, any regulation.

Colonel Clarke had the final defense presentation. He began with a lengthy analysis of the testimony of Lapus and Galang. The men were liars, he said, and their stories were "absurd and in view of the frank testimony of the grandson of General Ricarte in denial thereof, not worthy of belief." Apart from these accusations, Clarke argued, "there is no credible testimony in the entire record of trial which in any manner supports any contention that General Yamashita had ordered or had actual knowledge of the commission of any of the atrocities set forth in the bills of particulars." Without such knowledge, "he could not have permitted the commission of the atrocities. Before there could be permission, there would have to be knowledge of the acts or act to be permitted." Clarke was clearly using "permission" in its sense of affirmative assent, not passive failure to prevent.

"The only possible basis for imputing to General Yamashita any criminal responsibility for the commission of these atrocities is that of his status as the commanding general of some of the troops involved in the commission thereof." But, he went on, "the United States does not recognize a criminal responsibility predicated upon the status of the individual as a commanding general of troops, but does recognize the criminal liability attached to a commanding general for the improper exercise of that command."

But that liability, under the U.S. Army's own manual on the rules of land warfare, "is imposed on the persons who committed them and on the officers who ordered the commission thereof. A war crime of a subordinate committed without the order, authority or knowledge of the superior officer, is not the war crime of the superior officer."

The first sentence was an accurate summary of the army's manual, but the second sentence was Clarke's own. The provision he quoted stated only that "the fact that the acts complained of were done pursuant to order of a superior or government sanction may be taken into consideration in determining culpability, either by way of defense or in mitigation of punishment. The person giving such orders may also be punished." It did not address crimes done without the superior's "authority or knowledge" and so did not state that a crime committed without such authority or knowledge "is not the war crime of the superior officer." The defense of Yamashita would have been considerably strengthened had it done so.

"Throughout hours of questioning," Clarke argued, "General Yamashita told this commission the true facts as they existed during the period of time covering his command of the 14th Area Army in the Philippine Islands. The intensive cross examination of General Yamashita failed to develop any inconsistencies in his testimony."

Concluding, he appealed to the commission.

General Yamashita, appearing as a witness in his own behalf, has denied that he issued any orders directing the commission of any act of atrocity, that he had received any report of the commission of such acts, that he had any knowledge whatsoever of the commission of such acts, that he permitted such acts to be perpetrated, or that he condoned the commission of such acts. We respectfully request that this commission, after an analysis of the evidence adduced by the prosecution and the defense and after weighing this evidence in the scales of American justice, will exemplify the concepts and the standards of American justice, the keystone of American democracy, by returning a finding of not guilty of the charge.

"The defense did well," Mountz allowed. Reynolds adjourned for lunch. The afternoon would belong to the prosecution.

But there remained critical questions that no one had squarely taken on throughout the trial. What was the law here? What standard should the commission apply to determine whether Yamashita was guilty or innocent? Could a commander be found guilty on the basis of his troops' conduct alone? Or must there be, as the defense had argued, some finding that he had ordered their crimes, or at least had stood by and acquiesced in them? Would Yamashita's complete lack of knowledge, if that is what the commission believed, be a defense? Could he be convicted if he should have known, even if he did not actually know? If so, how does one determine what Yamashita should have known? What if his lack of knowledge was due to his own fault or negligence, or even his own affirmative actions to avoid knowing?

As we have seen, the law of command accountability in December of 1945 was looking into the void. No commander had ever been found guilty of a war crime unless he had personally taken part in it or had ordered his subordinates to commit it. If that were to be the standard, Yamashita surely deserved acquittal. There was no suggestion that he had even witnessed any of the crimes, nor was there any evidence, apart from the discredited Galang and Lapus and the ludicrous *Orders from Tokyo* propaganda film, of any order. Indeed, the testimony of Captain Sparnon of the Allied Translation and Intelligence Service that no incriminating order had ever surfaced all but proved the negative: that no such order had ever been issued. It was inconceivable that some such order had eluded Allied intelligence during and after the war as well as the investigators who had spent weeks preparing the case against Yamashita.

But the charge confronting Yamashita did not allege that he personally took part in the crimes or that he ordered them but, rather, that he had disregarded and failed to discharge his duty to control his troops, "permitting them to commit brutal atrocities and other high crimes." What, exactly, did that mean? What had to be proven to establish the guilt of the accused?

The structure of the commission was ill-suited to answer these questions. In a civilian trial or a court-martial, the responsibilities would be clear. There would be a judge, trained in the law, who would at the end of the trial instruct the members—the jury—on what the law was. The judge would explain to the jury the elements of the crime under the law and what facts must be established to prove each element. The jury would then determine whether the evidence did or did not establish each element beyond doubt and would render its verdict accordingly. If even one element is not proven, the jury must acquit on that charge. That division of responsibility ensures, as much as human failing allows, that jury verdicts are the result not of confusion or ignorance but of the application of the law to the facts.

That could not happen in Manila, because there was no judge in the room. The five generals were jurors. Reynolds had the title of "law member," but that was meaningless. He had no legal training nor any more authority than any of the other four. Without a judge, there was no one to instruct the generals on what the elements of the charge were. They were on their own in figuring out what the charge meant and how to apply it.

Until 1951, courts-martial in the American military were often conducted by nonlawyers. But they did not try enemy generals for war crimes. And they were given a detailed official manual of instructions that laid out the elements of any crime that might be tried, from unauthorized absence or disobedience of an order to assault, robbery, and murder, and what it took to prove each element. If they conscientiously followed the instructions in the manual, they would generally come out at the right place.

But there had never been a charge like this one, and so there was no manual, no instructions, no precedent, no checklist of elements. The five generals did not ask the experienced lawyers at the prosecution and defense tables to submit legal briefs that they could consider in reaching their decision. Nor, as far as the record shows, was there any guidance or instruction on those matters from military lawyers in General MacArthur's headquarters.

It is possible, though no evidence has ever come to light, that the commissioners were receiving instructions from MacArthur's headquarters on legal matters, including the elements of the charge that those lawyers had drawn up themselves. Such communications from a convening authority to the members of a court-martial or commission, concealed from the defense, would be grossly improper. Yet it seems very likely that MacArthur or his legal staff directed Reynolds to revoke his order that uncorroborated affidavits would not be accepted, and it plainly did dictate his abrupt reversal of his promise to allow the defense a continuance after the prosecution had rested its case. MacArthur's desire for a prompt conclusion was common knowledge, and his staff was receiving each day's transcript. It is therefore only natural to surmise that his headquarters was advising the untutored generals on the elements of the crime or even, less formally but equally improperly, telling them that the evidence was sufficient for a conviction.*

But whatever MacArthur's staff might have told the commissioners, neither the prosecution nor the defense could know with certainty what the prosecution had to prove to sustain a conviction. The defense, for its part, framed its

---

* MacArthur's theater judge advocate and staff might have been communicating with Major Kerr, though Lieutenant Mountz's letters, which provide candid insights into the prosecution strategy, say nothing about the matter. But there is nothing improper in a prosecutor consulting with his superiors on strategy and tactics.

case in closing argument around the proposition that it would not be fair—not just, not "American"—to convict Yamashita for crimes that he had not ordered or even condoned and did not know about or have any means to prevent if he had known. It was a plausible, even powerful, argument, but it was an appeal to fairness and honor and national values, not the law.

As the audience and the cast filled the ballroom after the lunch recess, Kerr waited for the generals to take their seats, and he stood up. Kerr did not divide the argument among his assistants; for the next two hours and fifty minutes, he stood alone before the commissioners and urged them to convict Yamashita.

Defense counsel had been organized and methodical; Kerr was animated and aggressive. He began by framing what he saw as the two "principal contentions" in the trial: "whether or not the accused did fail to perform a duty which he owed as commander of armed forces in the Philippines, and secondly, whether or not—if he did fail to perform that duty, if he were derelict in the performance of that duty—such constitutes a violation of the laws of war."

There was no question about the atrocities. "From Davao City in the south on Mindanao Island to north in Batan Island beyond the northern limits of Luzon, from practically one end of the Philippines to the other, these atrocities were committed in the Philippine Islands. There is no question as to those points in the charge having been adequately covered by the proof."

So on the first question, of whether Yamashita failed in a duty to control his troops, the first inquiry was: does the evidence establish that it *was* the duty of the accused to control his troops? Kerr read the testimony of Yamashita on that point. When Kerr had asked him, "Is it a recognized duty, among soldiers, of a commanding officer to control his troops so that they do not commit wrongful acts?" Yamashita had replied, "It is a recognized duty."

Yamashita had been speaking, of course, of an officer's military responsibility, what he had called "administrative" responsibility. This is what officers are supposed to do—lead their troops, look out for their welfare, deploy them, direct them, command them, control them. An officer who failed in those responsibilities would be subject, as Yamashita had said, to action from above—loss of command, reprimand, being passed over for promotion, assignment to a desk job or a backwater post, perhaps even dismissal. But that left open two questions: Was the duty to control one's troops also a requirement of international law? And if an officer failed to control his troops, was he criminally accountable for their acts? In 1945, international law had no answers to those questions.

Kerr left them unanswered as well. "The crimes having been committed, the atrocities having been established, of course the next question is, who is responsible? We contend that clearly under the laws of war, under international law, the commanding officer who was in command of those troops, who was in the theater, who owed the admitted duty to control those troops so that they would not commit those acts, is responsible." The laws of war hardly spoke "clearly" on that point, but Kerr had glided over it just as the defense had.

"Defense counsel has referred to these atrocities as having been committed by battle-crazed men under the stress and strain of battle," he argued, his voice rising. "That is not the evidence! That is not the evidence!* The atrocities which were established before this commission are atrocities—wrongful acts—committed by military units, or men then acting as a part of military units, under the command of noncommissioned officers or of officers. We submit, sir, that the evidence shows that these atrocities were carefully planned, carefully supervised; they were commanded."

Kerr moved on, challenging the claims of the defense. "The atrocities having been established, the command of the accused over the forces involved having been established, let us examine into the defense or the excuse offered by the accused. In explanation of his claim that he had no knowledge, he asserts that his communications were faulty." Kerr read portions of the testimony, much of it in conflict, about who could communicate with whom, and until when, and about what. "There was adequate communication during the period of the battle for Manila between Yamashita on the one hand and Yokoyama, and, on the other hand, between Yokoyama and Iwabuchi." And "there is nothing in the record to the effect that the accused did not have communications throughout with Batangas Province," the area south of Manila where troops under Colonel Fujishige committed brutal crimes.

> He says, "I received no reports." Is that satisfaction of the duty to control his troops? Does that constitute an adequate effort or any effort at all to control, to supervise his troops, to protect the civilian population? We contend it clearly was not an adequate or even any effort at all. He has not shown as a matter of defense that he could not have obtained the information as to what was going on in Batangas if he had desired to do so. Irrespective of any question of his actual knowledge, if we accept his position that he did not know, there still remains this stubborn fact: that he did not make an adequate effort to find out; else he would have known. And he has not shown that he could not find out so far as Batangas is concerned, nor so far as Manila is concerned.

Kerr continued his attack on Yamashita's credibility. "He contended that he did not have communications. They did have communications. Perhaps the accused did not endeavor to use those communications for the purpose of acquainting himself with the developments and the activities of the battlefront in

---

* Exclamation points are from the transcript of the trial.

Manila. Perhaps not! It was his duty to do so. It was his duty to know what was being done by his troops under his orders, under his commands."

On Yamashita's claim that he was preoccupied with the battle, Kerr was scornful. "Whenever the accused was asked upon the witness stand, 'Did you endeavor to find out what was going on?' the answer was invariably, 'No, I received no reports. I asked for no reports. I was too busy. I had many things to do. I was being pressed by the enemy.'"

"That, sir, is no answer," Kerr argued. "The performance of the responsibility of the commanding officer toward the civilian populations is as much, as heavy, a responsibility as the combating of the enemy. And if he chooses to ignore one and devote all of his attention to the other he does so at his own risk, because he is deliberately choosing then to disregard a substantial part of his duty as a commanding officer."

Kerr pressed his argument that Yamashita had simply ignored his duty to see that prisoners, civilians, and noncombatants generally were being adequately cared for, even when time allowed him to do that. "Why, sir!" Kerr proclaimed,

> The accused acknowledged that he did not even take the trouble to step the few steps from his headquarters buildings in Fort McKinley over to the prisoner of war camp where some 450 American prisoners of war were incarcerated to supervise the activities of his subordinate officers. He didn't even take that trouble! [Yamashita had testified that the POW camp at Fort McKinley was 1,500 meters, about a mile, from his office.] He had time to come down into Malacanang [the official residence of the Philippine president] for a social visit. He had time to drink with Ricarte and others in his own headquarters building, but he did not have the time because of press of duties to step those few steps or to ride in his car over there to the barracks where our prisoners of war were being starved, or improperly treated, according to the evidence. Our answer to that, sir, is not that he was too busy but that he was too disinterested. He did not care.

The defense had argued that atrocities would naturally not be reported up the chain of command to Yamashita; Kerr now turned the argument around. "The very method by which those executions were accomplished, the callous disregard, complete disregard of the prescribed procedure, shows that those men were acting under approval. Otherwise they would have never dared to be so arbitrary," he argued. "If those acts had been contrary to his desires, to his orders, certainly those men never would have dared to proceed on that basis."

Attacking relentlessly, Kerr belittled the evidence that Yamashita's orders for antiguerrilla actions specifically referred to "armed" guerrillas. "Yamashita gave orders for the control of guerrillas," he argued. "We maintain, sir, that if the accused saw fit to issue a general order to suppress guerrillas under circumstances as they then existed, according to his own testimony, he owed a definite, absolute duty furthermore to see to it that that did not open wide the gates of hatred of his men, leading them to wreak vengeance upon the civilian population. Obviously he did not do that. That is a part of his responsibility."

And the "trials" of suspected guerrillas were a mockery. "A trial in every nation of the world," Kerr said with considerable overstatement, "offers the person accused the opportunity to know what is the charge and the opportunity to defend himself, to answer it. And these poor people certainly had neither!"

Kerr did acknowledge, at several points, that there was no direct evidence that Yamashita had ordered any of these crimes. He did not even mention Lapus and Galang, a telling if tacit acknowledgment that they had been discredited. Nor, to his credit, did he refer at all to the *Orders from Tokyo* film, the prosecution's lowest blow and the trial's evidentiary nadir.

When it came to the elusive question of Yamashita's knowledge, and its significance for his guilt or innocence, Kerr did not handle it any more lucidly than the defense had. But the outline of his theory was beginning to emerge. He appeared to accept the fact that Yamashita did not know of these things. He never pointed to any specific evidence that he claimed would establish Yamashita's knowledge, and he never made the argument, at least not explicitly, that one might have expected: that the crimes were so widespread that Yamashita must have known about them and that he was lying when he said he did not. Kerr limited himself to arguing that communication with Manila and Batangas was good enough for Yamashita to have found out what was happening if he had made the effort. But he never quite went so far as to argue explicitly that Yamashita actually knew what was happening.

Likewise, Kerr argued that it was Yamashita's own fault—his own breach of duty—that insulated him from knowledge of what was happening in the POW camps. "If Yamashita didn't know it, it was his fault! He didn't choose to know it! He didn't inquire, he didn't require any reports, he didn't ask what they were doing, he did not investigate! There is no testimony even that he had any staff member look into that matter. He didn't care!"

A few minutes later, addressing the atrocities, he said, "Yamashita says that he didn't know that these things were happening in Manila. Our case is simply that it was his duty to know. It was possible for him to know. He should have known."

Kerr was smart to imply that the commission did not need to decide whether Yamashita actually knew of the crimes. He was setting the bar no higher than he thought he could clear, and given the defense's emphasis on Yamashita's lack of knowledge, Kerr avoided betting the verdict on that contentious point, arguing instead that a lack of knowledge was just as incriminating.

Kerr had been on his feet for more than two hours, addressing what he had said at the outset was the first of two questions to be decided: whether the accused had failed to perform his duty as a commander to control his troops. He had said little about the second: whether such a failure constituted a violation of the laws of war. With perhaps twenty minutes remaining in the trial day, he turned to that point.

He began with an admission, of sorts. "Truly, the application of the laws of war to a commanding officer on this theory has not frequently"—he would have been more accurate to say "not ever"—"been done or attempted. Nevertheless, we submit that it is well recognized in international law that a commanding officer does have a duty to control his troops in such a way that they will not commit these widespread, flagrant, notorious violations of the laws of war."

He began by quoting the Fourth Hague Convention of 1907, the treaty that had required that lawful combatants "be commanded by a person responsible for his subordinates." Kerr fixed on the word "responsible." It meant, he told the commission, that the commander of an army was

> responsible under international law for the proper conduct of its military operations; responsible to see to it that its members did conduct their operations in accordance with the laws and customs of war. That does not mean merely subordinate officers; that means everyone in the army, to see to it that they conducted their operations in accordance with the laws and customs of war. That alone is enough, as we see it, to establish the dereliction of duty on the part of Yamashita as a violation of the laws of war.

Kerr then frankly acknowledged that the definition and the interpretation were his own. "Confessedly," he said,

> this provision of the Hague Convention has not generally been so applied. In fact, I know of no case of any importance where it has been applied or where any effort has been made to apply it that way. However, there are many provisions in these international conventions, in the customs and laws of warfare, which have not as yet come before or had occasion to be passed upon by military tribunals or by any tribunals, and this may be one. We say this is the time for this tribunal to apply it.

The argument was candid, and his point that the customary law of war must evolve to meet changing circumstances was entirely valid, but his reading of the Hague Convention was a long stretch. The drafters of that convention had had no thought about a commander's responsibility for war crimes or about war crimes at all.* They were trying to define who was lawfully entitled to take up arms and kill the enemy, to distinguish lawful combatants from freelancers, marauders, and bandits. No one in those deliberations had suggested that "responsible" in this context should be taken to mean "criminally responsible in a court of law for crimes committed by those under him."

At this point, Kerr seemed to stumble, wandering off the path of his argument to cite a hodgepodge of legal rules and maxims from domestic American law dealing with negligence, strict liability, criminal conduct, and international relations, evidently in an effort to assure the commission that the principles of responsibility it needed to apply already existed elsewhere.

It must have been a confusing half hour for the five generals as they listened to Kerr argue that under the law of negligence—a field generally concerned with accidents, malpractice, and things that explode—"any man who, having the control of the operation of a dangerous instrumentality, fails to exercise that degree of care which under the circumstances should be exercised to protect third persons is responsible for the consequences of his dereliction of duty." And, reading from a legal digest, "The general conception of the courts, and the only one that is reconcilable with reason, is that the failure to do an act required or the doing of the act required is negligence as a mere matter of law, otherwise called 'negligence per se'"—a statement that, as Kerr read it, makes no sense at all.

Kerr pressed on, from a book on criminal law:

> That a person knows what he does is also sometimes called a presumption of law. If the term presumption of law is taken to mean something that the law declares to be universally true until rebutted, then it is not a presumption of law that all persons know what they are about, for there are many persons of whom the law declares just the contrary. But that a person who is cognoscenti [*sic*; cognizant?] should set up ignorance of fact as a ground of exculpation or of defense would be against the policy of the law, and hence, where there is no fraud or imposition . . .

And so on. It is doubtful that anyone, even the lawyers at either table, could follow his argument.

What Kerr was advocating was a mashup of negligence liability (which holds that persons must pay compensation to their victims for the foreseeable consequences of their actions or inactions if they failed to take the precautions that a reasonable person would have taken under the circumstances) and the law of strict liability (which generally holds that persons who control or operate

---

* See chapter 7.

something that they know or should have known to be unusually dangerous if mishandled must compensate victims for injuries caused when the thing gets out of control and causes injury, regardless of how careful they might have been). But such domestic legal constructs, which may vary considerably from one legal system to another, have never been a fertile source of international law. While one could, if pressed, articulate a plausible argument that these principles could be a sort of guide to how American tribunals might think about criminal accountability, Kerr's recitation of legal maxims fell well short of that. He was at the end of a long argument at the end of an exhausting trial, and it showed.

He eventually wound up, summarizing his case.

Now, in conclusion, sir, the prosecution believes without question that it has established the atrocities, the crimes, the murder, the rape, the destruction without military excuse or necessity of private and public property, the devastation of large parts of the Philippines. We have established that these acts were committed wrongfully by men under the command of the accused.

We have established that he failed to take steps which could have been taken to prevent those acts. We believe that the testimony shows an affirmative failure to act, a failure on the part of the accused to do those things which he as an army commander under the circumstance, with the experience he confessedly had, knew would have to be taken to prevent these foreseeable acts.

Jabbing his finger toward Yamashita, Kerr raised his voice.

We say he is responsible under the laws of war. We say that if Yamashita is responsible in any measure for the violations of the laws of war committed by the men under his command in the Philippines, anything less than the death sentence would be a mockery! We therefore respectfully recommend that if the accused is found guilty as charged, the sentence be death; and in view of the aggravated nature of the crimes, in view of the measure of the crimes, we recommend that the sentence in the case of death be carried out by hanging.

And with that, Kerr sat down. ("A good summation but I would not call it brilliant," Mountz concluded.) It was no surprise that the prosecution would ask for the death penalty, but in urging the commission to order hanging, Kerr was seeking a humiliating and ignominious death for a military officer, Japanese or American. Long tradition dictated that execution by firing squad—death from the enemy's arms—was a more honorable and fitting end for a warrior than the hood and noose of common criminals.

"Yamashita in his usual manner was calm as he heard the recommendation," according to the *Manila Times*. "His head was slightly inclined toward Hamamoto who translated, in hushed tones, the fateful recommendation. The furrowed lines on his brow did not alter as he took in the import of the plea."

Reynolds made the announcement: "The commission will announce its findings at two o'clock in the afternoon, Friday next," forty-eight hours away. The commissioners gathered up their papers and departed.*

Friday next was December 7—the date, in President Roosevelt's words, that would live in infamy.†

On December 6, with nothing to report, the dozen correspondents from the American, British, and Australian press who had sat through the trial and had heard nearly every witness appointed themselves as a jury and discussed the case. At the end, they cast their votes for the verdict. The outcome was unanimous: not guilty. The defense lawyers were not so sanguine. "Of the six of us," Reel said, "only Colonel Clarke had expressed a lingering hope for an acquittal." The rest of the defense team, Guy recalled, felt that the verdict "would unquestionably be 'guilty,' and that the sentence, surely as unquestionably, would be death."

December 7 was hot and humid. By 1:30, a crowd of Filipinos, American civilians and soldiers, and the reporters and film crews jammed the ballroom. There was no standing room. The prosecutors entered, and a few minutes later the spectators turned and watched as Yamashita and his lawyers came in and took their seats at the defense table. Yamashita, his demeanor unchanged on this day, showed no sign of nervousness.

A military police major strode to the front of the courtroom and faced the audience. "There will be no demonstrations," he said sternly. "When the judgment is pronounced, you will not utter any sound or make any display, either of pleasure or of dissatisfaction. I know there is a natural impulse to react to so dramatic an event, but in the interests of decorum, you will restrain yourselves."

---

* Reel's account of the trial states that at the conclusion of Kerr's summation, Reynolds read a statement "thanking all counsel, interpreters, stenographers, military police and others concerned for having co-operated with the commission in seeing to it that the trial was conducted with dispatch and without unnecessary disturbance." Those remarks do not appear in the record.

† It was widely assumed at the time, but never actually acknowledged by the commission, that the decision was scheduled to coincide with the anniversary of Pearl Harbor. Kerr later confessed that he was "startled" by the announcement, fearing that it would be seen as "intended vengeance for the Pearl Harbor attack," a perception he regretted as "indeed unfortunate." But if that was in fact the intent, Reynolds was off by a day. Because the Philippines are west of the international date line, Pearl Harbor was attacked on December 8, Philippines time.

At exactly 2:00, the crowd and the lawyers were called to attention as the five generals entered from the lawn overlooking Manila Bay and took their seats. In front of Reynolds, three radio network microphones were broadcasting live to the United States and around the world. Reynolds wasted no time on ceremony. He read the charge against Yamashita. The charge, he said,

is backed by bills of particulars specifying one hundred twenty-three separate items or offenses, most of which were presented for our consideration.

The crimes alleged to have been permitted by the accused in violation of the laws of war may be grouped into three categories:

(1) Starvation, execution or massacre without trial and maladministration generally of civilian internees and prisoners of war;
(2) Torture, rape, murder and mass execution of very large numbers of residents of the Philippines, including women and children and members of religious orders, by starvation, beheading, bayoneting, clubbing, hanging, burning alive, and destruction by explosives;
(3) Burning and demolition without adequate military necessity of large numbers of homes, places of business, places of religious worship, hospitals, public buildings, and educational institutions.

In point of time, the offenses extended throughout the period the accused was in command of Japanese troops in the Philippines. In point of area, the crimes extended throughout the Philippine Archipelago, although by far most of the incredible acts occurred on Luzon. It is noteworthy that the accused made no attempt to deny that the crimes were committed, although some deaths were attributed by defense counsel to legal execution of armed guerrillas, hazards of battle, and action of guerrilla troops favorable to Japan.

As Reynolds read, "an unearthly silence" came over the room, broken only by the sound of the newsreel cameras grinding in the background, Mountz wrote. "I know personally the perspiration began to drip off me as the suspense continued to mount."

Reynolds continued.

The commission has heard 286 persons during the course of this trial, most of whom have given eyewitness accounts of what they endured or what they saw. Testimony has been given in eleven languages or dialects. Many of the witnesses displayed incredible scars of wounds which they testified were inflicted by Japanese from whom they made miraculous escapes followed by remarkable physical recovery. For the most part, we have been impressed by the candor, honesty and sincerity of the witnesses whose testimony is contained in 4055 pages in the record of trial. We have received for analysis and evaluation 423 exhibits.

The prosecution has presented evidence to show that the crimes were so extensive and widespread, both as to time and area, that they must either have been willfully permitted by the accused, or secretly ordered by the accused. Captured orders issued by subordinate officers of the accused were presented as proof that they, at least, ordered certain acts leading directly to exterminations of civilians under the guise of eliminating the activities of guerrillas hostile to Japan. With respect to civilian internees and prisoners of war, the proof offered to the commission alleged criminal neglect, especially with respect to food and medical supplies, as well as complete failure by the higher echelons of command to detect and prevent cruel and inhuman treatment accorded by local commanders and guards. The commission considered evidence that the provisions of the Geneva Convention received scant compliance or attention, and that the International Red Cross was unable to render any sustained help. The cruelties and arrogance of the Japanese military police, prison camp guards and officials, with like action by local subordinate commanders were presented at length by the prosecution.

The defense established the difficulties faced by the accused with respect not only to the swift and overpowering advance of American forces, but also to the errors of his predecessors, weaknesses in organization, equipment, supply with especial reference to food and gasoline, training, communication, discipline and morale of his troops. It was alleged that the sudden assignment of naval and air forces to his tactical command presented almost insurmountable difficulties.

The situation was followed, the defense contended, by failure to obey his orders to withdraw troops from Manila, and the subsequent massacre of unarmed civilians, particularly by naval forces. Prior to the Luzon campaign, naval forces had reported to a separate ministry in the Japanese government, and naval commanders may not have been receptive or experienced in this instance with respect to a joint land operation under a single commander who was designated from the Army service.

As to the crimes themselves, complete ignorance that they had occurred was stoutly maintained by the accused, his principal staff officers and subordinate commanders. Further, that all such acts, if committed, were directly contrary to the announced policies, wishes and orders of the accused. The Japanese commanders testified that they did not make personal inspections or independent checks during the Philippine campaign to determine for themselves the established procedures by which their subordinates accomplish their missions. Taken at full face value, the testimony indicates that Japanese senior commanders operate in a vacuum, almost in another world with respect to their troops, compared with standards American general take for granted.

We have considered carefully the final statements of the prosecution and defense counsel. The accused is an officer of long years of experience, broad in its scope, who has had extensive command and staff duty in the Imperial Japanese Army in peace as well as war in Asia, Malaya, Europe, and the Japanese Home Islands.

Clearly, assignment to command military troops is accompanied by broad authority and heavy responsibility. This has been true in all armies throughout recorded history. It is absurd, however, to consider a commander a murderer or rapist because one of his soldiers commits a murder or a rape. None the less, where murder and rape and vicious, revengeful actions are widespread offenses, and there is no effective attempt by a commander to discover and control the criminal acts, such a commander may be held responsible, even criminally liable, for the lawless acts of his troops, depending upon their nature and the circumstances surrounding them. Should a commander issue orders which lead directly to lawless acts, the criminal responsibility is definite and has always been so understood. The Rules of Land Warfare, Field Manual 27-10, United States Army, are clear on these points.

It is for the purpose of maintaining discipline and control, among other reasons, that military commanders are given broad powers of administering military justice. The tactical situation, the character, training and capacity of staff officers and subordinate commanders as well as the traits of character, and training of his troops, are other important factors in such cases. These matters have been the principal considerations of the commission during its deliberations.

Reynolds then turned his eyes to the defense table. "The accused, his senior counsel and personal interpreter will take position before the commission."

Yamashita, Clarke, and Hamamoto stood and approached the general. Clarke had told Reynolds earlier that day that Yamashita wanted to make a final statement. The commissioners had asked for its text, and after reading it, they had approved the request, provided that it was read in English only.

When they were in position, Reynolds nodded and Hamamoto read Yamashita's words:

In my capacity as commander in chief of the Japanese 14th Area Army, I met and fought, here in the Philippines, numerically and qualitatively superior armed forces of the United States. Throughout this engagement I have endeavored to fulfill to the best of my ability the requirements of my position and have done my best to conduct myself at all times in accordance with the principles of fairness and justice.

I have been arraigned and tried before this honorable commission as a war criminal. I wish to state that I stand here today with the same clear conscience as on the first day of my arraignment, and I swear before my creator and everything sacred to me that I am innocent of the charges made against me.

With reference to the trial itself I wish to take this opportunity to express my gratitude to the United States of America for having accorded to an enemy general the unstinted services of a staff of brilliant, conscientious and upright American officers and gentlemen as defense counsel.

Yamashita looked at Reynolds. "Thank you," he said.
Reynolds looked back, and read the verdict.

General Yamashita: the commission concludes:

(1) that a series of atrocities and other high crimes have been committed by members of the Japanese armed forces under your command against people of the United States, their allies and dependencies throughout the Philippine Islands; that they were not sporadic in nature but in many cases were methodically supervised by Japanese officers and noncommissioned officers;
(2) that during the period in question you failed to provide effective control of your troops as was required by the circumstances.

Accordingly, upon secret written ballot, two-thirds or more of the members concurring, the commission finds you guilty as charged and sentences you to death by hanging.

Yamashita bent his head slightly as Hamamoto whispered Reynolds's words. He betrayed no emotion. The audience, duly warned, made no sound.

Reynolds turned to the military police. "The accused and Japanese members of the defense staff will be escorted from the courtroom." The room remained in dead silence as Yamashita, Muto, Utsunomiya, and Hamamoto, accompanied by Colonel Clarke, Lieutenant Colonels Feldhaus and Hendrix, Major Guy, and Captains Reel and Sandberg, were led from the ballroom.

"Its task completed," Reynolds said, "the commission adjourns."
The session had taken exactly fifteen minutes.

"What minutes of surprise and drama," Mountz wrote, "and in my humble opinion minutes when new history was written. They went right down the line on the question of command responsibility and failure to control his troops. It is a clear cut decision and the first real one in the history of warfare."

"Why must they hang us?" General Muto muttered. "Why can't they shoot us like true soldiers?"

Yamashita issued a written statement, in English, to the press a short time later:

I told the military commission that I never ordered, authorized, or condoned the commission of crimes by my troops. I also said that if I had known of the crimes before their commission, I would have done everything in my power to prevent them, and that if I had known of them afterwards I would have done everything in my power to punish them. From the conclusion of the military commission as read to me by its president, I see that the commission itself has recognized these facts. The finding of guilt was based solely on a conclusion that certain crimes were committed by troops under my command and that I "failed to provide effective control of those troops as was required by the circumstances." Considering the true facts of these circumstances I did everything I could and my conscience is clear.

With that, he was put in a Red Cross ambulance, guarded by military police, and driven from the High Commissioner's Residence, where he had lived for the past forty-one days, to the New Bilibid Prison in Manila. How long he would live there, he did not know.

What was stunning about the verdict was not the pronouncement of guilt, or the sentence of death, or even that the sentence should be carried out by a hangman. Whatever their hopes, whatever the assessment of the evidence, no one could be truly surprised that American generals in MacArthur's command would respond to the gruesome carnage of the Philippines by ordering the commanding general to pay with his life.

What was stunning was that the commissioners should say so little—virtually nothing—about what Yamashita was actually guilty of. Nearly all of Reynolds's statement was devoted to a brief summary of the evidence and the prosecution and defense contentions. As to the defense, that summary was accurate enough, but Reynolds had critically misstated the prosecution's case. He said that the prosecution had presented evidence of atrocities so widespread in time and territory "that they must either have been willfully permitted by the accused, or secretly ordered by the accused." In fact, the prosecution had argued neither of those theories; its contention was that Yamashita had failed in his duty to prevent the atrocities—a contention that Reynolds ignored. There was no evidence at all to support any finding that Yamashita had either secretly ordered or willfully permitted the atrocities.

To be sure, the commission was not obligated to explain its reasoning. It could have simply rendered a verdict of guilty or not guilty, as juries commonly do. But, as juries do, it would then have to give its verdict on each of the crimes charged. In the court-martial procedure of the time, and today, U.S. military regulations require that the charge of crime—murder, assault, disobedience, or whatever—be detailed in the specifications: the allegations of what the accused did, when and where and in what manner, to commit the crime. U.S. military regulations also required, then as now, that the court-martial (and thus the commission) enter a finding of guilty or not guilty as to each specification, followed by a finding of guilty or not guilty as to each charge. Here, the commission made no findings whatever on any of the 123 specifications, even though the prosecution had offered no evidence at all as to some of them.*

But the commissioners made no finding as to those specifications or any of the others. Reynolds's statement gave no indication at all as to whether they had concluded that Yamashita was responsible for all the deaths in Manila, or only those that had taken place after the naval forces had come under his tactical command, or only those that had taken place before he gave orders to abandon the city. It gave no indication of whether Yamashita was guilty of the crimes on Palawan, committed by air force officers when the air force was not under his command. Nor did it give any indication of whether he was guilty of the killings in a family on a remote island hundreds of miles from his headquarters, or of the deaths of prisoners of war who were on death's door before he ever set foot in the Philippines—all of which presented, at the very least, real questions of responsibility and compelling arguments for acquittal, even if one attaches guilt to every act that takes place under an officer's actual command.

The commission's explanation of its verdict, in essence, was that Yamashita was the commander, that atrocities had taken place, and that Yamashita had failed to prevent them. But his command, and the vast majority of the atrocities, were never in doubt, and his failure to prevent them was self-evident: they had happened.

So what had been the point of the trial? Why had all the pitiful victims been summoned to tell their anguished stories to the generals? Why had so much time and attention been spent on the details of which elements of the Japanese forces had been under Yamashita's command, his tactical authority, or his orders, and at what point? Why had weeks been spent on recounting horror after horror? Why, in short, did the trial need to consume more than a few hours? Why indeed was a trial, with all its trappings and procedures and formalities, necessary at all? Everything that was necessary to the commissioners' verdict, as Reynolds read it, was known and acknowledged, in substance if not in all its tragic detail, before the trial had begun forty days earlier.

---

* As previously noted (chapter 12), the prosecution introduced evidence on fifty-three of the original counts, and forty of the supplemental ones. That left thirty counts on which there had been no evidence at all.

The commission's failure to connect any of the evidence, or lack of it, with any of the verdict was compounded by its failure to address any aspect of a commander's accountability under the law. All it said was that a commander was not guilty of murder or rape because one of his soldiers committed murder or rape—an obvious truism—and that where the commander does not make an "effective attempt" to "discover and control" his troops' "widespread offenses," he "may be held responsible" for those acts "depending upon their nature and the circumstances surrounding them," including whether he had ordered them.

That carefully hedged statement said nothing at all, except that sometimes, in some situations, a commander could possibly be held responsible, depending on the nature of the acts and all the surrounding facts and circumstances. Nor was this noncommittal statement illuminated by the commission's assertion that among its "principal considerations" were the "tactical situation," the "character, training and capacity of staff officers and subordinate commanders," the "traits of character," and "training of his troops." It made no attempt to connect any of those "principal considerations" with any evidence or any law.

These are not idle questions. If a commander finds himself in a dire tactical situation, is his relative inattention to POWs and to the conduct of distant troops excused, to some extent? Or does such a situation actually place on him a greater responsibility to see that his troops adhere to their military mission and orders? If his "staff officers and subordinate commanders" lack adequate training, or upright character, can the commander himself be sympathetically judged, or should such defects make him more alert to the possibility of misbehavior, and thus more sternly judged because he did not take steps to control them—steps that a more fortunate commander would find unnecessary?

The commissioners seemed to accept the defense contention that Yamashita found himself faced with an overpowering enemy, incompetent predecessors, critical shortages, disrupted communications, shifting commands, untrained soldiers, poor morale, haphazard organization, and disobedient subordinates, none of which was his doing, for they characterized all of those as having been "established" by the evidence. Were these not exactly the "tactical situation," "capacity of staff officers and subordinate commanders," and "training of his troops" that it moments later cited as "principal considerations" in judging accountability? Yet the conviction—and especially its sentence of death, and by hanging—seemed to demonstrate that it did not take into account, in the slightest degree, any of these considerations in reaching its conclusions or even in mitigating his punishment. The commission could not have handed out a more severe and humiliating penalty had the accused been the most savage and rapacious marauder of the war, a general who orchestrated, ordered, and personally supervised every aspect of a reign of terror.

In his dispatch for the *New York Times*, Robert Trumbull made a prediction. "This trial, conducted entirely under the brief rules drawn up by Gen. Douglas MacArthur's legal staff, set precedents in trials of war criminals which were watched throughout the world. The verdict on Yamashita's culpability will undoubtedly be a precedent in such similar cases as may arise from now on throughout all history."

Marine Major Harry Pratt, the chief interpreter at the trial, who had stood by Yamashita's side and recited the verdict as it was being read, recalled years later, "It was a fascinating experience, but it was also one which I found, as a career officer, to be very worrisome. War crimes trials are a function of the victors. I could then and still find, that this law of command responsibility might well be charged against our own commanders under circumstances beyond their control."

That mattered little to the joyous crowds who danced in the streets of Manila that night. "Mamatay si Yamashita," they shouted. "Yamashita will die."

15

The Aftermath

The day after the verdict came down, Major Kerr went back to the High Commissioner's Residence to gather up some papers. The generals were there also. According to Mountz, who spoke to Kerr afterward and wrote home about it the next day, Kerr said they had

> quite an interesting time, discussing the various witnesses. One item of interest is that when Yamashita testified, he denied knowing anything about any of these atrocities. He also said that he had very poor staff officers, and his other officers were very poor, and undependable. The commission did not care for that, and felt that the defense had slipped in allowing him to take that position. Also they noted that neither Yamashita or his staff ever evidenced any horror at all the testimony produced.
>
> They said that if he had taken the stand and stated that he had good staff and officers and that it was necessary to depend upon them, and that he did so and had confidence in them, and that he could not understand them allowing such things to happen that did happen, and that he was shocked and distressed over it, and he certainly would see to the punishment, and that after all it was his responsibility, and that he accepted it as his responsibility and would assume all responsibility—then the commission stated that they doubted if any one of them would have voted for the death sentence.

If this account is accurate—it is, to be sure, secondhand hearsay, albeit from reliable sources—it is astonishing, for the transcript shows that Yamashita's testimony in fact was very close to what the generals told Kerr it should have been to save his life. Granted, the generals were participants in the trial and saw and heard Yamashita; no reading of the transcript decades later can replicate that experience. But the commissioners' account misstates what Yamashita actually said.

Yamashita did testify that when he arrived in Manila on October 9, 1944, he was disappointed in the headquarters staff officers left behind by his predecessor, who had paid little attention to discipline, training, or morale. Yamashita addressed this problem by bringing in as his chief of staff General Muto, whom he had long known, served with, and trusted—indeed, Muto had been by his side throughout the trial. Yamashita was in no position to replace the tactical officers—captains to colonels—whom his predecessor had let languish over two years of inaction in the Philippines. There were thousands of them, and few replacements would have been available at that stage of the war anyway.

In his testimony, Yamashita cast no aspersions on Muto or his other headquarters officers; nor on General Yokoyama, commander of the Shimbu Group, the most important Japanese army element that Yamashita had and the one closest to Manila; nor on Yokoyama's subordinates. In fact, at no time in his testimony did Yamashita ever blame his subordinate commanders or his staff for anything that happened after his arrival in October.

The problems he cited—interdiction of resupply from Japan by American planes and submarines, disruption of his landline communications, shortages of gasoline and food, the overpowering advance of the American army, increased guerrilla activity, Tokyo's fixation on Leyte, the inability to unify his command due to the inefficiency of the Japanese system—were not the fault of his staff or his commanders, and he never intimated that they were.

He did state that the new staff officers he brought in were "not familiar with the conditions in the Philippine Islands," which was a problem for him but no reflection on the newly arrived officers. Indeed, he admitted that on his arrival he too was unfamiliar with the Philippine situation.

He did lay blame on Admiral Iwabuchi for disobeying his orders, but Iwabuchi was not one of his staff officers, nor even a true subordinate commander, since Yamashita had only tactical control, and that only on paper. He never met Iwabuchi, who in any event flatly disobeyed the orders from Yamashita and Yokoyama to abandon the city. Any blame that Yamashita laid at Iwabuchi's feet could hardly be seen as disloyalty or buck-passing on Yamashita's part. He did sack the head of his military police after receiving complaints from Philippine authorities that the MPs were being too aggressive in their treatment of civilians, but this event was surely not what the commissioners had in mind.

The generals reportedly said that he should have acknowledged that it was necessary to depend on one's subordinates, but Yamashita had in fact said exactly that on cross-examination: "I gave definite instructions to the army division and other unit commanders, and I ordered that they were to carry out my instructions, and I entrusted them to do so, because this was a matter to which I could not personally look into."

Asked by Kerr, "Is it customary to check to determine whether or not the order has been obeyed?" he answered, "In matters of extreme importance such would be the case, but ordinarily I trust the integrity of the group, division and lower commanders."

And later: "The source of command and coordination with a command is, or lies in, trusting in your subordinate commanders. Under the circumstances I was forced to confront the superior U.S. forces with subordinates whom I did not know and with whose character and ability I was unfamiliar."

When Kerr gave him the opportunity to blame his subordinates, Yamashita declined:

"You desire to lay the blame and responsibility for these wrongs entirely upon subordinate officers and men, is that correct?"

"The persons who perpetrated these crimes should be punished and the immediate superior units should be subject to investigation and upon the findings they should receive either criminal punishment or administrative punishment."

The answer did not really respond to the question, but all Yamashita said was that those who committed the crimes, and their commanders, should be appropriately dealt with.

As to his own acknowledgment of responsibility, Yamashita never sought to shift the blame: "If the Japanese forces did these things and if I knew about it, it would be my duty to stop it." At another point, asked, "Is it a recognized duty among soldiers of a commanding officer to control his troops so that they do not commit wrongful acts?" Yamashita answered, "It is a recognized duty."

He was asked again: "[Is it] a recognized duty of a commanding officer to control his troops so that they do not commit atrocities?" and he repeated his answer: "It is his duty."

At another point, the following exchange took place:

"In other words, you were responsible for enforcing the Japanese military regulations?"
"Yes."
"And it would be your duty to see to it that the regulations were obeyed?"
"It is my duty as the commanding general to see that the rules are obeyed."

The only time that Yamashita stopped short of placing responsibility on the commander—on himself—was his refusal to accept criminal responsibility for the crimes of his troops regardless of what he knew or could do—the very charge that was laid against him:

Acts such as this must be stopped, but the location of the commanding officer and the time and the circumstances must also be taken into

consideration. . . . Even though he takes all the available means in order to prevent these acts, the location and the time and circumstances must be taken into consideration. However, if he has taken all possible means to stop them and still finds it impossible to prevent them he is subject to administrative responsibility. However, if the conditions are such that it is utterly impossible for him to take any action, then he would not even be administratively responsible.

The generals' statement that he never said that he "would see to the punishment, and that after all it was his responsibility, and that he accepted it as his responsibility and would assume all responsibility" was likewise unfounded:

> I believe that under the foregoing conditions I did the best possible job I could have done. However, due to the above circumstances, my plans and my strength were not sufficient to the situation, and if these things happened they were absolutely unavoidable. They were beyond anything that I could have expected. If I could have foreseen these things I would have concentrated all my efforts toward preventing it. If the present situation permits it, I will punish these people to the fullest extent of military law. . . . I absolutely did not order this, nor did I receive the order to do this from any superior authority, nor did I ever permit such a thing, or if I had known of it would I have condoned such a thing, and I will swear to heaven and earth concerning these points.

Asked on cross-examination, "You admit, do you, that you failed to control your troops in the Philippines?" Yamashita answered, "I have put forth my maximum effort in order to control the troops, and if this was not sufficient, then somehow I should have done more. Other people might have been able to do more, but I feel that I have done my very best."

Yamashita's consistent position, therefore, was not that the responsibility was not his, but rather that *because* the responsibility was his, he would have done everything he could to prevent the atrocities and to punish those who committed them, if he had known they were taking place. In any event, his testimony surely does not justify the commissioners' conclusion that he refused to accept responsibility, unless by that they meant he should have simply pleaded guilty to the charge and been done with it.

There was some truth to the generals' observation that Yamashita had never "evidenced any horror" at the testimony of the victims. Yamashita's demeanor throughout the trial was described by some as cold and stone-faced, by others as calm and dignified. In any event, it was not demonstrative. Given the theatrics of a trial as sensational as this one, he would have been wise to show more emotion as he sat at the defense table and to take time during his testimony to express his anguish and to condemn the conduct of Japanese troops as the grotesque and inhuman savagery that it was. But that was not in his character. "Yamashita was the consistent stoic," Captain Reel wrote after the trial. "His features never betrayed emotion. Whatever the thoughts and emotions he experienced, they were not reflected in his features, speech or actions."

On balance, however, the posttrial comments of the five commissioners to Kerr must raise the question of whether they saw and heard only what they wanted and expected to see and hear. That possibility is also suggested by a startling admission that General Lester, one of the commissioners, reportedly made in the conversation with Kerr. As recounted by Mountz, it was this:

> Gen. Lester then stated that he was in the hills when Yamashita surrendered, and he stated that Yamashita marched down with his troops and lots of them were sick and weak from hunger, and his officers, if any lagged behind, would turn around and behead them or bayonette [*sic*] them, and the M.P. of our army had a very hard time preventing these acts, and Yamashita was there and saw it, and still on the witness stand he told how none of his troops were ever kicked, beaten or mistreated by their officers.

The story is certainly false. Lester was not "in the hills when Yamashita surrendered." Lester had been the commanding general of the artillery elements in XIV Corps when it landed at Lingayen in January 1945 and fought its way to Manila. In May, according to entries in his service record in his own hand, he was reassigned as commander of U.S. And Philippine military police. Lester's post was in Manila; there was no reason for him to be in the trackless jungles at Kiangan, 150 miles away by air, on September 3, and there is certainly no record or account of his being there.

The officer who first laid eyes on Yamashita that day was a colonel, the chief of staff of the U.S. Army's Thirty-Second Division, and two contemporaneous accounts of the surrender made no mention that Japanese troops were beheading or bayoneting or otherwise mistreating anyone in the group. In fact, there were no troops, lagging or otherwise: one account stated that the surrender party consisted of Yamashita, Muto, Utsunomiya, Vice Admiral Okochi and another admiral, five staff officers, three "secretaries," three interpreters, and five orderlies—twenty-one men in all. The official history of the Thirty-Seventh Division, which was holding the area, states that Yamashita's party numbered twenty-three, including an "honor guard" otherwise not described. There were no military police in the American contingent; they did not enter the picture until later in the day, when Lieutenant Colonel Aubrey Saint Kenworthy received the Japanese group in Baguio. Kenworthy's detailed account of events contains no hint of any mistreatment, much less any stabbings and beheadings, which surely would have been reported to him had they occurred. Lester's tale that Yamashita countenanced the stabbing and beheading of his sick, hungry, and ragged soldiers as they straggled down to surrender—with Americans as eyewitnesses, no less—is wholly fictitious. Why he should have recounted it as fact to Kerr, and presumably to the other commissioners in the course of the trial, is a mystery.

By bringing it to bear in his deliberations he violated the cardinal principle of a fair trial: that the jurors are to base their decision on the evidence properly before them and disregard anything they might know, or think they know, from any other source. MacArthur's own regulations barred anyone from serving on the commission who was "disqualified by personal interest or prejudice" or who had "personally investigated" the case. Lester's dabbling in rumors did not rise to that level, perhaps, but by taking those rumors as true—even if they had been true—he disregarded his obligation to set aside extrajudicial information and base his verdict on the evidence adduced in the trial. Reel, who was unaware that Lester was anything other than a "desk general," noted that his "gestures, facial expressions and exaggerated mannerisms" made it clear that he was "antagonistic to the accused."

In any event, one can infer from this account that, although MacArthur's regulations required only a two-thirds vote—four of five—for a verdict and a sentence, the five generals were unanimous on both.

The trial was over, but the process was not. MacArthur's regulations specified that no sentence was to be put into effect until approved by the appointing authority, which in this case was General Styer, commander of the U.S. Army forces in the Philippines and MacArthur's hand-picked subordinate. The regulations gave him authority to uphold the sentence or reduce it, but that was something of a moot point, because the regulations also provided that no death sentence could be carried out until it was reviewed and confirmed by the Commander in Chief of U.S. Army Forces in the Pacific. That would be MacArthur himself. Since the Japanese surrender on September 2, MacArthur had also been Supreme Commander of the Allied Powers: the absolute ruler of occupied Japan. So Styer's office in Manila was but a quick stop—he upheld the result on December 12. In Tokyo, Colonel C. M. Ollivetti, MacArthur's theater judge advocate for the Pacific, assembled four of his most senior lawyers to begin the task of poring over the record, to come up with a recommendation for MacArthur.

But Yamashita's lawyers had already opened a far more audacious offensive. They wanted to take the case to the Supreme Court of the United States.

It was, to be blunt, a crazy idea. Except for small and rare categories of cases involving ambassadors or disputes between states, the Supreme Court hears only cases that have first been ruled upon by lower courts: a state supreme court or a federal court of appeals. The Philippines, a self-governing commonwealth about to become independent from the United States, had neither. Its own courts had not the slightest connection to the case of Yamashita or the slightest authority to tell MacArthur or Styer what to do. The trial had not even taken place in a court; it was a military operation from start to finish. And MacArthur's regulations specifically prohibited any review other than Styer's and his. That meant no courts.

There was, at best, a slight ray of light. In 1943, in the case of *Ex Parte Quirin*, the Supreme Court had heard and decided a case involving eight German saboteurs who had been captured after they came ashore in Florida and New York. President Roosevelt appointed a military commission to try them for war crimes, the allegation being that they had not been in uniform and thus, under the Hague Convention, were not legal combatants. Their lawyers went to the federal court in Washington, D.C., to seek a writ of habeas corpus to forestall the trial, claiming that the accused were being denied their constitutional right to a civilian jury. The court had summarily denied the writ, on the grounds that FDR's order had explicitly precluded any judicial review of military commission proceedings.

They appealed to the Supreme Court, which affirmed the denial. But the Court had not relied on FDR's prohibition on judicial review, citing "the duty which rests on the courts, in time of war as well as in time of peace, to preserve unimpaired the constitutional safeguards of civil liberty." FDR's order, the Court ruled, did not preclude the courts from ruling on the constitutionality of the proceeding in the first place. It proceeded to issue a lengthy opinion concluding that military commissions were lawful and that the accused were not entitled to a civilian trial with a jury. The commission then tried the saboteurs and convicted them all; six were executed, and the other two were sent to prison.

But at least the Supreme Court had been willing to take a military commission case and consider the defendants' objections to it, even if it had ultimately ruled against them. Yamashita, however, had a problem that the Germans did not. In habeas cases, a court must have jurisdiction over those holding the petitioners in custody. The Quirin trial had taken place in Washington, D.C.—in the very building that housed the Department of Justice—so the District of Columbia federal court had jurisdiction over the military authorities holding the Germans in custody there, and the Supreme Court could review the lower court's ruling.

No such pathway was open to Yamashita. His jailer was Styer in Manila, and Styer's boss, the Supreme Commander, was in Tokyo. No federal court in the United States had jurisdiction over either place, and there was no

American court in Manila. The only court in sight was the Supreme Court of the Philippines.

Yamashita's lawyers decided to go there. They could not have been expecting much, but the Philippine Supreme Court was not their real hope—they were taking a long shot to boost their chances with the U.S. Supreme Court by getting a ruling—even an adverse one—from a court, any court. On November 12, halfway through the trial, they had filed a petition for habeas corpus, asking the Philippine Supreme Court to halt the trial on essentially the same grounds as they had advanced to the commission: that the charge did not validly state a violation of the law of war and that MacArthur's rules for the conduct of the trial violated the Articles of War and the U.S. Constitution. They also sent off a habeas petition addressed to the U.S. Supreme Court itself, another long-shot hope, but one that might at least draw that Court's attention to what was happening in the Philippines.

The prosecutors were stunned. "Pandemonium reigned," Reel wrote, no doubt with some relish.

> Hurried conferences were held, opinions were written, radiograms winged back and forth between Manila and General MacArthur's headquarters in Tokyo. From members of the prosecution's headquarters we received reports that the commander-in-chief [MacArthur] was perturbed, that he had radioed orders to his Manila subordinates to ignore the Philippine Supreme Court, that it was well settled that the courts could not review the actions of a United States military commission—in short, that judicial interference should be avoided.

And avoid it they did. Styer left his office whenever the court's bailiff arrived to serve him with a copy of the papers—"just as an ordinary deadbeat dodges the sheriff," Reel wrote indignantly—but the court, undeterred, set the case down for a hearing two weeks later.

Lieutenant Colonel Walter Hendrix, who had devoted most of his time to this tactic and had taken little role in the trial itself, appeared before the Philippine Supreme Court on the appointed day. MacArthur ordered that no one from the prosecution or from the staffs of Styer or MacArthur was to show up.

Hendrix lit into MacArthur before the Philippine judges. His regulations, Hendrix argued with gusto and hyperbole, violate "every legal code in the world." They permitted the commission to operate on "no law at all." When one of the judges pointed out that it was up to MacArthur to establish those rules, Hendrix, shouting, answered, "There are two systems—one in Europe and one in the Pacific. Europe has the Allied system, the Pacific has only MacArthur's. Under MacArthur's system every law you could think of has been thrown out the window. That court has violated every law in the world. There are no legal men on the commission. There are others above [Reynolds] who want to see the trial brought to a close as soon as possible." He asked the court to give Yamashita due process of law.

That was a bit much for the judges. "I don't think the makers of our constitution had in mind persons like Yamashita, who came to our country as an invader," one of them told Hendrix. "Why don't you appeal directly to MacArthur?"

"I don't think I'll try that," Hendrix replied.

Yamashita was appealing to the Philippine court, Hendrix said, because he had nowhere else to appeal. "We contend that MacArthur has taken over the law into his own hands, disregarding the laws of the United States and of the constitution, and that he does not have authority from Congress and the President," Hendrix argued, to judges who surely must have wondered what that had to do with them. MacArthur "is a great soldier and a great general"—even Hendrix in his stridency knew better than to criticize this particular general's military acumen in front of Filipinos—"but not a great lawyer. Orders from MacArthur regarding the case are illegal. If you would hear the decisions of the court [sic], you would be shocked and amazed." He told the judges that of the 100 objections the defense had raised at trial, "only 12 have been sustained."

It was not a brilliant argument; anyone can bat .120 in court if he raises enough unfounded objections, and for all his rhetoric Hendrix had conspicuously avoided answering the question of what law, exactly, gave a Philippine court authority to tell MacArthur how to run any aspect of his generalship, including trials.

Hendrix and his colleagues had no hope of winning an order from the Philippine court. And even if they had, they knew MacArthur would ignore it. On November 28, three days after the hearing and just as Yamashita himself was taking the stand across town to testify, the court dismissed the case. "An attempt of our civil courts to exercise jurisdiction over the U.S. Army . . . would be considered a violation of this country's faith, which this Court should not be the last to keep and uphold." Just what faith would be violated, the court did not say, not that it mattered. The Philippine justices had shown the defense the door, but at least they had done so in an official order.

And the court had done the defense a favor: it had issued its decision almost immediately instead of holding it for weeks, by which time Yamashita might have been convicted, sentenced, and executed. Now the defense had what they wanted: an order from a civilian court denying their request to stop the trial. Whether that would cut the slightest ice in the Supreme Court of the United States was another matter altogether, but at least it was a ruling from a court, not an ad hoc panel of U.S. military officers.

They had precious little time. With Yamashita already on the stand, the end of the trial was in sight. If Yamashita were convicted and sentenced to death, they were well aware that MacArthur could order that the execution be carried out quickly, following the commission's verdict and his own review, which was entirely under his control. If Yamashita was sentenced on a Monday, he could be dead before the week was out.

Given the uncertainty of the situation, Yamashita's lawyers were desperately trying to cover all the bases. The petition for habeas corpus sent directly to the U.S. Supreme Court had requested the Court to issue the writ itself, which as a federal court it had jurisdiction to do. When the Philippine Supreme Court denied the habeas request made to it, the lawyers filed a second petition in the U.S. Supreme Court, requesting a writ of certiorari, a legal step by which the Court can review a lower court's decision. They also sought a writ of prohibition, archaic even in 1945, by which a court could order a lower court to stop what it was doing. The hope was that if the Supreme Court found some jurisdictional obstacle to one request, it might still act on another—if, of course, it wanted to hear the case at all.

On December 7, with Yamashita now sentenced, defense counsel sent an urgent cable to the clerk of the Supreme Court: "General Tomoyuki Yamashita sentenced to hang. It is feared sentence will be executed before Court can act on petition for writ [of] habeas corpus now before Court and on petition for writ [of] certiorari now en route to you. We urgently request Court to order Secretary of War to stay execution until Court can act on both petitions."

The pleas were not overlooked at the Supreme Court, which had received the habeas papers on December 3. Chief Justice Harlan Fiske Stone called the Solicitor General of the United States, whose office represents the U.S. government before the Court, to see if the army itself would defer any execution until the Supreme Court could decide what to do. The Solicitor General called the Secretary of War, who in turn cabled MacArthur, suggesting that he defer.

MacArthur refused. The Supreme Court had no jurisdiction, he told the secretary, and thus there was no reason to delay anything. He would proceed with the review. The secretary was not amused. He immediately ordered MacArthur to take no action while the Court considered the matter.

After six hours of discussion over two days on December 19 and 20, the justices decided to hear Yamashita's case. They scheduled an oral argument for January 7, 1946, less than three weeks away. They also ordered a stay of all proceedings in the case—a relief to Yamashita and his lawyers, for not even MacArthur would dare disregard an order of the Supreme Court. Yamashita would not go to the gallows until the Supreme Court had spoken.

On Christmas Day of 1945, Clarke, Sandberg, and Reel left Manila on a long journey to represent, for the first time in the Supreme Court's history, a convicted enemy war criminal.* At a prisoner-of-war camp in Manila, Ya-mashita—in an ill-fitting and threadbare U.S. Army work uniform, stripped of his general's uniform, his boots, and his medals—waited.

Meanwhile, in Tokyo, MacArthur's theater judge advocate and four of his staff lawyers were poring over the transcript, summarizing the trial and its issues for MacArthur's official review. As the defense attorneys were en route to Washington, MacArthur's lawyers produced a twenty-two-page single-spaced memo for the boss. It was to be the most detailed analysis of the trial to emerge from the entire process, and it was objective in many respects: the evidence for the prosecution and the defense was summarized in detail, and the discussion of the legal issues candidly acknowledged the absence of any precedent. But the authors were faced with a predicament familiar to government lawyers everywhere: should they write a confidential, impartial, objective analysis that might well conclude that the process had been flawed, or, knowing very well what the boss wanted, should their memo emphasize the strengths, minimize the weaknesses, and provide a legally defensible pathway to justify the desired outcome?

From a professional perspective, the lawyers' question was: who is the client? Was it MacArthur, or was it, in a larger sense, the government, that is to say, the United States? To whom did they owe their professional loyalty? There could be little doubt that what MacArthur wanted was a review that would support a decision to approve the conviction and death sentence. Whether he told the lawyers to prepare a memorandum to that end cannot now be known.† But it seems clear from the memorandum that if the lawyers wrestled with the question of what their role was, they resolved it in favor of providing MacArthur a conclusion and recommendation he welcomed.

After summarizing in some detail the evidence presented by each side, they turned to the legal questions: first, was the charge a valid one?

There can be "little doubt that the charge is sufficient," they wrote. "The doctrine that it is the duty of a commander to control his troops is as old as military organization itself and the failure to discharge such duty has long been regarded as a violation of the Laws of War." They cited only the provision of the Fourth Hague Convention of 1907 that defined lawful belligerents as those who are "commanded by a person responsible for his subordinates." But they noted, "It must, however, be conceded that only rarely, if at all, has punishment for failure to exercise control been meted out to an individual commander."

---

* In the Quirin case, the issue before the Supreme Court was whether the military commission properly had jurisdiction. The Court ruled that it did, and the accused saboteurs then proceeded to trial.

† MacArthur's memoir, *Reminiscences*, contains only the barest information about Yamashita, and his papers, nothing.

But that silence, the reviewing lawyers concluded, need not stand in the way of criminal punishment. "There is no reason, either in law or morality, why [the commander] should not be held criminally responsible for permitting such violations by his subordinates, even though that action has heretofore seldom or never been taken."

It was an assertion of breathtaking scope, for neither international law nor "morality" applied only to Japanese officers, or to defeated enemies. MacArthur's lawyers, wittingly or not, were creating a basis for the prosecution and conviction of any American commander who failed to prevent his troops from committing war crimes. And, without explicitly saying so, they had inserted no conditions on their conclusion—not the commander's knowledge or lack of it, nor his ability or inability to actually intervene, nor his diligence or negligence, nor his tactical situation. Indeed, the very proposition was directly contrary to the position taken by the United States at the Paris Peace Conference in 1919.

But citing official warnings by the Allies as early as 1943 that those responsible for war crimes would be "held accountable," MacArthur's lawyers took the long view.

> It should be borne in mind that International Law is not a static body of definite statutes but a living, growing thing. By solemn pronouncement, the United Nations gave warning that a new era had arrived with respect to the conduct of all persons, even high commanders, in their methods of waging war. In the enlightened and newly awakened conscience of the world, there is nothing either legally or morally wrong in now holding to strict accountability not only those who by their own acts violate the laws of humanity, but also those who knowingly or negligently permit such acts to be done. It is only by so holding commanders that any forward progress toward decency may be expected.

Intentionally or not, this view of international law for the postwar age mirrored that of Supreme Court Justice Robert H. Jackson, who was then chief counsel for the United States at Nuremberg, prosecuting twenty-two senior Nazis before the International Military Tribunal. In a letter written to President Harry Truman the preceding June, as Jackson was preparing to depart for London to draw up, with his British, Russian, and French counterparts, what would become in August 1945 the charter of that tribunal, he wrote,

> International Law is more than a scholarly collection of abstract and immutable principles. It is an outgrowth of treaties or agreements between nations, and of accepted customs. But every custom has its origin in some single act, and every agreement has to be initiated by the action of some

state. Unless we are prepared to abandon every principle of growth for International Law, we cannot deny that our own day has its right to institute customs and to conclude agreements that will themselves become sources of a newer and strengthened International Law.

Whether Jackson would have agreed with the expansive application of international law to Yamashita's case is an open question. He was at Nuremberg when the Supreme Court considered the case and took no part in the decision. But he was addressing a somewhat different issue: whether the Nazi invasion of European countries could validly be alleged as a "crime against peace," a charge that had not previously been criminally prosecuted, and whether those who orchestrated and directed those invasions could themselves be convicted of this newly articulated crime. Nothing in his view of the growth of international law suggests how he might have decided questions of a commander's responsibility for crimes. The charter of the Nuremberg tribunal said nothing about such accountability, and the issue did not arise in the international trial. It was to arise, however, in two American trials of German generals that followed the international Nuremberg tribunal.

Having concluded that the charge against Yamashita, however unprecedented, was legally valid, MacArthur's staff judge advocates turned to the question of whether their commander's procedures governing the trial had been fair. They had little difficulty with that. Acknowledging that the rules "varied in some important respects from those governing trials by court-martial, particularly with respect to the admissibility of evidence," they invoked Judge Advocate General Myron Cramer's formal opinion that the Articles of War enacted by Congress did not apply to trials of enemy war criminals. Furthermore, the rules were "in the main" the same as those followed in the trial of Quirin and his fellow saboteurs. And because the commissioners had "carefully followed" the rules given them, Yamashita "procedurally had a fair trial."

There was a significant gap in that analysis, however. Whether or not the rules themselves were fair, the lawyers did not address the question of whether the commissioners' actual rulings were. They did not discuss whether the admission of evidence, such as the *Orders from Tokyo* film or the prosecution's many written statements, compromised the fairness of the trial by denying the defense any meaningful cross examination, or whether the filing of fifty-nine additional counts on the eve of trial deprived Yamashita of fair notice of the charges, or whether the denial of a continuance during the trial impaired his ability to prepare his defense. To say that the commissioners "carefully followed" the rules was something of a sleight of hand; the rules allowed the commissioners to do pretty much whatever they wanted to.

The procedures thus dispatched, the lawyers turned to the important question of whether the evidence was sufficient to support the conviction. They concluded that the charge against Yamashita needed proof of three elements: first, that the atrocities were committed as alleged in the bill of particulars; second, that they were committed by members of the accused's command; and third—tracking the language of the charge itself—that "the accused unlawfully disregarded and failed to discharge his duty as commander to control the operations of the members of his command, permitting them to commit such atrocities."

As to the first two elements, there was of course no doubt. They noted, without discussion, that evidence had been adduced on 90 of the 123 specifications. Like the commissioners, they made no attempt to sort out which of the 90 were actually proven. They concluded that the evidence taken altogether was "clear, complete, convincing and, for the most part, uncontradicted by the defense." And they concluded that it was "abundantly proved" that the atrocities were committed by members of Yamashita's command. They noted that two of the most horrific incidents—the massacre of American POWs at Palawan and the transport of POWs on the *Oryoku Maru*—took place before either of those commands had been transferred to Yamashita, but they found it "unnecessary to decide" his accountability for those events, given the "overwhelming number of other atrocities" committed by troops under his command.

The third element was thus the key to the case, and they found that the evidence taken as a whole "impels the conclusion" that Yamashita was indeed responsible. They cited three aspects of the evidence to support this. First, they said, and without elaboration, "the atrocities were so numerous, involved so many people, and were so widespread that [the] accused's professed ignorance is incredible." In other words, Yamashita must have known.

Second, "their manner of commission reveals a striking similarity of pattern throughout," from which one might permissibly infer "that the atrocities were not the sporadic acts of soldiers out of control but were carried out pursuant to a deliberate plan of mass extermination which must have emanated from higher authority or at least had its approval." Their reasoning here, however, amounted to noting that the atrocities were carried out under the direction of commissioned or noncommissioned officers who used bayonets or swords "with a minimum expenditure of ammunition," and that the victims' bodies were buried, burned, or otherwise disposed of, and that there were some references made at the time to "orders of higher authorities." But these broad commonalities seem unconvincing proof of a master plan; soldiers acting on their own would have gone about the murderous work in much the same way, and there were far more differences among the acts that the lawyers left unmentioned. As to the "orders of higher authorities," they noted that "in a few cases Yamashita himself [was] mentioned as the source of the order," though not, they might have said, by anyone remotely in a position to know what an army group commander was thinking or saying.

"From the widespread character of the atrocities as above outlined, the orderliness of their execution and the proof that they were done pursuant to orders, the conclusion is inevitable," they concluded, "that the accused knew about them and either gave his tacit approval to them or at least failed to do anything either to prevent them or to punish their perpetrators. One cannot be unmindful of the fact that accused, an experienced officer, in giving such an order must have been aware of the dangers involved when such instructions were communicated to troops the type of the Japanese." But the memorandum cited no evidence of the accused "giving such an order"—because there was no such evidence.

The lawyers also gave some credence to the testimony of Galang, though they dutifully noted that his evidence was "somewhat weakened by proof that [Galang] was a confirmed collaborationist himself, and by the denial of the grandson that he interpreted the conversation." Still, they concluded, the testimony "cannot be wholly disregarded since it is entirely consistent with what later transpired in Manila." This was a fallacy. Galang's story at the trial, in November, was consistent only with what had *earlier* "transpired in Manila," and thus meaningless as an indicator of his credibility.

Acknowledging that "the accused was operating under some difficulty due to the rapidity of the advance of the Americans," the memo nonetheless discounted the significance of disruptions in communications. The lawyers noted that Yokoyama, commander of the Shimbu Group, maintained regular communications with Yamashita until April and managed some communication into June; what they did not note was that Yokoyama's communications with Iwabuchi in Manila were disrupted in February, nor did they note that there was no evidence of what, if anything, Iwabuchi actually communicated to Yokoyama. In fact, nowhere in the discussion of the evidence did the reviewing lawyers mention Iwabuchi, or Yamashita's orders that he evacuate the city.*

Like the prosecutors themselves, the reviewing lawyers did not venture any discussion of whether Yamashita's knowledge of events was material to the charge against him, nor of whether his ability or lack thereof to influence events in Manila from his shifting mountain redoubts was material to the

---

* In summarizing the defense case, the lawyers had briefly mentioned Yamashita's assertion that he had twice ordered that Manila be abandoned, but they did not refer to it again, an omission most notable in the substantive discussion of his responsibility for the crimes committed there.

charge. Taken as a whole, and with due regard for its setting out of the defense evidence and its acknowledgment of a lack of precedent, the memo contains nothing to suggest that Yamashita's guilt was even a close question or that the trial was anything less than scrupulously fair. Anything to the contrary simply went unmentioned. On the jurisdiction of the commission, there was "no reasonable question." Of the sufficiency of the charge, there was "little doubt." Questions about the commission's rulings were "without merit." There were "no errors injuriously affecting the substantial rights of the accused." The finding that the accused had a legal duty to prevent atrocities and had unlawfully disregarded that duty was "fully warranted." The death penalty was "appropriate to the offense."

The memorandum was exactly what MacArthur wanted.

Given the stay of proceedings ordered by the Supreme Court, however, he could do nothing with it. His formal approval of the conviction and sentence would have to await the Court's decision on the case—assuming, of course, that the decision would not overturn the conviction and remand the case for a new trial or, worse, invalidate the charge altogether. MacArthur, frustrated, could only postpone action, keep quiet, and await directions from higher authority: three of his least-developed talents.

16

The Supreme Court

The Court that heard Yamashita's case in January 1946 was almost entirely the creation of Franklin Delano Roosevelt. Chief Justice Harlan Fiske Stone had been appointed to the Court in 1925 by Calvin Coolidge, but it was Roosevelt who, in 1941, elevated him to Chief Justice. The senior Associate Justice was Hugo Black, the senator from Alabama, who in 1937 was the first of eight appointments by FDR in less than six years. Black was followed by former Solicitor General Stanley Reed in 1938; Harvard Law School professor Felix Frankfurter and Securities and Exchange Commission chairman William O. Douglas in 1939; former Michigan governor (and former governor general of the Philippines) Frank Murphy in 1940; former Attorney General and Solicitor General Robert H. Jackson in 1941; and former Washington University Law School dean Wiley Rutledge in 1943.* The junior justice, Harold Burton, had been a senator from Ohio when he was appointed a few months earlier by President Truman. With Jackson off prosecuting Nazi war criminals at Nuremberg, the 1945–1946 Court had eight sitting members.

All the justices had been in high political office or visible academic posts for years. In contrast to more recent Courts, only Rutledge had any judicial experience. Most had supported FDR's audacious and ultimately unsuccessful attempt to "pack the Court" with additional justices in 1937, in response to the Court's persistent invalidation of New Deal social and economic legislation. Reacting to the Court's authoritarianism of those years, all of FDR's appointees came from the school of judicial restraint. They saw the Court's proper role as giving broad deference to Congress to bring about regulatory reform and economic change, and after four years of war they were also distinctly disinclined to interfere with the authority of the President as Commander in Chief, or with the authority of those in uniform.

---

*The eighth appointment was James Byrnes, who served only from 1941 to 1942.

This Court's definition of war was broad, and it had an overlay of racism. In 1943, the Court had unanimously affirmed the conviction of Gordon Hirabayashi, an American citizen, for violating a curfew imposed by a military official—in California—directing that "all persons of Japanese ancestry" remain in their homes between 8:00 P.M. And 6:00 A.M. "The war power of the national government extends to every matter and activity so related to war as substantially to affect its conduct and progress," Chief Justice Stone had written. "We cannot close our eyes to the fact, demonstrated by experience, that in time of war residents having ethnic affiliations with an invading enemy may be a greater source of danger than those of a different ancestry."

The following year, as Yamashita was preparing his retreat to Baguio, a divided Court in *Korematsu v. United States* upheld the government's forced removal of Japanese and Japanese Americans from the West Coast to inland "relocation camps." Black, writing for the Court, was almost apologetic. "All legal restrictions which curtail the civil rights of a single racial group are immediately suspect," he began. "But exclusion from a threatened area [that is, the West Coast], no less than curfew, has a definite and close relationship to the prevention of espionage and sabotage. The military authorities, charged with the primary responsibility of defending our shores, concluded that curfew provided inadequate protection and ordered exclusion." In upholding the military order, Black wrote,

> We are not unmindful of the hardships imposed by it upon a large group of American citizens. But hardships are part of war, and war is an aggregation of hardships. . . . To cast this case into outlines of racial prejudice, without reference to the real military dangers which were presented, merely confuses the issue. . . . The properly constituted military authorities feared an invasion of our West Coast and felt constrained to take proper security measures, because they decided that the military urgency of the situation demanded that all citizens of Japanese ancestry be segregated from the West Coast temporarily, and finally, because Congress, reposing its confidence in this time of war in our military leaders—as inevitably it must—determined that they should have the power to do just this. . . . We cannot—by availing ourselves of the calm perspective of hindsight—now say that at that time these actions were unjustified.

Justice Jackson, dissenting, called the action a "military expedient that has no place in law under the Constitution." The exclusion, wrote Justice Murphy also in dissent, "goes over the very brink of constitutional power and falls into the ugly abyss of racism." And so it has come to be regarded since then—perhaps the most deplorable decision of the Court since the Dred Scott case in 1857 upheld the institution of slavery.*

But the case casting the longest and darkest shadow over Yamashita was the Court's 1942 decision in *Quirin*. Although the Court had given the commission defendants in that case a hearing, it had upheld the President's authority to convene military commissions. As it was later to do in *Hirabayashi* and *Korematsu*, the Court had taken a broad view of the President's authority to wage war and a strikingly broad view of what war was. "An important incident to the conduct of war," wrote Chief Justice Stone for a unanimous Court, "is the adoption of measures by the military command not only to repel and defeat the enemy, but to seize and subject to disciplinary measures those enemies who in their attempt to thwart or impede our military effort have violated the law of war." And that presidential authority, once established, precluded review by civilian courts. "We are not here concerned with any question of the guilt or innocence of petitioners," the Court noted—because they had not yet been tried. The only question was whether the commission had been validly convened and whether the charge validly stated a violation of the laws of war and thus was one that military commissions could try. The Court's affirmative answers to those two questions doomed Quirin and his mates.

The Court had changed little in the four years since that decision. The task for Yamashita's lawyers, clearly, was to persuade the justices that their case was different. They had respectable arguments. In *Quirin,* the Court had said it had the authority, indeed the obligation, to determine "whether any of the acts charged is an offense against the laws of war." The charge against Yamashita of failing to control his troops was both unprecedented and complex. In addition, the commission's rulings on evidence and continuances raised weighty constitutional issues of due process of law that the Court had had no occasion to consider in the Quirin case. But Yamashita was facing a Court that had consistently upheld the authority of the military to do what it needed to do to win the war, without judicial oversight, and that was quite ready to accept that military expertise could extend to judicial proceedings.

Colonel Clarke, Captain Reel, and Captain Sandberg landed in Washington on December 29, 1945, to face the daunting task of writing a brief and preparing an argument before the Supreme Court in nine days, an assignment to

---

* In 1987, the conviction of Hirabayashi was formally vacated by a federal court. In 1988, Congress authorized compensation, and an apology, to Fred Korematsu and 60,000 other Japanese Americans who were relocated, after a congressionally chartered commission concluded that the military order upheld by the Court was based on "race prejudice, war hysteria and the failure of political leadership."

which law firms routinely devote months. The Solicitor General of the United States, the Justice Department officer responsible for presenting the government's arguments to the Supreme Court, generously provided the defense team with office space, library access, and a secretary, and Army JAG detailed an experienced international lawyer to assist them. As they worked day and night on the brief, they learned that the Court had allotted six hours for oral argument, an exceptionally long time, and an encouraging sign that the Court was taking the matter seriously indeed.

They had little time to write their brief, but they had been living with the case every day for nearly three months and their arguments would closely track the legal points they had raised before the commission. To win a habeas case, they would have to convince the Court that U.S. laws were violated or that General MacArthur or the commission had abridged Yamashita's constitutional rights—assuming he had any to begin with. In the space of a week they produced a fifty-three-page typewritten brief and submitted it to the Court.

They first argued that the commission had not been lawfully convened, because commissions were wartime tribunals and the war had ended weeks before the charge was preferred. But that seemed just a warm-up to the main point: that the charge did not state a violation of the laws of war. Never before, they argued, had a commander been charged on the basis of acts committed by his troops, unless he had either ordered those acts or "had prior knowledge that the crime was to be committed, had the power in fact to prevent the crime, but failed to exercise his power and, instead, was personally present when the criminal design was carried out." (Their brief did not cite any such "prior knowledge" cases, because there had not been any of those, either.) Thus, criminal liability is "entirely dependent upon personal participation of some kind in the criminal act." While international law recognizes that combatants, to be lawful participants in battle, are to be commanded by a "person responsible" for them, "responsible" meant military authority; it was not intended to impose criminal accountability on the commander for the crimes of those combatants.

They focused on the ambiguity of the charge, which alleged that Yamashita—"petitioner" in the Court's usage—had failed to control his troops, "permitting" them to commit atrocities. "In no instance is it alleged that petitioner committed or aided in the commission of a crime or crimes," they wrote.

> In no instance is it alleged that petitioner issued an order, express or implied, for the commission of a crime. In no instance is it alleged that petitioner had knowledge of the commission of a crime by members of his command, or of a plan on the part of members of his command to commit crimes which petitioner failed to prevent. The charge alleges that he failed in his duty to control his troops, permitting them to commit certain alleged

crimes. But the bills of particulars set forth no instance of neglect of duty by the petitioner. They charge no act either of commission or of omission by the petitioner amounting to a "permitting" of the crimes in question.

"In essence, therefore," they argued,

the petitioner is not charged with having done something or with having failed to do something. He is charged merely with having been something, to wit: a commanding officer of a Japanese force whose members offended against the law of war. The heart of the charge is the proposition that commanding officers are rendered criminally liable regardless of fault for the acts of their troops. But it is a basic premise of all civilized criminal justice that punishment is adjudged not according to status, but according to fault, and that one man is not held to answer for the crime of another.

It was an argument clearly and forcefully stated. And the implication was clear: for the Court to rule against Yamashita, it must significantly expand the law of war. And the law of war applied to all, not just to Japanese generals. "The case at bar involves more than a precedent to brandish before a defeated enemy. It involves a precedent which we must also be ready to apply within our own forces and to acknowledge in all cases of friend and foe alike."

From the validity of the charge, they moved to the trial itself, arguing that MacArthur's directive "constituted such extreme departures from basic standards of fairness that the petitioner did not have a fair trial." Their points here were by now deeply familiar to them: the "extraordinary looseness" of MacArthur's regulations on evidence resulted in the admission of "highly prejudicial and unorthodox" depositions and affidavits that deprived the defense of any opportunity to cross-examine the declarant or probe his credibility. Hearsay was rampant throughout the trial, "sometimes three and four times removed from the source." The propaganda film *Orders from Tokyo* was "highly inflammatory and prejudicial." In addition, the commission had denied the defense sufficient time to prepare and had abruptly terminated their cross-examination of some prosecution witnesses.

The brief gave considerable attention to Article of War 25, the statute that prohibited the prosecution's use of depositions in capital cases. This was their strongest argument, for it depended neither on notions of what was fair, nor on whether enemy combatants had rights under the Constitution (a proposition no U.S. court had ever recognized), nor even on the proper deference that courts should pay to military authorities in wartime. Congress in the exercise of its constitutional authority to prescribe rules for the armed forces had enacted the Articles of War to regulate military trials, and Article 25 explicitly included commissions within its reach. Here, the commission, following the legal memorandum of the Judge Advocate General of the Army,* had categorically rejected the objections of the defense and had repeatedly accepted depositions—and many far less formal statements besides—when submitted by the prosecution. The issue was squarely before the Court.

The brief also raised two arguments of violations of the Geneva Conventions and then concluded with a heartfelt plea. "Turning for the moment from statute and doctrine," they wrote,

> let us examine the case as one of basic human right. The Anglo-Saxon nations take pride in their institutions of justice and in the guarantees of civil rights. It may seem to some that these fundamental guarantees were never intended for the benefit of a vanquished enemy general. But does not a defeated enemy represent that very example of a besieged and helpless human being caught in the net of overwhelming state power whom it was the impulse of the Bill of Rights to protect?

Even an enemy soldier, they went on,

> has fundamental human rights which inhere in him simply because he is a person; and it is of the deepest significance that our Constitution extends its most basic safeguards not to "citizens," not to certain kinds or categories of men, but to all "persons"—all human beings who are touched by our governmental machinery. The right to be tried fairly is such a fundamental human right. The gravity in this case does not lie only in the sentence—for soldiers always stand close to death—but rather in the obloquy of the judgment of iniquitous conduct which would tarnish the name of the accused for all time. . . . This was not a trial as Americans know the term, and it should not be allowed to stand.

They concluded with the words of Thomas Paine: "He that would make his own liberty secure must guard even his enemy from oppression; for if he violates this duty he establishes a precedent that will reach himself."

It was a remarkable argument, and not only for its eloquence. Clarke, Reel, and Sandberg were articulating a premise that was to become a fundamental principle of law but that in 1946 was entirely novel. No American court had ever held that the role of the judiciary was to protect "fundamental human rights" that inhere in all persons because they *are* persons, and to protect a "helpless human being caught in the net of overwhelming state power."†

---

* See Chapter 8.

† Clarke, Reel, and Sandberg signed the brief; in a gesture to their colleagues, they added the names of Hendrix, Feldhaus, and Guy as co-counsel.

This was the Court that, eighty-nine years earlier, had upheld the institution of slavery. In World War I it had affirmed convictions of antiwar activists for their criticism of U.S. participation in that war. In just the prior two decades, it had repeatedly struck down as a violation of due process of law congressional enactments to protect working men, women, and children from low wages, long hours, and unsafe workplaces. Its 1896 ruling in *Plessy v. Ferguson* upholding racial segregation was still the law of the land, and the ink was barely dry on its 1944 decision allowing American citizens to be taken from their homes and confined in distant and shoddy camps because their parents were Japanese.

For the United States, Solicitor General (SG) J. Howard McGrath* opposed every point. His argument was essentially that there was a line the Court should not cross, but if it did cross it, it should not cross the next one, or the one after that. The entire matter of captured enemy belligerents, the government's brief began, and particularly enemy belligerents who were charged with war crimes, was so intimately a part of the government's political and military policies that the Supreme Court had no business considering it and ought to dismiss the case on those grounds alone. It was an argument pitched to the Court's prevailing belief that it ought not to lightly overturn what was properly entrusted to Congress or the President, as their anti–New Deal predecessors had repeatedly done to presidential initiatives enacted by Congress.

And the SG had unimpeachable precedent: as long ago as 1829, Chief Justice John Marshall had enunciated the principle that the judiciary had no authority under the Constitution to act on the government's "interests against foreign powers." In any event, the SG went on, the Court had never departed from the "ancient doctrine" that nonresident enemy aliens had no access to U.S. courts at all. This was true, but not by much: the Quirin petitioners were "resident" only because they had been caught and arrested. But Yamashita could not claim even that connection. "An enemy soldier who only recently was engaged on the field of battle in attempting to overthrow this Government has no rights under the Constitution or laws of the United States and may receive no protection from its courts," the SG's brief argued. The last thing Yamashita had on his mind in 1944 and 1945 was overthrowing the U.S. government, but the point was made.

But if the Court did go on to actually consider Yamashita's claims, the SG contended, it should go no further than to satisfy itself that the military commission was properly convened and that it had jurisdiction to try Yamashita for war crimes. Though the defense had argued that there were flaws in the appointment procedure, the SG's brief carefully traced the authority of MacArthur to

---

*The brief was signed by McGrath and Assistant Solicitor General Harold Judson. (Some years later, the title of staff lawyers in the Office of the Solicitor General was changed to "Assistant to the Solicitor General," and it remains such today.)

direct General Styer to appoint a commission, and it refuted the contention that the authority to appoint a commission necessarily expired when the war ended.

But if the Court went even further than that, the SG went on, it should uphold the validity of the charge upon which Yamashita was tried. Here the government was on considerably less stable ground, because, like Yamashita, it had to make its case without the benefit of any precedent. But when a criminal charge—especially a capital charge—is without precedent, the onus lies more heavily on the prosecution to demonstrate its validity than on the defense to demonstrate its defect. The SG did what he could with what he had, arguing that the requirement that combatants be commanded by a "person responsible" for them imposed a legal obligation on the commander to control those combatants, and that a failure to do so was punishable as a crime. Yamashita was not charged with having merely "been" something, the SG argued, but with having failed to meet this legal obligation, and "there is nothing anomalous in affirming criminal liability for the consequences of inaction, where a duty to act exists." Whether that duty did in fact exist as a matter of law was the weakest part of the SG's argument, which is why the brief had erected so many barriers to the Court's even reaching it.

As to the various rulings by the commission, the SG had a ready answer if the Court should go that far: the rulings had not "prejudicially affected any of the accused's substantial rights." The brief did not go into any discussion of actual rulings or their context. It rested on the assertion that, with six defense counsel, time to prepare, and review by Styer and MacArthur, Yamashita had "every essential ingredient of such a trial as that concept is understood among civilized nations." It seemed a pro forma, almost dismissive, argument on the commission's rulings, but the Supreme Court seldom reviews evidentiary rulings of a trial judge, unless the rulings amount to a denial of statutory or constitutional rights—for example, the denial of the right of confrontation and cross-examination—and so the government's position was that Yamashita had no right to any particular trial process, let alone one with the guarantees of the U.S. Constitution.

The brief's conclusion yielded no ground:

International considerations of the utmost gravity, determining the extent to which this country may in wartime deal with those who have barbarously waged war against us, are presented by [this case]. Under established precedents, the Court should decline to intervene, since petitioner, an avowed enemy belligerent, is entitled to no rights in our courts in time of war. If, however, contrary to what we conceive to be the proper approach, the Court determines to examine petitioner's trial by military commission, we submit that such examination will not reveal any ground entitling petitioner to relief. The military commission had jurisdiction over petitioner's person and over the subject matter, it was properly appointed, the offense charged was a violation of the recognized laws of war, and the several procedural objections urged by petitioner are without substance and in any event unavailing on habeas corpus.

On January 7 and 8, 1946, in a full chamber, the Court heard oral argument from the three defense lawyers, wearing their service uniforms, ribbons, and insignia, and from Solicitor General McGrath and Assistant SG Harold Judson, each in that office's traditional morning dress: tailcoat, vest, and striped pants.*

The case was submitted. The eight justices would meet three days later at their weekly Friday conference to discuss and decide the case and begin the drafting of the Court's written opinion.

Stone and Frankfurter, two of the Court's most committed believers in judicial restraint, were firmly of the view that the Court should not interfere with what the military had done. Stone had written the Court's opinion in both *Hirabayashi* and *Quirin*, and Frankfurter was the Court's most ardent supporter of the President's authority—particularly this President's authority—to do what he thought necessary to win the war. We now know from the papers of some of the justices that Douglas and Reed readily agreed with Stone's views, expressed in a draft opinion. Black was slower to agree. He was troubled by what he saw as a denial of due process in the regulations and in the commission's sometimes capricious rulings on evidence, but those misgivings were overtaken by his belief that the Court had no jurisdiction in the first place over what MacArthur and the commission had done. Dealing with the enemy was the military's business, Black believed, and that included decisions on what to do with the enemy when the fighting was done. Still, he was not prepared to go as far as Stone proposed and rule that enemies tried by American authority had no right to due process of law in the first place.

Murphy and Rutledge were firmly on the other side, for reasons they were to express in lengthy dissenting opinions. Burton, the newest justice, was uncertain. Of the eight justices, Stone had five votes to deny habeas relief on the jurisdictional point, but, considering Black, only four sure votes to conclude that enemy combatants were not entitled to due process. He eventually brought Burton around to his views, but getting Black to join the Court's opinion was to require a significant concession by Stone.

---

* Morning dress is still worn today. No transcript of the oral argument was made, unfortunately, and Reel says very little about it in his book. Newspaper accounts are likewise scanty on the theatrics.

On February 4, 1946, a month after the oral argument, the Court issued its opinion. Written by Chief Justice Stone for himself and five other justices (all save Rutledge and Murphy), the opinion began on an unusual and gracious note. Noting the appointment of army officers as lawyers for Yamashita, Stone wrote, "Throughout the proceedings which followed, including those before this Court, defense counsel have demonstrated their professional skill and resourcefulness and their proper zeal for the defense with which they were charged."

Turning to business, the Court recalled the "governing principles" of cases such as these, as announced two years earlier in *Quirin:* although Congress had not created military commissions, in the Articles of War it recognized them as appropriate tribunals for trials alleging war crimes. But those commissions are not federal courts and their verdicts and rulings are normally reviewable only by military authorities, not by any court, including this one. This Court's authority, Stone went on, is limited to determining "whether the detention complained of is within the authority of those detaining the petitioner. If the military tribunals have lawful authority to hear, decide and condemn, their action is not subject to judicial review merely because they have made a wrong decision on the facts." Consequently, "we are not concerned with the guilt or innocence" of the accused.

However, the Court rejected the government's argument that it should dismiss the case outright on grounds that alien enemy combatants had no right even to come to court. Stone wrote that although Congress had restricted the appeals of those convicted by commissions, "it has not foreclosed their right to contend that the Constitution or laws of the United States withhold authority to proceed with the trial," nor did Congress—or could it—"withdraw from the courts the duty and power to make such inquiry into the authority of the commission as may be made by habeas corpus." Yamashita had his foot in the door.

On the question, then, of the authority to create the commission, the Court had little difficulty concluding that Roosevelt's 1942 order instituting military commissions—for the immediate purpose of trying Quirin—was broad enough to authorize this commission as well, and that MacArthur had all the authority he needed to convene it. It also dispatched the defense argument that whatever authority might have existed had expired when the war ended. As a formal matter, it noted that while Japan had surrendered, "peace has not been agreed upon or proclaimed."* More practically, it pointed out that if the authority to try war criminals by commission terminated with the surrender of the enemy, few trials could ever be held, for as a general matter only when the fighting had stopped could the army apprehend offenders and bring them to

---

* The formal peace treaty officially ending World War II was signed by forty-eight nations in San Francisco on September 8, 1951.

trial. These arguments had never been Yamashita's strong points anyway, and in their conference the eight justices had quickly rejected them.

The Court then took on the issue of whether the charge validly stated a violation of the law of war. They were entirely silent on the important and unresolved issue of whether "permitting" war crimes required some personal order, act, or participation by the commander. Rather, the questions were "whether the law of war imposes on an army commander a duty to take such appropriate measures as are within his power to control the troops under his command for the prevention" of war crimes "likely to attend the occupation of hostile territory by an uncontrolled soldiery" and, if so, "whether he may be charged with personal responsibility for his failure to take such measures when violations result."

In so stating the issue, the Court introduced an ambiguity of its own. Did "measures within his power" refer to his lawful authority to issue binding orders to the offenders or to his ability on the ground to learn what was happening, to communicate his orders effectively to the troops, and to see that those orders were appropriately received and followed? Yamashita plainly had the former power, but his ability to exercise it had been the most contentious issue at trial, with even the commissioners acknowledging that the American onslaught, the disrupted communications, the vast territory, and the shifting chain of command were real problems, even if not ultimately determinative of his guilt.

Stone's opinion did not answer that question directly, relying instead on the commission's conclusion that, for all his difficulties, Yamashita had "not taken such measures to control his troops as were 'required by the circumstances.'" Stone wrote, "We do not here appraise the evidence on which petitioner was convicted. We do not consider what measures, if any, petitioner took to prevent the commission" of atrocities, "or whether such measures as he may have taken were appropriate and sufficient to discharge the duty imposed upon him. These are questions within the peculiar competence of the military officers composing the commission and were for it to decide."

The result of this circuitous analysis seemed to be that a military tribunal can consider a commander's difficulties in issuing and enforcing orders, or not, as it wishes. Either way, its conclusion on the point will be final. So on the critical question of what it takes to prove a commander guilty, the Supreme Court took a pass.

Having concluded that the commander has a duty to take measures within his power—whatever that meant—to prevent atrocities, the majority turned to the central question: whether he is criminally accountable for a failure to do so. Its answer was clear: yes. It relied primarily on the requirement of the Fourth Hague Convention that lawful combatants be commanded by a "person responsible for his subordinates." It also noted that the convention required that an occupying power, having displaced the local authority, "shall take all measures in his power"—that ambiguity again—to "restore, and ensure, as far as possible, public order and safety." Furthermore, Stone noted, the First Geneva Convention made it the duty of commanders to see that its provisions on the humane treatment of the sick and wounded are carried out.

The flaw in this reasoning was that, as noted earlier, no one involved in the drafting or approval of the Hague Convention in 1907 had thought for a moment that it was imposing criminal liability for a failure of command. It was setting out the rules to ensure that those who fought would be lawful combatants and entitled to the protections due to prisoners of war only if they were in units led by a commander, wore uniforms, carried their arms openly, and themselves observed the laws of war. Remedies for violations were financial, not criminal. The convention provided that a government whose troops violate the convention "shall be responsible for all acts committed" by those forces and shall "be liable to pay compensation." It said nothing about the individual accountability of commanders. When that convention, and the First Geneva Convention, were drafted and approved, there was no case, let alone any accepted international law, imposing criminal accountability on a commander who had not ordered or participated in the crime. Nor had there been any such case since then.

The reasoning on the treaties was shaky, but Stone had another reason that seemed sounder:

> It is evident that the conduct of military operations by troops whose excesses are unrestrained by the orders or efforts of their commander would almost certainly result in violations which it is the purpose of the law of war to prevent. Its purpose to protect civilian populations and prisoners of war from brutality would largely be defeated if the commander of an invading army could with impunity neglect to take reasonable measures for their protection. Hence the law of war presupposes that its violation is to be avoided through the control of the operations of war by commanders who are to some extent responsible for their subordinates.

There is much sense in that, but the Court again refused to take the next step: to determine whether Yamashita, himself, in the Philippines, had issued orders or made efforts to "restrain" the atrocities, or whether he was, as a practical matter, able to do so, or even whether, as he claimed, his isolation and disrupted communications left him unaware of them. Neglect, after all, connotes a failure to take steps that one should have and could have taken. One has not neglected to do that which one was unable to do. Did Yamashita "neglect" to take such "reasonable measures," or was he prevented from doing so by the advancing enemy, his retreat to the jungle, the failure of communications, the insubordination of Iwabuchi's Manila force?

When the Court announces a new standard, it generally remands the case to the lower court to reexamine the evidence and determine whether it meets that standard. Here, there was no lower court to do that, and the Court did not do so itself. The Court thus created an anomaly: it announced a new standard of criminal accountability but disclaimed any jurisdiction or authority to determine whether that standard had been properly applied in the very case before it.

The Court then turned to the most prosaic, but the most intractable, obstacle to upholding the conviction: the unequivocal prohibition of Article of War 25 on the use of depositions by the prosecution in a capital case before a court-martial or a military commission. The articles were laws enacted by Congress; MacArthur could not ignore or overrule them. And if depositions were barred, surely MacArthur could not authorize the commission, as he had, to accept less reliable forms of hearsay—grossly less reliable, as the commissioners' rulings had repeatedly demonstrated.

If the Court were to rule that Article 25 meant just what it said, it would seem to have little choice but to set aside the conviction. Depositions and hearsay had so permeated the prosecution case that no fair judge could have concluded that they had been harmless and immaterial to the finding of guilt. While this would not have set Yamashita free—MacArthur could start over and try him again without depositions and hearsay—Yamashita and his lawyers would certainly have considered that a victory.

The Court avoided this outcome by engaging in much the same faulty analysis of the Articles of War that Judge Advocate General of the Army Cramer had done for the commission, though it did not refer to Cramer's memo. It concluded that the Articles of War did not apply to military commissions that were trying an enemy combatant for war crimes. This took some doing, as nothing in the articles explicitly excluded such commissions or even mentioned accused war criminals at all. But the Court held that Congress intended the articles to apply only to members of U.S. Armed forces. "The Articles recognized but one kind of military commission, not two," Stone acknowledged. "But they sanctioned the use of that one for the trial of two classes of persons, to one of which the Articles do, and to the other of which they do not, apply in such trials." As an enemy combatant, Yamashita "cannot claim the benefits of the Articles, which are applicable only to the members of the other class." So his commission "was not convened by virtue of the Articles of War, but pursuant to the common law of war. It follows that the Articles of War . . . were not applicable to petitioner's trial and imposed no restrictions upon the procedure to be followed. The Articles left the control over the procedure in such a case where it had previously been, with the military command."

To support this reasoning, the Court turned to another Article of War—Article 15—which makes clear that Congress did not intend to alter the traditional jurisdiction of commissions. But the Court's result was the judicial equivalent of pulling a rabbit out of a hat. And it does not stand up to analysis. It was true that, in Article 2, Congress had specified that members of U.S. forces—no mention of enemy forces—were "persons subject to military law." But that qualification, with a few exceptions not relevant here, was invoked only in the so-called punitive articles, defining crimes for which such persons could be tried. So, for example, Article 58 provides that "any person subject to military law" who deserts shall be punished by court-martial. Article 64 provides that "any person subject to military law" who willfully disobeys a lawful command of a superior shall be so punished, and so forth. Naturally there was no reason for Congress to apply the punitive articles to enemy combatants—what did the United States care if a Japanese soldier deserted, or disobeyed his superior?

Article 25, however, contains no such qualification. It allows the use of prosecution depositions "before *any* military court or commission in *any* case not capital" (emphasis added). Yamashita's case was born capital. There was simply no basis for the Court to rule that "any commission" meant "any commission except those trying accused war criminals."

Nor had Congress limited the articles as a whole to the category of "persons subject to military law." In fact it had done just the opposite. Article 23, for example, provides that "every person *not* subject to military law" (emphasis added) who disobeys a subpoena to appear as a witness before a commission or court-martial is guilty of a misdemeanor and shall be tried in federal civil courts. And Article 24 provides that "no witness" in a commission shall be compelled to incriminate himself. And Article 32 authorizes a commission to punish for contempt "any person" who disturbs its proceedings. While one might plausibly argue that Article 23 was intended to apply to civilians (enemy combatants would be arrested, not subpoenaed), Articles 24 and 32 certainly could include an enemy defendant such as Yamashita.

The conclusion is inescapable that Article 25 applied to all commissions, without regard to who was being tried, and that it had been repeatedly, unmistakably, and seriously violated, over the strenuous objections of the defense, throughout the trial. The Court's statement that the Articles "were not applicable" to Yamashita's trial and thus "imposed no restrictions" upon the commission was wrong.

The lasting significance of the Court's convoluted and erroneous reasoning is not that it misapplied the Articles of War as such. Congress repealed them in 1951 and replaced them with the Uniform Code of Military Justice, which has governed military trials ever since. The significance is that the justices were faced with a conviction that was obtained in violation of the laws of the United States and should therefore have been invalidated, and they did not do it.

The Court moved on, rejecting Yamashita's argument that his trial and conviction had violated Article 63 of the Geneva Convention of 1929 regarding prisoners of war, which provided that a sentence could be imposed on such prisoners only "in accordance with the same procedure as in the case of persons belonging to the armed forces of the detaining Power"—in other words, only according to the rules that would apply to American soldiers in courts-martial. The Court ruled that, given the context of this provision in the convention, it applied only to POWs who were tried for offenses committed in custody as prisoners, not for war crimes committed before their capture.*

Stone concluded his opinion with an awkward disclaimer. It is "unnecessary to consider what, in other situations, [the Due Process Clause of] the Fifth Amendment might require, and as to that no intimation one way or the other is to be implied." This was the rewrite job that Stone inserted to satisfy Justice Black, who had serious doubts about the fairness of the trial and the actions of the commissioners. Black agreed with the majority that the Court had no jurisdiction over military commissions, and he was content to rest the Court's decision on that ground. However, Stone in one of his drafts had concluded that the commission's rulings on evidence and procedure were consistent with the due process of law.

That was too much for Black. "If we are to apply the judicial concept of a 'fair trial,'" he had warned Stone during the drafting process, "I should be inclined to agree with the dissents." He was prepared to write a sharply worded concurring opinion, stating his own view that the procedures followed in the trial had been far from fair and that, if the Due Process Clause was applicable to enemy combatants, it had been violated in Yamashita's trial. A ruling that the Court had no jurisdiction to review the commission's conduct of the trial would avoid having to defend that conduct. And such a ruling would allow Black, at least, to go along with the majority's deference to military decision making without allowing it to taint due process jurisprudence that could spread to civilian trials at home.

Stone, who knew that Murphy and Rutledge were going to write stinging dissents of their own, was afraid of losing Black and having only four justices join his opinion. Five is still a majority, and in fact Black would have provided a sixth vote for the outcome based on his view of jurisdiction, but if Burton, the new justice who had yet to write an opinion in any case and was still

---

* When the Geneva Conventions were revised and updated in 1949, they explicitly applied these judicial protections to prisoners being tried for crimes committed before their capture, not merely during their captivity.

largely unknown to his colleagues, were to join Black's opinion, Stone would not have a majority for his opinion. The conviction would stand, but Stone's opinion would speak for only four justices and would not be the opinion of the Court itself.* That in turn would reflect badly on the Court (and MacArthur) and perhaps cast doubt on the wisdom of the impending execution. So Stone dropped his due-process analysis of the commission's work from his draft and inserted the terse disclaimer. Black, satisfied, signed on to Stone's opinion, as did Burton.†

There was no chance that Murphy or Rutledge was going to go along. They were both outraged at the way the case had been brought, charged, and tried, and they wrote lengthy and eloquent dissents that even today resonate with their invocation of justice and human rights. At a combined fifty-five pages, they were twice as long as Stone's opinion for the Court.

No one on the Court had a more intimate knowledge of the Philippines and its people than Frank Murphy. A former mayor of Detroit, he had been appointed Governor General (later, High Commissioner) of that commonwealth in 1933 by FDR and had lived there for three years. He was liked and respected by the Filipinos—a sentiment not always accorded his predecessors—for whom he was a vigorous advocate in Washington and a generous supporter in Manila. Returning to the States, he was elected governor of Michigan and then was appointed U.S. Attorney General before being named to the Court in 1940. No pacifist, he was the only member of the Supreme Court to volunteer for military service during the war, serving several reserve tours stateside, to the annoyance of Stone, who thought he had more important duties.

Overshadowed by Frankfurter, Douglas, Black, and Jackson then and almost forgotten today, he was until his death at age fifty-nine in 1949 a committed liberal who would have been entirely at home on the Warren Court of the 1950s and 1960s. He was a gifted speaker and an eloquent and inspirational if sometimes florid writer; those traits were on full display in his dissenting opinion.

"The significance of the issue facing the Court today cannot be overemphasized," he began. The "grave issue" was whether a military commission "may

---

* By long-standing Supreme Court practice, an opinion in which five or more justices join is the opinion of the Court itself, and has precedential value as such. An opinion of four or fewer is considered only to state those justices' own views. This calculus is separate from the decision to affirm or reverse the judgment under review, which is always by majority vote. The distinction arises because five (or more) justices may concur in the disposition of a case but have different reasons for their individual votes. A dissenting justice, on the other hand, disagrees with the disposition itself.

† Black reportedly expressed doubts privately a few months later about the correctness of the verdict.

disregard the procedural rights of an accused person as guaranteed by the Constitution, especially by the due process clause of the Fifth Amendment." For Murphy, the answer was plain:

> The Fifth Amendment guarantee of due process of law applies to "any person" who is accused of a crime by the Federal Government or any of its agencies. No exception is made as to those who are accused of war crimes or as to those who possess the status of an enemy belligerent. Indeed, such an exception would be contrary to the whole philosophy of human rights which makes the Constitution the great living document that it is. The immutable rights of the individual, including those secured by the due process clause of the Fifth Amendment, belong not alone to the members of those nations that excel on the battlefield or that subscribe to the democratic ideology. They belong to every person in the world, victor or vanquished, whatever may be his race, color or beliefs.

So much for the majority's deference to the military. "Such is the universal and indestructible nature of the rights which the due process clause of the Fifth Amendment recognizes and protects when life or liberty is threatened by virtue of the authority of the United States." The unprecedented charge and the commission's "biased view as to petitioner's duties and his disregard thereof," Murphy wrote, "is unworthy of the traditions of our people." And he warned, "No one in a position of command in an army, from sergeant to general, can escape those implications. Indeed, the fate of some future President of the United States and his chiefs of staff and military advisers may well have been sealed by this decision." In this case, he wrote, the Court was

> dealing with the rights of man on an international level. To subject an enemy belligerent to an unfair trial, to charge him with an unrecognized crime, or to vent on him our retributive emotions only antagonizes the enemy nation and hinders the reconciliation necessary to a peaceful world. . . .
>
> If we are ever to develop an orderly international community based upon a recognition of human dignity it is of the utmost importance that the necessary punishment of those guilty of atrocities be as free as possible from the ugly stigma of revenge and vindictiveness. Justice must be tempered by compassion rather than by vengeance. In this, the first case involving this momentous problem ever to reach this Court, our responsibility is both lofty and difficult. We must insist, within the confines of our proper jurisdiction, that the highest standards of justice be applied in this trial of an enemy commander conducted under the authority of the United States. Otherwise stark retribution will be free to masquerade in a cloak of false

legalism. And the hatred and cynicism engendered by that retribution will supplant the great ideals to which this nation is dedicated.

Murphy's departure from the bedrock principles of narrow judicial oversight of the military could not have been more profound. Where the majority had focused on the nature of military commissions and the constraints of habeas corpus review, Murphy catapulted the issue into one of international human rights and dignity. Murphy's invocation was its first mention in Supreme Court jurisprudence, nearly three years before the new United Nations organization would issue the Universal Declaration of Human Rights, universally accepted today as the governing statute of international human rights.

Murphy readily agreed with his brethren that the commission had been lawfully convened, but, he wrote, "I find it impossible to agree that the charge against the petitioner stated a recognized violation of the laws of war." Reviewing the military situation in the Philippines during Yamashita's command, Murphy emphasized that the charge did not allege, and the commission had not found, that Yamashita even knew of the atrocities that were being committed. The charge, he wrote, amounted to this:

> "We, the victorious American forces, have done everything possible to destroy and disorganize your lines of communication, your effective control of your personnel, your ability to wage war. In those respects we have succeeded. We have defeated and crushed your forces. And now we charge and condemn you for having been inefficient in maintaining control of your troops during the period when we were so effectively besieging and eliminating your forces and blocking your ability to maintain effective control. Many terrible atrocities were committed by your disorganized troops. Because these atrocities were so widespread we will not bother to charge or prove that you committed, ordered or condoned any of them. We will assume that they must have resulted from your inefficiency and negligence as a commander. In short, we charge you with the crime of inefficiency in controlling your troops. We will judge the discharge of your duties by the disorganization which we ourselves created in large part. Our standards of judgment are whatever we wish to make them."

Murphy also dismissed the majority's reliance on international treaties to impose a duty on a commander to control his troops. International law simply does not address that subject, he wrote, much less impose criminal liability for failing in such a duty, for the very good reason that judging a commander's duties in battlefield conditions is difficult and speculative, and untrustworthy when the victor is doing the judging. Even the official army publication on the rules of land warfare made no mention of command responsibility; it provided only that the person "giving the order" could be punished for the resulting crime.★

Murphy made clear his view that an allegation and proof that Yamashita knew of the atrocities and had done nothing, or too little, within his power to abate them would make for an "entirely different" case. But that had been neither alleged nor proven. "Instead the loose charge was made that great numbers of atrocities had been committed and that petitioner was the commanding officer; hence he must have been guilty of disregard of duty. Under that charge the commission was free to establish whatever standard of duty on petitioner's part that it desired."

It was all too much for Murphy. "At a time like this," he concluded,

> when emotions are understandably high it is difficult to adopt a dispassionate attitude toward a case of this nature. Yet now is precisely the time when that attitude is most essential. While peoples in other lands may not share our beliefs as to due process and the dignity of the individual, we are not free to give effect to our emotions in reckless disregard of the rights of others. We live under the Constitution, which is the embodiment of all the high hopes and aspirations of the new world. And it is applicable in both war and peace. We must act accordingly.

Justice Rutledge also dissented, in a forty-page opinion that rivaled Murphy's in its appeal to the nation's first principles. "More is at stake than General Yamashita's fate," he began.

> There could be no possible sympathy for him if he is guilty of the atrocities for which his death is sought. But there can be and should be justice administered according to law. In this stage of war's aftermath it is too early for Lincoln's great spirit, best lighted in the Second Inaugural,† to have wide hold for the treatment of foes. It is not too early, it is never too early, for the nation steadfastly to follow its great constitutional traditions, none older or more universally protective against unbridled power than due process of law in the trial and punishment of men, that is, of all men, whether citizens, aliens, alien enemies or enemy belligerents.

"I cannot believe in the face of this record that the petitioner has had the fair trial our Constitution and laws command," he continued.

★ This was true in 1946; the army publication was revised in 1956. See chapter 7.
† "With malice toward none, with charity for all."

At bottom my concern is that we shall not forsake in any case, whether Yamashita's or another's, the basic standards of trial which, among other guaranties, the nation fought to keep; that our system of military justice shall not alone among all our forms of judging be above or beyond the fundamental law or the control of Congress within its orbit of authority; and that this Court shall not fail in its part under the Constitution to see that these things do not happen.

The case was unprecedented, he wrote, acknowledging that

precedent is not all-controlling in law. There must be room for growth, since every precedent has an origin. But it is the essence of our tradition for judges, when they stand at the end of the marked way, to go forward with caution keeping sight, so far as they are able, upon the great landmarks left behind and the direction they point ahead. If, as may be hoped, we are now to enter upon a new era of law in the world, it becomes more important than ever before for the nations creating that system to observe their greatest traditions of administering justice, including this one, both in their own judging and in their new creation. The proceedings in this case veer so far from some of our time-tested road signs that I cannot take the large strides validating them would demand.

The road-sign metaphor may have been a bit labored, but Rutledge's oblique reference to the proceedings that were under way at Nuremberg suggested that, like Murphy, he could not view this case as simply a matter of applying settled and specialized rules of jurisdiction over military commissions; it was for him the end of one road and the beginning of another. With that in mind, he addressed first his belief that the commission was unconstitutional from start to finish. He agreed with all the other justices that it had been lawfully convened as a formal matter—that MacArthur had the authority to create it—but, he wrote, no commission could depart so clearly and so repeatedly from basic constitutional values and still retain its validity.

He listed the defects. Yamashita had been charged with a crime that was "defined after his conduct, alleged to be criminal, [had] taken place." Its language was "not sufficient to inform him of the nature of the offense or to enable him to make defense." He was "not charged or shown actively to have participated in or knowingly to have failed in taking action to prevent the wrongs done by others, having both the duty and the power to do so." A great deal of the evidence was "hearsay, once, twice or thrice removed," and some of it was "prepared *ex parte** by the prosecuting authority and include[d] not only

---

* Meaning with no participation of the other party.

opinion but conclusions of guilt." He was denied the right of confrontation and cross-examination.

"The matter is not one merely of the character and admissibility of evidence," he wrote.

> It goes to the very competency of the tribunal to try and punish consistently with the Constitution, the laws of the United States made in pursuance thereof, and treaties made under the nation's authority. . . . Whether taken singly in some instances as departures from specific constitutional mandates or in totality as in violation of the Fifth Amendment's command that *no* person [emphasis in the original] shall be deprived of life, liberty or property without due process of law, a trial so vitiated cannot withstand constitutional scrutiny. I cannot conceive any instance of departure from our basic concepts of fair trial, if the failures here are not sufficient to produce that effect.

With that overture, he turned one by one to the issues before the Court. As to MacArthur's convening order that allowed any evidence to come in, "a more complete abrogation of customary safeguards relating to the proof could hardly have been made. So far as the admissibility and probative value of evidence was concerned, the directive made the commission a law unto itself. It acted accordingly." Yet for all the voluminous evidence accumulated in the trial, "the commission's ultimate findings draw no express conclusion of knowledge, but state only two things: (1) the fact of widespread atrocities and crimes; (2) that petitioner 'failed to provide effective control . . . As was required by the circumstances.'"

"This vagueness, if not vacuity, in the findings," Rutledge wrote, "runs throughout the proceedings, from the charge itself through the proof and the findings, to the conclusion. It affects the very gist of the offense, whether that was willful, informed and intentional omission to restrain and control troops *known* by petitioner to be committing crimes or was only a negligent failure on his part *to discover* this and take whatever measure he then could to stop the conduct" (emphases in the original). In a lengthy footnote, he pointed out the ambiguity of the charge, which, he said, could cover either of these two readings. "Permitting" could mean either willful and intentional action (or inaction) in the face of the crimes, or it could mean simply "not preventing," which would be consistent with a lack of knowledge. "In capital cases such ambiguity is wholly out of place," he wrote.

Rutledge pointed out that Stone's opinion for the majority "nowhere expressly declares that knowledge was essential to guilt or necessary to be set forth in the charge." In short, Yamashita stood "convicted of a crime in which knowledge is an essential element, with no proof of knowledge" except perhaps evidence in "ex parte affidavits and depositions" that would be "inadmissible in any other capital case or proceeding under our system, civil or military."

Rutledge took particular issue with what he saw as the denial of the opportunity to present a defense, focusing not only on counsel's inability to cross-examine written statements but also on the last-minute addition of fifty-nine allegations in the supplemental bill of particulars, the denial of a continuance to investigate those new allegations, the commingling of the original and the supplemental charges soon after the trial began, the commission's abrupt reversal of its initial ruling not to allow any crime to be proven by affidavits alone, and the denial of a continuance again at the conclusion of the prosecution's case. "This sort of thing has no place in our system of justice, civil or military," he wrote. "Without more, this wide departure from the most elementary principles of fairness vitiated the proceeding. When added to the other denials of fundamental right"—the hearsay, the charge, the evidentiary rules—"it deprived the proceeding of any semblance of trial as we know that institution."

Rutledge then proceeded to a meticulous analysis of the Articles of War, demonstrating, as he put it, that MacArthur's regulations and the admission of extrajudicial evidence was "squarely in conflict" with Article 25's prohibition of depositions and with Article 38's requirement that commissions follow court-martial rules as far as practicable. He scorned the majority's conclusion ("as the Court strangely puts the matter") that the articles implicitly created "two types of military commission" and that "Congress intended the Articles of War referring in terms to military commissions without exception to be applicable only to the first type." This "highly strained construction" of the articles, he wrote, is "in plain contradiction" to their history, language, and purpose. His conclusion was blunt: "The commission was invalidly constituted, was without jurisdiction, and its sentence is therefore void."

Rutledge reserved his final words for Stone's refusal to apply the Fifth Amendment's Due Process Clause to Yamashita's conviction:

> I am completely unable to accept or to understand the Court's ruling concerning the applicability of the due process clause of the Fifth Amendment to this case. Not heretofore has it been held that any human being is beyond its universally protecting spread in the guaranty of a fair trial in the most fundamental sense. That door is dangerous to open. I will have no part in opening it. For once it is ajar, even for enemy belligerents, it can be pushed back wider for others, perhaps ultimately for all.
>
> The Court does not declare expressly that petitioner as an enemy belligerent has no constitutional rights, a ruling I could understand but not accept. Neither does it affirm that he has some, if but little, constitutional

protection. Nor does the Court defend what was done. I think the effect of what it does is in substance to deny him all such safeguards. And this is the great issue in the [case.]

"All this the Court puts to one side with the short assertion that no question of due process under the Fifth Amendment or jurisdiction reviewable here is presented," he concluded.

> I cannot accept the view that anywhere in our system resides or lurks a power so unrestrained as to deal with any human being through any process of trial. What military agencies or authorities may do with our enemies in battle or invasion, apart from proceedings in the nature of trial and some semblance of judicial action, is beside the point. Nor has any human being heretofore been held to be wholly beyond elementary procedural protection by the Fifth Amendment. I cannot consent to even implied departure from that great absolute.

Rutledge, like Yamashita's lawyers, ended with Thomas Paine: "He that would make his own liberty secure must guard even his enemy from oppression; for if he violates this duty he establishes a precedent that will reach to himself." He might well have added Paine's two preceding sentences, from First Principles of Government: "An avidity to punish is always dangerous to liberty. It leads men to stretch, to misinterpret, and to misapply even the best of laws."

And with that, the case of General Yamashita came to an end. From the laying of the charge in Manila to the decision of the Supreme Court, it had taken four months and two days.

What is most notable about the three opinions in the case is not that the justices disagreed but that they approached the case from such profoundly different perspectives. Although Murphy and Rutledge were careful to refute the majority's specific points, their true departure was on more fundamental grounds. Where Stone and his five colleagues had seen a military tribunal tasked with disposing of an episode arising in war, Murphy and Rutledge saw Douglas MacArthur and his five appointees applying—or misapplying—American law with disregard for the Constitution's great command that no person should suffer loss of life without due process of law. For them, the justices in the majority could not bring themselves to justify the obvious and continuous violation of due process and so had ignored it.

Ironically, the one safeguard of constitutional dimension that Yamashita was afforded—the zealous assistance of counsel—had yet to be recognized by the

Court as so inherently a requirement of due process that every serious state criminal trial must provide it.* But given the vagueness of the charge, the lack of any meaningful restrictions on the evidence that could be considered, the last-minute charges, the denial of cross-examination arising from the use of hearsay, and the rush—for what purpose?—to judgment, one would be hard-pressed, as Rutledge put it, to imagine a wider departure from "the most elementary principles of fairness." ("I didn't give the boys in the Yamashita case as much hell as I wanted to," Rutledge wrote to a friend a few months later. "I felt like turning loose with all the fire that Murphy poured on.")

The majority was not wrong in its conclusion that its only means of reviewing the conviction rendered by a military commission was by habeas corpus, and that the scope of that review was a narrow one. But the Court would not have had to take the giant step of ruling that enemy combatants were entitled to the constitutional protection of due process of law—a step it did take in 2004, in extending that protection to detainees at Guantánamo Bay. Even in 1946, the narrow focus of habeas corpus would have justified a new trial on grounds that the use of ex parte deposition testimony violated an act of Congress that explicitly prohibited such use in a capital case. The Court's convoluted analysis of Article of War 25 to avoid that result is quite unconvincing and leads only to the conclusion that the majority was determined to uphold the commission's verdict despite that fundamental and unequivocal barrier.

The Court could not, of course, uphold the conviction unless it upheld the validity of the charge. That the charge was unprecedented and ambiguous was clear; that it required no showing of actual misconduct by the accused—no order, no participation, no active permission, no neglect, and no knowledge—was clear as well. Lacking any legal authority of any kind from any source that such a charge was rooted in the common law of war or some treaty of the United States, the Court wove from the Hague Convention, and a few words from other treaties of even less relevance, a thin blanket to cover their conclusion that what Yamashita had not done was a violation of international law. Its justification—that it would make sense to have such a provision, because commanders are in charge and the whole purpose of the law of war is to prevent civilian casualties and to protect prisoners of war as much as possible—was reasonable enough as a general proposition, but the Court acknowledged early in its opinion, as it had two years earlier in *Quirin,* that the Constitution confers upon Congress, not the judicial branch, the authority to "define and punish . . . offences against the Law of Nations"—of which, the Court acknowledged, "the law of war is a part." The federal courts, like the other two branches of the federal government, "possess no power not derived from the Constitution," Chief Justice Stone had written in *Quirin.* In *Yamashita,* that restriction

---

* That ruling came in *Gideon v. Wainwright,* 372 U.S. 335 (1963).

required the Court to look for something adopted by Congress, and since Congress had never itself said a word about a commander's accountability, the only available source could be the treaties it had ratified. The majority's error lay in summoning the principle it needed from treaties that did not contain it.

Rutledge counted the Yamashita decision "the worst in the Court's history, not even barring Dred Scott." But that surely is an overstatement, even for Rutledge. "Great cases, like hard cases, make bad law," Justice Oliver Wendell Holmes had written in a 1904 Supreme Court decision. "For great cases are called great not by reason of their real importance in shaping the law of the future, but because of some accident of immediate overwhelming interest which appeals to the feelings and distorts the judgment."

Holmes's words are apt here. The appalling atrocities in the Philippines and the presence in the dock of the commanding general of the forces who had committed them were enough to make this a hard case. But once past that, the Court faced a vexing situation. In the words of Judge John M. Ferren, Rutledge's biographer, "Should the Court clear the way for the democratically elected branches of government to assume the moral and political responsibility for determining, ultimately, the rules for going forward against captured enemy commanders—subject only to the most limited scrutiny" by unelected judges? Or "should the only branch of government established by the Founders to protect the individual against majority passions resist procedural shortcuts—which, upon reflection in less stressful moments, might be seen to suggest vengeance more than justice?"

In fairness to Stone and his five fellow justices, the Court's determination to uphold the commission's verdict was less a product of vengeance than of judicial restraint—not a bloodthirsty desire to see a Japanese commander hang, but a deeply held aversion to intervening in military matters. And to the majority, this criminal trial of a Japanese soldier—like curfews and relocations imposed on Japanese civilians—was a military matter.[*]

The sand was now rapidly running through the hourglass for Yamashita. The Court dissolved the stay of proceedings it had imposed when it took the case, leaving MacArthur free to resume his formal review of the trial and announce

---

[*] This is not to deny the racial overtones of the Court's jurisprudence during this period, nor the larger racial context of the war. In the words of historian John Dower, "In the United States and Britain, the Japanese were more hated than the Germans before as well as after Pearl Harbor. . . . There was no Japanese counterpart to the 'good German' in the popular consciousness of the Western Allies," leading to a perception that "the Japanese were a uniquely contemptible and formidable foe who deserved no mercy and virtually demanded extermination." Dower notes that these stereotypes receded quickly at the end of the war in August 1945.

his decision on the sentence. Yet Yamashita's defense counsel, ever hopeful, managed to find a bright side to the way the Supreme Court had structured its decision. None of the eight justices had said that the trial had been fair. Two had written scathing and detailed condemnations of the entire process; the other six had declined to discuss the point.

The lawyers had no doubt that MacArthur was determined to see Yamashita executed. And the Court's decision had obliterated their lingering hope that MacArthur might yet be convinced that the trial—which had been conducted according to the very regulations he had approved—had been unfair. But their objective now was to spare Yamashita's life, and the decision had perhaps strengthened an argument they had made after the trial ended, as the official transcript was being prepared for MacArthur's review.

Clarke and his colleagues had hurriedly written and attached to the record a "recommendation for clemency" to MacArthur. "This is the first time in the history of the modern world," they wrote,

> that a commanding officer has been held criminally liable for acts com-
> mitted by his troops. It is the first time in modern history that any man has
> been held criminally liable for acts which according to the conclusion of
> the commission do not involve criminal intent or even gross negligence.
> The commission therefore by its findings created a new crime. The accused
> could not have known, nor could a sage have predicted, that at some time
> in the future a military commission would decree acts which involved no
> criminal intent or gross negligence to be a crime, and it is unjust, therefore,
> that the punishment for that crime should be the supreme penalty.

They hoped that maybe—just maybe—the split decision of the Court would now give MacArthur pause. Maybe the strident dissenting opinions of Justices Murphy and Rutledge, the only analyses of the trial to come from someone other than defense counsel and military lawyers subordinate to MacArthur, would, if thoughtfully read, lead him to appreciate that there was more to the case than he might have anticipated when he put the process in motion. Mac-Arthur, the absolute ruler of Japan, was deeply involved with the writing of a new constitution, transforming a country that for nearly eighty years had been led by a divine emperor into a democracy under the rule of law. Might this not be the opportunity to stay the hangman, to demonstrate, however implicitly, that even a military leader of a defeated enemy could be punished short of execution, when two members of the victor's highest court had so vigorously raised their voices in protest?

The Court's decision had come down in midafternoon on February 4, 1946, which was February 5 in Tokyo. The news was radioed to MacArthur, with the assurance that copies of the opinions were being sent immediately by air and would arrive within a few days for his review.

Twenty-four hours later, with the Court's opinions en route, MacArthur announced his decision: The sentence would stand. Yamashita would be executed, by hanging.

His statement was pure MacArthur. In its entirety, it read:

It is not easy for me to pass penal judgment upon a defeated adversary in a major military campaign. I have reviewed the proceedings in vain search [*sic*] for some mitigating circumstances on his behalf. I can find none. Rarely has so cruel and wanton a record been spread to public gaze. Revolting as this may be in itself, it pales before the sinister and far reaching implication thereby attached to the profession of arms. The soldier, be he friend or foe, is charged with the protection of the weak and unarmed. It is the very essence and reason for his being. When he violates this sacred trust he not only profanes his entire cult but threatens the very fabric of international society. The traditions of fighting men are long and honorable, based upon the noblest of human traits—sacrifice.

This officer, of proven field merit, entrusted with high command involving authority adequate to responsibility, has failed this irrevocable standard; has failed his duty to his troops, to his country, to his enemy, to mankind: has failed utterly his soldier faith. The transgressions resulting therefrom as revealed by the trial are a blot upon the military profession, a stain upon civilization and constitute a memory of shame and dishonor that can never be forgotten. Peculiarly callous and purposeless was the sack of the ancient city of Manila, with its Christian population and its countless historic shrines and monuments of culture and civilization, which with campaign conditions reversed had previously been spared.

It is appropriate here to recall that the accused was fully forewarned as to the personal consequences of such atrocities. On October 24—four days following the landing of our forces on Leyte—it was publicly proclaimed that I would "hold the Japanese Military authorities in the Philippines immediately liable for any harm which may result from failure to accord to prisoners of war, civilian internees or civilian non-combatants the proper treatment and the protection to which they of right are entitled."

No new or retroactive principles of law, either national or international, are involved. The case is founded upon basic fundamentals and practices as immutable and as standardized as the most natural and irrefragable of social codes. The proceedings were guided by that primary rational [*sic*] of all judicial purposes—to ascertain the full truth unshackled by any artificialities or narrow method of technical arbitrariness. The results are beyond challenge.

> I approve the findings and sentence of the Commission and direct the Commanding General, Army Forces in the Western Pacific, to execute the judgment upon the defendant, stripped of uniform, decorations and other appurtenances signifying membership in the military profession.

It was an astounding statement. Putting aside the orotund invocation of soldierly virtues and the stilted syntax, it utterly contradicted the plain facts of the case. Even the prosecutor and the members of the commission had acknowledged that there were "mitigating circumstances," albeit insufficient to stand in the way of conviction and execution. And MacArthur only obliquely intimated that this was a case of command accountability at all, rather than personal involvement in the ordering or commission of the atrocities. His assertion that "no new or retroactive principles of law" were involved contradicted even his own staff's acknowledgment that "only rarely, if at all, has punishment for failure to exercise control been meted out to an individual commander."

Rather than characterizing his regulations as appropriate measures for a trial of this type, he praised his search for "truth unshackled by any artificialities or narrow method of technical arbitrariness." To say that the procedural safeguards of the Constitution and rules of evidence can sometimes subordinate full disclosure is one thing; to dismiss them as artificial and arbitrary technicalities is contemptuous. His assertion that the results were "beyond challenge" can only have been intended as an insult to the lengthy challenges of two Supreme Court justices whose opinions he had not waited to read.

Finally, as MacArthur surely intended, his order that Yamashita be executed "stripped of uniform, decorations and other appurtenances signifying membership in the military profession" heaped disgrace on the humiliation of hanging. Not content to see his adversary on the gallows, MacArthur seemed determined to send him there stripped of not only his uniform but his dignity as well.

MacArthur, or a subordinate, immediately ordered the Japanese press to publish no unfavorable comment on the confirmation of the sentence or on MacArthur's statement. Lindesay Parrott of the *New York Times* reported that many Japanese expressed "considerable shock" that Yamashita was to be denied his uniform and decorations for having "'profaned' the honorable traditions of military service," he wrote. "While most Japanese undoubtedly expected the execution of the death sentence, probably none expected the additional disgrace—which comes as a blow worse than execution to the proud inheritor of the 'Bushido' cult."

MacArthur's other insult, to the Supreme Court, did not go unnoticed there. Later in February, the Court rejected without a hearing the habeas corpus petition of General Homma, also convicted of war crimes in the Philippines, though on stronger evidence than had been marshaled against Yamashita. Murphy and Rutledge again dissented. "Hasty, revengeful action is not the American way," Murphy wrote. In an obvious rejoinder to MacArthur, he added, "All those who act by virtue of the authority of the United States are bound to respect the principles of justice codified in our Constitution. Those principles, which were established after so many centuries of struggle, can scarcely be dismissed as narrow artificialities or arbitrary technicalities. They are the very life blood of our civilization."

Yamashita's lawyers did the last thing they could do for their client. They delivered a petition for clemency to the White House, asking President Truman to commute the sentence to life imprisonment. The lawyers' hopes rose when they were given an audience with Major General Harry H. Vaughan, Truman's military aide, to make their case. Vaughan was courteous but noncommittal. The next day the War Department issued a terse and unsigned statement: "The President will take no action on the petition for clemency," it read. "General MacArthur has been given this information."

In Japan, some 86,000 people had signed a petition urging MacArthur to commute the sentence, or at least to allow Yamashita the honorable death of hara-kiri. In Manila, Filipinos had clamored for a public execution in the devastated remains of Manila's old city of Intramuros. Both were to be disappointed. While the focus of the case was in Washington, Yamashita had been transferred to a prison camp at Los Baños, about 40 miles south of Manila, where, with thousands of other Japanese prisoners, he sat with little to do, on grounds where civilian internees had once been held in the custody of the army he had once led. He received the news, as he received all news, calmly, and he prepared himself to die. He was sixty years old.

He had an unexpected wait. Though MacArthur had authorized Styer to carry out the execution immediately, Styer delayed for almost two weeks; his reasons remain unclear today. On Friday night, February 22, 1946, Styer issued the order for the execution, to take place within hours.

A Buddhist monk was brought to Yamashita's tent. But Yamashita did not pray. Instead, he dictated his final words to the monk, who wrote them down. First published in 1981 and translated into English only in 2005, he addressed the letter not to his wife—whom he had not seen since leaving Tokyo for Manila some sixteen months earlier—but to the "Japanese People." He said:

> Due to my carelessness and personal crassness, I committed an inexcusable blunder as the commander of the entire Army and consequently caused the deaths of your precious sons and dearest husbands. I am really sorry and cannot find appropriate words for sincere apologies. . . . For a person like

me who constantly faced death, to die is not at all difficult. . . . But I would
like to say something on this point, as I am just about to die and thus have
great concern about Japan's future. . . .

Please stand up firmly after the ravages of war. That is my wish. I am a
simple soldier. Faced with execution in a very short time, a thousand emotions overwhelm me. But in addition to apologizing, I want to express my
views on certain matters.

. . . First, is about carrying out one's duty. . . . In a free society, you should
nurture your own ability to make moral judgments in order to carry out
your duties. Duties can only be carried out correctly by a socially mature
person with an independent mind and with culture and dignity. . . . You are
expected to be independent and carve out your own future. No one can
avoid this responsibility and choose an easy way. Only through that path can
eternal peace be attained in the world.

Second, I would like you to promote education in science. No one can
deny that the level of Japan's modern science, apart from certain minor
areas, is well below world standards. . . . We made the greatest mistake—unprecedented in world history—by trying to make up for the lack of materials and scientific knowledge with human bodies. . . . I am not saying this is
the only reason, but it was clearly one important reason for Japan's defeat. . . .
If there is any method to defend against atomic bombs—the weapon that
has made obsolete all past warfare—it would simply be to create nations all
over the world that would never contemplate the use of such weapons.

. . . The science that I mean is not science that leads mankind to destruction. It is science that will develop natural resources still to be tapped, that
will make human life rich, and will be used for peaceful purposes to free
human beings from misery and poverty.

Third, I want to mention the education of women. . . . My hope is that
you will break out of your old shell, enrich your education, and become
new active Japanese women, while maintaining only the good elements of
existing values. The driving force for peace is the heart of women. Please
utilize your newly gained freedom effectively and appropriately. Your freedom should not be violated or taken away by anyone. As free women, you
should be united with women throughout the world and give full play to
your unique abilities as women.

. . . Please do your best in educating your own children. Education does
not begin at kindergarten or on entry to elementary school. It should begin
when you breastfeed a newborn baby. . . . It is not enough for a mother to
think only about how to keep her children alive. She should raise them to
be able to live independently, cope with various circumstances, love peace,
appreciate cooperation with others and have a strong desire to contribute to
humanity when they grow up. . . .

These are the last words of the person who took your children's lives away from you.

Shortly before 3:00 a.m., an escort detail of American soldiers arrived, and Yamashita was made to undress and put on some old Army fatigues, tailored to look as little as possible like a uniform. His hands were bound behind his back and, accompanied by the monk, he was led out of his tent into a weedy sugar cane field and toward a brightly lit wooden gallows. MacArthur had dispatched three generals to Los Baños to witness the event.

Yamashita had a written statement, in English, probably translated by someone at the prison camp. An interpreter distributed it to the small gathering.

I know that all you Americans and American military affairs officers always have tolerance and rightful judgment. When I have been investigated in Manila court, I have had a good treatment, kindful attitude from your good-natured officers, who all the time protect me. I never forget for what they have done for me, even if I have died. I don't blame my executioners. I will pray God bless them.

Please send my thankful words to Colonel Clarke, and Lieutenant Colonel Feldhaus, Lieutenant Colonel Hendrix, Major Guy, Captain Sandberg, Captain Reel, at Manila court.

Yamashita then spoke in Japanese: "I will pray for the Emperor's long life and his prosperity forever." Robert Cromie of the *Chicago Daily Tribune* noted, "He appeared stoical."

He climbed thirteen steps to the scaffold. The hangman placed a noose over his head and fitted it to his neck. The trap was sprung and he fell.

His body was sewn into a blanket and carried on a canvas stretcher to a grave marked by a white wooden post. It bore no name.

Three months later, his wife received an official communication from the United States government. It informed her that her husband had been "executed as a war criminal."

17

The Forties
Nuremberg and Tokyo

Throughout Yamashita's trial and in the Supreme Court decision, neither the prosecution nor the commission nor the Court had come to grips with the question of what Yamashita actually knew about the rampage in the Philippines. Did he know—and, if so, what—or didn't he? The defense position was clearly that he did not know, but the defense never built a cohesive argument from that assertion. Was a lack of knowledge sufficient to exonerate him? Or would the commission have to delve into the question of why he did not know, and perhaps into the question of whether he should have known? Would the answers to these questions determine his guilt or innocence?

The Supreme Court majority also ignored those questions, leaving the dissenters to argue that the prosecution had failed to prove any knowledge on Yamashita's part. So the question remained: in the prosecution of a commander for the crimes of his troops, should the prosecution have to prove that he knew— or at least, taking all the circumstances into account, should have known—that those troops were committing crimes? In other words, would ignorance of the facts—at least when it was not due to any willful blindness or any intentional shirking of duty—be a defense to a charge based on command accountability?

The issue is fundamental, because in the American canon of law, one is not held criminally responsible for what one did not do, unless one had a duty under the law to do something and culpably failed to do it. Yet because no other commander had ever been charged on the basis of command accountability, there was no precedent in the law, no guidance in regulations, not even any real discussion of the issue in the learned treatises on the international law of war. Whatever dim light illuminated the issue arose from omission: no charge had ever been brought, and no jurist or scholar had ever suggested such a basis; nor had the official manual of the U.S. Army on the laws of land warfare ever clearly stated that a commander could be held liable for the crimes of his troops.

In fact, the army's regulations on the law of war—which were for practical purposes the regulations of the entire U.S. Armed forces, since no other branch

of service issued any of its own—had shifted several times on the issue of command accountability, which it treated simply as an aspect of a soldier's liability
for following his superior's orders. The first statement came in the army's first
edition of the regulations, in 1914. "Individuals of the armed forces will not be
punished for [violations of the law of war] in case they are committed under
the orders or sanction of their government or commanders. The commanders
ordering the commission of such acts, or under whose authority they are committed by their troops, may be punished by the belligerent into whose hands
they may fall." So soldiers who were ordered or authorized to commit war
crimes were not answerable; instead, the commander who ordered or authorized them would be.

To be sure, there is some ambiguity over what was meant by "authority." Did
it mean "authorization," that is, affirmative permission, short of an order? Or does
"under whose authority" mean "within whose organization?" In context, it seems
to mean the former. Thus, the soldier would be protected, but the commander
punished, for crimes that were ordered or "authorized," but by implication the
commander's knowledge of the crimes by itself would not be sufficient for guilt.

This provision was repeated in the 1934 and 1940 editions of the regulations.
In November 1944, however, the Army deleted it, probably in the realization
that trials for Nazi criminals, just then being incubated, could ill afford to allow
a "just following orders" defense yet could hardly forbid it if the army's own
regulations allowed it. So the army revised its rule: "Individuals and organizations who violate the accepted laws and customs of war may be punished
therefor. However, the fact that the acts complained of were done pursuant to
order of a superior or government sanction may be taken into consideration in
determining culpability, either by way of defense or in mitigation of punishment. The person giving such orders may also be punished."

A superior's order was thus no longer an automatic defense for those who
committed war crimes, though it could be "taken into consideration" in determining guilt or punishment. And the person giving such orders could be
punished as well. Nine months later, the Charter of the International Military
Tribunal at Nuremberg, drafted in large part by Justice Robert Jackson, the U.S.
chief of counsel, removed the discretion when it came to guilt: "The fact that
the defendant acted pursuant to order of his Government or of a superior shall
not free him from responsibility, but may be considered in mitigation of punishment if the Tribunal determines that justice so requires." The Nuremberg
charter said nothing about command accountability, nor did the Allies rely on
that principle in presenting the case against the Nazi defendants.

The next edition of the army's manual, issued in 1956 and still current today,
embroidered the following-orders defense somewhat: "The fact that the law
of war has been violated pursuant to an order of a superior authority, whether

military or civil, does not deprive the act in question of its character of a war crime, nor does it constitute a defense in the trial of an accused individual, unless he did not know and could not reasonably have been expected to know that the act ordered was unlawful."

The 1956 manual's test was a dual one, with both subjective and objective components: the superior's order is not a defense unless the subordinate who acted on it did not himself know that it was illegal and, furthermore, unless a reasonable person in the subordinate's shoes would not have known it was illegal, either.

In addition, the 1956 regulations, for the first time, explicitly provide for command accountability. The responsibility of a commander for crimes committed by subordinates

> arises directly when the acts in question have been committed in pursuance of an order of the commander concerned. The commander is also responsible if he has actual knowledge, or should have knowledge, through reports received by him or through other means, that troops or other persons subject to his control are about to commit or have committed a war crime and he fails to take the necessary and reasonable steps to insure compliance with the law of war or to punish violators thereof.

Had that been the standard governing the charge against Yamashita, the prosecution would have been required to prove that Yamashita did indeed actually know about the crimes or that he should have known about them through reports or "other [unspecified] means," and that he then failed to take "necessary and reasonable" steps to prevent or punish them. That would seem to have been an impossible burden for the prosecution to have met. At the least, that standard would have required conscientious commissioners to pay close attention to the situation on the ground, to determine just what reports or other knowledge, if any, Yamashita had actually received, and what necessary steps he could reasonably have taken in light of that knowledge.

This requirement of actual knowledge, or knowledge that one should have had, did not arise in a vacuum. After the International Military Tribunal (IMT) issued its judgment and disbanded in 1946, the United States stayed on at Nuremberg to stage an additional twelve trials, against twelve groups of German defendants, including doctors, financiers, judges and lawyers, and several groups of military officers. These trials, each presided over by a panel of three judges from American state courts, thirty-six judges in all, did not have the international stature of the IMT, but their lengthy and carefully reasoned judgments have contributed significantly to the jurisprudence of the law of war.

Two of those trials confronted the issue of a commander's accountability for the crimes of subordinates. The first was brought against Wilhelm List and nine other German generals in the Balkans. It is often called the Hostages Case because its primary focus was on the German practice of taking civilians hostage to deter local partisans from killing German soldiers, and executing the hostages in reprisal when such killings occurred.

The judges concluded, with obvious reluctance, that the customary law of war had allowed this practice, under certain narrow conditions. The evidence, however, showed that hostage taking and reprisal killings had been widespread and poorly controlled, often serving as a cover for the murder of Jews, Communists, and political enemies. At trial, many of the generals claimed that they were unaware of the extent of the practice or of its abuses, blaming subordinate commanders acting without authority.

The judges took the claim seriously. They ultimately rejected it, not because knowledge was irrelevant but because the evidence showed that the German generals in the Balkans in fact knew, or should have known from reports sent to their headquarters, that the crimes were taking place. The commanders "had mail, telegraph, telephone, radio and courier service for the handling of communications," the *List* judges noted. "Reports were made daily, sometimes morning and evening. Ten-day and monthly reports recapitulating past operations and stating future intentions were regularly made. They not only received their own information promptly but they appear to have secured that of the enemy as well. We are convinced that military information was received by these high ranking officers promptly, a conclusion prompted by the known efficiency of the German armed forces."

The judges thus made knowledge an essential element of accountability. And if knowledge could not be proven directly, as for example by the commander's statements at the time, it could be proven indirectly by looking at the reports sent to him. "An army commander," the judges ruled,

> will not ordinarily be permitted to deny knowledge of reports received at his headquarters, they being sent there for his special benefit. Neither will he ordinarily be permitted to deny knowledge of happenings within the area of his command while he is present therein. It would strain the credulity of [this] Tribunal to believe that a high ranking military commander would permit himself to get out of touch with current happenings in the area of his command during wartime.

In response to the claim that some of the generals had in fact been absent from their headquarters, on leave or at the front, and had therefore been unaware of what was happening in their subordinate units, the judges announced a two-part rule. "As to events occurring in his absence resulting from orders, directions, or a general prescribed policy formulated by him, a military commander will be held responsible in the absence of special circumstances. As to events, emergent in nature and presenting matters for original decision, such commander will not ordinarily be held responsible unless he approved of the action taken when it [later] came to his knowledge."

The tribunal was clearly seeking, as the Yamashita commission had not, a balanced approach that held commanders to their duty of overseeing their troops while still taking into account the realities of combat. Once the evidence established that communications were efficient and unimpeded and that reports were regularly sent to a commander's headquarters, that commander could not deny knowledge of what was in those reports, unless he was in fact absent from his headquarters, had not authorized the excesses, and did something about them if and when he learned of them afterward.

This formulation was to have—and still has—an enormous influence on the concept of command accountability. It requires the prosecution to present what might be called a snapshot of the commander's state of mind at a crucial but often momentary point in time. It requires proof either that he knew what was happening or was at fault, through negligence or inefficiency, in not knowing. But the *List* tribunal was also implying that if a commander's lack of knowledge was due to disrupted communications, or a failure of his subordinates to report the truth, or his being out of touch—and assuming none of that was his own fault—then the commander would be acquitted. "In determining the guilt or innocence of these defendants," the judges wrote, "we shall require proof of a causative, overt act or omission from which a guilty intent can be inferred before a verdict of guilty will be pronounced. Unless this be true, a crime could not be said to have been committed unlawfully, willfully, and knowingly as charged in the indictment."

This was the first meaningful analysis of command accountability by any tribunal. The judges' decision made no reference to the Supreme Court's conclusion in Yamashita's case that the criminal accountability of a commander had been established in 1907 by the Hague Convention. But their silence implicitly rejected that analysis in favor of a nuanced weighing of the evidence centered squarely on a commander's knowledge or lack of it.

The judges convicted eight of the generals and acquitted two. In each of the convictions, they specified exactly the orders given and the reports written and received establishing that defendant's knowledge of crimes against noncombatants and other innocent victims by troops under them. (The two acquitted were chiefs of staff, and the court absolved them because they had no command authority.) And although the judges concluded that "the evidence in this case recites a record of killing and destruction seldom exceeded in modern history," no one was executed. Two of the generals were sentenced to life imprisonment, the others to terms of imprisonment ranging from seven to twenty years.

Nine months later, in November 1948, a different panel of American judges handed down a decision in the High Command Case against Wilhelm von Leeb and a dozen other senior German field generals, charged with passing on to their subordinates illegal orders they had received from their superiors on the German General Staff or from Hitler himself. The orders were among the most notorious of the Third Reich: that captured Russian soldiers who were commissars—political officers—be executed; that captured Allied commandos be "slaughtered to the last man"; that civilians suspected of opposing German forces in occupied territories be executed swiftly, without trial. There was abundant evidence that the orders had led to the killing of tens of thousands of civilians and innocent combatants. The question before the tribunal was whether the defendants were guilty of those crimes because they or their staffs had transmitted the orders onward to subordinate units.

The tribunal stated, "For a defendant to be held criminally responsible, there must be a breach of some moral obligation fixed by international law, a personal act voluntarily done with knowledge of its inherent criminality under international law." Noting that the defendants were not lawyers but "field commanders [who] were charged with heavy responsibilities in active combat," the judges ruled that "to find a field commander criminally responsible for the transmittal of such an order, he must have passed the order to the chain of command *and* the order must be one that is criminal upon its face, or one which he is shown to have known was criminal" (emphasis added).

For orders that were obviously criminal—"criminal on their face"—no inquiry into the commander's state of mind was necessary. "By any standard of civilized nations," the judges stated, such orders were "contrary to the customs of war and accepted standard[s] of humanity. Any commanding officer of normal intelligence must see and understand their criminal nature. Any participation in implementing such orders, tacit or otherwise, any silent acquiescence in their enforcement by his subordinates, constitutes a criminal act on his part."

But for other orders—those that were lawful in form but resulted in widespread abuses and atrocities in the field—the judges applied a different standard, focusing, as in the Hostages Case, on what the commander knew at the time he acted or failed to act. "Modern war such as the last war entails a large measure of decentralization. A high commander cannot keep completely informed of the details of military operations of subordinates and most assuredly not of every administrative measure. He has the right to assume that details entrusted to responsible subordinates will be legally executed," the judges wrote.

Criminality does not attach to every individual in [the] chain of command from that fact [of command] alone. There must be a personal dereliction. That can occur only where the act is directly traceable to [the commander] or where his failure to properly supervise his subordinates constitutes criminal negligence on his part. In the latter case it must be a personal neglect amounting to a wanton, immoral disregard of the action of his subordinates amounting to acquiescence. Any other interpretation of international law would go far beyond the basic principles of criminal law as known to civilized nations.

That was quite a remarkable statement, unprecedented in the law of war. Not only did the court reject the notion that a commander could be held accountable without "personal dereliction" on his part; it ruled that such dereliction must be serious indeed, rising to the level of "criminal negligence"—a "wanton, immoral disregard" amounting to acquiescence in the crimes of his subordinates.

"Criminal responsibility is personal," the court stated. "The act or neglect to act must be voluntary and criminal. The occupying commander," it added, "must have knowledge of these offenses and acquiesce or participate or criminally neglect to interfere in their commission, and [the] offenses committed must be patently criminal."

Unlike the judges in the Hostages Case, this tribunal did acknowledge the Supreme Court's Yamashita decision but distinguished it. It reasoned that Yamashita had full authority over his operations, whereas the German crimes "were mainly committed at the instance of higher military and Reich authorities."

The distinction, however, seems awfully weak. While it is true that after the loss of Leyte, Yamashita was on his own in the Philippines, with few if any orders from Tokyo or Southern Army headquarters, by no stretch could his actions be characterized as "criminal negligence" or immoral disregard amounting to tacit acquiescence. Even if one assumes that he knew what was happening, not even the Manila commission went so far as to suggest that he consciously stood by and watched, "wanton[ly]" and "immoral[ly]" allowing the carnage to continue unabated while refusing to halt it. A more likely explanation for the High Command court's accommodation of the Yamashita decision was that it did not wish to embarrass the U.S. Army by pointing out that it had convicted and executed Yamashita under a standard of command accountability that the court had just rejected, and on evidence that the court would almost surely have found insufficient.

The Hostages and High Command decisions were the first in history to articulate a reasoned standard by which to judge a commander's accountability for crimes he had not ordered. But they came three years too late to save General Yamashita.

Meanwhile, a second international tribunal was lumbering down the runway, in Tokyo. On January 19, 1946, while the Supreme Court was deliberating Ya-mashita's case, MacArthur, the viceroy of Japan, promulgated the charter for the International Military Tribunal for the Far East (IMTFE), which would eventually try twenty-five Japanese military and civilian officials for murder, war crimes, and crimes against peace.

The IMTFE is inevitably compared to Nuremberg, and invariably comes off a distant second. It was a beast of a trial, with eleven judges from eleven nations. Every victim of Japanese aggression, and then some, sent a judge: not only the United States, Britain, France, and the Soviet Union, as at Nuremberg, but also Australia, New Zealand, China, India, the Philippines, Canada, and the Netherlands.* And every nation sent a team of prosecutors, all under the direc-tion of the Chief of Counsel Joseph Keenan, a U.S. Justice Department assistant attorney general of no particular renown. The trial convened on May 3, 1946, and after two and a half years and 818 days of trial announced its judgment on November 1, 1948. It heard 419 witnesses in person, accepted the depositions of another 779, and compiled a transcript of nearly 50,000 pages of testimony and another 30,000 pages of exhibits. Two hundred and thirty-two lawyers took part. The opinion extended to 1,781 pages and took nine days to read aloud in court, not including a dissenting opinion by the judge from India, which was just as long and mercifully was not recited aloud. The closing arguments alone consumed forty-seven days, more than the entire Yamashita trial. Every defen-dant was convicted.

The question naturally arises: why did MacArthur not simply hold Yamashita to be tried in Tokyo? When he ordered Yamashita to the military commission in Manila on October 1, 1945, planning for the Tokyo trial was already well under way in Washington. Seventeen of the twenty-five defendants eventually selected for trial had served in uniform in the 1937–1945 period, eleven of those as field commanders. Both the Philippines and Britain, the colonial master of Singapore, had scores to settle with Yamashita. His leadership of the air force during the late 1930s, his extended inspection tour of Germany in 1941, and his consultations with the German General Staff, even a photo opportunity with Hitler himself, plus his leadership of the Twenty-Fifth Area Army in its invasion of Malaya on the first day of the war, would easily have qualified him to be included among the defendants charged with planning, launching, and waging aggressive war, what-ever his own reluctance to follow that course. And the Philippine atrocities were

---

* The U.S. Appointed a Massachusetts state court trial judge, but he departed after the trial was under way and was replaced by the recently retired Judge Advocate General of the Army, General Myron C. Cramer.

prominent at that trial. Indeed, Akira Muto, Yamashita's chief of staff in the Philippines and a major witness at his trial, was made a defendant and was convicted and hanged, in large part because of the atrocities there. Given MacArthur's silence on his thinking, we will never know the answer.

The IMTFE's unwieldy structure and glacial pace (it recessed for the entire summer of 1947 to allow defense counsel time to prepare their case) and the fact that its lengthy opinion, filling ten times the pages of its Nuremberg counterpart, was not published for decades afterward have given it a decidedly inferior place in history that is not entirely justified. Its opinion is carefully reasoned and painstaking in its detail, covering the sweep of Japanese expansionism, militarism, political intrigue, and war from the early 1930s until surrender. Its contribution to the jurisprudence of command accountability, however long delayed in its publication and dissemination, is substantial. Its teaching on the command accountability of civilian government officials has informed several recent decisions of the International Criminal Tribunal for the Former Yugoslavia.

The IMTFE laid out a nuanced road map of accountability. It did so in its discussion of abuses and neglect of POWs and civilian internees, but its conclusions would apply to crimes against civilians whatever their location. Starting with the proposition that responsibility for the well-being of prisoners and internees rests with the government in whose custody they are, the judges included in the cohort of those responsible the members of the government and the departmental officials tasked with supervising prisoner matters, as well as the military officers commanding units holding prisoners and the jailers themselves. All of these, the IMTFE announced, have a "duty to secure proper treatment of prisoners and to prevent their ill treatment by establishing and securing the continuous and efficient working of a system appropriate for these purposes." Civilian and military officials become criminally accountable if they fail to establish such a system, or fail to secure its "continued and efficient" operation. Each of them must take "the same pains to ensure obedience to his orders in this respect as he would in respect of other orders he has issued on matters of the first importance."

Here, the IMTFE judges addressed the issue of the responsible official's knowledge, in a way that largely followed the decisions of the High Command and Hostages cases. An official or military commander would not be held responsible unless he either had knowledge that crimes were occurring and failed to "take such steps as were within [his] power" to stop them or was "at fault for having failed to acquire such knowledge." And fault, the judges made clear, required proof of "negligence or supineness" on the part of the official: a personal dereliction of duty.

The tribunal made clear that this element of fault was to be kept in perspective. It is not enough, it said, for the official to show that he "accepted assurances from others more directly associated with the control of the prisoners if having regard to the position of those others, to the frequency of reports of such crimes, or to any other circumstances he should have been put upon further enquiry as to whether those assurances were true or untrue." But it seems fair to infer from the context that here, too, the "should have" standard means that the commander was at fault, through his own negligence or conscious decision, in not making further inquiry—in other words, that he is entitled to rely on the reports of subordinates unless he has some reason to doubt their veracity or completeness. In that equation, evidence that crimes are "notorious, numerous and widespread as to time and place are matters to be considered in imputing knowledge."

Though the tribunal's formulation may at first reading seem to be caught up in "on the one hand; on the other hand" balancing, it is actually just a series of yes-or-no questions. First, was the accused an official responsible for the treatment of prisoners and internees? Second, if so, did he either fail to establish a system of reporting or, having established one, fail to oversee its proper administration? If the answer to both questions is yes, the next question is: did he know that prisoners were being mistreated? Actual knowledge can be proven directly, or it can be inferred—he must have known—if the mistreatment is so "notorious, numerous and widespread" that he could not have remained unaware of it. But if he did not have actual knowledge, the fourth and final question is whether he was at fault in not knowing, keeping in mind that "fault" really does mean fault. It would not include an inability to receive information because the enemy has forced him into an isolated command post; or because communication is disrupted due to terrain, weather, faulty equipment, or enemy action; or because the reports he receives on the matter seem to be adequate and regular in reporting nothing amiss. So if the answer to both the first two questions and to either the third or the fourth is yes, the commander or other official is to be held accountable, by the tribunal's analysis.

Its opinion is incomplete in one important respect: it implicitly assumes that a commander with knowledge would be able to deal effectively with the situation. The judges did not address the possibility that, even fully aware, a commander would be unable to fix it. Assuming a commander in the mountains knows of atrocities in the city and orders the subordinate commander to cease and abandon the city, an inquiry must be made as to whether he was able to enforce the order. Given the tribunal's attention to the matter of fault, it would presumably exonerate a commander who was not. As obvious as that might be, the Supreme Court's analysis in Yamashita's case left no room for it.

The Tokyo tribunal ended in November 1948 with the conviction of all twenty-five defendants of the crime against peace—the planning, launching, and waging of aggressive war. In addition, ten were convicted of ordering atrocities against civilians and prisoners of war or of disregarding their duty to prevent them. Seven were ordered to be executed by hanging, sixteen were given life imprisonment, and two others were given shorter prison terms.

By this time, the Allies were done with war crimes trials, and weary of them. The international trial at Nuremberg had concluded more than two years earlier, and testimony in the Ministries Case, the last of the twelve subsequent U.S. trials against various Nazi defendants, ended a few days after the Tokyo judgment. The Allies themselves were no more: Churchill had decried the Iron Curtain across Europe, the Marshall Plan was rebuilding western Europe, the Truman Doctrine had instituted the policy of containment that was to last through the Reagan administration, the Soviet Union was blockading Berlin, and the United States was airlifting supplies daily to the isolated city. Communism was the West's enemy; the sooner the Nazis were forgotten, the better.

In Japan, MacArthur was in his fourth year of what he would later tell Congress was "the greatest reformation recorded in modern history." His final piece of war crimes business was to uphold the sentences imposed by the Tokyo judges, which he did on November 24, 1948, with surpassing grandiosity.

"No duty I have ever been called upon to perform in a long public service replete with many bitter, lonely and forlorn assignments and responsibilities is so utterly repugnant to me," he proclaimed. "It is not my purpose, nor indeed would I have that transcendent wisdom which would be necessary, to assay the universal fundamentals involved in these epochal proceedings designed to formulate and codify standards of international morality by those charged with a nation's conduct." Many will disagree with the court, he acknowledged, "but no mortal agency in the present imperfect evolution of civilized society seems more entitled to confidence in the integrity of its solemn pronouncements. If we cannot trust such processes and such men we can trust nothing." In directing the execution of the sentences, he appealed to all to "pray that an Omnipotent Providence may use this tragic expiation as a symbol to summon all persons of good will to a realization of the utter futility of war—that most malignant scourge and greatest sin of mankind—and eventually to its renunciation by all nations."

Seven defendants were executed within a month. The sixteen given life imprisonment were all released within ten years.

America was done with war crimes.

18

The Seventies

My Lai

On the morning of March 16, 1968, near the east coast of South Vietnam, Second Lieutenant William L. Calley led his platoon of twenty-five American soldiers on a combat assault operation in the village of My Lai, known as "Pinkville" or "My Lai 4" in local army parlance. Calley's unit, three months in the country and untested by combat, was eager for action. Intelligence reports had identified My Lai 4 as the headquarters of a battalion of the North Vietnamese Army. On Saturday morning the civilians would have left for market, leaving the village to the enemy soldiers.

The intelligence was wrong. The families who lived there had not gone to market, and there were no enemy soldiers. The next several hours were one of the most shameful chapters in American military history. The men of the platoon, led by Calley himself, murdered, raped, and brutalized hundreds of men, women, and children, laying waste to the community and nearly everyone in it. Children barely old enough to walk were cut down by automatic rifle fire; schoolgirls were raped and then murdered; old women were shot in the back as they tried to flee; the modest huts were set on fire; not even the animals were spared. Some 400 Vietnamese were murdered that day, the great majority of them women, children, and old men.

By midday, the carnage was over, and the soldiers, spent and exhausted, returned to their base camp a few miles away. Reports were made of a victorious engagement with the enemy. The army public information office, as usual, issued a press release. The next day, the *New York Times* reported on an inside page, "American troops caught a North Vietnamese force in a pincer movement on the central coastal plain yesterday, killing 128 enemy soldiers in daylong fighting." The operation took place "in an area of sand dunes and scrub brush" and brought the number of enemy dead that week to 569. It was a routine report, and completely fictitious.

Nothing more was said for nearly a year, and nothing more might ever have been said, but for Ron Ridenhour, an American soldier in his final months in

Vietnam, who was hearing troubling stories about Pinkville from his buddies in Calley's platoon. On March 29, 1969, discharged and back home in Phoenix, Arizona, Ridenhour sent a five-page typewritten letter recounting what he had heard to the Secretary of Defense and several members of Congress. After laying out the details he had been told, Ridenhour wrote, "Exactly what did, in fact, occur in the village of 'Pinkville' in March, 1968 I do not know for *certain,* but I am convinced that it was something very black indeed"—black enough, Ridenhour wrote, to require "a widespread and public investigation of this matter."

Ridenhour's letter got the army's attention. General William C. Westmoreland, the army's chief of staff and its top commander in Vietnam at the time of the massacre, directed the Inspector General (IG) of the Army to investigate. When he read the IG's report in August 1969, Westmoreland referred it to the army's criminal investigation division, which conducted its own investigation. Calley—now a first lieutenant—was recalled from Vietnam to Fort Benning, Georgia, to await the outcome. On September 5, army JAG prosecutors formally charged Calley with killing 109 "Oriental human beings, occupants of the village of My Lai 4, whose names and sexes are unknown, by means of shooting them with a rifle."

Fort Benning's public information office issued a brief and bland press release that day, stating that Calley was "charged with violation of [Uniform Code of Military Justice] Article 118, murder, for offenses allegedly committed against civilians while serving in Vietnam in March 1968." There was no mention of the number of victims, of My Lai, or of any other details, and the announcement drew only cursory press coverage.

But in Vietnam, *New York Times* reporter Henry Kamm noticed. He made his way to a settlement near My Lai and met there with survivors of the massacre. On November 17, his story made the front page of the newspaper: "Vietnamese Say G.I.'s Slew 567 in Town." The next day, Ron Haeberle, a civilian in Cleveland, Ohio, who had been an army photographer with Calley's platoon that day, called the *Cleveland Plain Dealer* and told them he had photographs—not the official photographs of the operation, but color photos taken on his personal camera. The paper published some of the photos a few days later, depicting the stark results of ghastly acts: bodies of men, their entrails spilling onto the ground; tiny bodies riddled with bullet holes; women tied to a post, clutching their babies, their faces contorted in frantic screams; mounds of bodies, arms and legs askew; victims unrecognizable because their heads had been cleaved in two.

The photos, republished in *Life* magazine and then throughout the world, would have caused a sensation no matter what their political context, but coming as they did in November 1969, when opposition to the war in Vietnam was mounting by the week in the United States, they transformed politics. Those who opposed the war, and many who previously had not, were appalled that American soldiers—"American boys," average age barely twenty-one—could be so callous and dehumanized as to commit such horrors. Those who supported the war as righteous opposition to a Communist insurgency saw instead the unavoidable cruelties of a treacherous guerrilla war and were outraged at the unpatriotic reaction of the war's opponents, who had no idea of the dangers American boys faced every day. Slight and unassuming, Calley became a lightning rod in a riven nation.

If the immediate question was how this could have happened, the second was why it took so long—twenty months, from March 1968 to November 1969—to come to light. Within a week of the banner headlines, Westmoreland called in Lieutenant General William Peers, a well-regarded soldier who had earned his spurs in the OSS leading guerrillas in China during World War II and had commanded a corps in Vietnam. Westmoreland told Peers to investigate whether the army had conducted an adequate investigation following the event—though it must have been obvious to all that it had not—and whether Calley's chain of command, which had extended to Westmoreland himself, had covered up the slaughter prior to Ridenhour's letter.*

Working nonstop over the next three and a half months, Peers and his staff delivered to Westmoreland on March 14, 1970—two years almost to the day after the massacre—a 341-page single-spaced report, meticulous in its detail and documented with three volumes of exhibits and appendices. Although his instruction from Westmoreland was to investigate only what the army had done after that day in My Lai, Peers decided sensibly enough that he could not assess the army's response unless he first established what had happened and who was in charge.

Peers's report was to bring back to life the issue of the accountability of commanders after twenty years of dormancy, and shake the U.S. military to its foundations. What Peers found was that the soldiers in My Lai that day, "while under the supervision and control of their immediate superiors" had committed, singly and together, murder, rape, sodomy, maiming, and assault on civilians, killing at least 175 and perhaps as many as 400 Vietnamese, and had laid waste to the hamlet, not only its people but its dwellings, crops, wells, and livestock.

But determining who had been in charge was not easy. Early 1968 had been a harried and hectic time in Vietnam. A coordinated offensive at the Tet holiday in January had been a stunning political success for the North Vietnamese Army and its Viet Cong guerrilla allies in the South. In the aftermath, as

---

* President Johnson appointed General Westmoreland Chief of Staff of the Army on March 23, 1968, one week after the My Lai massacre, long before it became known.

American forces in Vietnam were increased, Westmoreland and his staff shuffled the military's organization, creating new units and chains of command.

Calley's platoon was one of five in C Company—Charley Company—commanded by Captain Ernest Medina, one of three companies in an ad hoc task force under Lieutenant Colonel Frank Barker. The task force was a temporary battalion-size unit of about 700 men in the Eleventh Infantry Brigade,* commanded by Colonel Oran Henderson and itself only recently arrived in Vietnam. The brigade was in turn part of the Americal Division, a newly created patchwork command under Major General Samuel Koster. Koster reported eventually to Westmoreland at headquarters, Military Assistance Command Vietnam (MACV).

On the day of the massacre, Koster, the division commander, had received a sketchy report from Barker, who reported twenty civilian deaths, which he attributed to victims having been caught in cross fire between U.S. troops and the enemy. But a helicopter pilot, Warrant Officer Hugh Thompson, had a different and far more ominous account. Flying low over the village that day, he saw to his consternation the bodies of civilians, and American soldiers confronting women and children huddled in groups, but no enemy troops. He landed his helicopter, confronted Calley, and rescued several children, airlifting them to a nearby hospital. On his return to base, he reported his action to his company commander "in most serious terms," Peers reported. "Those who were present heard the terms 'killing' and 'murder' used freely with estimates of the dead in My Lai running over 100."

The next day, Thompson's company commander went to division headquarters and reported to Koster's assistant commander, a brigadier general, that there had been "lots of unnecessary killing, mostly women, children and old men," and that Thompson's account had been confirmed by others. The assistant commander repeated the account to Koster, who ordered Henderson, the brigade commander, to "investigate" the allegations. But Koster did not transmit the troubling information to any higher headquarters, despite regulations requiring him to do so. Instead, Peers found, he adopted "a 'close-hold' attitude concerning all information relating to this incident."

Peers did not hide his scorn for Henderson's "investigation"—putting quotes around the word, or calling it "so-called investigative efforts"—which consisted of little more than gathering thirty to forty men of C Company, complimenting them on their operation, and then asking if any of them had "witnessed

---

* In the army's combat organization at the time, a brigade was roughly the size of an infantry regiment. But while regiments were permanent organizations with fixed (usually three) battalions and supporting elements, brigades were flexible in their configuration, often comprising (as the Eleventh Brigade did), air and artillery units as well as infantry battalions.

any atrocities." No one spoke up. Henderson also met with Thompson, which, Peers found, "should have provided a full awareness of the nature and extent" of the encounter. Yet Henderson reported orally to Koster (as task force commander Barker had, two days earlier) only that some twenty civilians had been killed in a cross fire and that there was no factual basis for Thompson's troubling report. "Henderson deliberately misrepresented both the scope of his investigation and the information that he had obtained," Peers concluded. Koster accepted the report as the end of the matter.

A few weeks later, when Koster received reports from Vietnamese sources of some 400 killings that day in My Lai, he ordered Henderson to put the report of his investigation in writing. Henderson dutifully submitted a two-page memo, dismissing the latest news as obvious Viet Cong propaganda. Koster accepted it, and did nothing further.

Peers's conclusions were categorical: "Within the Americal Division, at every command level from company to division, actions were taken or omitted which together effectively concealed" the entire incident, including acts and omissions that "constituted deliberate suppression or withholding of information." Henderson's investigation, in particular, was singled out as having been "knowingly false and deceptive." Yet Koster accepted Henderson's initial report and his subsequent false "investigation" at face value and neither followed up with Henderson nor forwarded any information to Westmoreland's headquarters, despite regulations and many opportunities to do so.

In all, said Peers, there was "a serious obstruction of justice" following the crimes at My Lai. He identified by name twenty-eight officers whose "omissions and commissions" made them complicit, in Peers's view, in the obstruction. Ten of them were in the direct chain of command from Calley up to Koster.* All of Peers's accusations were based on the individual officers' failures to report, to investigate, or otherwise to follow regulations. None was based on command accountability.

Calley was court-martialed and convicted of the murders of twenty-two civilians—the only man convicted in the entire episode—based on his personal participation in the slaughter.†

---

* The remainder were chaplains, U.S. Advisers to the army of South Vietnam, and officers in other units, all of whom, Peers found, had failed to report or adequately pursue information of the atrocities that came to them in the days following the massacre. Peers's mandate was not to investigate the actions of individual soldiers in the massacre itself, and his report said little about Calley and Medina, who by that time had already been formally charged.

† Calley was sentenced to life imprisonment, but this was reduced on review to twenty years, and on further review the Secretary of the Army reduced it to ten years. His sentence was overturned by a federal court and he was freed; when that decision was reversed on appeal and his conviction reinstated, the army did not return him to prison. He was paroled by

Medina was also tried by a court-martial, on four charges of murder and assault and a fifth charge of premeditated murder of "not less than 100" Vietnamese civilians—a charge that was based on command accountability in that Medina, knowing that his subordinates were engaged in murder, refused to intervene and stop it. It was the first trial since 1948 to invoke that standard of accountability.

At the conclusion of the evidence, the military judge reduced the premeditated murder charge to involuntary manslaughter and then instructed the jury that in order to convict on that charge, they must find that Medina had "actual knowledge" that his troops were committing war crimes. "You will observe," the judge instructed them, that "legal requirements placed upon a commander require actual knowledge plus a wrongful failure to act." He reiterated the point: "While it is not necessary that a commander actually see an atrocity being committed, it is essential that he know that his subordinates are in the process of committing atrocities, or are about to commit atrocities."

The instruction was plainly wrong. According to the army's manual on the law of war, a commander is responsible "if he has actual knowledge, or *should have* knowledge, through reports received by him or through other means" (emphasis added) that his subordinates are committing crimes, and fails to intervene. Medina, who had been on the outskirts of the village for several hours, denied that he knew what Calley's platoon was doing inside it. Testimony by other witnesses was confused and contradictory, and the jury evidently found in Medina's denial a reasonable doubt as to his actual knowledge. He was acquitted of the charge, and of all others as well. Had the judge instructed the members correctly, Medina's actual knowledge would have been irrelevant; a panel of military officers would surely have concluded that a company commander whose troops were engaged in combat nearby "should have knowledge" of what they were doing.

Barker, the task force commander, had been killed in action a few weeks after My Lai. Henderson, the brigade commander, was tried by court-martial for dereliction of duty in failing to conduct a proper investigation and for perjuring himself in the Peers inquiry. The perjury charge was dropped during his trial, and he was acquitted on the dereliction charge. Koster, who had gone on to become superintendent of the U.S. Military Academy at West Point, was originally charged in the cover-up, but that charge was withdrawn. Secretary of the Army Stanley Resor reduced him in rank to brigadier general, issued him a letter of censure, and revoked his Distinguished Service Medal—a humiliating rebuke but not a criminal one. Several other officers not implicated in the

the Secretary of the Army in 1975, having served six months in prison and three years under house arrest at Fort Benning.

massacre itself but who learned of it afterward had all charges dropped without trial; some were issued letters of reprimand.*

My Lai was a failure on many levels, first and most obviously that of the atrocity itself. This was followed by a cover-up: though many officers knew the truth—or at least some of the truth—no one in a position of authority pursued the matter. Worse, a brigade commander dissembled and lied when told to investigate by a two-star general; the general then accepted the patently inadequate result and put a lid on any further reporting. Westmoreland, to his credit, took Ridenhour's letter seriously, ordered the inspector general to investigate the crimes, referred the IG's report for criminal prosecution, and ordered a no-nonsense general to investigate the cover-up. And he did so with what must surely have been apprehension that the findings might lead directly to his own headquarters. But the criminal prosecution was a disaster. Only two officers were charged with murder, and only Calley, the lowliest officer involved in the entire affair, was convicted of anything.

When Secretary Resor disciplined Koster, he said, "As the division commander, General Koster must surely be held responsible for ascertaining the accuracy of the information which he had about Mylai, as that information indicated that his troops might have been guilty of serious misconduct. Any other conclusion would render essentially meaningless the concept of command responsibility accompanying senior positions of authority."

But Koster's demotion was based on his own evasion of duty when presented with information that demanded decisive action, not on "the concept of command responsibility" in the legal sense. The true concept of command responsibility—criminal accountability—was ignored. Neither the brigade commander nor the division commander, let alone anyone higher, was in any way held accountable on any such concept.

The outcome was so jarringly inconsistent with the standard by which General Yamashita was executed that it is difficult even to compare the two episodes. To be sure, My Lai was one horrific day; the people of the Philippines suffered many horrific days over several months. But without doubt every commander from Medina up to at least Koster "disregarded and failed to discharge his duty as commander to control the operations of the members of

---

* Only one enlisted soldier was tried for the crimes, and he was acquitted. Charges were dismissed for lack of evidence against several others. At the time, military personnel who had been discharged could not be tried by court-martial, and a good many members of Calley's platoon thus were effectively immune from prosecution. In 1996, Congress enacted a statute making violations of the law of war a federal crime, not just a military one. Now discharged soldiers can be brought to trial in a civilian court, though to date none ever has been.

his command, permitting them to commit brutal atrocities," in the words of the charge against Yamashita. Indeed, Medina admitted that he had lost control of his troops and that he knew it; still, he was acquitted. And while no one above Koster, including Westmoreland, had any actual knowledge of the atrocities, that lack had not precluded the Yamashita commission and the Supreme Court from convicting Yamashita.

In the midst of this legal shambles, the ghost of Yamashita stirred. It began with a book—*Nuremberg and Vietnam: An American Tragedy*—written by Telford Taylor, Justice Jackson's deputy at Nuremberg and, on Jackson's departure, the chief of counsel for the twelve subsequent trials (with the rank of brigadier general), and in 1970 a professor of law at Columbia University. Despite its title, the slender volume was (and remains, forty years later) a most readable and sensible introduction to the law of war.

Taylor's agenda went beyond an explanation of that law and beyond the crimes of My Lai itself. He asked troubling questions about the entire war. "What are the Nuremberg legal principles, and what is their meaning today as applied to American involvement in Vietnam?" he asked. "Are the people of the United States able to face the proposition that Jackson put forth in their name, and examine their own conduct under the same principles that they applied to the Germans and Japanese at the Nuremberg and other war crimes trials?" The Yamashita case in particular, Taylor wrote, and "the principles that it exemplifies, are of great importance in establishing the reach of criminal responsibility" for the actions of American soldiers in Vietnam. "The integrity of the nation is staked on those principles, and today the question is how they apply to our conduct of the war in Vietnam, and whether the United States Government is prepared to face the consequences of their application."

Taylor found much reason for dismay with the conduct of the war:

> forced resettlement of millions of rural families with utterly inadequate provision for their health and human dignity; complicity in the torture of prisoners by our wards, the South Vietnamese; enthusiasm for body counts overriding the laws of war on the taking of prisoners; devastation of large areas of the country in order to expose the insurgents; outlawry of every visible human being in the free-fire zones; slaughter of the villagers of [My Lai] even to the infants-in-arms.

To hold only individual soldiers and junior officers accountable for overt war crimes missed the larger point, Taylor argued; they were only fighting the war in the way political and military leaders at the highest levels wanted it fought, and so the atrocities at My Lai were not wild aberrations but the foreseeable, if unintended, consequences of policies initiated and directed at echelons far higher than those criminally charged. "The ultimate question of 'guilt' in the trials of the [My Lai] troops," Taylor argued, "is how far what they did departed from general American military practice in Vietnam as they had witnessed it."

Taylor quoted a U.S. sergeant in Vietnam who saw nothing to criticize in the wake of the My Lai disclosures. "Our job is to destroy the enemy," the sergeant wrote. "I want to come home alive [and] if I must kill old men, women or children to make myself a little safer, I'll do it without hesitation." To this Taylor responded, "One may indeed sympathize with the desire to 'come home alive,' but if that aim now requires the slaughter of all the Vietnamese who might be sympathetic to the Vietcong, then all our talk of 'pacification,' to say nothing of the Hague Conventions, is the sheerest hypocrisy, and we had better acknowledge at once that we are prepared to do what we hanged Japanese and German generals for doing."

It is the senior officers, Taylor wrote, up to and including the Joint Chiefs of Staff, who bear command responsibility for the conduct of operations in Vietnam.

> From General Westmoreland down they were more or less constantly in Vietnam, and splendidly equipped with helicopters and other aircraft, which gave them a degree of mobility unprecedented in earlier wars, and consequently endowed them with every opportunity to keep the course of the fighting and its consequences under close and constant observation. Communications were generally rapid and efficient, so that the flow of information and orders was unimpeded. These circumstances are in sharp contrast to those that confronted General Yamashita in 1944 and 1945, with his forces reeling back in disarray before the oncoming American military powerhouse.

And if, in the words of Douglas MacArthur, Yamashita had "failed his duty to his troops, to his country, to his enemy, to mankind; has failed utterly his soldier faith," what was one to say of American commanders?

Taylor did not advocate actual war crimes trials for Westmoreland and other high commanders. He acknowledged that there was no political support for that. But more was at stake than their individual fates. "Whether or not individuals are held to criminal account is perhaps not the most important question posed by the Vietnam war today [1970]," Taylor wrote. But the fate of the My Lai defendants "can not be fairly determined without full inquiry into the higher responsibilities. Little as the leaders of the Army seem to realize it, this is the only road to the Army's salvation, for its moral health will not be recovered until its leaders are willing to scrutinize their behavior by the same standards that their revered predecessors applied to Tomoyuki Yamashita 25 years ago."

Reviewing Taylor's book in the *New York Times*, Princeton professor Richard A. Falk, a distinguished international law expert and an outspoken critic of the war, noted that the book explained well the problems of war crimes and their prosecution but was vague on a more important point.

> Taylor does not help us answer the question—Should Yamashita standards be applied?—much less the dilemma of practical conscience—how can it be applied when the potential criminals also happen to be the rulers of the most powerful country in the world? What Taylor never himself faces up to is how the United States government, as perpetrator, can ever be expected to pass judgment upon itself, or more profoundly, whether the passing of adverse judgment, precisely because it is so well-founded, would not mean the end of the Republic.

This vision of national political suicide may seem overdrawn today, but Falk had identified the difficulty in Taylor's analysis: the Yamashita standard could never be applied to American generals because the consequences would be unthinkable. The American government, still in the midst of a draining and failing war, would be condemning not only its own military leaders but the very objectives it had sent those leaders into war to pursue, the very policies it had directed them to implement.

A few weeks later, in January 1971, Taylor raised the stakes of the discussion. On the Dick Cavett television show and in a next-day interview with the *New York Times*, Taylor stated explicitly that Westmoreland might well be convicted were he to be tried under the Yamashita standard. Cavett pressed him on whether Secretary of State Dean Rusk and Secretary of Defense Robert McNamara might also be convicted.

Taylor answered, "If you were to apply to them the same standards that were applied in the trial of General Yamashita, there would be a very strong possibility that they would come to the same end as he did."

"Then you imply they would be found guilty?" Cavett asked.

"Could be found guilty," Taylor replied. "And the American people cannot face their own past and cannot face the principles that they laid down and applied to Germans and Japanese unless they're willing to have the principles work the other way too."

Taylor emphasized that he was not speaking only, or even primarily, of My Lai. He considered the widespread civilian deaths and destruction inherent in incessant bombing, artillery barrages, and "free-fire" zones, and the forced evacuation of Vietnamese people and the failure to care for them, "far more serious" than that one episode. He dismissed the significance of the Calley and

Medina trials. "That's not the level at which the real responsibility for these things originated," Taylor said.

A few days later, the *Times* printed a lengthy letter from Frank Reel, written twenty-five years to the week after he had argued the case of his client before the Supreme Court of the United States. "Might be convicted?" Reel quoted Taylor. "Under the Yamashita rule as set down by the United States Supreme Court, Westmoreland would be convicted." Quoting the Hague Convention cited by the Court's majority, Reel wrote that the Court had decided that "the protection of civilians in a war zone rests on the rule that an armed force 'must be commanded by a person responsible for his subordinates.' So simple and pointed was this finding of guilt based on the theory of 'command responsibility,'" Reel wrote, "that the late Justice Frank Murphy wrote in his Yamashita dissent: 'No one in a position of command in an Army from sergeant to general can escape those implications. Indeed, the fate of some future President of the United States and his Chiefs of Staff and military advisers may well have been sealed by this decision.'"

Reel did not suggest that the outcome he had fought so passionately to avoid for an enemy general should now be applied to American generals as well. The Yamashita decision was wrong then, he wrote, and it is wrong today. "Shall we admit that we are horrified at the thought of trying General Westmoreland and former President Johnson for these capital crimes?" he asked.

> The concept of punishing a man, not for anything he has done but because of a position he has held, is abhorrent. It smacks of totalitarian tyranny rather than Anglo-Saxon law. The case of General Yamashita was a lone and disgraceful departure from this most important touchstone of human freedom.
>
> The answer to the dilemma is not a cynical decree that we have one law for the vanquished and another for ourselves. Rather, it is frankly to face the fact that the Yamashita case and also some other of the post–World War II war crimes trials were exercises in vengeance rather than law. The case of Yamashita was not only a grievous miscarriage of justice—it made bad law.

He ended on a curious note. "Inherent in the World War II convictions for 'violation of the laws of war' is the assumption that there are good ways to kill and bad ways to kill; that it is criminal to shoot unarmed civilians at point-blank range but legal to bomb them from the skies," he wrote. "We cannot progress in our long struggle to become civilized if we persist in attempting to legalize methods of conducting an essentially criminal pastime." Reel seemed to be disparaging the very validity of laws of war. He reiterated the point in an op-ed piece in the same newspaper a few weeks later. The laws of war, "like the rules of heraldry, serve to glorify war and hide its true import," he wrote. "It is akin to playing Pontius Pilate to describe the Vietnam business as a 'dirty war,' implying that there is some other kind. Man's long struggle to become civilized is impeded by such assumptions. It is time we grew up—and quit."

In 1972, after Calley was convicted and Medina acquitted, after only Henderson was tried for the cover-up and was acquitted, after three enlisted men were acquitted in three trials, Taylor gave his assessment of the whole process. "It is apparent that the Army's procedures for the prevention, detection, and punishment of war crimes have failed abysmally," he wrote. Addressing the many calls for clemency for Calley, Taylor wrote, "Calley's personal guilt is beyond question, but the idea that he alone should bear criminal responsibility is absurd. . . . Clemency for Calley should be granted, if at all, on the basis that it is unfitting and unprincipled to punish one man for the crime of many." He urged, as he had before, "a national commission of inquiry" to investigate "at a minimum the military operational directives in force in Southeast Asia, the standards of training and discipline with regard to observance of the laws of war, and the processes of military justice in dealing with war crimes. Only by treating the end of the courts-martial as the beginning of serious efforts to confront the facts and learn from experience," he concluded, "can the failure of the judicial process be redeemed, and the stain of Mylai lightened."

No such inquiry was ever held.

19

The Twenty-First Century
Tribunals

In the 1970s, America was in no mood to exhume General Yamashita. When U.S. forces withdrew in 1975, Vietnam became in much of the public's mind a synonym for U.S. ignominy and defeat, best buried and forgotten.

The United States continued the cold war until the Soviet Union disintegrated in 1991. Soon after, Yugoslavia followed. Ever since the end of World War II, Yugoslavia had been an uneasy amalgam of Bosnians, Serbs, Croats, Slovenes, and Montenegrins, peoples of different cultures, religions, and ethnicities, a federation held together by its president Josip Tito, who steered a high-wire course of nonalignment, playing East against West. But with his death in 1980 the tightrope slackened, and Yugoslavia disintegrated into sovereign states. Ethnic tensions led to savage violence, with the dominant Serbs lashing out against the neighboring Croats and particularly the predominantly Muslim Bosnians. The Serbs created concentration camps run by commandants and guards whose cruelty recalled memories of the notorious Nazi camp of Jasenovac, where Croats had been the persecutors of Serbs and Jews. In the 1990s, Serb armies, paramilitaries, and death squads roamed the countryside in a horrific campaign of "ethnic cleansing"—a new name for genocide. Later, Serb attacks against ethnic Albanians in Kosovo would lead President Bill Clinton to call in NATO forces, and overt conflict eventually ended with the signing of the U.S.-sponsored Dayton Accords in 1995.

But in the meantime something happened that was without precedent in the postwar world. In 1993, the United Nations created a brand new court, whose purpose was to bring to trial and to justice those responsible for the savagery. The International Criminal Tribunal for the Former Yugoslavia (ICTY) was given jurisdiction to prosecute war crimes, crimes against humanity, genocide, and breaches of the Geneva Conventions that had been committed there since the breakup.

Such an endeavor would have been quite impossible during the cold war. Virtually every international initiative of that era was politicized, and neither the United States nor the USSR would have countenanced a truly independent international tribunal with the power to convict, sentence, and jail people.* In a post–cold war world, however, the United States became a firm supporter of international justice and of an international court to levy it—for a while, anyway. Following the Rwandan genocide of 1994, the United Nations created the International Criminal Tribunal for Rwanda (ICTR). The ICTY sits in The Hague, the ICTR in Tanzania.

The international law experts who wrote the statute of the ICTY† did something that had not been done at Nuremberg or Tokyo, and certainly not in Manila or at any time since. It drafted a provision that defined command accountability, and it authorized the prosecutors and judges to apply it to persons in positions of authority.

In doing so, the framers of the ICTY were not writing entirely on a clean slate. In 1974, after several years of discussion and deliberation, a delegation of international lawyers and policymakers gathered in Geneva to finalize two additions (known as protocols) to the venerable Geneva Conventions, which had last been revised in 1949. Unlike the pre–World War I Hague Conventions, which had aimed to regulate the tactics, weapons, and stratagems of warfare, the Geneva Conventions focused on the protection of noncombatants: the wounded, prisoners of war, and civilians caught up in the paths of armies. But by the 1970s those conventions were showing their age. As Vietnam famously demonstrated, wars were no longer being fought on battlefields by uniformed soldiers confronting each other in organized military units. The "national liberation" movements of those decades and the transformation of combat into guerrilla war and insurgencies led many to conclude that new rules, or at least updated rules, were necessary to keep the Geneva Conventions current and effective.

Finalized in 1977, Articles 86 and 87 of Additional Protocol I to the Geneva Conventions require nations that adopt the protocol to take appropriate steps within their domestic political and legal systems to punish "grave breaches" of the Geneva Conventions—simply put, war crimes—"which result from a failure to act when under a duty to do so." And it is a commander's duty "to prevent and, where necessary, to suppress and to report" such crimes to competent authorities. Commanders who are aware that their subordinates are committing or about to commit war crimes must take the necessary steps to prevent them and, where appropriate, to punish those subordinates. The protocol provides that commanders are not to be absolved from responsibility for the crimes of a

---

* The ICTY, like the subsequent International Criminal Tribunal for Rwanda and later the International Criminal Court, has no capital punishment. The maximum sentence of each is life imprisonment.

† The statutes of the ICTY and the ICTR are quite similar, and references here to the ICTY statute include the ICTR statute as well.

subordinate "if they knew, or had information which should have enabled them to conclude in the circumstances at the time," that the subordinates were committing or were about to commit such breaches.

These provisions were intended to establish two important concepts: first, commanders do in fact have a duty to prevent and, where appropriate, to punish subordinates* who commit war crimes. In the Yamashita case, the Supreme Court had conjured such a duty, but the protocol was the first treaty to make it explicit in international law.

Second, the protocol took the step the Court had not taken: addressing the matter of the commander's knowledge as an element of that duty, or, to be more exact, as an element of judging his accountability if he fails to prevent or punish such crimes. The protocol specifies that accountability inheres in such failure, but only for commanders who actually know, or who have "information which should have enabled them to conclude in the circumstances at the time" of present or imminent war crimes, and who do not then "take all feasible measures within their power" to stop the crimes or punish the perpetrators.

The point on knowledge and information, though important, is significantly narrower than it might have been, because the authors of the protocol avoided becoming enmeshed in what a commander "should have known." That would have opened the door for the prosecution of commanders who were clueless about crimes because they were not careful enough or competent enough or organized enough to ensure that relevant information came to them. To avoid liability in such situations, the protocol reaches only commanders who actually know of lawlessness or, failing that, have actual information that should alert them to present or imminent lawlessness.

The protocol is a treaty,† not a criminal statute to be applied in an actual prosecution, but had its standard of accountability been applied in Manila in 1945, it surely would have presented a formidable obstacle to Yamashita's conviction. There was no evidence that he actually knew about Japanese crimes, or that he had enough information about the situation in Manila and elsewhere to conclude that such crimes were being committed. His failure to receive regular reports about the status of POWs or the actions of Japanese forces would have been beside the point. Only actual information would have counted. (The

---

* Article 87 refers not only to subordinates in the military sense—armed forces under their superiors' command—but also to persons under their "control," meaning civilians (or soldiers, for that matter) who are not technically subordinates but whose actions are nonetheless directed or controlled by the commanders. It may also include civilians in occupied territories. For simplicity's sake, all such persons are referred to here as "subordinates."

† Protocol I has been widely adopted—by 171 nations, not including the United States, as of 2012—though not quite as widely as the Geneva Conventions themselves, which have 194 signatories, virtually every nation in the world.

treaty itself does not address the situation of commanders whose ignorance of material information is intentional—who direct that no information be given to them—but the explanation of the drafters suggests that willful ignorance should be no excuse.)

The protocol also obligates commanders, once they have actual knowledge or sufficient information, to take measures that are both "feasible" and "within their power" to prevent or punish the crime. As the official explanation of the protocol points out, "it is a matter of common sense" that commanders can only do what they can do. The protocol thus makes allowances for commanders who, whatever their information, are powerless to act on it—as, for example, when the enemy's overpowering force has driven them into the hills and the jungle and disrupted their communication and their ability to control events. It would be entirely consistent with the protocol's explicit, but realistic and limited, definition of command accountability to absolve commanders who, whatever their state of mind, simply were unable to act in any effective way.

Against this background, the scholars and judges who drafted the statute of the ICTY in the early 1990s wrote rules on command accountability for prosecutors, defense counsel, and judges to apply to real prosecutions of real people—the first time such rules had ever been written. The result is Article 7 of the ICTY statute, which begins with a straightforward rule: a person who "planned, instigated, ordered, committed or otherwise aided and abetted in the planning, preparation or execution" of a war crime, a crime against humanity, or genocide is "individually responsible" for the crime. The point, however self-evident, is meant to distinguish commanders who order crimes or otherwise participate in their planning or execution from those whose accountability depends on what their subordinates do.

On the question of command accountability, the language of the ICTY statute appears to vary from the language of Protocol I in two respects. First, where Protocol I requires proof that commanders "knew, or had information which should have enabled them to conclude in the circumstances at the time" of crime, the ICTY statute requires proof that the commander "knew or had reason to know." Second, where Protocol I requires commanders to "take all feasible measures within their power" to prevent or punish the crime, the ICTY statute requires that the commander "take the necessary and reasonable measures" to do so.

The ICTY has ruled, however, that there is no significant difference between the two documents. The ICTY statute's "knew or had reason to know" is the same as Protocol I's "knew, or had information." Thus the ICTY prosecutor must prove that the commander did in fact have identifiable information about imminent or ongoing crimes. And the ICTY statute's requirement that the commander take "necessary and reasonable measures" to prevent or punish the crimes is equivalent to Protocol I's requirement that commanders take "all feasible measures within their power" to do so. So the ICTY prosecutor must also prove that the commander did in fact have both the authority and the actual ability to take appropriate steps.

In its nineteen years in existence, the ICTY, as of early 2012, has indicted 161 people (the last indictment came in 2004) and has convicted 64 and acquitted 13. Thirty-five cases are ongoing, either at the trial or appeal level, and some forty-one cases have been withdrawn, transferred to a national court, or dismissed because the defendant died before or during trial. It is aiming to wind up all cases and go out of business in 2013 or so.

The ICTY has been a prolific source of jurisprudence on command accountability, for several reasons. The prosecutor's office has tended to choose as defendants men of significant responsibility—government ministers, senior military commanders, concentration camp commandants, and the like—and to leave the low-level thugs to national courts in Bosnia-Herzegovina and other former Yugoslav republics. Many cases focus on a single locale or episode and arraign several defendants who allegedly worked together, which naturally creates questions of who was in charge of whom and who had responsibility for what.

But one problem of the ICTY is that, with three judges on each case and opinions and judgments that often run to several hundred pages, there are lengthy and sometimes convoluted explanations of the court's reasoning for each verdict. When the ICTY sat for the first time, on the bench were judges from Egypt, Italy, Canada, Nigeria, France, China, Costa Rica, Australia, Pakistan, Malaysia, and the United States. The ICTR is similarly eclectic. Though all the judges are bound by the same statute, they naturally approach the cases from the perspectives of diverse legal systems, each with its own concepts of criminal law and individual responsibility. It will be no surprise that twenty-five judges do not always agree on every aspect of law and that reaching a common view of a concept as subtly defined as command accountability has proven challenging.

Over time, however, some important principles have emerged. For one, the definition of a commander has been expanded to include not only formal military commanders but civilians as well—cabinet ministers and others who exercise significant control over armies. The court has also created a distinction between de jure commanders (those duly appointed by lawful authority) and de facto commanders (those who in fact control or command troops, whether officially appointed or not) and has applied the command-accountability rules to both. This has been significant in a theater of war and crime where paramilitary, nationalist, or terrorist groups can be as visible and as lethal as uniformed army units, and sometimes more so. Both these constructs have recognized that the nature of responsibility is dynamic and that courts must shape a law of war that realistically reflects what actually happens in combat.

But in one fundamental respect, the court, in its judgments both at trial and on appeal, has failed to articulate a workable construct for command accountability. The court has persistently focused its rulings almost exclusively on the state of mind of accused commanders at the time their responsibility arises. To determine command accountability (for which the ICTY uses the traditional term "command responsibility"), it seeks to determine the commanders' knowledge, their intentions, and their diligence or "carefulness" at the time they allegedly failed in their duty to prevent subordinates from committing crimes. As in the Hostages and High Command cases, the command-responsibility standard, by asking what commanders knew or what information should have alerted them to find out more, essentially requires judges to take a snapshot of commanders' mental state at the specific and sometimes fleeting point in time when they failed to take action to prevent or terminate crime by others.

This is where the ICTY has stumbled. Capturing the contents of a person's mind at a given moment is tricky at best and is difficult to do accurately. There is often no direct and unambiguous evidence; what a commander knew or intended must be inferred from what he actually did, and that can be subject to conflicting accounts and interpreted in varying ways. In Yamashita's trial, for example, staff officer Nishiharu testified that when he told Yamashita that captured Filipino guerrillas would be "handled" or "investigated," the general, reading some papers, nodded—once—and said nothing. What did that fleeting act say of his knowledge or intent, if anything at all?

The difficulty is compounded by disagreement among some judges over whether the command-responsibility standard requires commanders to actively seek out information that would inform them of the actions of their subordinates or only holds them accountable if there was information actually available to them at the time that would put them on notice of misbehavior. The ICTY's appeals panel has ruled that the latter is the case: commanders have no duty but to act on information that they actually have, not on information they might have taken steps to discover.

But this has led the ICTY onto still more treacherous ground. "Information" is infinitely variable. How specific, or extensive, or reliable, or corroborated, or ominous, must it be, in order to give a commander "reason to know" of illegal acts and thus trigger a responsibility to act? Here again, judges have tried to quantify the unquantifiable—one appeals panel suggesting that even general information would be sufficient, and another suggesting that information must be "alarming." But at what point does information become "alarming" rather than "general"?

On top of that, the judges are acting years after the events, limited to the evidence of witnesses who may have faded or faulty memories or who may be sympathetic, or hostile, toward the defendant. Assessing credibility and reconciling conflicting accounts of events is a judge's (or jury's) task, but it is a distinctly difficult one when something as intangible as the state of another's knowledge is at issue and must be determined by indirect and often ambiguous evidence.

The difficulty of assessing a commander's state of mind, the information available, and the crime has been aggravated by the ICTY's requirement that the commander's information must exactly match the crimes that are ultimately committed if he is to be found guilty. For example, if a commander knows that a certain platoon about to embark on an action is an unruly gang of drunken roughnecks prone to ransacking and rape, he is not held responsible if the platoon engages in an orgy of murder. In one case, the ICTY acquitted a commander of the torture of civilians committed by his troops, reasoning that

> in order to determine whether an accused "had reason to know" that his subordinates had committed or were about to commit acts of torture, the court must ascertain whether he had sufficiently alarming information . . . to alert him to the risk of acts of torture being committed, that is of beatings being inflicted not arbitrarily but for one of the prohibited purposes of torture. Thus it is not enough that an accused has sufficient information about beatings inflicted by his subordinates; he must also have information—albeit general—which alerts him to the risk of beatings being inflicted *for one of the purposes provided for in the prohibition against torture.* [Emphasis added.]

The authoritative international Convention against Torture defines torture as severe pain inflicted on a person for such purposes as obtaining a confession or intimidating or coercing the victim. So what the ICTY has ruled is that if a commander has information that his troops are abusing innocent civilians, but does not have information that they are doing so for one of these "prohibited purposes," he has no information that they are engaging in torture, and so he is not criminally accountable for torture. Thus the court is put to the task of comparing the information the commander has with the crime the subordinates actually commit, to determine whether the commander had the requisite knowledge of the actual (or imminent) crime at the critical moment when he failed to intervene. If there is no match, there is no guilt.

As a result, the jurisprudence of responsibility has become detached from the realities of combat. It has led to a single-minded focus on the commander's knowledge or state of mind at a critical moment, isolating it from other relevant factors in favor of evidence that is often scant or conflicting, to determine a state of mind that is abstract to begin with. What lies behind this misadventure is that the present concept of command accountability rests on a legal fiction: that the defendant committed the crime that his subordinates committed. It is a fiction because the commander's true act is not having committed murder or mistreatment or abuse of prisoners. It is having been derelict in his duty of command.

The law has never acknowledged what every commander should understand: he is accountable if he has been seriously irresponsible or negligent in carrying out his duties. He may be removed from command for incompetence in battle or other serious failure to carry out his responsibilities, and may be prosecuted for failing to take appropriate measures to prevent troops under his command from mistreating civilians and prisoners of war and other noncombatants. To recognize that command accountability, properly understood, derives from the dereliction of a commander's duty is to expose the flaw of the current doctrine that purports to examine only what a commander knew, or might have known from the information at hand at a particular moment in time, and then purports to compare that state of mind to what actually happened at the crime scene. The ICTY, virtually the sole judicial source of command accountability doctrine in the past twenty years, has in case after case gone deeply into what it can make of the commander's mind, taking a snapshot and magnifying it into ever more pixels, seeking to determine whether there is a match between his state of mind and the way the murdered, raped, or tortured victims met their fate at the hands of his troops. The verdict of guilt or innocence turns on that inquiry.

But courts do not work under laboratory conditions. The passage of time, the chaos of the circumstances, the perspective of the participants, the limitations of memory, and the conflict of accounts, even if brought together in a dispassionate analysis, are often enough to derail any attempt to reconstruct accurately a person's state of mind. When that process must take place in an adversarial procedure that pits prosecutor against defendant and requires the evidence to comply with rules of admissibility and interpretations of law, the judges' task of re-creating a state of mind at a particular point cannot be carried out with any assurance of a just and reliable outcome.

It would be more fruitful, more reliable, and more fair for the court to examine the commander's overall performance of duty, including such matters as whether he took action beforehand to educate his troops on proper conduct, or whether he issued orders forbidding the mistreatment of civilians and prisoners, or whether he delegated responsibility to his staff to provide him with regular reports on such matters, and whether those reports were complete, candid, and accurate. The court should not ignore, as it must do now, issues such as the commander's action or inactions in earlier, similar situations; the command climate created by higher authorities; the volatility of ethnic or religious differences; and the intelligence, education, and training of the troops.

To hold commanders fully and fairly accountable when their troops violate the law requires that we abandon the present law of command responsibility that looks only to the time frame between the commander's acquisition of knowledge or information and the commission of the crime, that looks backward from the crime that was committed to divine what the commander knew or should have known about the possibility that just such a crime would be committed. What we want to encourage, after all, is a responsible exercise of command that minimizes or precludes the commission of crimes in the first place. We want commanders to train and lead their troops to avoid mistreatment, to emphasize the distinction between enemy forces and civilians, to warn that mayhem can impede the successful accomplishment of the mission, to acquaint them with the international laws that prohibit mistreatment of non-combatants, to emphasize that misconduct will be punished, and to back up training, education, and orders with action. None of these things, regrettably, is taken into account in conventional command-responsibility law.

No new laws are necessary to accomplish this recasting of the inquiry into the commander's actions. Every military code holds soldiers criminally responsible for dereliction of duty. When they negligently or intentionally fail to obey a lawful order, or otherwise fail to do what they are supposed to do, they can be court-martialed. Commanders can be disciplined for dereliction of duty when they fail, for no acceptable reason, to lead their troops responsibly, whether because of cowardice, incompetence, insubordination, or similar abdications of a commander's duty. There is good reason, therefore, for international courts to follow a similar analysis and to focus on the overall failure to take reasonable steps in the training and supervision of troops when such failure has caused, or contributed to, the commission of war crimes, crimes against humanity, or genocide. A commander's state of mind on the likelihood of crime, including his knowledge and his available information, is relevant, but it need not continue to be the exclusive touchstone of guilt or innocence. The touchstone is whether in his leadership up to that point he has negligently or intentionally created the conditions that have given rise to the crimes.

It is very probably true that a verdict of guilt, under this analysis, will always depend on the actual commission of such crimes, for it would be difficult to establish that a commander was derelict in his duty to prevent crimes if in fact none has been committed. But when such crimes have taken place, the inquiry must be wider than the commander's knowledge or information at a particular moment. To abandon the present command-accountability doctrine, therefore, is simply to broaden the universe of relevance to include all aspects of a commander's duty, not merely his knowledge or information. The more serious the crime of the subordinates, the more severe should be the punishment of the commander. This change would be nothing more than aligning the realities of the law to the realities of command in war, while advancing the very purpose of the law of war—to regulate the conduct of those who take part in it so as to protect as much as possible those who do not.

20

Today

However important the principle of command accountability might be, it is but a larger part of that body of treaties, customs, and jurisprudence that we call the law of war, or these days, the law of armed conflict. Discussing command accountability sooner or later leads to much larger questions: Is there any sense in having laws of war? Is there any sense to the laws of war? Such fundamental questions have been asked for about as long as those laws have existed, and they cannot be lightly dismissed. Many thoughtful people see a fundamental anomaly, even a contradiction, in the idea of regulating through law the conduct of those trying to kill one another, who are in fact sent into battle by the state for the purpose of killing one another. Nations have solemnly entered into treaties that allow bombs of astonishing ferocity but not land mines, that allow killing an enemy who is running away but not one who lies incapacitated, that require that an enemy who surrenders or is captured be provided the same food, shelter, clothing, and medical care that would be provided to one's own troops, insofar as possible. Would any nation, any army, adhere to these rules if victory or defeat hung in the balance? Can we fairly expect any rifleman in combat to adhere to them when he fears, as he always does, for his own life or safety?

And how can there be any law worth the name when its enforcement is so capricious? The vanquished cannot punish the victors' crimes, and the victors only rarely punish their own, and certainly never their generals and their political leaders. Is not all enforcement of the laws of war merely victors' justice, which is to say no justice? In his opening statement to the tribunal at Nuremberg, Justice Jackson told the judges, "We must never forget that the record on which we judge these defendants today is the record on which history will judge us tomorrow. To pass these defendants a poisoned chalice is to put it to our own lips as well." But no nation has ever lifted the Nuremberg chalice to its own lips.

And where, one asks, is the sense or consistency in a legal regime that forbids the slaughter of women and children in a village but allows aerial bombardment that cannot avoid the demolition of the village and all who live there? That prohibits the poisoning of wells but not the devastation of forests and farmland? That prohibits the use of poison gas but not the deadly miasma of radiation? Why, indeed, have nations not come together to ban the use of atomic weapons, if not because the powerful nations that build and stockpile those weapons will tolerate no law that impedes their global strategies, be they offensive or defensive?

Criticisms that the laws of war are inconsistent, unrealistic, and unequally applied, and that they were devised in any event to serve the needs and strengthen the arms of the most powerful nations, cannot be easily or convincingly refuted by the historical record. That record is replete with tragedy and suffering that would seem more than sufficient to support the skepticism, even cynicism, that has always attended the laws of war.

But should we account the laws of war a failure, even failure wrapped in hypocrisy, simply because they have not eliminated the cruelties and sufferings and injustices of warfare from the earth? No legal system has ever succeeded in abolishing injustice—after all, as Jackson reminded us, our criminal laws have not eliminated crime. And is it not reason enough to prohibit the poisoning of wells and the use of gas and land mines that those weapons cannot be confined to enemy combatants and linger dangerously long after the war is over? The laws of war aim not to abolish war itself but, rather, to confine it to agreed bounds that limit its cruelty. The failure to abolish nuclear weapons is the result of superpower rivalries, but is that any reason to forsake more modest steps than can be, and have been, taken?

And as to victors' justice, goes the argument, that is better than no justice at all. In a perfect world, perhaps, victors and vanquished alike would stand before a stern and impartial tribunal, but in our imperfect world is that any reason not to hold Nazis and other criminals to account for their crimes? The tribunals at Nuremberg earn high marks for the fairness of their procedures and the impartiality of their judgments. To apply the epithet of "victors' justice" is only to acknowledge that no one from the Allied Powers was brought before them, and that aggressive war—the "crime against peace"—had never been charged and tried as an international crime. But does that make the defendants, who certainly waged aggressive war, any less deserving of punishment? Summary execution would surely not have accomplished something better.

Even critics of the laws of war would not shrug off the Holocaust, or the rape of Nanking, or the sack of Manila, or the slaughter at Srebrenica as merely the unavoidable consequences of war. Those crimes were not committed in warfare at all; they were, to say the least, vicious murders of defenseless civilians that it has been the highest purpose of the laws of war to prohibit and punish for over a century. And for all the abuses of prisoners of war relentlessly carried

out by the Japanese and the Soviets in World War II or by the North Vietnamese a quarter century later, many more prisoners in the custody of others were
treated humanely and survived.

Telford Taylor, posing the question of why we maintain those laws, had a
pragmatic answer: "They work. Violated or ignored as they often are, enough of
the rules are observed enough of the time so that mankind is very much better
off with them than without them. . . . If it were not regarded as wrong to bomb
military hospitals, they would be bombed all of the time instead of some of the
time." And he had a second and no less humane answer: such laws "diminish
the corrosive effect of mortal combat on the participants. War does not confer
a license to kill for personal reasons," he wrote. "War is not a license at all, but
an obligation to kill for reasons of state; it does not countenance the infliction
of suffering for its own sake or for revenge."

To be fair, few of those who criticize the laws of war go so far as to propose
their abolition. Their point is not that the laws never do good, but that they
are so frequently ignored, so easily violated, and so inconsistently enforced that
we delude ourselves to think that they effectively deter inhumane and criminal
conduct. By this view, the world does not really have a law of war, only what
it *calls* a law of war.

It is a criticism with some truth in it, but it overlooks undeniably constructive developments of the past two decades. The creation of the international
tribunals for Yugoslavia and Rwanda in the mid-1990s goes far to erase the
stigma of victors' justice. No Croats or Bosnians sit in judgment of Serbs (or
vice versa); no Tutsis sit in judgment of Hutus. Their jurisdiction is limited to
specific territories at certain times, but they are truly international courts—created by the United Nations, staffed by prosecutors and judges from a score or
more of nations, adjudicating cases alleging genocide, war crimes, and crimes
against humanity. None of these crimes could remotely be considered ex post
facto, due to the groundbreaking work of the tribunals at Nuremberg and Tokyo years earlier, establishing such acts as international crimes long before the
breakup of Yugoslavia and the meltdown of Rwanda.*

The creation of the International Criminal Court at the dawn of the twenty-
first century takes the concept one important step further: it is a permanent
sitting court, created by a treaty that by 2012 had been ratified by 120 nations,
with worldwide jurisdiction over those same crimes (and, eventually, over the
crime of aggressive war as well). It is explicitly a court of last resort, empowered

---

* This is not to overlook the spate of limited ad hoc tribunals that have been created in
recent years to deal with atrocities in Cambodia, Sierra Leone, and elsewhere, and the sporadic expansion of national jurisdiction over international crimes, such as Spain's assertion of
judicial authority over the crimes of General Augusto Pinochet in Chile.

to act only if the national courts that ought to prosecute and judge such crimes are unable or unwilling to do so. And it is still a young tribunal—as yet no case has reached a final verdict upheld on appeal—but its significance should not be underestimated. "Historic" is a word worn thin by overuse, but how else could one characterize the world's first permanent international criminal court? "Victor's justice," if that means unprecedented charges heard by judges appointed by conquering armies, has become an anachronism—thanks in large part to the law developed by those very judges.

There is a serious fundamental problem, however, with laws of war that were devised and developed for a form of warfare that has been steadily disappearing since the end of World War II. They were constructed on the premise that wars are fought by nation-states that send their armies and navies into battle against each other, seeking the subjugation of the enemy by force of arms, led by generals and admirals who command organized units and subordinate leaders of smaller organized units through a defined chain of command, all of whom issue explicit orders. Such wars begin with armed hostilities, continue with casualties and the capture of enemy prisoners, and end in victory and defeat when one side forces the other into surrender or obliterates it.

Few wars have been fought that way, and to such a definitive conclusion, in recent years. Since World War II, state-sponsored wars engaging air, armor, and massed infantry in a fight to the finish have largely given way, first to guerrilla warfare and then to insurgencies and asymmetric warfare: improvised explosive devices, car bombs, and suicide bombers. The objective of such violence is not conquest by force of arms but attrition and exhaustion through the weakening of political will to continue. Prisoners of war have become as rare as fifes and drums. In Afghanistan, remotely piloted drones hover in the sky, directed by soldiers in Nevada or by civilians at the Central Intelligence Agency. The Defense Department has created a Cyber Command to carry on, or defend against, hostile action through electronic disruption of computer networks. In this environment, there is no point in the Hague Convention's requirement that combatants wear insignia visible at a distance and carry their arms openly.

It is likewise true that in today's warfare, even organized armies no longer adhere to the straightforward organizations and chains of command that characterized the combat arms of World War II. International coalitions, multilateral organizations, multinational forces, special operations, and joint commands require complex and decentralized administrative and command structures to carry out intricate and sometimes conflicting objectives of combat, pacification, counterinsurgency, support for indigenous armies, and nation-building. Orders from senior echelons have in significant measure been replaced by statements of purpose and objectives that delegate significant tactical decisions down to the battalion, company, and even platoon commander.

Changes in warfare have been accompanied by changes in how we define war itself. The attacks on New York City and the Pentagon on September 11, 2001, were crimes, not acts of war in any historical or conventional sense. The perpetrators were a score of civilians, sponsored by no state, commanded by no general, wearing no uniform, carrying no firearms, bound by no treaties, giving not even lip service to any law. Even the wars in Afghanistan and Iraq, though begun as conventional military invasions, devolved into protracted insurgencies, the enemies' weapons not tanks and infantry battalions but concealed and treacherous devices. The targets of hostile action are not only those in the theater of combat but civilians in passenger trains in Spain, buses in London, hotels in Indonesia, airplanes in the United States. While the new international tribunals still apply the laws of war, drawing on Nuremberg and Tokyo as well as their own organic charters, the forms of the laws, even the premises on which they proceed, are unsuited to the terrorism that has displaced the warfare for which the Geneva Conventions were intended.

But as the laws of war are growing archaic, the difference between war and crime is growing ever less distinct. President George W. Bush insisted that the United States was at war with terrorism itself, but he declared the Geneva Conventions inapplicable to it. He ordered that terrorists, and those who support them, be tried by military commission, not by federal courts. Yet by rejecting the alternative of bringing those accused before the nation's civilian courts, he put the U.S. government in an irreconcilable contradiction. If the global war on terrorism is a real war, why are those who have been captured subjected to "enhanced interrogation" and outright torture, in plain violation of the Geneva Conventions? And if they are just brutal criminals, why are they brought before military tribunals? For that matter, what authority do military commissions have to try anyone for terrorism, or conspiracy to commit it?

It is not at all clear whether this trail of confusion and contradiction can yet yield trials that are consistent with the U.S. Constitution and its laws, with judgments that are based on reliable evidence and that inspire public confidence that the guilty have been fairly convicted and the innocent acquitted. The Military Commissions Act of 2009 has addressed some of the more glaring deficiencies of the tribunals ordained in 2002. But among the many issues yet to be untangled in whatever courts or commissions are given the responsibility, there is one principle of particular importance: those who exercise authority and control over subordinates who carry out the violence must be identified, charged, fairly tried, and fairly judged. Commanders must be held accountable.

Unlike most other aspects of the law of war, and of customary international law generally, the doctrine of command responsibility—command accountability—has a clear birthplace: the case of General Yamashita. The birth process had three stages: the charge, the trial and conviction, and the Supreme Court's decision. The first was a product of vindictiveness, the second the result of the commissioners' subservience to the wishes of their commander, and the third the result of the Court's refusal to intervene in any aspect of the military's conduct of war, even its treatment of the vanquished enemy under color of law.

The doctrine was not only created in the Yamashita case; it was created specifically *for* Yamashita. And it was created in order to convict him, by devising a link previously unknown in the law that attributed to him crimes that he did not order, did not participate in, very probably did not know about, and almost certainly could not have done anything about even if he had known of them.* Moreover, the charge and the conviction leapfrogged entirely over the issue of whether he should have known of them, or should have done anything different from what he did, or was able to do anything different if he had wanted to. It announced no standard of command accountability. It simply proceeded to the conclusion, explicitly stated in the charge, that Yamashita was guilty of the crimes because he lost control of his troops, thereby "permitting" their crimes. But that ambiguous "permitting" depended not on any actual permission but, rather, on the self-evident fact that he was no longer in control. The reason he was not was accurately stated by Justice Murphy: Yamashita failed to control his troops because American forces succeeded in destroying his ability to do so.

The misbegotten nature of the charge was compounded, moreover, by the trial itself. It was conducted not by judges who could render a thoughtful analysis of accountability but by five generals of the victorious army, none of them trained in the law, and none of them under any illusion but that their duty was to deliver a conviction to MacArthur. The trial exhibited some outward appearances of due process of law, but in the end it was simply theater. The charge itself doomed Yamashita from the outset. That he was the commander, that the forces were out of his control, that they committed horrendous atrocities: of all of this there was never any doubt. Had the prosecution forsaken the mournful victims whom it paraded through the ballroom to relate their horrors to Manila and the world, it could have presented its entire case against Yamashita in an afternoon.

No one can second-guess his lawyers for their bold and successful maneuver to bring the case before the Supreme Court of the United States. Their client had nothing to lose, and they presented their case skillfully, leading two of the Court's members to express their dissents with eloquence that still resonates

---

* In 2000, Congress passed the Japanese Imperial Government Disclosure Act (Public Law 106-567) and directed an interagency working group under the auspices of the National Archives "to locate and disclose" any U.S. government documents that related to Japanese war crimes. None of the documents contained any order by Yamashita relating to the atrocities in the Philippines. The final report of the working group was released in April 2007.

sixty-five years later. But the Court's affirmance of the conviction elevated and validated what would have been a soon-forgotten kangaroo tribunal in the far Pacific into a lingering and troublesome precedent that courts ever since have struggled to understand and apply. It remains the only Supreme Court case in history that has addressed the issue of command responsibility, however inartfully it did so.

The Nuremberg tribunals in the High Command and Hostages trials tried diligently to accommodate the cases before them to the Supreme Court's Yamashita decision—naturally enough; they were American judges. Given the opacity of that decision, those tribunals strove to find some sensible standard by which a commanders' accountability could be judged. In doing so, they focused on the commander's knowledge: an issue the Manila commission had never come to grips with and the Supreme Court had ignored. They applied the principle that commanders could be held accountable for the crimes of their troops, but at the same time they avoided, or at least mitigated, a harsh rule that commanders were always accountable for the crimes of their troops, which a literal reading of the Supreme Court's opinion might have justified.

When a decade later the U.S. military issued its first (and still current) pronouncement on command accountability, it incorporated the Nuremberg tribunals' analysis that a commander is responsible if he has "actual knowledge, or should have knowledge." That authoritative formulation in turn influenced the 1977 Geneva Protocol, so that in the 1990s the newly created international tribunals for Yugoslavia and Rwanda adopted the same standard, with some embroidery that focused on information at hand. That standard in turn is found today in the statute of the International Criminal Court.

In matters of justice to the enemy, if terrorists are the enemy, the Supreme Court has abandoned its 1946 deference to the military, and in large part even to the President. In a series of decisions from 2004 to 2008, it rejected the Bush administration's attempts to consign alleged terrorists to indefinite detention without charge or due process of law. The Court also overturned the military commissions ordained by President Bush, because they violated the Geneva Conventions' requirement of "judicial guarantees which are recognized as indispensable by civilized peoples."

The United States, which had ignored the Yamashita precedent after the Vietnam War, did so again after the Iraq War thirty-five years later. In 2004, shocking photographs from the Abu Ghraib prison in Baghdad demonstrated that American soldiers had humiliated, bullied, raped, and tortured Iraqi captives and had probably caused the death of at least one. Donald Rumsfeld appeared before a congressional committee and said, "These events occurred on my watch. As secretary of defense, I am accountable for them and I take full responsibility." He didn't mean it literally, of course, not in the sense that Yamashita was accountable and responsible. Prosecutions were confined to eleven enlisted guards and supervisors, at the rank of staff sergeant and below, and one officer, a lieutenant colonel, who was acquitted. The United States devised the Yamashita precedent, but it has never lifted the chalice to its own lips.

But Yamashita's ghost lingers in the law. Born in an unprecedented and ambiguous charge by a vindictive American general, nurtured by a misbegotten trial by his subordinates, deferentially upheld by America's highest court, shaped by two panels of American judges at Nuremberg, and incorporated into official American policy and international tribunals, it has loomed over the international law of war for too long.

The need to hold commanders accountable for derelictions of duty that result in crimes against those whom the laws protect is too important to depend on this ill-considered rationale and its discredited history. It is time to inter the apparition with its namesake.

Epilogue

Tomoyuki Yamashita was buried in a grave marked by a white wooden post at the Los Baños camp, near the gallows on which he died. His remains were reportedly later removed to Tokyo and interred in the Tama Reien Cemetery.

General of the Army Douglas MacArthur was Supreme Commander for the Allied Powers in Japan and, during the Korean War, commanded United Nations forces until removed from both posts by President Truman in 1951. He had served fifty-two years in the U.S. Army. He died in 1964 and was given a state funeral. He is interred in the MacArthur Memorial in Norfolk, Virginia.

Robert Kerr left active duty soon after the trial and returned to his native Oregon, where he established a successful practice, specializing in representing agricultural cooperatives. He retired from the U.S. Army Reserve as a colonel. His former law partner (and later Chief Justice of the Oregon Supreme Court) Edwin J. Peterson recalled him as "one of the best lawyers, if not the best, that I ever knew." Yamashita's was the only case he ever tried.

Frank Reel practiced law in Tarrytown, New York, until his death in 2000 at age ninety-two. His book *The Case of General Yamashita* was published in 1949 by the University of Chicago Press and was reissued in the wake of the My Lai controversy in 1971. In the Fiftieth Anniversary Report of his Harvard class of 1928, he wrote, "My professional, business, political, and even military lives have been studded with anti-establishment rebellion."

Major General Russel B. Reynolds served as Chief of the Special Services Division, U.S. Army, from 1946 until his retirement in 1949. He died in 1970 and is buried at Arlington National Cemetery.

Major General Leo Donovan was the presiding officer of the military commission that in 1946 tried General Masaharu Homma, commander of Japanese troops in the Philippines during the 1942 Bataan death march. Homma was convicted and executed by firing squad. Donovan retired thereafter and died in 1950. He is buried at Arlington National Cemetery.

Major General James Lester commanded an army division in occupied Japan after the war and retired to San Francisco in 1953. He died in 1958 and is buried at Arlington National Cemetery.

Brigadier General Egbert Bullene was promoted to major general and named chief of the Army Chemical Corps in 1951 and retired in 1955. He died in 1958 and was buried at San Francisco National Cemetery.

Brigadier General Morris Handwerk served in various training and administrative commands in Japan and the United States until his retirement in 1951. He died in 1967 and was buried at Arlington National Cemetery.

Chief Justice Harlan Fiske Stone died on April 22, 1946, some ten weeks after the Yamashita decision, after collapsing during a session of the Court. Justice Frank Murphy and Justice Wiley Rutledge died within a few weeks of each other in the summer of 1949; Murphy was fifty-nine; Rutledge was fifty-five.

Justice Hugo Black served on the Court until his death in 1971, thirty-four years after he took his seat. Black and Justice William O. Douglas, who joined Stone's majority opinion and who served for thirty-six years until his retirement, were instrumental in the Warren Court's expansion of constitutional protections in the 1950s and 1960s. Both are buried at Arlington National Cemetery.

Notes

All quotations from the trial are taken verbatim from the official U.S. Army transcript on the dates indicated at the beginning of a chapter's notes or as "Tr." with the date. All dates are 1945, unless otherwise indicated.

NYT = *New York Times*
CDT = *Chicago Daily Tribune* (now *Chicago Tribune*)
CDN = *Chicago Daily News*
MT = *Manila Times*
WP = *Washington Post*
NYHT = *New York Herald Tribune*

Prologue

Cosgrave: Tr. October 31.

"Hirohito has surrendered": *NYT*, August 17.

Dan Shaw: *NYT*, August 28; *CDN*, August 28.

"I am taking this opportunity": *NYT*, August 28; *CDT*, August 28.

"The Army and Navy groups": Gerwig, "Surrender at Baguio," 2.

"Division Commander's Account of Yamashita's Surrender": in Frankel, *37th Infantry Division*; Kenworthy, *Tiger of Malaya*, 1–38.

"As he walked toward me": Frankel, *37th Infantry Division*, 377.

"Yamashita's face twitched": Frankel, *37th Infantry Division*, 378.

"General": Frankel, *37th Infantry Division*, 378.

"Clearly and emphatically": Gerwig, "Surrender at Baguio," 4.

Terms of surrender: "Instrument of Surrender of the Japanese and Japanese-Controlled Armed Forces in the Philippine Islands to the Commanding General United States Army Forces, Western Pacific, Camp John Hay, Baguio, Mountain Province, Luzon, Philippine Islands, 3 September 1945," http://avalon.law.yale.edu/wwii/j6.asp.

"How could we win": Kenworthy, *Tiger of Malaya*, 38.

Chapter 1. Law and War

"War consists": T. Taylor, *Nuremberg and Vietnam*, 19–20.

Rome and Greece: Josiah Ober, "Classical Greek Times," in *Laws of War*, ed. M. Howard, Andreopoulos, and Shulman, 12–26.

Henry the Fifth: Act 1, scene 2.

Jus in bello: Among others, see T. Taylor, *Nuremberg and Vietnam,* 58–77; Guthrie and Quinlan, *Just War.*

"We would have all such offenders": *Henry the Fifth,* act 3, scene 6.

"'Tis expressly against the law of arms": *Henry the Fifth,* act 4, scene 7.

Geneva Conventions: International Committee of the Red Cross, www.icrc.org/ihl.

Lieber Code: "General Orders No. 100: The Lieber Code. Instructions for the Government of Armies of the United States in the Field," avalon.law.yale.edu/19th_century/lieber.asp.

Wirz: Chipman, *Tragedy of Andersonville.*

Hague Convention (IV), 1907: "Laws of War: Laws and Customs of War on Land (Hague IV); October 18, 1907," www.icrc.org/ihl.

Llandovery Castle: Mullins, *Leipzig Trials*, 107–134; T. Taylor, *Nuremberg and Vietnam*, 21–25.

Chapter 2. Tomoyuki Yamashita

Except where otherwise indicated, details of Yamashita's early years are from Potter, *Life and Death of a Japanese General,* the only English-language biography based on original sources, including interviews with Yamashita and, later, his widow. John Deane Potter, the chief Pacific war correspondent for the *London Daily Express,* spoke and read Japanese. He quotes from Yamashita's diary, which I was unable to locate. A reliable source in Japan told me privately that Yamashita did not keep a diary in the Philippines.

For details of Japanese militarism and the conflict between the Control and the Imperial Way cliques, see also Drea, *Japan's Imperial Army,* chaps. 7–10; Storry, *History of Modern Japan,* chap. 8; Toland, *Rising Sun,* part 1; Duus, Myers, and Peattie, *Japanese Wartime Empire*; and Edgerton, *Warriors of the Rising Sun.*

"If only I had been cleverer": Potter, *Life and Death of a Japanese General,* 16.

"Before Vienna": Potter, *Life and Death of a Japanese General,* 22.

"We will not let you die alone": Potter, *Life and Death of a Japanese General,* 27.

Hitler as unimpressive little clerk: Potter, *Life and Death of a Japanese General,* 33.

Chapter 3. Malaya and Singapore

An enormous amount has been written on the Malaya and Singapore campaigns. See particularly Allen, *Singapore*; Attiwill, *Fortress*; Boi, *Syanon Years*; Bond and Tachikawa, *British and Japanese Military Leadership*; Bradley, *Cyril Wild*; Churchill, *Second World War,* vol. 3, *Grand Alliance,* and vol. 4, *Hinge of Fate*; Farrell, *Defence and Fall of Singapore*; Farrell and Hunter, *Sixty Years On*; Forbes, *Hellfire*; Kratoska, *Malaya and Singapore*; Leasor, *Singapore*; Shinozaki, *Syonan*; C. Smith, *Singapore Burning*; Tachikawa, *General Yamashita*; Thompson, *Battle for Singapore*; Tsuji, *Singapore*; Warren, *Singapore*; Wigmore, *Australia in the War.*

Before the first bombs on Pearl Harbor: Wilkins, "Anatomy of a Disaster."

"Singapore was Britain's pivotal point": Tsuji, *Singapore,* 216.

"Beware that troops": Churchill, *Grand Alliance,* 637–638.

Three divisions: Tsuji, *Singapore,* 35.

Bicycles: Tsuji, *Singapore,* 183.

"Wherever bridges were destroyed": Tsuji, *Singapore,* 183–184.

"the long-legged Englishmen": Tsuji, *Singapore,* 185.

"In all the war": Churchill, *Grand Alliance,* 620.

"considerable initiative": Kratoska, *Malaya and Singapore,* 38.

"The majority of them": Silver, *Bridge at Parit Sulong,* 63.

"The resulting clatter": Toland, *Rising Sun,* 269n.

"I want my troops to behave with dignity": Potter, *Life and Death of a Japanese General*, 61.

Yamashita discipline: Farrell, *Defence and Fall of Singapore*, 374.

"We must encourage": Potter, *Life and Death of a Japanese General*, 68–69.

"Do not despise": Potter, *Life and Death of a Japanese General*, 68–69.

"one who enforced": Tsuji, *Singapore*, 68.

"It is a fine thing": Tsuji, *Singapore*, 150.

Other British wounded: Potter, *Life and Death of a Japanese General*, 68–69.

"Here we have": Churchill, *Hinge of Fate*, 45.

"The battle must be fought": Churchill, *Hinge of Fate*, 100.

"The chief troubles": Churchill, *Hinge of Fate*, 101.

"I had put my faith": Churchill, *Hinge of Fate*, 49.

"Indian troops": Warren, *Singapore*, 261.

Yamashita note "I, the High Command": There are several versions of this note in various English-language sources, none of them exactly alike, which is odd because the note was written in English. None of the sources indicates where the original is now. This text is taken from Wigmore, *Australia in the War*, 353, a careful account that also substantially agrees with Bradley, *Cyril Wild*, 26. Tsuji, *Singapore*, 262–263, has additional text, but this is not corroborated elsewhere. See also Toland, *Rising Sun*, 274, and Forbes, *Hellfire*, 162–163.

"gallant stand": Toland, *Rising Sun*, 275.

"I was sure": Churchill, *Hinge of Fate*, 105.

Surrender at Ford plant: Toland, *Rising Sun*, 275; Forbes, *Hellfire*, 165.

"That's the end": Forbes, *Hellfire*, 87.

Surrender of Singapore: The most detailed accounts—substantially but not exactly in agreement on the confrontation of Yamashita and Percival—are in Toland, *Rising Sun*, 276–277; Bradley, *Cyril Wild* (a biography of General Percival's aide at the surrender); and Allen, *Surrender of Singapore*.

"a bluff": Toland, *Rising Sun*, 276n.

"I now realized": Potter, *Life and Death of a Japanese General*, 89.

"I fear that we shall not be able" and subsequent discourse: Toland, *Rising Sun*, 276–277.

"On this occasion": Potter, *Life and Death of a Japanese General*, 89–90.

"the worst disaster": Churchill, *Hinge of Fate*, 92.

"Perhaps the most disastrous campaign": Leasor, *Singapore*, 108.

"It was the greatest land victory": Toland, *Rising Sun*, 277.

"He told me afterward": Potter, *Life and Death of a Japanese General*, 90; see also Allen, *Singapore*, 183.

"It was surprising": *CDT*, December 3.

"If by any chance": Tsuji, *Singapore,* 272.

"The Army will not hold a celebration": Tsuji, *Singapore,* 275.

altar: Tsuji, *Singapore*, 275.

cross: Singapore National Archives, www.roll-of-honour.com/Overseas/Singapore JapaneseInvasion.html.

Kempetai: Farrell, *Defence and Fall of Singapore*, 384; Allen, *Singapore*, 184.

"a holiday spirit": Wigmore, *Australia in the War*, 511.

Watchmaker's shop: Tsuji, *Singapore*, 279.

British and Australian POWs: Wigmore, *Australia in the War*, 515–520.

"Some of our men": Potter, *Life and Death of a Japanese General*, 91.

More than 50,000 prisoners: Wigmore, *Australia in the War*, 522.

"Tiger of Malaya": Forbes, *Hellfire*, 109.

Yamashita note: Kinvig, *Scapegoat*, 322.

Parit Sulong: The incident at Parit Sulong is described in Silver, *Bridge at Parit Sulong*; Mant, *Massacre at Parit Sulong*; and Ward, *Snaring the Other Tiger*.

"The area became a frightful shambles": Silver, *Bridge at Parit Sulong*, 183.

"The more able-bodied": Silver, *Bridge at Parit Sulong*, 183.

Footnote, Nishimura's trial: For trenchant criticism of the trial and the outcome, see Ward, *Snaring the Other Tiger*.

"The sight of the wounded men": Silver, *Bridge at Parit Sulong*, 187.

"On the night of 17 February": Hirofumi, "Battle of Singapore."

Sook ching **campaign lasted three or four days:** Farrell, *Defence and Fall of Singapore*, 385; Allen, *Singapore*, 36; Kratoska, *Malaya and Singapore*, 99–100.

5,000 Chinese killed: Bradley, *Cyril Wild*, 139.

Range of estimated number of deaths: Hirofumi, "Battle of Singapore."

Footnote, "The methods of torture": Kratoska, *Japanese Occupation of Malaya,* 115.

Diary entry: Hirofumi, "Battle of Singapore."

Carried out by Tsuji: Ward, *Snaring the Other Tiger*, 80–81.

Tsuji inserted: Thompson, *Battle for Singapore*, 124.

Circumvent Yamashita: Thompson, *Battle for Singapore*, 100.

"meticulously planned": Ward, *Snaring the Other Tiger*, 80–81.

First footnote, "operations and intelligence" and "In an army of ultraconservatives": Norman and Norman, *Tears in the Darkness*, 372–373.

Tsuji ordering slaughter of American prisoners: Toland, *Rising Sun*, 295.

Homma stunned: Toland, *Rising Sun*, 317–318.

Yamashita did not know: Ward, *Killer They Called a God*, 298.

Second footnote, "protected by the US military" and Tsuji escape: Hirofumi, "Battle of Singapore."

Heads on pikes: Kratoska, *Malaya and Singapore*, 94; Ward, *Killer They Called a God*, 115–116.

"As already announced": Kratoska, *Malaya and Singapore*, 97–98.

"a poisonous insect": Toland, *Rising Sun*, 533n.

Wild chief investigator: Ward, *Snaring the Other Tiger*, 55–56; Bradley, *Cyril Wild*, chaps. 7 and 8.

Wild early career: Rowland, *A River Kwai Story*, 32–34.

"I have a wider knowledge": Silver, *Bridge at Parit Sulong*, 279.

Interrogation of Yamashita and report to Mountbatten: Bradley, *Cyril Wild*, chap. 7.

Emperor's birthday and "Today we celebrate": Shinozaki, *Syonan*, 40–44.

Transfer to Manchuria, no stop in Tokyo: Potter, *Life and Death of a Japanese General*, 95–96.

Chapter 4. Leyte

Chief sources for accounts of the battle on Leyte: Cannon, *Leyte*; Falk, *Decision at Leyte*; Morison, *Leyte*; Vego, *Battle for Leyte*; and Esposito, *West Point Atlas of War*. The definitive biography of General MacArthur is James, *Years of MacArthur*; see also Manchester, *American Caesar*; Petillo, *Douglas MacArthur*; and MacArthur, *Reminiscences*.

"be commenced immediately": U.S. Army, Japan, Office of the Military History Officer, Japanese monograph 24, 69.

"a superb tactician": Cannon, *Leyte*, 50.

Difficulties facing Yamashita: Falk, *Decision at Leyte*, 49–56; Lael, *Yamashita Precedent*, 7–10.

"The source of command": Falk, *Decision at Leyte*, 56.

"under the great disadvantage": Kenworthy, *Tiger of Malaya*, 69.

"Imperial General Headquarters": Falk, *Decision at Leyte*, 73.

"The Army and the Navy always quarreled": Cannon, *Leyte*, 53–54.

Chain of command: Cannon, *Leyte*, 46; Falk, *Decision at Leyte*, 72–73.

"the line of command": Kenworthy, *Tiger of Malaya,* 70.

"Where's Leyte?": Kenworthy, *Tiger of Malaya*, 71; Cannon, *Leyte*, 51; Falk, *Decision at Leyte*, 106.

"The transports": Kenworthy, *Tiger of Malaya*, 71.

Stratton interview and "None of his answers": Stratton, "Tiger of Malaya," 143.

"to pay particular attention": Kenworthy, *Tiger of Malaya*, 71.

"to issue strict warning": Kenworthy, *Tiger of Malaya*, 72.

MacArthur orders and "The President of the United States": Falk, *Decision at Leyte*, 20.

"The Philippines is American territory": Cannon, *Leyte*, 4.

Roosevelt approval: Cannon, *Leyte*, 9.

"more men": Cannon, *Leyte*, 23.

Imperial Headquarters' plan: Falk, *Decision at Leyte*, 48; Lael, *Yamashita Precedent*, 10.

"impossible to execute": Falk, *Decision at Leyte*, 48.

No interest: Falk, *Decision at Leyte*, 26.

"I have returned": Cannon, *Leyte*, 154.

"decisive victory": Lael, *Yamashita Precedent*, 10.

Yamashita furious: Falk, *Decision at Leyte*, 64, 106.

One division: Cannon, *Leyte*, 22; Falk, *Decision at Leyte*, 70.

"The communications network": Falk, *Decision at Leyte*, 81.

Logistics and resupply: Falk, *Decision at Leyte*, 107; Lael, *Yamashita Precedent*, 10.

"dumbfounded and indignant": Falk, *Decision at Leyte*, 107.

"muster all possible strength": Falk, *Decision at Leyte*, 107; Lael, *Yamashita Precedent*, 10–11.

Word to Suzuki: Falk, *Decision at Leyte*, 107–108.

Yamashita unable to communicate: Falk, *Decision at Leyte*, 94, 101–104; Cannon, *Leyte*, 104.

Lack of provisions: Cannon, *Leyte*, 324.

"as long as any officers": Cannon, *Leyte*, 252.

Japanese fire discipline: Cannon, *Leyte*, 250–252.

"beautifully camouflaged": Cannon, *Leyte*, 290.

Soil: Cannon, *Leyte*, 248.

"It was bitter": Manchester, *American Caesar*, 405.

Messages had to be sent by hand: Cannon, *Leyte*, 294.

Message to Suzuki arrived November 12: Falk, *Decision at Leyte*, 255.

Telephone and telegraph destroyed: Cannon, *Leyte*, 295–296.

One division: Cannon, *Leyte*, 313–314.

Relying on foot soldiers: Cannon, *Leyte*, 324.

"forced to eat coconuts": Cannon, *Leyte*, 359.

"It was pitiful": Cannon, *Leyte*, 358.

No further assistance to Thirty-Fifth Army: Cannon, *Leyte*, 359–360.
Yamashita message to Suzuki: Cannon, *Leyte*, 362, 364.
Casualty figures: Cannon, *Leyte*, 367–368; Lael, *Yamashita Precedent*, 12.
"In their determination": Cannon, *Leyte*, 369.
"the Leyte campaign was a tragic nightmare": Falk, *Decision at Leyte*, 318.
"We never had a chance": *CDT*, November 26.
Negotiated end: Esposito, *West Point Atlas of War*, 80.
"After the loss of Leyte": Tr. November 28.

Chapter 5. Luzon

Main sources for Luzon operations are R. Smith, *Triumph in the Philippines*; Morison, *Liberation of the Philippines*; Esposito, *West Point Atlas of War*; Connaughton, Pimlott, and Anderson, *Battle for Manila*; Holzimmer, *General Walter Krueger*; Norman and Norman, *Tears in the Darkness*.

"be left to the discretion": Falk, *Decision at Leyte*, 307.
over 200,000 soldiers: R. Smith, *Triumph in the Philippines*, 93–95.
"understrength": R. Smith, *Triumph in the Philippines*, 90.
Forces under Yamashita's command: R. Smith, *Triumph in the Philippines*, 92–93.
"dread kamikazes": R. Smith, *Triumph in the Philippines*, 46.
Luzon defense: U.S. Army, Japan, Office of the Military History Officer, Japanese monograph 114, 1–3; Lael, *Yamashita Precedent*, 13.
Japanese telephone, and environment: U.S. War Department, *Handbook on Japanese Military Forces*, 316.
"Crucially": Rottman, *World War II Battlefield Communications*, 7.
Maintaining wire communications: Rottman, *World War II Battlefield Communications*, 37.
Radio problems: Rottman, *World War II Battlefield Communications*, 37.
Telephones unavailable: U.S. War Department, *Handbook on Japanese Military Forces*, 303.
"It is extremely difficult": U.S. War Department, *Operations*, 282.
messenger on foot: Lael, *Yamashita Precedent*, 36.
"American headquarters": Stratton, "Tiger of Malaya," 140.
Transfer of commands: R. Smith, *Triumph in the Philippines*, 96.
Iwabuchi's force: U.S. Army, Japan, Office of the Military History Officer, Japanese monograph 114, 7.
Lingayen: Manchester, *American Caesar*, 406; Lael, *Yamashita Precedent*, 22.
Transfer of operational control: R. Smith, *Triumph in the Philippines*, 242; Lael, *Yamashita Precedent*, 26–27.
"mirrored a picture": R. Smith, *Triumph in the Philippines*, 241.
Iwabuchi's forces, Yokoyama's response: R. Smith, *Triumph in the Philippines*, 242; Lael, *Yamashita Precedent*, 26.
"You men": U.S. Army, Japan, Office of the Military History Officer, Japanese monograph 114, 12.
"Iwabuchi's Plan": R. Smith, *Triumph in the Philippines*, 246.
"Once started": R. Smith, *Triumph in the Philippines*, 246.
Filipino guerrillas: U.S. Army, Japan, Office of the Military History Officer, Japanese monograph 114, 13.
communication often interrupted or lost altogether: Lael, *Yamashita Precedent*, 36.
"In addition": Lael, *Yamashita Precedent*, 36.
Yokoyama had no true picture: R. Smith, *Triumph in the Philippines*, 271.
Yokoyama order: R. Smith, *Triumph in the Philippines*, 272.

No control: U.S. Army, Japan, Office of the Military History Officer, Japanese monograph 114, 14–16.

Yokoyama-Iwabuchi communications: U.S. Army, Japan, Office of the Military History Officer, Japanese monograph 114, 17–18; R. Smith, *Triumph in the Philippines*, 273.

"all communications": R. Smith, *Triumph in the Philippines*, 273.

Suicide: U.S. Army, Japan, Office of the Military History Officer, Japanese monograph 114, 20.

Largest urban battle: R. Smith, *Triumph in the Philippines*, vii.

Japanese defenses: R. Smith, *Triumph in the Philippines*, chap. 13.

Urban combat: R. Smith, *Triumph in the Philippines*, chaps. 14–16.

University buildings: R. Smith, *Triumph in the Philippines*, 289.

New Police Station: R. Smith, *Triumph in the Philippines*, 282–283.

2,000 shells: R. Smith, *Triumph in the Philippines*, 287.

Casualties: R. Smith, *Triumph in the Philippines*, 307.

"The devastation of Manila": Manchester, *American Caesar*, 412.

"I watched": MacArthur, *Reminiscences*, 247.

"The forces of MacArthur and Yamashita": Lael, *Yamashita Precedent*, 32.

Casualties: R. Smith, *Triumph in the Philippines*, 692–694.

"The Filipino people": Hastings, *Inferno*, 556.

"a perspective": Hastings, *Inferno*, 426.

Chapter 6. Military Commissions

First American code of military law: Winthrop, *Military Law and Precedents*, 20–22.

"Officers and Soldiers": Winthrop, *Military Law and Precedents*, 947.

"well and truly try": American Articles of War of 1776, sec. 14, art. 3, in Winthrop, *Military Law and Precedents*, 968.

"The court-martial is only an instrumentality of the executive power": Winthrop, *Military Law and Precedents*, 54.

"As a court of law": Winthrop, *Military Law and Precedents*, 54.

André commission: Fisher, *Military Tribunals*, 11–13.

Scott commissions: Fisher, *Military Tribunals*, 32–40.

"any court for the trial": Fisher, *Military Tribunals*, 33.

"necessarily resulted": Fisher, *Military Tribunals*, 33.

"an addition": Fisher, *Military Tribunals*, 34.

"as nearly as practicable": Fisher, *Military Tribunals*, 35.

commission statistics: Fisher, *Military Tribunals*, 35.

"worked like a charm": Fisher, *Military Tribunals*, 33.

Civil War commissions: Neely, *Fate of Liberty*, 168.

"insurgents and marauding": Fisher, *Military Tribunals*, 48.

"the rules and principles": Winthrop, *Military Law and Precedents*, 42.

"Persons acting independently": Winthrop, *Military Law and Precedents*, 784 and n57.

Claim of military status: Neely, *Fate of Liberty*, 167–175.

Charge against Wirz: Chipman, *Tragedy of Andersonville*, 32.

Congressional authority: Winthrop, *Military Law and Precedents*, 833; Fisher, *Military Tribunals*, 41–51.

Review of proceedings: Winthrop, *Military Law and Precedents*, 833.

"should be regulated": Fisher, *Military Tribunals*, 48.

"constituted in a similar manner": Fisher, *Military Tribunals*, 49.

"Prisoners were sometimes taken": Neely, *Fate of Liberty*, 41.

"Trials by military commissions": Neely, *Fate of Liberty*, 41.

Suspension of habeas corpus and 1863 act: Neely, *Fate of Liberty*, chap. 3.

Vallandigham case: *Ex Parte Vallandigham,* 68 U.S. 243 (1863); Neely, *Fate of Liberty*, 65–68; Fisher, *Military Tribunals*, 56–58.

Second case: *Ex Parte Milligan*, 71 U.S. 2 (1866); Fisher, *Military Tribunals*, 58–60.

Philippines: Fisher, *Military Tribunals*, 80–81.

"In the absence": Winthrop, *Military Law and Precedents*, 841–842.

Chapter 7. The Charge: The Accountability of Command

All quotations from the trial in this chapter are from the transcript of October 8.

Yamashita cell: *Canberra Times*, September 5.

Hamamoto: *Harvard Crimson*, June 18, 1952; Harvard College Class of 1927, Sixty-Fifth Anniversary Report, 42; Terami-Wada, "Lt. Shigenobu Mochizuki and the New Philippine Cultural Institute," 107n10.

MacArthur authority for trials: Lael, *Yamashita Precedent*, 59–61.

"speed is of the essence": Lael, *Yamashita Precedent*, 67–69.

"real motives or feelings": James, *Years of MacArthur*, 3: 98.

"wanted justice": Stratton, "Tiger of Malaya," 142.

"public disclosure": Redford, *Trial*, 12.

First order, laying out rules and regulations: GHQ U.S. Army Forces, Pacific, "Regulations Governing the Trial of War Criminals," AG 000.5 (24 Sep 45) (hereafter "Regulations").

Second order: GHQ U.S. Army Forces, Pacific, "Trial of War Criminals," AG 000.5 (24 Sep 45).

Third order: GHQ U.S. Army Forces, Pacific, "Trial of General Tomoyuki Yamashita," AG 000.5 (24 Sep 45).

"When troops flee": McNeilly, *Sun Tzu*, 295.

Convicted as a principal: Article 77, Uniform Code of Military Justice, 10 U.S.C. sec. 877.

"Every Officer commanding": "Article 11th, Massachusetts Articles of War, Adopted by the Provisional Congress of Massachusetts Bay, April 5, 1775," reprinted in Winthrop, *Military Law and Precedents*, 948–949.

Two Philippine cases: Parks, "Command Responsibility," 10.

MacArthur well knew: Lael, *Yamashita Precedent*, 69–71.

Fourth Hague Convention: "Convention (IV) Respecting the Laws and Customs of War on Land and Its Annex: Regulations Concerning the Laws and Customs of War on Land. The Hague, 18 October 1907," ICRC International Humanitarian Law—Treaties and Documents, www.icrc.org/ihl.nsf/full/195.

"Persons acting": Bordwell, *Law of War*, 80.

"Experience has convinced": Bordwell, *Law of War*, 80.

"The root of this indisposition": Hall, *Treatise on International Law,* 555.

Lieber Code: Article 51, avalon.law.yale.edu/19th_century/lieber.asp.

"an order emanating": Oppenheim, *International Law*, 105.

Brussels conference: Scott, *Texts of the Paris Peace Conferences*, 382–383.

"cause the laws of war": Hall, *Treatise on International Law*, 557.

Brussels declaration adopted: Hall, *Treatise on International Law*, 558.

"When once it is recognized": Amos, *Political and Legal Remedies*, 231.

Report of the Lansing committee: All quotations are from the Commission on the Responsibility of Authors of the War and on Enforcement of Penalties, *Report Presented to the Preliminary Peace Conference,* March 29, 1919, reprinted in *American Journal of International Law* 14 (1920): 95–154 (hereafter 1919 Report).

"abundant evidence of outrages": 1919 Report, 113.

"There is no reason": 1919 Report, 116.

"There is little doubt": 1919 Report, 117.

International criminal tribunal: 1919 Report, 122–123.

"standard certain": 1919 Report, 134.

"subordinating him": 1919 Report, 136.

"unalterably opposed": 1919 Report, 143.

"negative criminality": 1919 Report, 129.

"It is one thing": 1919 Report, 143.

Commission final report: 1919 Report, 121.

"The purpose of constituting a high tribunal": 1919 Report, 129.

"when he knows of": Douglass, "High Command Case," 686–687.

French and Canadian regulations: Parks, "Command Responsibility," 18–19.

Nuremberg Charter: Nuremberg Trial Proceedings, Vol. 1: "Charter of the International Military Tribunal," avalon.law.yale.edu/imt/imtconst.asp.

Footnote, effect of Article 7: Green, "Command Responsibility," 328.

Rights of due process: "Regulations," sec. 14.

Appointment of defense counsel: Reel, *Case of General Yamashita,* 5–11.

"Yamashita is being tried": Reel, *Case of General Yamashita,* 8.

Headlines: *CDT,* October 8; *MT,* October 10.

"Yamashita was already convicted": Guy, "Defense of Yamashita," 57.

"I don't see how": *WP,* October 29.

Trial settings: Descriptions of the trial setting are based on U.S. Army films viewed at the National Archives, Record Group 111: Records of the Office of the Chief Signal Officer, 1860–1985. Several clips excerpted from these films can be accessed at www.criticalpast.com among the clips from 1945, under "Manila Philippines."

Seventy-two reporters: Letters of George E. Mountz, Allen County Public Library, Fort Wayne, Indiana (hereafter Mountz), October 9.

Spectators: *MT,* October 9; Reel, *Case of General Yamashita,* 27.

"If feasible": "Regulations," sec. 8.

Commission members: Information on the members of the commission is from their service records maintained at the National Archives and Records Administration, National Personnel Records Center, Military Personnel Records Branch, St. Louis, Missouri, and from the following obituaries: *NYT,* March 12, 1958 (Lester); *Meyersdale (Florida) Republican,* September 21, 1967 (Handwerk); Arlington National Cemetery (Donovan); and *NYT,* February 23, 1958 (Bullene).

"Yamashita was the consistent stoic": Reel, *Case of General Yamashita,* 15, 50–51.

"He stood about 5′7″ tall": Guy, "Defense of Yamashita," 54–56.

"he hesitated": Mountz, October 9.

"Yamashita maintained": *MT,* October 9.

"The arraignment": *NYHT,* October 9.

"plump and potbellied": *CDT,* October 9.

"I have never": Reel, *Case of General Yamashita,* 51.

"This was a tour de force" and interpreters: Reel, *Case of General Yamashita*, 145–146.

Kerr career: Author's telephone interview with Edwin J. Peterson, former law partner, March 30, 2010.

"smart as a whip": Mountz, October 9.

Recommended by Carpenter: Lael, *Yamashita Precedent*, 72–73.

"I never want to meet": Reel, *Case of General Yamashita*, 34.

Staff: Mountz, October 28.

"I am as near bushed": Mountz, October 28.

"such a fat file": *NYT*, October 8.

Interview of Yamashita: Reel, *Case of General Yamashita*, 12–26.

"It was a wonderful show": Mountz, October 9.

"If those crimes": Reel, *Case of General Yamashita*, 25.

"We cut him short": Reel, *Case of General Yamashita*, 16.

"was the story of a man": Reel, *Case of General Yamashita*, 17.

"I was naturally unprepared": Reel, *Case of General Yamashita*, 19–20.

"The Japanese army": Reel, *Case of General Yamashita*, 22.

Yamashita did not learn until February 13: Reel, *Case of General Yamashita*, 23.

"Thus we saw revealed": Reel, *Case of General Yamashita*, 24–25.

"There were no secrets": Reel, *Case of General Yamashita*, 25–26.

"didn't, in the slightest": *Modesto (CA) Bee*, June 9, 1974.

Psychiatrists' interview: Reel, *Case of General Yamashita*, 65–72; transcripts of interviews in author's possession.

Chapter 8. The Prosecution: The Hearsay Problem

All quotations from the trial in this chapter are from the transcript of October 29.

Defense lawyers outraged: Reel, *Case of General Yamashita*, 77.

"About 4:30": Mountz, October 23.

"The more I see": Mountz, October 28.

Regulations dictated by MacArthur: James, *Years of MacArthur*, 3: 94.

"settled rule of law": Maltby, *Treatise on Courts Martial*, 43–44.

1945 army manual: U.S. War Department, *Military Justice Procedure*, 88–89.

"The principal evil": *Crawford v. Washington*, 541 U.S. 36, 50, 59 (2004).

"Admitting": *Crawford*, 541 U.S. At 61–62.

Cramer Memo: Memorandum for General John M. Weir, Assistant Judge Advocate General, Director, War Crimes Office, Subject: "Applicability of Articles of War to Trials of War Criminals by Military Commissions," n.d., NARA Record Group 331, SCAP, Legal Section, Manila Branch, Entry UD 1336.

None since the Civil War: Winthrop, *Military Law and Precedents*, 838.

Supreme Court had struck down even Lincoln's commissions as unconstitutional: *Ex Parte Milligan*, 71 U.S. (4 Wall.) 2 (1866).

Rules of Land Warfare: U.S. War Department, *Rules of Land Warfare, Field Manual 27-10*, 1940 ed., secs. 346, 347, 356.

Footnote, "The offenses denounced": *Digest of Opinions of the Judge Advocate General of the Army (1912–1930)* 30 (June 25, 1921): sec. 1282.

Chapter 9. The Prosecution: The Victims

All quotations from the trial in this chapter are taken from the transcripts of October 29 through November 3.

"queen of tearjerkers": *Manila Bulletin*, November 26, 2006.

"lovely 26-year old brunette": *NYT*, October 29.

"made a very good witness": Mountz, October 30.

Footnote, Valdes's appointment: *MT*, November 15.

"Bonbons" headline: *WP*, November 1.

"You men": Reel, *Case of General Yamashita*, 88–90.

"The case is progressing": Mountz, November 1.

Gripping and staring: *Sydney Morning Herald*, November 3.

"story rivaling in horror": *CDT*, November 2.

Head bent: *Sydney Morning Herald*, November 3.

"imperturbable": *CDT*, November 2.

"sitting quietly": *Sydney Morning Herald*, November 3.

"So everyone took pictures": Mountz, November 2.

"Yamashita, seemingly ignorant": *CDT*, November 2.

"Calm and apparently unconcerned": *MT*, November 3.

"He looked incredibly tame": *Time*, November 12.

Fourteen-page report: Exhibit 192.

Saturday sessions: Mountz, November 2.

Kerr "fed up": Mountz, November 5.

"An orgy of murder": *NYT*, November 2.

"the usual pattern": *NYT*, November 3.

Chapter 10. The Prosecution: The Defense Scores

Except as noted, all quotations from the trial in this chapter are from the trial transcript of November 3 through November 13.

"Imagine the judge asking": Mountz, November 4.

"Yesterday": Mountz, November 4.

"He did not do so well": Mountz, November 5.

"MANILA, Tuesday, Nov. 6—Big tears": *NYT*, November 6.

"As she testified": *Time*, November 19.

Santo Tomas: Hattendorp, *Japanese Occupation*; Cogan, *Captured*; Kerr, *Surrender and Survival*.

"was not deleteriously influenced": Pearson, "Morbidity and Mortality," 1013.

Sexual activity: Pearson, "Morbidity and Mortality," 999.

Worsening conditions: Cogan, *Captured*, 136.

Treatment of internees: Cogan, *Captured*, 120–121.

Calories: Pearson, "Morbidity and Mortality," 1003.

Footnote, calorie comparison: Academy of Nutrition and Dietetics (2012). www .eatright.org/Public/content.aspx?id=6805 and www.eatright.org/Public/content.aspx?id =6831.

"democracy of hunger": Cogan, *Captured*, 137.

Weight loss: Pearson, "Morbidity and Mortality," 1003.

Deaths at Santo Tomas: Pearson, "Morbidity and Mortality," 1010–1111.

"Neither a POW camp": Cogan, *Captured*, 108–109.

"a loose, poorly defined state": Cogan, *Captured*, 114.

Reunion: Cogan, *Captured*, 113.

Transfer of camp control: Tr. 1455.

Inspections: Cogan, *Captured*, 118; Tr. 1935.

Snapshots: Mountz, November 10.

"We are getting our evidence": Mountz, November 13.

"Language problems dogged the trial": Boardman, *Yamashita Trial*, 29.

"While high Japanese officers": *NYT*, November 11.

Royal Warrant: Taylor, *Final Report*, 254–257.

MacArthur "disturbed by reports": Lael, *Yamashita Precedent*, 90; James, *Years of Mac-Arthur* 3: 95.

"pushed to prompt conclusions": Redford, *Trial*, 34.

"This phrase obviously means" and "However": Tr. October 29.

"Ang Kim Ling, the youngest witness": *NYHT*, November 13.

"a bad slip": Mountz, November 13.

"a devious journey": Reel, *Case of General Yamashita*, 134.

"against my better judgment": Redford, *Trial*, 26–28.

"unaffected, childlike spontaneity": Reel, *Case of General Yamashita*, 136.

"alert appearance": *CDT*, November 13.

Chapter 11. The Prosecution: The Conclusion

Except as noted, all quotations from the trial in this chapter are taken from the trial transcript of November 14 through November 20.

Final week: Tr. November 13.

Eight-page U.S. Army colonel's report: Prosecution Exhibit 318.

Location and task of Kobayashi's force: Connaughton, Pimlott, and Anderson, *Battle for Manila*, 187.

"I was momentarily": Sakakida, *Spy in Their Midst*, 175–176.

Orders from Tokyo (film, 1945): UCLA Film and Television Archive, Los Angeles. Viewed July 17, 2009. Quotations from author's notes of narration.

"a flaming spectacle": *NYT*, November 16.

Footnote, "A Christian nation": Douglas MacArthur, Address to Congress, April 19, 1951. www.pbs.org/wgbh/amex/macarthur/filmmore/reference/primary/macspeech 05.html.

"a colored movie on the burning & destruction of Manila": Mountz, October 2.

Hoping to tie Yamashita down: Mountz, November 14.

"Unity of command": Morison, *Liberation of the Philippines*, 197.

"I think we got enough in": Mountz, November 16.

"I can face death": *NYHT*, November 17.

"a hard-boiled commander": *NYHT*, November 20.

Spectators snickered: *NYHT*, November 20.

Chapter 12. The Defense: Setting The Stage

Testimony and commission proceedings in this chapter taken from the trial transcript of November 20 through November 28.

Motion for finding of not guilty: "Regulations," sec. 17e.

"Reynolds was obviously displeased": *NYHT*, November 20.

Muto's appearance: *MT*, November 22; *CDT*, November 21.

Muto's account was an accurate one: The U.S. Army's history of the Philippines campaign relied on Muto's testimony as a primary source, corroborating it with much other information, including American operational reports and postwar interrogations of Japanese officers. R. Smith, *Triumph in the Philippines*, 89 n2, 90–92, 92n12.

"He really sang": Mountz, November 21.

"Cross-examination of Lt. Gen. Akira Muto": *CDT*, November 23.

"To be sure": Eichelberger, *Our Jungle Road*, 211.

"an unimpressive little figure": *CDT*, November 26.

"a very elderly-appearing": *NYT*, November 28.

Chapter 13. *The Defense: Yamashita Testifies*

Testimony and commission proceedings taken from the transcript of November 28 to December 3.

"In America, is it considered proper": Reel, *Case of General Yamashita*, 145.

Yamashita appearance: *MT*, November 29.

Yamashita raises voice: *NYHT*, November 29.

"Staring at his interpreters": *NYHT*, November 29.

"Booted, spurred, beribboned": *CDT*, November 29.

"One could sense": *NYHT*, November 29.

"steady as a chant": *NYHT*, November 29.

"Three hours of searching cross-examination": *NYHT*, November 30.

Footnote, POWs under international law: Convention (III) Relative to the Treatment of Prisoners of War, August 12, 1929 ("Third Geneva Convention"), Articles 21, 42, 91–93.

Yamashita spoke slowly: *NYHT*, December 1; Reel, *Case of General Yamashita*, 148.

"a dramatic forty-five minute oration": *NYT*, December 1.

"Major Kerr repeatedly attempted": *NYT*, November 30.

"If his speech": *NYHT*, December 1.

"In their misery": *Time*, December 10.

"leaving everyone thoroughly confused": *NYT*, December 4.

"had confused": *WP*, December 4.

Geneva Convention: Convention (III) Relative to the Treatment of Prisoners of War (1929), Articles 45, 46, 66.

Eighteen hours on the witness stand: Guy, "Defense of Yamashita," 59.

"The commission may sentence": "Regulations," sec. 20.

"approved by the officer": "Regulations," sec. 21.

Chapter 14. *The Verdict*

Quotations from the transcript are taken from December 5 (closing arguments) and December 7 (verdict).

"the fact that the acts complained of": U.S. War Department, *Rules of Land Warfare, Field Manual 27-10*, as amended by Change No. 1, November 15, 1944, adding section 345.1 and amending section 347.

"Thank you": *NYHT*, December 5.

"The defense did well": Mountz, December 5.

Jabbing his finger: *NYHT*, December 5.

"A good summation": Mountz, December 6.

"Yamashita in his usual manner": *MT*, December 6.

First footnote, Reynolds's statement: Reel, *Case of General Yamashita*, 166.

Second footnote, Kerr "startled": Redford, *Trial*, 36–37.

Reporters' poll: Reel, *Case of General Yamashita*, 174.

"Of the six of us": Reel, *Case of General Yamashita*, 174.

"**would unquestionably**": Guy, "Defense of Yamashita," 64.
Yamashita not nervous: Reel, *Case of General Yamashita*, 168.
"**There will be no demonstrations**": Reel, *Case of General Yamashita*, 168.
"**an unearthly silence**": Mountz, December 7.
No sound: Guy, "Defense of Yamashita," 64.
"**What minutes**": Mountz, December 7.
"**Why must**": *WP*, December 8.
Yamashita statement: *MT*, December 8.
Ambulance: *MT*, December 8.
"**This trial**": *NYT*, December 7.
"**It was a fascinating experience**": Camp, "Talking with the Enemy," 19.
"**Mamatay si Yamashita**": *MT*, December 8.

Chapter 15. The Aftermath

Quotations of the testimony of Yamashita are from the transcript on November 28, 29, and 30.

Conversation with the commissioners: The account of this conversation is based on Mountz, December 9.

"**Yamashita was the consistent stoic**": Reel, *Case of General Yamashita*, 52.

Account of Yamashita's surrender: Gerwig, "Surrender at Baguio," 2; Kenworthy, *Tiger of Malaya*, 28–38.

"**disqualified by personal interest**": "Regulations," sec. 8.

"**gestures, facial expressions and exaggerated mannerisms**": Reel, *Case of General Yamashita*, 40, 44.

Two-thirds vote: "Regulations," sec. 9.

MacArthur's regulations specified: "Regulations," sec. 21.

Quirin case: *Ex Parte Quirin*, 317 U.S. 1 (1942); Fisher, *Nazi Saboteurs*.

"**Pandemonium**": Reel, *Case of General Yamashita*, 187; Lael, *Yamashita Precedent*, 92–93.

"**just as an ordinary deadbeat**": Reel, *Case of General Yamashita*, 189.

MacArthur's order that no one attend the Philippine Supreme Court: Redford, *Trial*, 42; Lael, *Yamashita Precedent*, 92–93.

Hendrix argument: *NYHT*, November 23; *WP*, November 24.

No hope of winning an order: Reel, *Case of General Yamashita*, 197.

Philippine Supreme Court decision: *Yamashita v. Styer*, G.R. No. L-129 (December 19, 1945), www.lawphil.net/judjuris/juri1945/dec1945/gr_l-129_1945.html. The decision was announced on November 28; the written decision followed. *NYT*, November 28.

"**An attempt**": *MT*, November 29.

Cable to the clerk of the Supreme Court: Reel, *Case of General Yamashita*, 203.

Supreme Court receives papers: *CDT*, November 4.

MacArthur refuses: Redford, *Trial*, 97.

Supreme Court schedules oral argument: Lael, *Yamashita Precedent*, 100.

Lawyers depart: Reel, *Case of General Yamashita*, 202–209.

MacArthur staff review of verdict: GHQ, U.S. Army Forces, Pacific, Office of the Theater Judge Advocate, "Review of the Record of Trial by a Military Commission of To-moyuki Yamashita, General, Imperial Japanese Army, December 26, 1945."

"**International Law is more than a scholarly collection**": "Report to the President by Mr. Justice Jackson, June 6, 1945." International Conference on Military Trials: London, 1945, avalon.law.yale.edu/imt/jack08.asp.

Chapter 16. The Supreme Court

Supreme Court: See generally Feldman, *Scorpions.*

Curfew: *Hirabayashi v. United States*, 320 U.S. 81 (1943).

Relocation: *Korematsu v. United States*, 323 U.S. 214 (1944).

Footnote 2, compensation and apology to Japanese Americans: Civil Liberties Act of 1988, 50 U.S.C. App. 1989–1989d.

Quirin case: *Ex Parte Quirin*, 317 U.S. 1 (1942).

Defense working arrangements in Washington: Reel, *Case of General Yamashita*, 210.

Brief in support: Brief in Support of Motion for Leave to File Petition for Writs of Habeas Corpus and Prohibition and of Petition for Writ of Certiorari, *In Re Yamashita*, No. 61 Misc., October Term 1945.

A proposition no U.S. court had ever recognized: Urofsky, *Division and Discord*, 64–65.

Brief in opposition: Brief for the Respondents in Opposition, *In Re Yamashita*, No. 61 Misc., October Term 1945.

Marshall principle: *Foster v. Neilson*, 27 U.S. 253, 307 (1829).

Court's deliberations in conference: Lael, *Yamashita Precedent*, 103–107; Mason, *Harlan Fiske Stone,* 666–671; Urofsky, *Division and Discord*, 65–67.

Judgment and opinions: *In Re Yamashita*, 327 U.S. 1 (1946).

Footnote, Revision of Geneva Conventions: Convention (III) Relative to the Treatment of Prisoners of War (1949), Article 85.

"If we are to apply": Mason, *Harlan Fiske Stone,* 668.

Footnote 10, Black's doubts: James, *Years of MacArthur,* 3: 101.

"I didn't give the boys as much hell": Ferren, *Salt of the Earth*, 305.

Due process extended to enemy combatants at Guantánamo in 2004: *Hamdi v. Rumsfeld*, 542 U.S. 507 (2004).

"the worst in the Court's history": Ferren, *Salt of the Earth,* 320.

"Great cases, like hard cases": *Northern Securities Co. v. United States,* 193 U.S. 197 (1904).

"Should the Court clear the way": Ferren, *Salt of the Earth*, 314.

Footnote, "In the United States and Britain": Dower, *War without Mercy,* 8–9, 13. And see Prevost, "Race and War Crimes."

Recommendation for clemency: Reel, *Case of General Yamashita*, 233.

Court's decision sent to MacArthur: James, *Years of MacArthur*, 3: 96.

MacArthur decision: MacArthur, *Reminiscences*, 295–296.

"considerable shock": *NYT*, February 8, 1946.

"Hasty, revengeful action": *In Re Homma,* 327 U.S. 759 (1946).

"The President will take no action": *WP*, February 9, 1946.

Japanese petition: James, *Years of MacArthur*, 3: 95.

"Due to my carelessness": Tanaka, "Last Words."

"I know that all you Americans": *CDT*, February 23, 1946; *Argus (Melbourne)* (newspaper), February 25, 1946.

"He appeared stoical": *CDT*, February 23, 1946.

Notice to his wife: Oki, *Higeki no shogun.*

Chapter 17. The Forties: Nuremberg and Tokyo

"Individuals of the armed forces": U.S. War Department, *Rules of Land Warfare*, 1914 ed., sec. 366; U.S. War Department, *Rules of Land Warfare*, 1934 ed., sec 352; U.S. War Department, *Rules of Land Warfare, Field Manual 27-10*, 1940 ed., sec. 347.

"Individuals and organizations who violate": U.S. War Department, *Rules of Land Warfare, Field Manual 27-10,* 1940 ed., as amended November 15, 1944, sec. 345.1.

Nuremberg charter: Nuremberg Trial Proceedings, Vol. 1, "Charter of the International Military Tribunal," art. 8, avalon.law.yale.edu/imt/imtconst.asp.

"The fact that the law of war has been violated": U.S. War Department, *Rules of Land Warfare, Field Manual 27-10,* 1956 ed., secs. 501, 509.

Hostages Case: U.S. Military Tribunal, Nuremberg, "The Hostages Trial: Trial of Wilhelm List and Others," in *Law Reports of Trials of War Criminals,* selected and prepared by United Nations War Crimes Commission, 8: 34–92.

High Command Case: U.S. Military Tribunal, Nuremberg, "The German High Command Trial—Trial of Wilhelm von Leeb and Thirteen Others," in *Law Reports of Trials of War Criminals,* selected and prepared by United Nations War Crimes Commission, 12: 1–127.

Tokyo trial: Quotations are from the *Judgment of the International Military Tribunal for the Far East,* part A, chapter II(b). See Pritchard and Zaide, *Tokyo War Crimes Trial;* Boister and Cryer, *Tokyo International Military Tribunal: A Reappraisal* and *Documents on the Tokyo International Military Tribunal;* Totani, *Tokyo War Crimes Trial;* Minear, *Victors' Justice;* Horwitz, "Tokyo Trial"; Picigallo, *Japanese on Trial.*

Planning for the Tokyo trial: U.S. State Department, *Foreign Relations of the United States,* 6: 926.

"The greatest reformation": Douglas MacArthur, Address to Congress, April 19, 1951. www.pbs.org/wgbh/amex/macarthur/filmmore/reference/primary/macspeech05.html.

MacArthur's statement upholding Tokyo sentences: Minear, *Victors' Justice,* 166–167.

Chapter 18. The Seventies: My Lai

Accounts of the massacre at My Lai include Hersh, *My Lai 4;* Bilton and Sim, *Four Hours in My Lai;* Peers Commission Report (hereafter Peers Report), in Goldstein, Marshall, and Schwarz, *My Lai Massacre;* Belknap, *Vietnam War on Trial.*

"American troops": *NYT,* March 17, 1968.

Ridenhour letter: Peers Report, 34–37.

Investigation and charge: Hersh, *My Lai 4,* 81–128.

"Vietnamese Say G.I.'s": *NYT,* November 17, 1969.

"while under the supervision": Peers Report, 314–315.

"in most serious terms": Peers Report, 47.

"lots of unnecessary": Peers Report, 48.

"a 'close-hold' attitude": Peers Report, 49.

"should have provided": Peers Report, 49.

"Henderson deliberately misrepresented": Peers Report, 50.

Koster accepted the report: Peers Report, 51–52.

Conclusions: Peers Report, 319–345.

"constituted deliberate suppression or withholding of information": Peers Report, 52.

"knowingly false and deceptive": Peers Report, 307.

"a serious obstruction of justice": Peers Report, 317.

"omissions and commissions": Peers Report, 318.

Medina trial: K. Howard, "Command Responsibility," 10–11.

Footnote, 1996 statute: 18 U.S.C. sec. 2441.

"As the division commander": *NYT,* May 20, 1971.

Medina admitted losing control: K. Howard, "Command Responsibility," 10.

"**What are the Nuremberg legal principles**": Taylor, *Nuremberg and Vietnam*, 12–13.
"**the principles that it exemplifies**": Taylor, *Nuremberg and Vietnam*, 53.
"**The integrity of the nation**": Taylor, *Nuremberg and Vietnam*, 94.
"**forced resettlement**": Taylor, *Nuremberg and Vietnam*, 152.
"**The ultimate question**": Taylor, *Nuremberg and Vietnam*, 160.
"**Our job**": Taylor, *Nuremberg and Vietnam*, 169.
"**From General Westmoreland**": Taylor, *Nuremberg and Vietnam*, 181.
"**Whether or not**": Taylor, *Nuremberg and Vietnam*, 182.
"**Taylor does not help**": *NYT*, December 7, 1970.
"**If you were to apply**": *NYT*, January 9, 1971.
"**Might be convicted**": *NYT*, January 19, 1971.
"**like the rules of heraldry**": *NYT*, March 31, 1971.
"**It is apparent**": *NYT*, February 2, 1972.

Chapter 19. The Twenty-First Century: Tribunals

International Criminal Tribunal for the Former Yugoslavia, www.icty.org; International Criminal Tribunal for Rwanda, www.unictr.org.

Additional Protocol I to the Geneva Conventions of 1949: "Protocol Additional to the Geneva Conventions of 12 August 1949, and relating to the Protection of Victims of International Armed Conflicts (Protocol I), 8 June 1977," www.icrc.org/ihl.nsf/full/470.

First footnote, civilians as subordinates: "Protocol Additional to the Geneva Conventions of 12 August 1949," ICRC Commentary, sec. 3555, www.icrc.org/ihl.nsf/COM/470–750112.

Only commanders who actually know: "Protocol Additional to the Geneva Conventions of 12 August 1949," ICRC Commentary, sec. 3545.

Commentary of the drafters on willful ignorance (parenthetical): ICRC Commentary, sec. 3546.

"**it is a matter of common sense**": "Protocol Additional to the Geneva Conventions of 12 August 1949," ICRC Commentary, sec. 3548.

Statute of the ICTY: Updated Statute of the International Criminal Tribunal for the Former Yugoslavia, www.icty.org, art. 7.

No significant difference: Mucić et al. (Celebići Camp), No. IT-96-21, Appeals Chamber (hereafter AC), ICTY, February 20, 2001, paras. 235–241. www.icty.org/x/cases/mucic/acjug/en/cel-aj010220.pdf.

ICTY prosecutor must prove: Mettraux, *Law of Command Responsibility*, 209.

ICTY case statistics: *ICTY Digest*, no. 108 (January 2012), www.icty.org.

Definition of commander: *Prosecutor v. Delalić*, ICTY, Trial Chamber (hereafter TC), IT-96-21-T, November 16, 1998. www.icty.org/x/cases/mucic/tjug/en/98116_judg_en.pdf.

De jure and de facto commanders: *Prosecutor v. Delalić*, TC, November 16, 1998.

Disagreement on seeking out information: *Prosecutor v. Blaskić*, ICTY, TC, March 3, 2000, www.icty.org/x/cases/blaskic/tjug/en/bla-tj000303e.pdf; Blaskic AC, ICTY, July 29, 2004, www.icty.org/x/cases/blaskic/acjug/en/bla-aj040729e.pdf; Delalić TC, November 16, 1998.

Appeals panel ruling on seeking out information: Blaskic AC, July 29, 2004.

Commanders have no duty but to act: Mettraux, *Law of Command Responsibility*, 209nn77–78.

Disagreement on nature of information: Delalić AC, February 20, 2001, para. 238; Krnojelac AC, www.icty.org/x/cases/krnojelac/acjug/en/krn-aj030917e.pdf, September 17, 2003, paras. 155–171.

"In order to determine": Krnojelac AC, September 17, 2003, para. 155l.

Definition of torture: "Convention against Torture and Other Cruel, Inhuman, or Degrading Treatment or Punishment," article 1, www.hrweb.org/legal/cat.html.

No match, no guilt: Strugar, ICTY, TC, January 31, 2005, www.icty.org/x/cases/strugar/tjug/en/str-tj050131en.pdf, para. 373; Oric TC, June 30, 2006, www.icty.org/x/cases/oric/tjug/en/ori-jud060630e.pdf, para. 577; Hadzihasanovic AC (Decision on Interlocutory Appeal), July 16, 2003, www.icty.org/x/cases/hadzihasanovic_kubura/acdec/en/030716.htm, para, 204; see Bantekas, "On Stretching the Boundaries," 1197, 1199.

Chapter 20. Today

"We must never forget": International Military Tribunal, *Trial of the Major War Criminals*, 2: 101.

As Jackson reminded: "International Conference on Military Trials: London, 1945. Report to the President by Mr. Justice Jackson, October 7, 1946," avalon.law.yale.edu/imt/jack63.asp.

"They work": T. Taylor, *Nuremberg and Vietnam*, 40–41.

Creation of the International Criminal Court: www.icc-cpi.int.

Cyber Command: U.S. Department of Defense, News Release, May 21, 2010.

Bush memo on Geneva Conventions: "Humane Treatment of Taliban and al Qaeda Detainees," www.pegc.us/archive/White_House/bush_memo_20020207_ed.pdf.

Bush memo on military commissions: "Detention, Treatment, and Trial of Certain Non-Citizens in the War against Terrorism," www.fas.org/sgp/news/2001/11/bush111301.html.

Military Commissions Act of 2009: 123 Stat. 2190, 10 U.S.C. 948a et seq.

Footnote, Working Group: Drea, "Introduction," in Drea et al., *Researching Japanese War Crimes Records*, 7–14.

Supreme Court decisions: *Hamdi v. Rumsfeld*, 542 U.S. 407 (2004); *Hamdan v. Rumsfeld*, 548 U.S. 557 (2006); *Boumediene v. Bush*, 553 U.S. 723 (2008).

"judicial guarantees": Common Article 3 of the Geneva Conventions.

"These events occurred on my watch": *NYT*, May 8, 2004.

Bibliography

Addicott, Jeffrey F., and William A. Hudson Jr. "The Twenty-Fifth Anniversary of My Lai: A Time to Inculcate the Lessons." *Military Law Review* 139 (1993): 153–185.

Akashi, Yoji. "General Yamashita Tomoyuki: Commander of the Twenty-Fifth Army." In *Sixty Years On: The Fall of Singapore Revisited*, edited by Brian P. Farrell and Sandy Hunter. Singapore: Eastern Universities Press, 2002.

Akashi, Yoji, and Mako Yoshimura. *New Perspectives on the Japanese Occupation in Malaya and Singapore, 1941–1945*. Singapore: National University of Singapore Press, 2008.

Allen, Louis. *Singapore, 1941–1942*. London: Frank Cass, 1993.

———. "The Surrender of Singapore: The Official Japanese Version." *Durham University Journal* 50, no. 1 (December 1967): 1–6.

Aluit, Alfonso J. *By Sword and Fire: The Destruction of Manila in World War II, 3 February–3 March 1945*. Manila: National Commission for Culture and the Arts, 1994.

Amos, Sheldon. *Political and Legal Remedies for War*. New York: Harper & Brothers, 1880.

Anderson, David L., ed. *Facing My Lai: Moving beyond the Massacre*. Lawrence: University Press of Kansas, 1998.

Attiwill, Kenneth. *Fortress: The Story of the Siege and Fall of Singapore*. New York: Doubleday, 1960.

Ballantine, Joseph W. "Mukden to Pearl Harbor: The Foreign Policies of Japan." *Foreign Affairs* 27 (July 1949): 651–664.

Bantekas, Ilias. "On Stretching the Boundaries of Responsible Command," *Journal of International Criminal Justice* 7 (2009): 1197–1208.

Barclay, Glen St. John. "Singapore Strategy: The Role of the United States in Imperial Defense." *Military Affairs*, April 1975, 54–59.

Barker, A. J. *Yamashita*. New York: Ballantine Books, 1973.

Barnett, Louise. *Atrocity and American Military Justice in Southeast Asia*. New York: Routledge, 2010.

Belknap, Michal R. *The Vietnam War on Trial: The My Lai Massacre and the Court-Martial of Lieutenant Calley*. Lawrence: University Press of Kansas, 2002.

Bien, Peter J. "General MacArthur and the Yamashita Decision, September 1944–February 1946." Unpublished paper. Carlisle, Pa.: U.S. Army War College, Carlisle Barracks, 1989.

Bilton, Michael, and Kevin Sim. *Four Hours in My Lai*. New York: Penguin Books, 1992.

Boardman, Eugene P. "The Yamashita Trial Changes the Rules." *Marine Corps Gazette,* June 1946, 25–31.

Boi, Lee Geok. *The Syonan Years: Singapore under Japanese Rule, 1942–1945*. Singapore: National Archives of Singapore, and Epigram, 2005.

Boister, Neil, and Robert Cryer. *Documents on the Tokyo International Military Tribunal*. Oxford: Oxford University Press, 2008.

———. *The Tokyo International Military Tribunal: A Reappraisal*. Oxford: Oxford University Press, 2008.

Bonafé, Beatrice I. "Finding a Proper Role for Command Responsibility." *Journal of International Criminal Justice* 5 (2007): 599–618.

Bond, Brian, and Kyoichi Tachikawa, eds. *British and Japanese Military Leadership in the Far Eastern War, 1941–1945*. London: Frank Cass, 2004.

Bordwell, Percy. *The Law of War between Belligerents: A History and Commentary*. Chicago: Callaghan, 1908.

Bradley, James. *Cyril Wild: The Tall Man Who Never Slept*. West Sussex, England: Woodfield, 1991.

Caffrey, Kate. *Out in the Midday Sun: Singapore, 1941–45*. London: Andre Deutsch, 1974.

Camp, Dick. "Talking with the Enemy: Major Harry Pratt and the Yamashita Trial." *Leatherneck*, October 2008, 14–19.

Cannon, M. Hamlin. *Leyte: The Return to the Philippines*. United States Army in World War II. Washington, D.C.: Center of Military History, U.S. Army, 1954.

Capozzola, Christopher. "A Tale of Two Treasons: Adjudicating War Crimes and Collaboration in Manila, 1945." Paper presented at the American Society of Legal History Conference, Dallas, November 12, 2009.

Carnahan, Burrus M. *Lincoln on Trial: Southern Civilians and the Law of War*. Lexington: University Press of Kentucky, 2010.

Chipman, N. P. *The Tragedy of Andersonville: Trial of Captain Henry Wirz, The Prison Keeper*. San Francisco: Blair-Murdock, 1911. Reprint, Birmingham, Ala.: Notable Trials Library, 1990. Page citations are to the reprint edition.

Churchill, Winston S. *The Second World War*. Vol. 3, *The Grand Alliance*. Vol. 4, *The Hinge of Fate*. Boston: Houghton Mifflin, 1950.

Clark, Roger S. "Medina: An Essay on the Principles of Criminal Liability for Homicide." *Rutgers-Camden Law Journal* 5 (1973): 59.

Coates, Lt. Gen. John. "'Out-Generalled, Outwitted, and Outfought'—Generals Percival and Bennett in Malaya, 1941–42." *Australian Army Journal* 2, no. 1 (Winter 2004): 201–214.

Cogan, Frances B. *Captured: The Japanese Internment of American Civilians in the Philippines, 1941–1945*. Athens: University of Georgia Press, 2000.

Commager, Henry Steele. *The Story of the Second World War*. Boston: Little, Brown, 1945. Reprint, Washington, D.C.: Brassey's, 2004. Page citations are to the reprint edition.

Commission on the Responsibility of the Authors of the War and on Enforcement of Penalties. Report presented to the Preliminary Peace Conference, March 29, 1919. *American Journal of International Law* 14 (1920): 95–154.

Congressional Research Service, Library of Congress. "Terrorism and the Law of War: Trying Terrorists as War Criminals before Military Commissions." December 2001, updated December 11, 2001. http://www.fas.org/irp/crs/RL31191.pdf.

Connaughton, Richard, John Pimlott, and Duncan Anderson. *The Battle for Manila*. Novato, Calif.: Presidio Press, 2002.

Currie, David P. "The Constitution in the Supreme Court: The Second World War, 1941–1946." *Catholic University Law Review* 37 (1987): 1–38.

Damaska, Mirjan. "The Shadow Side of Command Responsibility." *American Journal of Comparative Law* 49 (2001): 455–496.

Daws, Gavan. *Prisoners of the Japanese: POWs of World War II in the Pacific.* New York: William Morrow, 1994.

Deacon, Richard. *Kempetai: A History of the Japanese Secret Service.* New York: Berkley Books, 1985.

Dickerson, Lt. Col. George W. "Defeat on Leyte." *Infantry Journal,* July 1949, 30–33.

Douglass, John Jay. "High Command Case: A Study in Staff and Command Responsibility." *International Lawyer* 6 (1972): 686–705.

Dower, John W. *Cultures of War.* New York: W. W. Norton, 2010.

———. *Embracing Defeat: Japan in the Wake of World War II.* New York: W. W. Norton, 2000.

———. *War without Mercy: Race and Power in the Pacific War.* New York: Pantheon Books, 1986.

Drea, Edward J. *In the Service of the Emperor: Essays on the Imperial Japanese Army.* Lincoln: University of Nebraska Press, 1998.

———. *Japan's Imperial Army: Its Rise and Fall, 1853–1945.* Lawrence: University Press of Kansas, 2009.

Drea, Edward, Greg Bradsher, Robert Hanyok, James Lide, Michael Petersen, and Daqing Yang. *Researching Japanese War Crimes Records: Introductory Essays.* Washington, D.C.: Nazi War Crimes and Japanese Imperial Government Records Interagency Working Group, 2007. http://www.archives.gov/iwg/japanese-war-crimes/introductory-essays.pdf.

Duus, Peter, Ramon Myers, and Mark R. Peattie, eds. *The Japanese Wartime Empire, 1931–1945.* Princeton: Princeton University Press, 1996.

Eckhardt, William G. "Command Criminal Responsibility: A Plea for a Workable Standard." *Military Law Review* 97 (1982): 1–34.

———. "My Lai: An American Tragedy." *UMKC Law Review* 68 (1999): 671–704.

Edgerton, Robert B. *Warriors of the Rising Sun: A History of the Japanese Military.* New York: W. W. Norton, 1997.

Eichelberger, Robert L. *Our Jungle Road to Tokyo.* New York: Viking Press, 1950.

Esposito, Vincent J., ed. *The West Point Atlas of War: World War II. The Pacific.* West Point, N.Y.: U.S. Military Academy, 1959.

Falk, Stanley L. *Decision at Leyte.* New York: W. W. Norton, 1966.

Farrell, Brian P. *The Defence and Fall of Singapore, 1940–1942.* Gloucestershire, UK: Tempus, 2005.

Farrell, Brian P., and Sandy Hunter. *Sixty Years On: The Fall of Singapore Revisited.* Singapore: Eastern Universities Press, 2002.

Feldman, Noah. *Scorpions: The Battles and Triumphs of FDR's Great Supreme Court Justices.* New York: Twelve, 2010.

Felton, Mark. *Japan's Gestapo: Murder, Mayhem and Torture in Wartime Asia.* South Yorkshire, UK: Pen & Sword Books, 2009.

Ferren, John M. *Salt of the Earth, Conscience of the Court: The Story of Justice Wiley Rutledge.* Chapel Hill: University of North Carolina Press, 2004.

Finn, Richard B. *Winners in Peace: MacArthur, Yoshida and Postwar Japan.* Berkeley: University of California Press, 1992.

Fisher, Louis. *Military Tribunals and Presidential Power: American Revolution to the War on Terrorism.* Lawrence: University Press of Kansas, 2005.

———. *Nazi Saboteurs on Trial.* 2nd ed. Lawrence: University Press of Kansas, 2005.

Forbes, Cameron. *Hellfire: The Story of Australia, Japan and the Prisoners of War.* Sydney: Pan Macmillan Australia, 2005.

Frankel, Stanley A. *The 37th Infantry Division in World War II.* Washington, D.C.: Infantry Journal Press, 1948.

Friedman, Leon. *The Law of War: A Documentary History.* New York: Random House, 1972.

Gailey, Harry M. *The War in the Pacific.* Novato, Calif.: Presidio Press, 1995.

Garner, James W. "Punishment of Offenders against the Laws and Customs of War." *American Journal of International Law* 14 (1920): 70–94.

Gerwig, Robert. "Surrender at Baguio: A Record of Events and Proceedings Relating to the Surrender of Japanese Forces in the Philippines at Baguio, Luzon, 2 September 1945." Witness to War: Preserving the Oral Histories of Combat Veterans. www.witnesstowar .org/content/materials/Robert%20Gerwig.pdf.

Glueck, Sheldon. *War Criminals: Their Prosecution and Punishment.* New York: Alfred A. Knopf, 1944.

Goldstein, Joseph, Burke Marshall, and Jack Schwarz. *The My Lai Massacre and Its Cover-up: Beyond the Reach of Law?* New York: Free Press, 1976.

Goodman, Ryan. "The Detention of Civilians in Armed Conflict." *American Journal of International Law* 103 (2009): 48–74.

Green, L. C. "Command Responsibility in International Humanitarian Law." *Transnational Law and Contemporary Problems* 5 (1995): 319–372.

Greenspan, Morris. *The Modern Law of Land Warfare.* Berkeley: University of California Press, 1959.

Guardia, Mike. *American Guerrilla: The Forgotten Heroics of Russell W. Volckmann.* Philadelphia: Casemate, 2010.

Guthrie, Charles, and Michael Quinlan. *Just War: The Just War Tradition. Ethics in Modern Warfare.* London: Bloomsbury, 2007.

Guy, George F. "The Defense of Yamashita." *Wyoming Law Journal* 4 (1949): 153–180. Reprint, in *Yearbook of the Supreme Court Historical Society,* 1981, 53–70. Page citations are to the reprint edition.

Haley, John O. Review of *The Tokyo International Military Tribunal: A Reappraisal,* by Neil Boister and Robert Cryer, and *The Tokyo War Crimes Trial: The Pursuit of Justice in the Wake of World War II,* by Yuma Totani. *Journal of Japanese Studies* 35 (2009): 445–451.

Hall, William Edward. *A Treatise on International Law.* Edited by A. Pearce Higgins. 7th ed. Oxford: Clarendon Press, 1917.

Hansen, Victor. "What's Good for the Goose Is Good for the Gander, Lessons from Abu Ghraib: Time for the United States to Adopt a Standard of Command Responsibility towards Its Own." *Gonzaga Law Review* 42 (2006–2007): 335–414.

Harries, Meirion, and Susie Harries. *Soldiers of the Sun: The Rise and Fall of the Imperial Japanese Army.* New York: Random House, 1991.

Hasian, Marouf, Jr. *In the Name of Necessity: Military Tribunals and the Loss of American Civil Liberties.* Tuscaloosa: University of Alabama Press, 2005.

Hastings, Max. *Retribution: The Battle for Japan, 1944–45.* New York: Alfred A. Knopf, 2008.

———. *Inferno: The World at War, 1939–1945.* New York: Alfred A. Knopf, 2011.

Hattendorp, A. V. H. *The Japanese Occupation of the Philippines.* Vol. 2. Manila: Bookmark, 1967.

Hayashi, Saburo. *Kogun: The Japanese Army in the Pacific War.* Quantico, Va.: Marine Corps Association, 1959.

Heberer, Patricia, and Jurgen Matthaus, eds. *Atrocities on Trial: Historical Perspectives on the Politics of Prosecuting War Crimes.* Lincoln: University of Nebraska Press, 2008.

Hébert, Valerie Geneviève. *Hitler's Generals on Trial: The Last War Crimes Tribunal at Nuremberg.* Lawrence: University Press of Kansas, 2010.

Hersh, Seymour M. *My Lai 4: A Report on the Massacre and Its Aftermath.* New York: Random House, 1970.

Higgins, A. Pearce. *The Hague Peace Conferences*. London: Cambridge University Press, 1909.

Hirofumi, Hayashi. "The Battle of Singapore, the Massacre of Chinese and Understanding of the Issue in Postwar Japan." *Asia-Pacific Journal: Japan Focus*, 28-4-09, July 13, 2009. http://www.japanfocus.org/-Hayashi-Hirofumi/3187.

Hodges, M. Douglas. "The Juridical Character of Nonstatutory Military Tribunals." Thesis, Judge Advocate General's School, 1963.

Holzimmer, Kevin C. *General Walter Krueger: Unsung Hero of the Pacific War*. Lawrence: University Press of Kansas, 2007.

Horwitz, Solis. "The Tokyo Trial." *International Conciliation* 28, no. 465 (1950): 475–584.

Howard, J. Woodford. *Mr. Justice Murphy: A Political Biography*. Princeton: Princeton University Press, 1968.

Howard, Kenneth A. "Command Responsibility for War Crimes." *Journal of Public Law* 21 (1972): 7–22.

Howard, Michael, George Andreopoulos, and Mark R. Shulman, eds. *The Laws of War: Constraints on Warfare in the Western World*. New Haven: Yale University Press, 1994.

Hoyt, Edwin P. *Japan's War: The Great Pacific Conflict, 1853 to 1952*. New York: McGraw-Hill, 1986.

———. *Three Military Leaders: Heihachiro Togo, Isoroku Yamamoto, Tomoyuki Yamashita*. Tokyo: Kadansha International, 1993.

Huber, Thomas M. "The Battle of Manila." cgsc.leavenworth.army.mil/carl/download/csipubs.

Ikehata, Setsuo, and Ricardo Treta Jose, eds. *The Philippines under Japan: Occupation Policy and Reaction*. Manila: Ateneo de Manila University Press, 1999.

Ikehata, Setsuo, and Lydia N. Yu Jose, eds. *Philippines-Japan Relations*. Manila: Ateneo de Manila University Press, 2003.

International Military Tribunal. *Trial of the Major War Criminals before the International Military Tribunal (Blue Series)*. Vol. 2. Nuremberg, Germany, 1947–1949.

James, D. Clayton. *The Years of MacArthur*. Vol. 2, *1941–1945*. Vol. 3, *Triumph and Disaster, 1945–1964*. Boston: Houghton Mifflin, 1975, 1985.

Jose, Ricardo T. "Test of Wills: Diplomacy between Japan and the Laurel Government." In *Philippines-Japan Relations*, edited by Ikehata Setsuo and Lydia N. Yu Jose. Manila: Ateneo de Manila University Press, 2003.

Karig, Walter, Russell L. Harris, and Frank A. Manson. *Battle Report: Victory in the Pacific*. New York: Rinehart, 1949.

Karnow, Stanley. *In Our Image: America's Empire in the Philippines*. New York: Ballantine Books, 1989.

Kawashima, Midori. "The Records of the Former Japanese Army concerning the Japanese Occupation of the Philippines." *Journal of Southeast Asian Studies* 27 (March 1996): 124–131.

Kenworthy, Aubrey Saint. *The Tiger of Malaya*. New York: Exposition Press, 1953.

Kerr, E. Bartlett. *Surrender and Survival: The Experience of American POWs in the Pacific, 1941–1945*. New York: William Morrow, 1985.

Kheng, Cheah Boon. *Red Star over Malaya: Resistance and Social Conflict during and after the Japanese Occupation of Malaya, 1941–1946*. Singapore: Singapore University Press, 1983.

Kinvig, Clifford. *Scapegoat: General Percival of Singapore*. London: Brassey's, 1996.

Kratoska, Paul. *The Japanese Occupation of Malaya: A Social and Economic History*. Honolulu: University of Hawai'i Press, 1997.

———, ed. *Malaya and Singapore during the Japanese Occupation*. Singapore: Journal of Southeast Asian Studies Special Publication Series, 1995.

Lael, Richard L. *The Yamashita Precedent: War Crimes and Command Responsibility.* Wilmington, Del.: Scholarly Resources, 1982.

Lamont-Brown, Raymond. *Kempetai: Japan's Dreaded Military Police.* Gloucestershire, UK: Sutton, 1998.

Lawrence, T. J. *International Problems and Hague Conferences.* London: J. M. Dent, 1908.

Leasor, James. *Singapore: The Battle That Changed the World.* Garden City, N.Y.: Doubleday, 1968.

Levie, Howard S. *Terrorism in War: The Law of War Crimes.* Dobbs Ferry, N.Y.: Oceana Publications, 1993.

Ling, Cheah Wui. "Post–World War II British 'Hell-ship' Trials in Singapore: Omissions and the Attribution of Responsibility." *Journal of International Criminal Justice* 8 (2010): 1035–1038.

Lippman, David H. "The Tiger of Malaya." *World War II* 17, no. 7 (March 2003): 70–77.

MacArthur, Douglas. *Reminiscences.* New York: McGraw Hill, 1964.

———. *Reports of General MacArthur.* Prepared by his general staff. Reprint ed. 2 vols. Vol. 1, *The Campaigns of MacArthur in the Pacific.* Washington, D.C.: Center of Military History, 1994.

Maltby, Isaac. *A Treatise on Courts Martial and Military Law.* Boston: Thomas B. Wait, 1813.

Manchester, William. *American Caesar: Douglas MacArthur, 1880–1964.* Boston: Little, Brown, 1978.

Mant, Gilbert. *Massacre at Parit Sulong.* Kenthurst, NSW, Australia: Kangaroo Press, 1995.

Marmon, Thomas C., Joseph E. Cooper, and William F. Goodman. "Military Commissions." Paper, Judge Advocate General's School, 1953.

Marston, Daniel, ed. *The Pacific War Companion: From Pearl Harbor to Hiroshima.* London: Osprey, 2005.

Martinez, Jenny S. "Understanding Mens Rea in Command Responsibility." *Journal of International Criminal Justice* 5 (2007): 638–664.

Mason, Alpheus Thomas. *Harlan Fiske Stone: Pillar of the Law.* New York: Viking Press, 1956.

May, Richard, and Mariske Wierda. *International Criminal Evidence.* Ardsley, N.Y.: Transnational, 2002.

McCarthy, Mary. *The Seventeenth Degree: How It Went, Vietnam, Hanoi, Medina, Sons of the Morning.* New York: Harcourt Brace Jovanovich, 1974.

McNeilly, Mark. *Sun Tzu and the Art of Modern Warfare.* Oxford: Oxford University Press, 2001.

McPherson, James M. *Tried by War: Abraham Lincoln as Commander in Chief.* New York: Penguin Books, 2008.

Meloni, Chantal. "Command Responsibility: Mode of Liability for the Crimes of Subordinates or Separate Offence of the Superior?" *Journal of International Criminal Justice* 5 (2007): 619–637.

———. *Command Responsibility in International Law.* The Hague: T. M. C. Asser Press, 2010.

Mercado, Stephen C. *The Shadow Warriors of Nakano: A History of the Imperial Japanese Army's Elite Intelligence School.* Washington, D.C.: Brassey's, 2002.

Mettraux, Guénaël. *The Law of Command Responsibility.* Oxford: Oxford University Press, 2009.

Minear, Richard H. *Victors' Justice: The Tokyo War Crimes Trial.* Ann Arbor: University of Michigan Center for Japanese Studies, 2001.

Minow, Martha. "Living Up to Rules: Holding Soldiers Responsible for Abusive Conduct and the Dilemma of the Superior Orders Defense." *McGill Law Journal* 52 (2007): 1–54.

Morison, Samuel Eliot. *Leyte—June 1944–January 1945*. Vol. 12 of *History of United States Naval Operations in World War II*. Boston: Little, Brown, 1958.

————. *The Liberation of the Philippines: Luzon, Mindanao, the Visayas, 1944–1945*. Vol. 13 of *History of United States Naval Operations in World War II*. Boston: Little, Brown, 1959.

————. *The Two-Ocean War: A Short History of the United States Navy in the Second World War*. Annapolis, Md.: Naval Institute Press, 1963.

————. *Victory in the Pacific, 1945*. Boston: Little, Brown, 1960.

Morton, Louis. *The Fall of the Philippines*. The United States Army in World War II. Washington, D.C.: Department of the Army, 1953.

Moyer, Homer E., Jr. *Justice and the Military*. Washington, D.C.: Public Law Education Institute, 1972.

Mullins, Claud. *The Leipzig Trials: An Account of the War Criminals' Trials and a Study of German Mentality*. London: H. F. & G. Witherby, 1921.

Murphy, Peter. "No Free Lunch, No Free Proof: The Indiscriminate Admission of Evidence Is a Serious Flaw in International Criminal Trials." *Journal of International Criminal Justice* 8 (2010): 539–574.

Neely, Mark E., Jr. *The Fate of Liberty: Abraham Lincoln and Civil Liberties*. New York: Oxford University Press, 1991.

Nersessian, David L. "Whoops, I Committed Genocide! The Anomaly of Constructive Liability for Serious International Crimes." *Fletcher Forum on World Affairs* 30 (2006): 81–106.

Norman, Michael, and Elizabeth M. Norman. *Tears in the Darkness: The Story of the Bataan Death March and Its Aftermath*. New York: Farrar, Straus & Giroux, 2009.

O'Brien, William V. "The Law of War, Command Responsibility and Vietnam." *Georgetown Law Journal* 60 (1972): 605–664.

Ogawa, Tetsuro. *Terraced Hell: A Japanese Memoir of Defeat and Death in Northern Luzon, Philippines*. Rutland, Vt.: Charles E. Tuttle, 1972.

Oki, Shuji. *Higeki no shogun: Ningen Yamashita Tomoyuki*. Tokyo: Nihon Shuhosha, 1959. Translations from this document by Kay Makino.

Oppenheim, L. *International Law*. 3rd ed. Vol. 2. London: Longmans, Green, 1921.

Parks, William H. "Command Responsibility for War Crimes." *Military Law Review* 62 (1973): 1–104.

Paust, Jordan J. "My Lai and Vietnam: Norms, Myths and Leader Responsibility." *Military Law Review* 57 (1972): 99–187.

Pearson, Emmet F. "Morbidity and Mortality in Santo Tomas Internment Camp." *Annals of Internal Medicine* 24, no. 6 (June 1, 1946): 988–1013.

Peers, W. R. *The My Lai Inquiry*. New York, W. W. Norton, 1979.

Petillo, Carol Morris. *Douglas MacArthur: The Philippine Years*. Bloomington: Indiana University Press, 1981.

Picigallo, Phillip R. *The Japanese on Trial: Allied War Crimes Operations in the East, 1945–1951*. Austin: University of Texas Press, 1979.

Potter, John Deane. *The Life and Death of a Japanese General*. New York: Signet/New American Library, 1962. (Published in the U.K. As *A Soldier Must Hang*. London: Frederick Muller, 1963.)

Prevost, Ann Marie. "Race and War Crimes: The 1945 War Crimes Trial of General Tomoyuki Yamashita." *Human Rights Quarterly* 14 (1992): 303–338.

Pritchard, R. John. "The International Military Tribunal for the Far East and Its Contemporary Resonances." *Military Law Review* 149 (1995): 25–36.

Pritchard, R. John, and Sonia Magbanua Zaide, eds. *The Tokyo War Crimes Trial: The Complete*

Transcripts of the Proceedings of the International Military Tribunal for the Far East in Twenty-Two Volumes, and The Tokyo War Crimes Trial: Index and Guide. New York: Garland, 1981.

Redford, L. H. "The Trial of General Tomoyuki Yamashita: A Case Study in Command Responsibility." M.A. thesis, Old Dominion University, 1975.

Reel, A. Frank. *The Case of General Yamashita.* Chicago: University of Chicago Press, 1949.

Richards, Peter Judson. *Extraordinary Justice: Military Tribunals in Historical and International Context.* New York: New York University Press, 2007.

Rottman, Gordon L. *World War II Battlefield Communications.* Oxford: Osprey, 2010.

Rowland, Robin. *A River Kwai Story: The Sonkrai Tribunal.* Crows Nest, NSW, Australia: Allen & Unwin, 2007.

Russell, Edward (Lord Russell of Liverpool). *The Knights of Bushido.* New York: Skyhorse, 2008.

Sakakida, Richard. *A Spy in Their Midst: The World War II Struggle of a Japanese-American Hero.* As told to Wayne S. Kiyosaki. Toronto: Madison Press Books, 1995.

Schabas, William A. *An Introduction to the International Criminal Court.* 3rd ed. New York: Cambridge University Press, 2007.

Scott, James Brown, ed. *Texts of the Paris Peace Conferences at the Hague, 1899 and 1907.* Boston: Ginn, 1908.

Shakespeare, William. *The Life of Henry the Fifth.* Rev. ed. New Haven: Yale University Press, 1955.

Shinozaki, Mamoru. *Syonan—My Story: The Japanese Occupation of Singapore.* Singapore: Asia Pacific Press, 1975.

Shulimson, Jack. "The Marine War: III MAF in Vietnam." 1996 Vietnam Symposium: After the Cold War: Reassessing Vietnam. April 18–20, 1996. www.vietnam.ttu.edu/ events/1996_Symposium/96papers/marwar.htm.

Sides, Hampton. *Ghost Soldiers: The Epic Account of World War II's Greatest Rescue Mission.* New York: Anchor Books, 2001.

Silver, Lynette Ramsay. *The Bridge at Parit Sulong: An Investigation of Mass Murder, Malaya, 1942.* Sydney: Watermark Press, 2004.

Smith, Colin. *Singapore Burning: Heroism and Surrender in World War II.* London: Viking Press, 2005.

Smith, Robert Ross. *Triumph in the Philippines.* Washington, D.C.: Center of Military History, U.S. Army, 1963.

Solis, Gary D. *The Law of Armed Conflict: International Humanitarian Law in War.* New York: Cambridge University Press, 2010.

Solis, Gary D., and Fred L. Borch, eds. *Geneva Conventions.* New York: Kaplan, 2010.

Steinberg, David. "Jose P. Laurel: A 'Collaborator' Misunderstood." *Journal of Asian Studies* 24, no. 4 (August 1965): 651–665.

———. "The Philippine 'Collaborators': Survival of an Oligarchy." In *Southeast Asia in World War II: Four Essays,* edited by Josef Silverstein, 67–86. Monograph Series, no. 7. New Haven: Yale University Southeast Asia Studies, 1966.

Steinberg, David Joel. *Philippine Collaboration in World War II.* Ann Arbor: University of Michigan Press, 1967.

Steinberg, Rafael. *Return to the Philippines.* New York: Time-Life Books, 1979.

Storry, Richard. *A History of Modern Japan.* Baltimore: Penguin Books, 1960.

Stratton, Samuel S. "Tiger of Malaya." *U.S. Naval Institute Proceedings* 80 (February 1954): 137–143.

Straus, Ulrich. *The Anguish of Surrender: Japanese POWs of World War II.* Seattle: University of Washington Press, 2003.

Stryszak, Michael. "Command Responsibility: How Much Should a Commander Be Expected to Know?" *USAF Academy Journal of Legal Studies* (2002): 27–81.

Suverkrop, Don. "WWII and the 32nd Division in the Philippines and Japan, 1944–1946." With Gilbert Gia. www.gilbertgia.com /hist_articles/war/WWII_32nd_DIVISION .pdf.

Swinson, Arthur. *Four Samurai: A Quartet of Japanese Army Commanders in the Second World War.* London: Hutchinson, 1968.

Tachikawa, Kyoichi. "General Yamashita and His Style of Leadership: The Malaya/Singapore Campaign." In *British and Japanese Military Leadership in the Far Eastern War, 1941–1945,* edited by Brian Bond and Kyoichi Tachikawa. London: Frank Cass, 2004.

Tanaka, Yuki. "Last Words of the Tiger of Malaya, General Yamashita Tomoyuki." *Asia-Pacific Journal: Japan Focus,* September 22, 2005. http://www.japanfocus.org/-Yuki-TANAKA/ 1753.

Taylor, Telford. *Final Report to the Secretary of the Army on the Nuernberg War Crimes Trials under Control Council Law No. 10.* Washington, D.C.: Government Printing Office, 1949.

———. *Nuremberg and Vietnam: An American Tragedy.* Chicago: Quadrangle Books, 1970.

Terami-Wada, Motoe. "Lt. Shigenobu Mochizuki and the New Philippine Cultural Institute." *Journal of Southeast Asian Studies* 27, no. 1 (March 1966): 104–123.

Thompson, George Raynor, and Dixie R. Harris. *The Signal Corps: The Outcome, United States Army in World War II.* Washington, D.C.: Office of the Chief of Military History, 1966.

Thompson, Peter. *The Battle for Singapore.* London: Portrait/Piatkus Books, 2005.

Thompson, Richard J., Jr. *Crystal Clear: The Struggle for Reliable Communications Technology in World War II.* Piscataway, N.J.: IEEE Press, 2007.

Tillotson, Lee S. *The Articles of War Annotated.* 2nd rev. ed. Harrisburg, Pa.: Military Service Publishing, 1943.

Toland, John. *The Rising Sun: The Decline and Fall of the Japanese Empire, 1936–1945.* New York: Random House, 1970.

Totani, Yuma. *The Tokyo War Crimes Trial: The Pursuit of Justice in the Wake of World War II.* Cambridge, Mass.: Harvard University Press, 2008.

Tsuji, Masanobu. *Singapore: The Japanese Version.* Translated by Margaret E. Lake. Sydney: Ure Smith, 1960.

United Nations War Crimes Commission, ed. *Law Reports of Trials of War Criminals.* London: Published for the United Nations War Crimes Commission by His Majesty's Stationery Office, 1949.

Urofsky, Melvin. *Division and Discord: The Supreme Court under Stone and Vinson, 1941–1953.* Columbia: University of South Carolina Press, 1997.

U.S. Army. *Service Forces Manual, Civil Affairs Handbook: Philippine Islands.* Secs. 11 and 12, *Transportation Systems and Communications,* September 7, 1944.

U.S. Army, Japan, Office of the Military History Officer. Japanese monographs, nos. 3–9, 24, 45, 114, and 117 (1946).

U.S. Army, Judge Advocate General of the Army. *A Manual for Courts-Martial.* 1928, corrected to April 20, 1943.

U.S. Department of the Army. *Report of the Department of the Army Review of the Preliminary Investigations into the My Lai Incident (Peers Commission Report), 1970.* www.loc.gov/rr/frd/ Military_Law/pdf/RDAR-Vol-I.pdf.

U.S. House of Representatives, Committee on Armed Services. *Investigation of the My Lai Incident.* 91st Cong., 2nd Sess. (July 15, 1970).

U.S. National Archives and Records Administration, Nazi War Crimes and Japanese Imperial

Government Records Interagency Working Group. *Researching Japanese War Crimes Records: Introductory Essays.* 2006.

U.S. State Department. *Foreign Relations of the United States, 1945.* Vol. 6. Washington, D.C.: Government Printing Office, 1969.

U.S. War Department. *Handbook on Japanese Military Forces, Technical Manual 30-480 (1 October 1944).*

———. *Military Justice Procedure, Technical Manual 27-255 (February 1945).*

———. *Operations, Field Manual 100-5 (15 June 1944).*

———. *Rules of Land Warfare, 1914 (revised 1934).*

———. *Rules of Land Warfare, Field Manual 27-10, 1940 (revised 1956).*

van der Vat, Dan. *The Pacific Campaign: The U.S.–Japanese Naval War, 1941–1945.* New York: Touchstone/Simon & Schuster, 1991.

Vego, Milan. *The Battle for Leyte, 1944: Allied and Japanese Plans, Preparations, and Execution.* Annapolis, Md.: Naval Institute Press, 2006.

Ward, Ian. *The Killer They Called a God.* Singapore: Media Masters, 1992.

———. *Snaring the Other Tiger.* Singapore: Media Masters, 1996.

Warren, Alan. *Singapore, 1942.* London: Talisman, 2007.

Waterford, Van. *Prisoners of the Japanese in World War II.* Jefferson, N.C.: McFarland, 1994.

Webb, James. *The Emperor's General.* New York: Broadway Books, 1999.

Weintraub, Stanley. *15 Stars: Eisenhower, MacArthur, Marshall.* New York: New American Library, 2007.

Whitman, John W. "Captured British Supplies Fed the Japanese War Machine during the Conquest of Malaya." *World War II* 15, no. 6 (February 2001): 12–14.

Wigmore, Lionel. *Australia in the War of 1939–1945.* Series 1, Army. Vol. 4, *The Japanese Thrust.* Canberra: Australian War Memorial, 1957.

Wilkins, Thomas S. "Anatomy of a Disaster: The Fall of 'Fortress Singapore,' 1942." *Journal of Military History,* January 2009, 221–230.

Williamson, Jamie Allan. "Some Considerations on Command Responsibility and Criminal Liability." *International Review of the Red Cross* 90, no. 870 (June 2008): 303–317.

Winthrop, William. *Military Law and Precedents.* 2nd ed. Washington, D.C.: Government Printing Office, 1920.

Index

About the Author

Allan A. Ryan clerked for Supreme Court Justice Byron R. White, was a U.S. Marine Corps judge advocate, and was Assistant to the Solicitor General of the United States. As the first director of the U.S. Department of Justice's Office of Special Investigations in the 1980s, he was the chief prosecutor of Nazi war criminals who had escaped to America. He teaches the law of war at Boston College Law School and Harvard University and is author of *Quiet Neighbors: Prosecuting Nazi War Criminals in America.* He and his wife, Nancy, live in Norwell, Massachusetts. For additional information on *Yamashita's Ghost,* see www .yamashitasghost.com.